AF526702

WISDOM OF ŚAṄKARA SERIES

Vol. 1	Īśa Upaniṣad, Kena Upaniṣad, Kaṭha Upaniṣad, Praśna Upaniṣad
Vol. 2	Muṇḍaka Upaniṣad Māṇḍūkya Upaniṣad with Gauḍapāda Kārikā
Vol. 3	Taittirīya Upaniṣad Aitareya Upaniṣad

Forthcoming

Vol. 4	Chāndogya Upaniṣad
Vols. 5 & 6	Bṛhadāraṇyaka Upaniṣad
Vol. 7	Bhagavadgītā
Vols. 8, 9 & 10	Brahmasūtras

THE WORD SPEAKS TO THE FAUSTIAN MAN
VOLUME THREE

The Word Speaks to the Faustian Man

A translation and interpretation of the Prasthānatrayī and Śaṅkara's bhāṣya for the participation of contemporary man

Som Raj Gupta

Volume Three

MOTILAL BANARSIDASS PUBLISHERS
PRIVATE LIMITED • DELHI

First Edition: Delhi, 1999

ISBN: 81-208-1545-9

Also available at:
MOTILAL BANARSIDASS
41 U.A. Bungalow Road, Jawahar Nagar, Delhi 110 007
8 Mahalaxmi Chamber, Warden Road, Mumbai 400 026
120 Royapettah High Road, Mylapore, Chennai 600 004
Sanas Plaza, 1302, Baji Rao Road, Pune 411 002
16 St. Mark's Road, Bangalore 560 001
8 Camac Street, Calcutta 700 017
Ashok Rajpath, Patna 800 004
Chowk, Varanasi 221 001

PRINTED IN INDIA
BY JAINENDRA PRAKASH JAIN AT SHRI JAINENDRA PRESS,
A-45 NARAINA, PHASE I, NEW DELHI 110 028
AND PUBLISHED BY NARENDRA PRAKASH JAIN FOR
MOTILAL BANARSIDASS PUBLISHERS PRIVATE LIMITED,
BUNGALOW ROAD, DELHI 110 007

CONTENTS

PREFACE

When they philosophise, philosophers do not, as a rule, use their linguistic inheritance the way most men and women do. Words and their referents seem to get interfused in their discourse, though many among them may not, in fact do not, go to the extent of proclaiming them as one, the name and the named, even the word and the concept. Yet philosophers often use them interchangeably except when they are trying to formulate their respective ontologies. Many among them formulate these, words and their referents, as interconstitutive. There have indeed been some among them who have been staunch 'realists', though to find a staunch 'realist' would not be an easy task these days, one who would proclaim language and facts as absolutely independent realities. Yet the word and the referent are obstinate enough to remain distinct in some, indistinct, sense; they may depend on each other but they refuse to merge into each other. The creativity of the philosopher–scientist, his original insights and formulations, unmistakably 'declare' this difference, show it forth even in the absence of an actual formulation. This becomes evident when a philosopher is forced to formulate a new concept and coin a new term, his linguistic–conceptual inheritance having proved inadequate to express what he has to say. Though the philosopher himself does not know precisely what his new concept is before he has actually articulated it, though, one may even say, the concept does not come to be the concept before its articulation, one cannot, if one is attentive to the creative process, but recognise that something is unmistakably there to precede the articulation, a prelinguistic and preconceptual something in the process of becoming a linguistic concept. This germ and referent of articulation does not owe its birth to our linguistic–conceptual inheritance but to, as it were, a prelinguistic dimension in man, a dimension which remains concealed from most people but which a philosopher–scientist taps for the enrichment of what they call knowledge and thought. Most insights and findings owe their birth to this dark interiority in man which most people, even thoughtful people, unable or unwilling to face it, mystify and obscure by the use of such expressions as 'intuition' and 'genius'. This, their homage, is, however, an unconscious recognition of its existence, of this fount of discoveries and insights. Our preoccupations with 'man' and his world succeed but poorly in making us oblivious, completely oblivious, of it. Every original thought bears witness to its being and its truth, every insight and every creative hypothesis.

It may, however, be argued that this prelinguistic germ is nothing but prearticulated concept and that a prearticulated concept is only, so to say, a prearticulated word, that the word too has its prearticulate state and its articulate state as a concept or a percept has, that the philosopher's or the scientist's originality lies not in forging a new, original, word but only in unconcealing or uncovering a part of the concealed 'utterance'. This view visualises language as having two faces or aspects: the communal and the noncommunal, the articulate and the inarticulate. However, if one understands language as utterance, as an intersubjective, communicative phenomenon, then the prearticulated word will not be a word of our common understanding, for the word is, for this understanding, nothing if not an articulation. What is the shape of the word at the prearticulate level? one might ask. And what is the meaning of the concept in that state? The word is not the word nor the concept the concept in that state, the state outside a communal context, where there are no others and no classes to constitute each other. Words and concepts are social things, obtain only in a linguistic community, are, perhaps, themselves socialities, they do not obtain in the dark interiority of the creative source, which, if it is there, must be prelinguistic and preconceptual.

In the domain of the articulate, language, however, functions as referential, as constituted by otherness. The referent too is found as constituted by language. The name and the named thus refuse to part company but they do not become one. Between the word and the referent— the concept or the object— there falls an unformulated and unformulable schism, a divide. Not, however, at the prearticulate level. There the word and the referent are not interconstitutive, for the one has not yet taken shape and the other has not yet been identified and placed. The philosopher/scientist through his original articulation breaks that 'unity' [can we call it unity?] to turn it, not into clear cut distinctions, but into an ambiguity. This breaking of the unity [?] we often term bringing into the open, into light, into clarity. But the articulation fails to be a real opening, remains dark and unclear. For the referent cannot be identified as such, even after articulation. Language can only point to it, ever points to it but fails to reach it. It is an orientation towards the referent which ever eludes its grasp, for what it points to is not an object as such, a nonlinguistic thing but something already linguised, already linguistic, so to say. Still the referent retains itself, it does not coincide with the articulation, with what we in our times call interpretation.

This is indeed true of what we call interpreted phenomena, things that are there in the world. What about concepts? Can concepts be fully enclosed within the confines of words or language? Are words and concepts one? There is in every concept a tendency to exceed itself. A concept is always problematic, falsifiable, open to change and transformation, even replacement, rendering it impossible for words to contain or confine it. The fragility of concepts is notorious or, if you will, celebrated. You do not arrive at a concept which in its very formulation is not questionable. So a tension constitutes the relationship between the concept and the word. We find it daily enacted, sometimes tragically, between thinkers, original thinkers, and the common people. The latter would have a concept fully articulated, stable, clear and unambiguous; if a particular word does not fit in, then another word should do; for a thinker, the word, the concept merely given, the concept frozen into a word, is ever a dead thing. He finds the frozen concept, the concept as the word, always, ever, questionable, the new concept–word as much as the old concept–word. In other words, when the philosopher articulates a new concept, he is not quite successful in his endeavour, for his articulated concept remains, will ever remain, questionable. The word as well as the concept, or, to be more precise, the word–concept thus remains, ever and always, problematic. A darkness envelops the philosopher–scientist's 'light'; there is no clarity which is not obscurity, no articulation which is not dumb.

There are some men and women other than the scientist or the philosopher for whom the dark presence within them is too alive, too immediate to be reduced into a generality, to a concept or a term, that everybody's word. There are occasions when it becomes forbidding, threatening to disrupt and destroy them and their world. The philosopher–scientist succeeds, to an extent, to tame that dark presence into the communicable word, the conceptual word, the word that is/can be anybody's word because the presence does not present itself before him as an existential threat but only as a problem, a serious problem, of understanding, understanding of himself and the world. He can tame it because it is, relatively speaking, weak, disrupting only his conceptual framework, not his existential context. When the dark isolation truly becomes an existential threat, it refuses to become a part of our daily world and our conceptual discourses. It comes very near to undo us, our world and our reality principles. Men and women live in deep pain when this demonic darkness comes to possess them, this choking and killing force, that will not let them feel, think, even, sometimes, breathe. They find it killing because they do not know, cannot say, what it is, this demon within them, do not know how this dweller within their little self, whose existence most human beings do not even suspect, has the power to disrupt, even to destroy, their entire world.

It is not that the men and women, whom this 'nothingness' will not let rest, easily give in to it; they too would tame it, would reduce it into language, but language not of generalities, not language of terms, but language of words, intimate words about which I, if I ever come to stumble upon them, will/can only say that they are mine alone, uniquely mine, and will not consent to be anybody else's unless and until that somebody else becomes me through an intent and intimate contemplation of them. The proximity with which that forbidding, but my own, undersoul presses upon me compels me to respond to it personally and in words personal. I find those words intimate, personal, inextricably related to me and my being because they are the saviours of the person in me, save me from the anonymity of the nothing within and the anonymity of the generality without. Personal identity cannot be affirmed or asserted in propositional terms. It can only be shown forth, shown forth by the unexpressed intimacy one feels in the presence of these words born out of the encounter of one's soul and undersoul. Only the intimate language of a poet can reveal it, reveal it through its presence, not through utterance, only the intimate speech of the intimate presence, of the darkness—for in that moment the darkness itself seems to speak and not the man. Not the language of self affirmation which makes of me a concept or its illustration. The innocent words of the poet can give us some moments in which we can be almost ourselves, moments which our normal social relationships, even our familial relationships, often fail to give, except when we act originally, not as 'they' but as the me's isolated from others but open to the intimations within, intimations of the self-same dark interiority.

To that interiority we owe all our knowledge and all our light, all our goodness, howsoever little or howsoever fleeting and those rare moments for which we ever remain grateful, the rare moments when we feel we have almost come to be ourselves. All that we value and cherish we owe to it, to that anonymity in us which most of us would sleep over, or, when it would not consent to be ignored, would flee from. We forget that what we would term chaos, confusion or disorder in us is the creative centre of all that is original and out of the ordinary in any civilisation and culture. Every civilisations, we must remember, even the most scientific, is 'mystical' in inspiration. Any civilisation that fails to find order in this chaos and life in this death cannot hope to survive as a living civilisations. It will come to ruin because it will be peopled not by persons but by categories, not by ends but by means. Can any civilisation treat man as an end in himself when it cannot recognise the person in him? Modern civilisation should seriously ponder upon this question.

Poetry is, thus, the utterance of the impersonal to save and reveal the person, save him, through its rhythm and imagery, from the generality that he is in our social, and, more often than not, in our personal, life. Lingering on each and every syllable, on its suppression as much as on its expression, postpones the expression of 'the total idea' of the poem in question. Yet I have the patience and the leisure to give myself up to this lingering, to this hampered expression, because it can, for a moment, make me the person I would be. In the same way, the imagery of a poem resists our attempt to treat a thing as a mere member of a class or a link in a causal or conceptual chain; it lets the thing before us stand out and stay as itself and by itself to make us, for the moment we contemplate it, stay with it and for it and, staying with it and for it, stay with ourselves and by ourselves. Unfortunately, not many among us pause to realise that a single syllable, a single word, can give us what a whole life and all the learned philosophico–scientific discourses may, and, for most, do, fail to give: a moment of being oneself.

The rhythm and music of a poem thus releases me, for some moments, from the tyranny of the syntax, and, with that, from the tyranny of the linguistic context, from the *langue,* and from the other of the linguistic context, the world. There is enough space in a single sound unit to absorb and accommodate me and my world. And in a single word or a single image. The syntax, of course, is there and also the context of the structure and body of language and the context of the world but they do not infringe upon me, upon my leisure and my autonomy, when I am in the grip of this creativity, when my soul is at peace with my undersoul and pays all the heed to it. They are willing to wait, those contexts, even to be marginalised for a moment for this moment of intimacy, even to be ignored. For it is the syllable, the single syllable, the single image that will constitute me, sustain me, introduce me to myself. So little do I demand then, so little do I need that I can find enough leisure to rest in that moment, to become, so to say, a being-in-the-moment. This being-in-the-moment, the being deplaced and decontextualised, however, is a being of and for the moment. I cannot, I find, sustain this moment, cannot (despite the feeling of plenitude and fullness) be fully that moment, because this speech too is, despite its leisured pace and absorbing sensusousness, ultimately a movement towards the whole, towards the articulation of the entire poem, which will be a poem among poems, a moment of language and of the world. The syntax will eventually triumph, the context will assert itself, with all the hamperings placed in its way, and so will the world. The moment cannot stay for long, the syllable, the image and the word. Human beings do not easily consent to be themselves for long, they would rather assert than *be.*

So the self that this word of the poet reveals or creates, reveals or creates gently, unobtrusively, 'silently', is undone by this very word itself, by its inevitable orientation towards the referent and towards the context of the referent, the class-context or the world-context. The poet will question the darkness, ask it who it is but only to the extent it consents to be expressed, made manifest, in *human* words. I *almost* suggested above that this dark fertility itself creates a poem, not, to be sure, every kind of poem but only the poem that a poet is said to create at what are called 'his most inspired moments'. But even 'the most inspired poem' is not the pure utterance of the enigmatic muse. It too has the element of the human in it, some contribution, to use a prosaic term, made by the poet himself. Even in his most authentic moment, the poet does not fully integrate with the muse, does not fully become the darkness to utter with the darkness and as the darkness. Howsoever open to it he may be, whatever be the depth of his passivity and nonassertiveness, of his breathless waiting for the peal of the word, he retains his identity as passivity at least, as waiting, as the listener of the peal. This much of contribution he does make, diligently make, this 'human' contribution of passive opening out. This does not always happen easily or spontaneously. Some have to struggle for it, for the words of the sociality in them continue to intrude into and mingle with the findings of the passivity in them, rendering their expulsion difficult, sometimes impossible. Many are too vain even to try to distinguish between the stale words and the creative words, between the findings of the *me* and the assertions of the generality. Most great poetry thus remains a mixture of inspiration and fabrication. Even on the rare moments when the muse replaces the man, it is the *human* muse that replaces him, not the *deinon* or the *deva,* the god, not the darkness and the mystery. I say '*human* muse' because the man does not die, he only becomes passive, a recipient passivity, which does not fail to personalise the muse. It is for this reason that the poetic voice is the poet's own voice, and nobody else's voice, neither of the 'they' nor of the god.

So the man in the poet does not lose himself, he remains the being that he is, the being-with-others, a being along with the world. He remains so, though not actively. He does become passive, consents to be marginalised and pushed aside, but he does not cease to be. The man in him ever waits to reassert himself, at the very first opportunity. The moment of release the poet finds is, therefore, a passing moment, a moment of escape, not a moment of ontological transformation. The poet does not really and truly become the person to remain the person. With the passing away of the moment, that intimate moment, passes away the person too, the person or what seemed like him.

How to be person, to be oneself, is the passion of our life, colouring all our activities, our thoughts, our aspirations. Our possessions cannot make us persons nor can our daily actions nor our thoughts, frivolous or serious. These can enrich the sociality in us or make of it a poor thing but they cannot free us from it. They can augment the sense of mine but cannot make me the me I would be. They make of me a title, a generality, not a self, not a being. Nor can the creativity of a philosopher–scientist nor of the poet, not even in his most inspired, most authentic moment. Should man, unlike the philosopher and the poet, take the plunge into the dark chaos, that total disorder and confusion, or what seems to us, creatures of the group and order, like these, take the plunge to be himself? He will not take that plunge as long as the human blood and human breath flow and move within him, as long as he would cling to his human self or identity, that being-with-against-others and being-in-out-of-the-world. But some are there who will, are almost destined to, take the daring step, those who have drunk the bitter cup of life, who have seen through the veils of illusions that we daily weave, illusions secular and sacred, seen through them without the further illusions of bitterness and cynicism. They can see through the veils because they live aware of their death, not the death that beings-along-with-others know of, an event among other events, but death that the dying man has to 'die': the end of all the world and its affairs, its past, present and future. Such men as can die with the dying can enter into those dark and killing depths which the world sleeps over, which the philosopher–scientist would sabotage into what we call knowledge and the poet into what we call plenitude and beauty and being ourselves. They cannot be bewitched by these seductive things because they have drunk enough of the bitter draught. They enter into the realm of 'death', enter into it because the other death, what we call life, has nothing left to offer them. What do they find there? Simply nothing as the majority of people take that to be? Or, chaos as the scientist would take it, or confusion as a conceptualist will find it? Or the No-person that the poet would fear and avoid? Those who had the courage to plunge into that forbidding nothingness did not, they affirm, perish in it; they rose up all transformed. Some say that they dived into it as crows but came up as swans, others that they dived as the sons of men but came up as the sons of God, or as God himself. Others rose up as the Word, the abode of all that is, was or could be, the healing of the divide between the word and the referent, between the name proper and the name common, the divide that renders our knowledge ignorance, our reality a falsehood, our goals a mockery, our self no-self.

The Word they become is, they say, their name, their true name as well as the name of others, the name at once proper and universal, the name uniquely mine, uniquely yours and of everybody else, of every being and every thing. And it is also me, you and everything and every being. In what we call life, my proper name does not inform me, it is only a label, a sign totally adventitious to me. What seems to inform me is a common name, which does not inform me but negates me, renders irrelevant the person that I am or would be. Only the name that is at once proper and universal can truly inform me. And that name cannot remain *my* name, it will be me, my self. [All these thoughts which can barely be hinted at here have received our considered attention in our study of the Upaniṣads.] The poet, we saw, found the word/s that seemed to bear witness to the person in him. But they did not become him, those words, they remained *his* words. And the word which is only *mine* and not *me*, does not, cannot, stay with me to become my proper, informing name. However, when the word and the I coalesce, when the former becomes *properly* my proper name, others will not remain others, all will share in the same name to become the me that will be the all. The person that the poet found was, therefore, only a seeming person, not the real person, because he was not all the persons. The poet stays at a word or a syllable through exclusion, exclusion of the structure and texture of language, he does not become the word or the syllable to find it as the all. All genuine poetic utterance is, therefore, a joy and a pain, a promise trembling insecure at the threshold of being, insecure because the threshold will not be crossed and the promise never fulfilled. And the threshold is not crossed because the poet would be, and remain, merely himself, would not be the real person, the person that is all the persons. The poet is a creature of misery when the creative mood finally deserts him, 'like the woman wailing for her demon lover.' Like 'the woman' he only forgot that he was human, a mere generality; he had no real, genuine proper name, no real, genuine self, the person he had become was more of a semblance than of reality. His demon too could not convert him into himself and, therefore, deserted him as did the woman's. And like the woman's too is his ambivalence towards the dispenser of his 'being', the ambivalence that makes of the latter both a terror and an attraction, a seductive death as it were. The Word, on the contrary, is the home, the being of all, is my self as well as yours, of the world and of whatever might lie beyond it, 'before' its origin and 'beyond' its end. In that Word alone do I truly find myself and whatever else I seek, or would know or be. All discourses seek it, all endeavours would find it, all aspirations and all desires. But one can find the Word only by being it, you cannot find it otherwise, you cannot hear it. For the moment you hear it, it will cease to be the Word, will turn into something else. For the Word-become, therefore, there is no Word, not the Word we can talk about. To call the Word 'Word' is a falsehood, a false attribution. Similarly, when the Word is heard, it will not remain the Word; it will turn into a word, a distortion of it, an impoverishment of it. They say that the Word manifests itself as the Heard Word, as the *śruti*, the word which can only be heard but has no speaker, for what we call its speakers: seers, prophets, sages: are none else than the Word itself. The Word that does not hear itself cannot also 'hear', know, that it is the speaker. The *antevāsins*, those who live in the proximity of the sage, of the prophet or the seer or what seems like these, alone can hear the Word. For these alone, the *antevāsins*, the Word is the Word, not for the Word-become seer. But does the Word, can it, remain the same Word, can it remain even the Word, for these hearers of the Word? Will it not become a part of the human discourse, a kind of human discourse, 'an expression of a culture', 'a product of a particular language game', or, if nothing else, at least a kind of human language? The Word which is not the Word for itself cannot remain the Word for its hearer, too. The latter however can call it the Word because despite its peal and its articulation, despite its modification into the *śruti*, it has something in it which is more than the human word it has changed itself into. How can we say, wherein find the sign and indication to assert, that this word of which there was no speaker is different from every human word, every human discourse?

The *śruti*, the Word Heard, the revelation, is always anthropomorphised by most human hearers, by the faithfuls no less than by the rationalists and the humanists. The humanists and the rationalists find it a mere cultural document, every book of revelation, to be understood and assessed in the context of its cultural *milieu*. The Vedas that are said to be *apauruṣayas*, authorless, are not taken to be so by the rationalists or realists. They are considered to be human words, conditioned by human situations, with all the limitations of those situations. There is no sanctity attached to them, as indeed to any other revelation; they have to be assessed by modern man in terms of his own understanding and framework but with a mind open enough to assess his own world view from their point of view and modify it, if possible. This is the most reasonable approach that modern man can put forward and, on occasions, acts upon. For the faithfuls, on the other hand, the *śruti* is the word of God, the word that redeems and saves, the word of the Truth itself. They do not, would not, care to understand the implications of '*apauruṣaya*': the coming together of the name and of the named, of the speaker and speech, of knowledge and reality, of me and the other, of my proper name and the common name. Their Word is not the Word but a word and their God is no God but a man speaking like man. [The Vedic vision of the Word the reader will find explained in the pages of this and earlier volumes, more specifically in my analysis, in the present volume, of the *sūkta* 10.71 of the *Ṛg Veda*.]

If the Word is not the Word for itself, that is to say, for what we call a sage, a seer or a prophet nor can it be for the hearers of it, for those who hear the sage utter it, then why is it called the Word? The *śruti* is said to be the Word manifested, manifested in the form of human language as a seer is said to be the Word manifested in the form of the human person. Those who self-submit to it do find, they say, this apparently human language exceeding itself as it were, transform itself and them into the Word, the Word that knows not itself. Even those who do not thus give themselves up to it, who retain their human identity, even their rational pursuations and the creed of the scholar, cannot but notice a difference between the *śruti* and our human discourses. Human discourses, they know, reveal and conceal, relate and alienate, communicate and dissimulate, exalt and degrade, guide and cheat, make the seemingly ugly look beautiful and the beautiful look ugly, render the simple complex and the complex simple, even ordinary. They all remain dualities, all our discourses, and speak about dualities to dualities. They cannot undo the duality, cannot take one to the referent, cannot make one oneself, cannot give one the truth, the truth as it is 'to and for itself', but only interpretations of these. There are no doubt some thinkers who may go to the extent of equating reality with interpretations, as the idealists equated it with ideas but the majority will concede these limitations of the human discourse and the divide that obtains between it and reality— even the most committed humanists among them. For the dilemma remains ineliminable for every thoughtful humanist: How could there be me without language and the world, and how could language be there without me and the world, and how could the world be there, the world we think we know and live in, without me–others and language? It is no use calling them coprimordialities as some followers of Wittgenstein would like to do. When things cannot be without each other, cannot even be conceived so, it is mere confusion to use mere names. In our experience, we do find these three together, but do we ever pause to visualise, ever imagine, what becomes of language, of me and others and of the world when they are contemplated, *experientially*, as 'coprimodialities'? I cannot visualise this without flowing into the others, into the world, its entire space; I cannot do this without finding the word as me and me as the word. If I succeed in doing this and cannot know where I end and the world begins, who I am and what the world is, who the speaker is and what/who the word [where will be 'who', 'which', 'what', then?], I will be in such an undecidable state, I will be such a nondecision, that I will have no breath left to talk about me and the world and language and their interconstitutive and internegating functions. There will be no me, no world and no language to relate in any terms, neither those of distinction nor those of identity nor, for that matter, of ambiguity.

We were, however, considering how the *śruti* can be recognised, is, in fact, recognised as different from all human discourses despite its concealment by the human ear. The *śruti* is different from human discourses because it would lead man out of these dualities, the dualities that these discourses are and proclaim. It does not concern itself with what we call 'human' concerns but would ask man to rise above them, that is, above himself. It does, no doubt, ask man to relate himself with others, not with other humans alone, but with animals, domestic and wild, with birds, even with the elements. When it asks man to care for others through charity, through hospitality and through service, one may well imagine, as indeed many of the faithfuls and the nonfaithfuls have imagined, that it expresses concern for human affairs and human society and human wellbeing. But its equal call for care of the animals and of the elements severely qualifies its 'humanistic concerns'. Human community, rational, communicative community, has the material world as its constitutive other, for that is the world which communicative, linguistic, concepts can reveal or, more accurately speaking, constitute. To flow into inanimate things, to be inert with a stone, to blow with a puff of breeze and to flutter with a leaf or to fall with it when the breeze turns into a gust is to undo the me that perceived and experienced these phenomena and occurrences as phenomena and occurrences; it is also to undo them, undo the concepts, undo the referential and the interpretative language, in truth, the entire world. To be what he perceives is devastating for man the communality and the material world, the constitutive other of that communality. What will happen to me and the world and language when I, following the lead given by the *śruti*, extend with the earth to its horizons, to the quarters, up to the sky and flow on and on beyond the sky towards ... (?). Space will not remain space then, space that extends for ever and ever and is experienced as such, as continuous extending, as temporality as it were. And will not I too turn into this extending, I and the world becoming one, and in becoming one becoming innocent of myself and of the world? And if I find myself too passive to extend with the earth, I may, again following the instruction of the *śruti*, merely contemplate a most ordinary thing before me, contemplate it passively, so passively that I become, so to say, that thing. I will find, in that moment of deep concentration, a concentration which will be an occurrence and not an act, the entire world and infinity itself dwelling in the little thing before me, the little thing swallowing up me too into itself. So the way the *śruti* asks us to relate can be devastatingly disruptive, disruptive of the whole interpreted world, not merely of the little thing before me and the little being that I am.

What about the claims that the faithfuls are never tired of making about the truth value of its alleged 'propositions', claims that the not-faithfuls find so unconvincing? Those who study these so-called propositions with care cannot fail to notice that there is no truth that the *śruti* proclaims which it will not disclaim, no virtue that it upholds which it will not disown. To be sure, it would not do it conceptually but what may be called existentially, through outliving a truth or virtue by living it. Thus it does *not* ask man to disclaim all truths and disown all virtues and *retain* himself, his judgement and his thinking. On the contrary, it asks man to live every truth it proclaims and practise every virtue it enjoins. Let man, to give but one example, live as the body, as the senses, as breath, as thought, as judgement, let him live these 'truths' and the bliss of contemplation, the last 'truth' of his experience. When he does that, he will find how he outlives all these states, one after the other, eventually to [find himself] as what can only be termed untruth. The *śruti* reveals this way how every doctrine, when lived through, disowns itself, every truth, every state of being, every virtue. [How it does this will be found in the pages of this and the preceding volumes].

So the *śruti* relates but only to derelate and derelates only to relate. Its revelations are concealments, its concealments revelations, its truths falsehoods, its falsehoods truths. It finds depths on the surface and the surface in the depths, the mortal as the immortal and the immortal as the mortal, earth as heaven and heaven as earth. It leads man into godhood and godhood into manhood and affirms to deny and denies to affirm. It leads one to bliss to reveal it a misery, to truth to reveal it untruth. This it does not in order to proclaim the cult of the ambiguous but to undo man and his concepts, for his goal will not be attained to until he has undone himself and his concepts. For that is the goal cut out for him, his fate, his destiny, his mortal destiny. And he has to own it up, this destiny, this his *moira* of being reduced to nothingness, to 'untruth'. In this post-modern age, we have come to proclaim ourselves as prophets of the ambiguous. We believe we perceive the ambiguous everywhere: in our truths, in our norms, in our values, in our relationships. It is because we *think* we *perceive* the ambiguous, because we *think* we *know and understand* it, and proclaim it with every force and conviction that we find ourselves in a mess. How has it happened that we have found untruth in truth, nonbeing in being and *vice versa* and managed to retain ourselves, our conceptualisations, our formulations to proclaim this so-called truth? How is that, despite my loud proclamations of the ambiguous, I cannot share in the stoniness of the stone and the stone share in my consciousness and in my speech? How is it that it does not share in my perception of it? For the real seer of the ambiguous is one who floats between polarities, who flows into the other to let the other to flow into him, not one who proclaims the concept of the ambiguous. This cannot happen unless and until we become the ambiguity life–death, unless we find life and death reconciled with each other. Until that happens, it is no use talking about the ambiguous. Only the man who lives in death 'knows' what the ambiguous is, not the man who *lives* and still has the audacity to enunciate the doctrine of the ambiguous.

We cannot become ambiguities, cannot live as ambiguities as long as we can think in and through concepts, as long as we think and affirm and deny. Ambiguity, genuine ambiguity, can only show itself forth, it cannot be formulated. The *śruti* does not, therefore, ask man to conceptually find, merely conceptually, unrighteousness in righteousness, untruth in truth and *vice versa*. It asks man to orient himself towards the other, the beyond and the ideal and death and find out if the other is the other, the beyond the beyond and death death. When man does orient himself this way, he will turn into innocence and the world into *samatvam*, into sameness, the nondual that will not consent to be conceptualised in our terms. The paradox, the momentous paradox, is that our conceptual dualities turn out to be no dualities when they are lived and not merely formulated.

This is precisely the case with language too. Language shares in the trait of the ambiguous with its interpretations. But for those who merely advocate ambiguities, it is, existentially speaking, an *absolutus*. For these proclaimers of the ambiguous, words are simply *there*, unambiguously there. That is why they can pick them up and use them. They do not pause to contemplate the word they so unheedingly use, do not live to mingle into it, would not be it. When I stay between the word and myself, I shall not be able to utter the word, nor hear it, there will be not enough distance between me and the word for speaking and hearing. In that silence-like speech, where will be this thing I call myself, this word that I speak, this world I live in and speak about? Again, the paradox is that you come to this silence–speech not through distancing yourself from language, but by flowing into language, flowing into it to own it up as your being. Those who declare language as the informing principle of reality have only to be language to know how language turns into something else, which is neither me nor language, nothing that any term can encompass or express. That very state of being, that profound reconciliation of me and the word, of the name and the named, is what is called the Word.

The *śruti* prepares us for this contemplation of the word before us, to dwell in it so that we become that word and the word us. For this purpose, it asks the miserable cruel and insensitive man to be sensitive and compassionate; the selfish and calculating man to be large hearted and generous; the self centred man to open out; the realist to become aware of the depth and mystery of things; the worldling to hear the call of the beyond, and one who would *be*, would sleep over mortality, to remember death. When, after a long probation, man succeeds in shedding his cruelty and insensitivity, his self-centred calculations and greediness, when he turns concernful and caring, and never forgets that he is not a being to be but a being not be, when man succeeds in accomplishing this, he will become serene and innocent enough to linger on the word before him, stay there still and restful. A being towards death, a true being towards death, is not anxious to interpret, for all frameworks, all contexts, all forms of life are of no account for him. He will simply be, this man who lives as if he were not [again, another paradox]. Whatever thought articulates itself in him, a passing thought, will not be related to a framework, that passing thought itself will be enough for this passivity and mortality. I will not commit the mistake of describing what that word-become state is. The *śruti* itself will give us many a hint in this regard. But it does say that the word-become is the Word-become and that seeming silence is the source from whence peals the redemptive word, the word of the *śruti*. Of our human discourses too is that the source and of the other of these discourses, our world. However, these do not, cannot, lead us to the source because they are the various facets of the process of sleeping over, of not heeding, the call of the Word.

So the *śruti* which to us linguistic beings appears a mere discourse, a discourse among discourses, will turn into the Word when we, following its lead, prepare ourselves for the contemplation of its word, a single word, *aum* or some other. All moral preparation, spiritual endeavours and penances are meant for this purpose, to create in us that innocence which can give itself up to the word as if it were the all. This clearly runs counter to all human discourses which are man-centred and man serving, augmenting thereby his tragedy. The ravages wrought by the 'achievements' of these discourses, these logos insulting discourses, especially those inspired by the Faustian passion, have received our attention in the present work and need not be mentioned here. One may, however, pause a little on the sorry state to which philosophy has brought itself as a result of its humanistic preoccupations, oblivious of its own creative springs. We have *rigorously* landed ourselves into trivialities, thought ourselves into despair, lost every sense of direction and concern for the search for meaning. Our goals and purposes have degenerated into 'values', mere creatures of man, of his language games, to be trifled and flirted with, not to live for and die for. Consumer culture has become the bane of this civilisation, the source of most of our troubles. But we cannot even make a plea for outliving it, a convincing plea, because we have lost all touch with meaning and purpose. They have become, more or less, our fabrications, with no objective validity about them. As for truth, we have already equated it with interpretation, our interpretation. In our infatuation with ourselves, we forget that we are born in interpretations, we do not precede them. If we too are indispensable for interpretations, we are indispensable not so much as their creators as their inheritors, as their creatures. In our arrogance, we have forgotten that language is a gift to us, it is not our creation. That is how it constitutes us and we it. The *śruti* makes us aware of this truth and commands us not to be mere users of words but their contemplators, of a single word, to find it the Word, our self, the self of each and of all. Until we do that our life will remain a futility and tragedy, our knowledge ignorance, our happiness a misery.

We moderns killed god to replace him with man but succeeded in killing both god and man. Today, man is as much a chimera as god is. With the arrogance of modernity to augment his ego, modern man may feel comfortable with himself. With the cynicism of postmodernism to support him, he may sleep over his existential *angst.* But how long can the comfort last and the oblivion sustain a mere nothing? Human imagination cannot visualise their indefinite continuity, cannot visualise that this civilisation will not meet its end sooner than later. We have chosen to ignore the source, the darkness, the creativity, we have chosen to celebrate the effect, the light and the given, the fact and the concept. We forget that the fact and the concept, the light and the given are death, the darkness and the source, life. We even forget that our knowledge, our science, which we think is *our* discourse, the discourse of our reason and observation, owes its inspiration and life to that darkness, to that source. We forget that that is our purpose, our goal, our truth, and that what we call our purposes, our goals, our 'values' are mere aberrations of it. We must remember, always remember, the source of our knowledge, we will bring only ruin upon ourselves if we do not remember that source, that innocence. For only that knowledge can bear the right fruit, only that security can sustain, only that comfort can refresh and renew which does not make us forget the source, the goal, the ground of our being. Our discourses will turn ruinous if we allow ourselves to be overwhelmed by what they promise in terms of knowledge and power, forgetful of the source of these 'triumphant' songs of 'humanity'. We must revive our awareness of the source, and our orientation towards it, to keep our obsessive passion for knowledge and power within limits. And it is only revelation, only the *śruti*, the word heard and not spoken, that can make us aware of that innocence within us and lead us to it to turn us into the Word and, eventually, to die with the Word. It is time we realised that we have had enough of discourses and enough of knowledge, more than enough of them.

The song of the siren is tempting, the lure of knowledge is irresistible. It is casting its spell on India, too, despite her long tradition of devotion to the *śruti*. Her intellectuals have almost given themselves up to the culture of discourse, they have almost killed the god, disowned the innocence, rejected the darkness for the sake of man, of knowledge and of light. The darkness is all confusion for most of them, the innocence all chaos. Many among them do not even suspect that it exists somewhere within them, such is the extent of their obsession with modernity, with rationality, with science. They forget that concepts and ideas, which they have merely picked up, picked up as abstractions, have been emergences in the West, the expressions of 'creative' experiences and situations in its history. They do not realise that emergences, when fossilised into abstract ideas or values, often turn into tyrannies and falsehoods and that imitation can only be of abstractions and not of emergences. Other traditions can be fruitful only to the extent they can be lived and experienced, not as impositions. The difficulty with modern civilisation is that it has already, out of arrogance of its success and power, fossilised, in practice though not always in theory, its emergences into abstractions, open ended sustenances into nonrelative principles and norms, rendering them thereby into instruments of power and domination. If we Indians pick up , merely pick up, these 'principles' and 'norms', we will pick them up not as persons but as instruments, as means for progress, for power, for technology. And instruments, we know, can neither begin nor sustain a rational discourse, for that too requires awareness of the presence of the opaque within us, even if it sabotages this awareness into itself, attributes that which it owes to that darkness to itself. So, we will not succeed even in that sphere, unless we come upon ideas as emergences through our encounter with the darkness . We will have to be 'irrational', to an extent, to be rational, originally and not imitatively.

Rational–scientific discourse that disowns its own source is a forgetting of it, negates, as we have seen, the opportunity occasionally given to man to be the person. Will our economic–scientific progress, if and when we Indians succeed in accomplishing it, be of much avail if we cease to be *persons* and live only as means and instruments? Market economy, which we want to adopt, will not let the person emerge, not even what is called welfare economy. For the latter, too, envisages, practically, man not as a person awake to the illuminating darkness within him but a mere unit of the totality called society, who will become a useful unit if his needs and wants are taken due care of. So, ultimately, success is the criterion, success in the discourse oriented towards mastery of nature. *Welfare* economy, welfare economy in the true sense, is not the economy that sustains us as instruments of production and consumption but as persons, which does not, will not, hinder the flow of the creative spring in us. Only that science is enlightened which helps sustain our orientation towards 'the not-being', 'the untruth' within us, sharpens our awareness of it. And only that economics is a welfare economics which does not pervert that orientation into a consumeristic one. Neither our knowledge of nature nor our mastery of it, nor the systems of social and economic relationships should make us forget where our life is, our welfare is and our purpose is. Unfortunately, our knowledge, our arts, our actions can, and often do, prevent us from drinking at the fount of life. The arrogance of knowledge and power, the insensitivity that goes with addiction to pleasures, the resultant decadence of a consumer culture have, in these our times, achieved precisely this, more than this: most of us do not even suspect that there is such a spring flowing in each one of us. We have to subdue this arrogance, we have to restrain our desires and orient ourselves to simplicity, in life and in thought, to save ourselves from this bestiality which we have come to confuse with humanity. 'Being human' has really become a nauseating phrase. How crudely it makes us forget that we are all disinherited beings! To regain our humanity, our openness to Being, our urge for transcendence, we must, have to, heed the call of the *śruti,* its call to hear the voice of the Word in its words. We can be persons, come to be ourselves, only if we give ourselves up to that call, not when we expect truth to obey our call. Modern world has to remember this truth, the 'developed' part of it as well as the 'developing' part of it. Some modern thinkers have voiced, in convincing terms, their anguish over the destructive trends in modern civilisation. But the agony has failed to disillusion most of them of their faith in the human discourse; they would only ask for recognition of the relative legitimacy of the discourses other than the scientific. They, most of them, continue to remain 'human' to perpetuate, unwittingly, the inhumanity of humanism. The commitment of modern civilisation to rationality, to theory laden observation, to conceptual thinking remains, in practice, full and unqualified, with all the criticism of these attitudes and approaches. This commitment is so deep, so fatal, that these attitudes are only conceptually criticised, not outlived. We must soften down our commitment to discourse and listen to the Word, we must sacrifice knowledge for innocence, cognitive acquisitiveness for opening out, if we would avoid the suicidal consequences of modern cynicism and consumerism. We have to choose if we would live as *persons* or as mere means.

It is a matter of some satisfaction that these volumes have been kindly received by philosophers, scholars and reviewers. In the preface to the second volume I expressed my deep sense of gratitude to Professor Paul Ricoeur, Professor Jean-François Lyotard and Professor Raimundo Panikkar for their very encouraging responses and to the scholars who had reviewed Volume 1, or otherwise responded to it. Some reviews appeared or reached me after the publication of the second volume. I take the opportunity offered by this preface to express my thanks to Professors Fred Dallmayr and J.N. Mohanty and the editor of 'Philosophy East and West' for the two reviews published therein, a stimulating review of Volume 1 by Professor Dallmayr and a perceptive, and, to borrow a word from the review itself, inspiring review of Volume 2 by Professor Mohanty. Professor V.Y.Kantak wrote a very appreciative review of volume 2, which appeared in the 'Journal of Indian Council of Philosophical Research'. I thank him, thank him with emotion, and also its present editor, Professor Daya Krishna. And so do I thank Professor Michel Adam and the editor of *Revue philosophique*, Paris, for a generous review of the first volume. Professor Panikkar, Dr. Karan Singh, Dr. Kapila Vatsyayan and Professor Namwar Singh continue to be encouraging. I shall be failing in my duty if I do not mention, with thanks, the debt I owe to my friend and a profound Pāṇiṇt scholar, Mr Śivanārāyaṇa Śāstrī.

This volume had the support of a senior fellowship granted by the Department of Culture, Ministry of Human Resource Development. I take this opportunity to express my deep appreciation of the support.

Mr. N.P. Jain is as cooperative as ever and Sunjay Sharma as helpful, patient and supporting in editing the work as before. I should not, of course, blame him for the many faults this volume doubtless has. My feelings towards my wife and children remain what they were before. There has been no disillusionment to qualify them.

This volume has been in press for almost two years. I am happy that it is now going to be published.

Delhi **Som Raj Gupta**
January, 1999

LIST OF ABBREVIATIONS

1.	AiĀ	Aitareya Ārṇyaka
2.	AitU	Aitareya Upaniṣad
3.	Āp	Āpastamba Dharma Sūtras
4.	BG	Bhagavadgītā
5.	BṛU	Bṛhadāraṇyaka Upaniṣad
6.	ChU	Chāndogya Upaniṣad
7.	GK	Gauḍapāda Kārikā
8.	ĪśaU	Īśa Upaniṣad
9.	Kaṭh(a)U	Kaṭha Upaniṣad
10.	Ken(a)U	Kena Upaniṣad
11.	Manu	Mānava Dharmaśāstra (Manusmṛti)
12.	Mā(ṇḍ)U	Māṇḍūkya Upaniṣad
13.	MB	Mahābhārata
14.	Mu(ṇḍ)U	Muṇḍaka Upaniṣad
15.	Pr(aśna)U	Praśna Upaniṣad
16.	SB	Śātapatha Brāhmaṇa
17.	ŚB	Śāṅkara-bhāṣya
18.	ŚveU	Śvetāśvatara Upaniṣad
19.	TB	Taittirīya Brāhmaṇa
20.	TaitU	Taittirīya Upaniṣad

Note: In this work, the *mantras* of the Upaniṣads are printed in a larger type than the type adopted for the author's commentary. Śaṅkara's *bhāṣya* is given in a smaller type and is always preceded by ***ŚB*** (Śāṅkara-bhāṣya).

SCHEME OF TRANSLITERATION

Vowels	a ā i ī u ū ṛ ṝ ḷ e ai o au
anusvāra	ṃ
visarga	ḥ
Consonants	
gutturals	k kh g gh ṅ
palatals	c ch j jh ñ
cerebrals	ṭ ṭh ḍ ḷ ḍh ḷh ṇ
dentals	t th d dh n
labials	p ph b bh m
semi-vowels	y r l v
sibilants	s as in *sun*
	ś palatal sibilant
	ṣ cerebral sibilant
aspirate	h

For the reader not familiar with Sanskrit

a may be pronounced as *u* in *but*
ā as *a* in *father*
i as *i* in *if*
ī as *ee* in *feel*
u as *u* in *full*
ū as *u* in *rule*
e as *ay* in *play*
ai as *y* in *my*
o as *o* in *globe*
au as *ow* in *now*
ṛ as *ri* in *ritual*
ḷ as *li* in *lick*
g as *g* in *go*
c as *ch* in *church*
ś and *ṣ* as *sh* in *shun*
ṃ at the end of a word and before labials as *m*, elsewhere as *n*
This is only a rough scheme.

TAITTIRĪYA UPANIṢAD

An Upaniṣad of the *Yajur Veda*

TAITTIRĪYA UPANIṢAD

Part 1

Sīkṣāvallī

Chapter 1

ŚB From which is born all this transient world, into which is it dissolved, and by which is it sustained, to that do I bow, that which has consciousness as its being.

I ever bow to those teachers who in the past did explain the Upaniṣads word by word and sentence by sentence through means that lead to knowledge true.

By the grace of my teacher shall I explain this essence of the *Taittirīya* part of the Vedas for the sake of those who would have an exposition clear of it.

The transient world is ever and always a world to be, a world with a past to escape from and a future to escape into. A never ending struggle is it between past and future, with no real present dimension informing it. Not that it ever had a beginning, an absolute beginning without a past. There would have been no world if it had one, an absolute beginning. Equally, there will never be a time when it would have no future. For that too will mean its end. The world can be only a world to be, not a world that has come to be. The same is true of things in the world. There is no thing which has a present dimension, which means it has no genuine past and future dimensions. One cannot find it as a presence, nor can one understand it in terms of past and future, in terms, that is, of cause and effect, or, for that matter, in terms of whole and part.

Our concepts and categories are hopelessly inadequate to encompass what we call the world. Totally adventitious to it are they, even the concept 'world'. This last term too is merely another name for cause–effect, part–whole relationships. The way to approach the truth of the world does not lie through these categories. One has to outlive them, these concepts and categories and let what *is* do what it will. Before this passive opening out, this noninterfering disposition, things will present themselves as events, as occurrences, not as fixed and inert things; material things will turn into mental events, the external will become the internal, the internal external. Consciousness would emerge as witness to this dance of coming to be and ceasing to be, one giving place to another, without effort, without reason.

Those who think as prisoners of categories will ever find consciousness problematic, this most proximate fact for one who can be indolent, nonself-referentially indolent, *vis-a-vis* his percepts and thoughts, his feelings and ideas. Before a man in this mood, if indeed it could be termed as a mood, thoughts arise like ripples from a contentless, thought-free source to collapse into it almost immediately. Or like shadows. Thoughts they are not but what may be called thing–thoughts or thought–things. One cannot in that 'mood' know where and how to demarcate between what one used to call mind and world. From that dark passivity rises the world, the thought–world, in it does it dwell and into it does it disappear.

It is only the man who has been seized by that peaceful darkness, that passive depth in him, who can see, with utmost clarity, why we mortals are so desperately in search of causes and effects. He will know the cause of our futile search, not when he is in that lucid 'mood' but when he has come back to what we, in our blindness, call normal moods. He will find that nothing comes to be itself as a phenomenon except when it meges in this simple contentless awareness. However, when phenomena merge into that awareness, the latter too will cease to be. Awareness, consciousness contentless and pure, is thus not the true being of the world. But to us, creatures who are burdened with consciousness of things, that awareness alone is truth, the source and end of the world. We have to accept that alone as our self, our being, our truth. We have to give ourselves up to it, sacrifice ourselves into it, to be the truth itself, the truth that is not consciousness. Our way to that absolute truth lies through consciousness alone; there is no sudden leap into it.

This is what the Upaniṣads reveal to us and this is how the commentator will explain this 'truth' to us. His exposition has behind it the massive authority of a tradition, the tradition of a truth realised and experienced. It is not the product of a theory, the result of a hypothesis. No belief is assumed in this exposition, no truth is presumed. It is an invitation to the death of our human thought, its categories and frameworks, an invitation to an absolute opening out. Exposition of the Upaniṣad is to be taken up for this very purpose, for the purpose of distancing man from all that he knows and thinks himself to be. The great teachers who explained the Upaniṣads word by word and sentence by sentence did so to undo the illusion that man was what he imagined or could ever imagine himself to be or that the world was what he interpreted or could ever interpret it to be. That indeed is knowledge for the Upaniṣads which undoes what we think is knowledge. And that is the knowledge that the commentator would generate among those who would care to study his works.

ŚB The preceding part of this text--the *Taittirīya Āraṇyaka*—has revealed the *nitya-karmans,* the holy acts that men must do in every condition and situation, must do them until the knowledge of the self dawns upon them. For their purpose is to cleanse men of the stain of all the sins they have accumulated through their worldly pilgrimage, birth after birth. It has also revealed *kāmya-karmans,* those scriptural acts men may resort to, to fulfil those desires which ordinary human acts are unable to fulfil. Now commences *brahma-vidyā,* revelation of the ultimate real, which will undo the very cause of doing, be it in the form of holy acts or secular acts, acts done for self-purification or for fulfilment of certain desires.

Of every kind of act, desire is the cause. That alone prompts one to act. Those whose desires have been fulfilled come to get absorbed in the self. In that state no desire can possibly stir up to compel them into any action. Fulfilment of desires comes to be possible only when man's desires become exclusively oriented towards the self, when he discards all desires for the not-self and longs only to know himself and be himself. The self can fulfil all desires because the self is Brahman itself, the reality entire, the very Absolute. The knower of the self alone, the *śruti* will declare, attains to the supreme state of being (2.1.1.). Therefore, only he attains to this highest state of being who abides in the self alone and does not resort to the not-self, to any object, [unlike a worldly man who would resort to it] as if it were his very self. This comes to be possible when *avidyā,* ignorance, which confounds the self with the not-self, is eliminated. The Upaniṣad will declare how such a man attains to the state without fear (2.7.1), how he attains to the self that is made of bliss (2.8.5).

Objection: Let not man do any act the *śruti* forbids him to do nor resort to any *kāmya-karmans,* Vedic acts meant for the fulfilment of certain otherwise unappeasable desires. Let him bear with patience all that his *prārabdha-karmans* [literally, acts that have already commenced bearing their fruit] unfold before him in the form of his present life. If, in addition to this, he takes care to do the *nitya-karmans,* obligatory acts, he will save himself from the stain of sin. This way, he will come to be established in his self without any other effort, will attain to liberation from birth and death. Or he may attain to liberation of another sort, liberation in the form of the matchless ecstasy they call *svarga,* heaven, which, you know, is attainable through holy acts themselves. Thus through acts may one attain freedom from acts.

Vedāntin: There is no end to the number of acts one has done in the innumerable lives one has lived through in one's worldly pilgrimage. Many of them may have become ripe for bearing their fruit, others may have to wait for this ripening. To diverse and opposite results many of them may lead. How can one possibly exhaust in just one life the acts that are not yet ripe enough to bear fruit? One would be quite reasonable in inferring that they would give rise to new births to cause further new acts. And texts in their hundreds, revelatory as well traditional, will lend their authority to one's inference. 'Those,' says the *śruti*, 'those who do noble deeds here will be born out of noble wombs' (ChU 5.10.7). And echoes the *smṛti:* 'Acts which have yet to bear their fruit [cause the soul to be born again].' (Āp. 2.2.2.3)

Opponent: *Nitya-karmans*, obligatory acts, are meant precisely to undo the acts that are yet to bear their fruit, acts good and evil alike. What would be your response if we were to make this contention?

Vedāntin: *Nitya-karmans*, it is said, are to be resorted to, to ward off *pratyavāya*, that is to say, evil consequences. That, verily, is what the word *pratyavāya* indicates: evil consequence. The evil belongs to future, the result of nonperformance of the obligatory holy deeds, the *nitya-karmans*. These deeds are ineffective against the actions done in the past lives and this life, actions that are yet to show forth their results. Even if one were to concede, for the sake of the argument, that these holy deeds can undo the said actions, it is only evil actions they will undo, only the evil effect of such actions, not the noble deeds or their results. For *nitya-karmans* and noble deeds, which will bring only good to man, have no discord with each other. Good deeds are opposed to evil deeds, not to other good deeds.

Moreover, unless all that is, is realised as the self, desire, the generator of action, will not die down. When desire does not die, action too will not die out, not completely. And desire is always for the other. Only he who sees and perceives the other will be its victim, not he who perceives and sees only the self. The self is; as we have already pointed out, the Absolute itself. In that self, the self which is all that is, there can be no desire, it is ever and always attained.

There is one more point to take into consideration. The contention that if one does not do *nitya-karmans*, one will bring evil unto oneself is also an unsound contention. For evil emerges through doing something, through doing something evil, not just by not doing something, by not doing good deeds. That which is not cannot give rise to that which is. Therefore, any disinclination on the part of a man towards doing the *nitya-karmans* speaks of the evil he has accumulated through the sins committed in the past; it is that evil that brings about his fall, not the mere nonperformance of the holy acts. In this regard, the following words (from Manu) should prove instructive:

> Not doing the *nitya karmans* and doing the prohibited ones, man gets attached to his senses. Thus does he bring about his fall. (11.44).

The use of the present participle in 'Not doing the *nitya-karmans*' is quite appropriate. [It speaks of the propensity to evil that he has inherited from his past lives, rendering him unfit for holy deeds]. If a man brought about his fall simply by not doing something, he would generate that which is out of that which simply is not, making nonsense of all valid means of knowledge. Therefore, your contention that man will be established in the self automatically if he merely abstains from forbidden deeds and *kāmya-karmans* and takes care to perform the obligatory acts, has no ground to stand on.

Another contention of yours too is not a sound one, the contention that the matchless ecstasy they call heaven—the result of holy deeds—is itself the state of liberation. For liberation is eternal and the eternal can have no beginning. It would, however, have one if it were brought about by holy deeds but that would not be liberation the eternal. No deeds can bring it about.
Opponent : What about the holy deeds that are done in association with meditation? Surely, these two, in combination with each other, can give rise to eternal liberation!
Vedāntin: What you say is self-contradictory? How can the eternal have a beginning?
Opponent: Suppose we say liberation is coming to end of the worldly mode of being. Cessation of that mode will then have a beginning but no end. For that which comes to end does not come into being again. In this sense, eternal liberation may be said to have a beginning.
Vedāntin: Liberation is positive; it cannot, therefore, be compared to cessation. Moreover, it makes no sense to say that cessation has a beginning. As existence can be associated with particular existents, nonexistence cannot be associated with particular nonexistents that one could talk about it in terms of beginning or end. It is a mere thought imagined as the counter analogue of existence, its negation. Men do, as a matter of fact, particularise existence into existents like a pot or a piece of cloth—particularise one existence into many existents and talk about their respective existence, the existence of a pot or that of a piece of cloth, for example. They cannot, of course, particularise nonexistence in the same way and speak about particular nonexistents as they would speak about particular existents. However, the fact remains that they do happen to talk about it in terms analogical to those they use in relation to existence and associate it with qualities and actions as if it were a substance. But this is mere imagining. Unlike an existent, e.g. a lotus, nonexistence has no qualifiers. If it had, it would cease to be nonexistence; it would be existence itself.

Modern thinkers, by and large, would talk about existents, not about bare existence. Existence makes sense to them only in relation to things, not in itself. For Śaṅkara, on the contrary, existence is the thing itself and what we call things are its mere qualifiers. The latter have no being apart from it. It is true that we become aware of existence only through these qualifiers, through what we call things or existents: it is through them that existence shows itself forth: yet existence alone is the thing. What we call things do not really come to be things, they never come to *be*. About nonexistence, however, Śaṅkara speaks almost in the same vein as many a modern thinker would speak about existence. There are no nonexistents to show forth nonexistence. Therefore it can have no ontological pretensions. Our talk about it consists only of the non-referential analogues of our talk about existence. It speaks of our semiological compulsions rather than of propositional truth. Those who equate reality with interpreted reality will, however, equate existence with nonexistence. This, Śaṅkara would say, bespeaks of the hold that *avidyā*, primordial ignorance, has over them. For no interpreted phenomena, he would say, ever come to partake of existence; they ever remain adventitious to it.

ŚB Opponent: The eternal soul is the doer of meditation and holy acts. That being the case, its meditation and acts too will be a continuity. The liberation that will result from this continuity will be everlasting liberation.
Vedāntin: Doership that inflicts every embodied being is an uninterrupted process; it flows on continuously as do the waters of the Ganges. It is nothing else than suffering itself, this doership. So will be the continuous flow of holy deeds and meditation, the result of doership: they too will be a continuous flow of misery. Even if this continuity be equated with liberation, its cessation will mean the end of liberation. Liberation means establishment in one's self. And establishment in one's self comes to be possible only when *avidyā*, ignorance that confounds the self with the not-self and the not-self with the self, and desire and action—the trio that constitutes the material cause of bondage—get eliminated. For the self itself is Brahman. With its realisation alone can *avidyā* be eliminated. For that purpose, for the revelation of that self, is commenced this Upaniṣad.

Vidyā is called *upaniṣad* because it loosens, puts an end to the conception, birth and age of those who are devoted to it. Or, because it takes one near Brahman or because the highest good inheres in it. The book [under discussion] too is called 'upaniṣad' because it too has the same end in view [to bless man with liberation].

Aum! śaṃ no mitraḥ śaṃ varuṇaḥ. śaṃ no bhavatv aryamā.
śaṃ na indro bṛhaspatiḥ. śaṃ no viṣṇur urukramaḥ.
namo brahmaṇe. namaste vāyo. tvam eva pratyakṣaṃ brahmāsi.
tvām eva pratyakṣaṃ brahma vadiṣyāmi.
ṛtam vadiṣyāmi. satyaṃ vadiṣyāmi. tan mām avatu.
tad vaktāram avatu. avatu mām. avatu vaktāram.
auṃ śāntiḥ śāntiḥ śāntiḥ

Aum! May Mitra be propitious to us,
May Varuṇa and Aryaman be so
and Indra and Bṛhaspati

and Viṣṇu, the far striding.
Adoration to Brahman!
Adoration to thee, Vāyu!
Thou indeed art Brahman the visible!
Thou shall I proclaim Brahman the visible!
Thou shall I call ṛta
and thou the truth!
May that protect me
and him that speaks.
May that protect me and the speaker!
Aum! peaceful be the world and the elements,
peaceful the heavens and the gods,
peaceful the creatures that live and move.

ŚB Mitra is the deity as the day without and as the outgoing breath within. Let that god be propitious to us, shower joy and happiness upon us. Varuṇa is the deity called night. Within he dwells as the incoming breath. Aryaman is the sun god in the world. In man he is present in the form of the eye. Indra is the god that dwells within and without in the form of strength and energy. And Bṛhaspati is the god that identifies himself with speech and the faculty that determinates, the faculty called *buddhi*. Viṣṇu, the far-striding, is the god the stride [the god who encompasses all, pervades all]. This way all these [cosmic] gods that dwell in the body [too] may be propitious to us. 'May be' should be understood as associated with each and every god.

All that is, from the breath that moves within man to the vast expanse of the world, is not what he takes it to be; everything has anthropo-cosmic-divine dimension, it is not the little thing that it appears to our poor, small selves, poor and small because we do not know how to flow out of ourselves. The air I breathe in is not mere breath, it is also day, more than breath and more than day; it has dimensions which speech known to man cannot encompass, unless that speech too reveals its cosmic and divine depths, or, shall we say, 'unless that speech too *realises* its cosmic and divine dimension'? And the air I breathe in is also consmotheandric; this breath also is the all concealing night and has dimensions immeasurable for man. In the meeting point of day and night, of the outgoing and the incoming breath, the point in which one flows out into the other and the other into one, day into night and night into day, outgoing breath into incoming breath and incoming breath into outgoing breath, in this meeting point lies the key to the opening out of man to the divine and the cosmic in him. That is why the pious participate in the intermingling of day and night and the *yogins* in the interflow of the outgoing breath and the incoming breath. Through this mingling in that intermingling they seek to find the awesome depths that lie hidden in them, in the day and the night and in the breath that no one cares even to notice. When these depths open themselves out to mortal man, he ceases to be a mortal; he dies to become *Virāj*, to become *Hiraṇyagarbha*, to become *Īśvara*—to become God the immanence, God the creator, God the transcendental. When man perceives that his eye is not merely his eye, his strength not merely his strength, his speech not merely his speech, when he finds the cosmic in each of these and the divine, when he finds that the little step he takes can span the entire world and its mystery, then does he become the seer of all in each.

This short prayer dramatises the ecstasy of opening out when it changes into address and praise. It also shows what kind of disposition the Upaniṣad demands of the man who would learn the secret of its wisdom.

ŚB Until these gods turn benign to man, he will not become fit recipient of the words of revelation, many an obstacle will stand in his way to prevent him from opening out to them; they will not come to stay and dwell with him. Nor will he ever come to be their speaker. This prayer is said so that gods may turn gracious enough to let the seeker of truth be suffused with the redemptive words of the *śruti*.

The prayer is meant for the revelation of the concealed quarters of the word. One-fourth of it is already vouchsafed to man, the *Ṛg Veda* tells us (1.164.45). When gods turn benign, the cosmic quarter will open out and so will the heavenly. The last quarter will still remain concealed to the cosmotheandric being, the knower of the cosmotheandric word. To know that quarter the cosmotheandric man will have to become the Absolute—to know the Word Absolute. The prayer assumes a different tone and colour when we remember this last point.

ŚB Now he who seeks to know Brahman bows down to, worships *Vāyu*, the god that blows [as wind in the world and as breath in man] so that all that stands between him and the revelation of Brahman may be appeased and propitiated. For it is his privilege, of this god, to dispense success to the efforts and endeavours of mortals. It is for this reason, the reason that he ordains the fate of all endeavours, that *Vāyu* is equated with Brahman, the Absolute. For that Brahman, for that *Vāyu*, are offered adorations. The seeker of Brahman bows down before this god with all humility. In the text the reference to the agent who offers the prayer is implicit. 'Adoration to thee, *Vāyu*' thus means 'I offer adoration to thee *Vāyu*.' '*Vāyu*' here signifies both its visible and invisible aspects.

Vāyu, as breath, is more proximate to man than senses, the eye and the like, more immediately present. For this reason, it is addressed as Brahman the visible, Brahman proximate and immediate, for this reason, the man in search of truth says, 'Thou shall I proclaim Brahman the Absolute.' *Ṛta* too he calls it, *ṛta,* the scriptural law firmly planted in the mind. Of that law too breath is the guardian. Awareness of this fact prompts him to equate *Vāyu* with *ṛta,* the law. Whatever is accomplished by speech and by body is accomplished under the tutelage of breath. For this reason I, says the seeker of truth, shall call you truth, for truth is what the speech act and the body act accomplish.

Brahman, the Absolute, is present in man in the form of breath. That is its visible face and that is the guardian of the law and of truth. He who mingles with the rhythmic motion of breath, serenely flows with its ebb and tide, their rhythms equalised through yogic practice, he alone will know what is right, what is the law. And he alone will be the man of truth. This worship of *Vāyu,* of breath, this way sets aflame the *naciketa-agni,* the fire of innocence, to burn away all impurities. The *Praśna Upaniṣad* calls this fire of innocence, *udāna,* the uprising breath. From earth does this life-fire rise to reach *antarikṣa,* the domain of air. The human correlate of earth is the region of the navel and what lies below it and the *antarikṣa,* the mid region, has its counterpart in the region between the navel and the head. *Vāyu* is called the law of righteousness because it alone can orient man to the transcendental urge in him, freeing him from the narcissistic fury of the anus and the genitals, of hunger and sex. Not until man frees himself from the narcissism of these urges will he be truly righteous and truly truthful. Only then will what he does through his speech and body, his word and act, become truth, not before. The act done under the tutelage of this breath, this life-fire, alone will be truth. And so will be the word when it submits itself to breath. When speech does not articulate itself through breath but mingles with it, then alone will it find itself, find the three-fourths lost to it. *Vāyu* reveals its cosmic aspect when it rises above the navel, its divine aspect when it reaches the crown of the head. And the word too reveals its hidden depths there, for it thunders there as *nāda,* as *praṇava,* the divine song and the divine word, to transform man into *ātman.* And itself too, for there the divide between the word and its referent will disappear.

The seeker of this truth, this word, calls upon *Vāyu* to protect him and his teacher. If the god does not care to protect the teacher, the teacher will not speak the word as the word but as man. Therein lies the glory of the teacher, in his being the word when he speaks the word. Then does he become the revelation, then does he speak as the *ātman.* When the teacher speaks the word as the word and the student turns into breath, serene and gentle, the teacher's word will turn into *nāda*, into sound immortal, to absorb the personality of the student into itself, his thoughts, his feelings, his percepts and his concepts. Then will the student flow out of his human confines to dwell as space and live as time, to dwell as *diś* and live as *kāla*. *Virāj* will he then become, the Cosmic Man and his teacher the Lord, *Īśvara*, the dwelling place of all that is and all that is not. At that moment, the word will reveal its cosmodivine depths, the word of the teacher and of the Veda. The Veda known to him, however, will be only three-fourths of the Veda, to use the metaphor of the *Ṛg Veda*, not the Veda entire. It is to the man undone by *praṇava*, to man as all, that the Veda will reveal itself as the Lord. But even then he will only be the knower of the Veda, not its speaker, that is, not the Veda itself, for the Veda is its own speaker, it has no speaker other than itself. In other words, he will be the recipient of wisdom, not its teacher. To be the teacher, cosmic man will have to die into Brahman.

This Upaniṣad will show him the path to that state, will show him the way to plumb into the fourth part of itself, of the Upaniṣad itself.

ŚB May that self of all called *Vāyu*, continues the student, protect me by suffusing me with *vidyā*, with wisdom as revelation, the wisdom that I seek—may that *Vāyu* the Brahman that I adore. And may that Brahman protect the speaker, the teacher. May it bless him with the power to speak the word. The repetition of 'May that protect me and the speaker' shows the student's sense of the worth of the revelatory wisdom he seeks. The three times repeated *śāntiḥ*, peace, at the end of the invocation is a prayer for the 'peace' of all the theanthropocosmic hindrances in the way to enlightenment.

Chapter 2

ŚB The Upaniṣads are primarily concerned with the revelation of the referent of their discourse. There should, therefore, be no slackening in one's effort to learn and understand the meaning of the text in question. For this purpose is commenced, first of all, the chapter on instruction, on pronunciation of words.

1. śīkṣāṃ vyākhyāsyāmaḥ. varṇaḥ svaraḥ. mātrā balam. sāma santānaḥ. ityuktaḥ śīkṣādhyāyaḥ.

We shall explain the instruction regarding pronunciation. In this regard what one has to learn are letters, accents, quantity, stress, uniformity, combination. Thus has been spoken the lesson on pronunciation.

ŚB *Śīkṣā*, instruction, means instruction regarding pronunciation of letters, words, etc. One may also say that the things learnt, namely, letters and the like, themselves are *śīkṣā*. *Śīkṣā* is the Vedic form of the Sanskrit *śikṣā*. That *śīkṣā* the *śruti* will explain, will speak of clearly and in each and every aspect. That is the meaning of the word *khyā* when preceded by prefixes *vi* and *ā*. *Khyā* is used here instead of *cakṣiṅ*, the root with the same meaning.

Now letters are *a* and others. Accents are *udātta*, elevated, i.e., the higher pitch, *svarita*, the sounded, the middle pitch and *anudātta*, not elevated, the lower pitch. *Mātraḥ*, quantities, are short, long and protracted. Stress is the kind of effort required in pronunciation. Uniformity means the medium mode of articulating letters. Combination is *saṃhitā*, placing together, it means euphonic combination. All this is, should be, taught. Thus has been spoken the chapter incorporating *śikṣā*. 'Has been spoken' indicates that the said chapter has been concluded.

The written word enshrines within itself the state of being of the speaker in the absence of the hearer of the word. When a speaker speaks to the other, his speech is qualified by the presence of the other. The other regulates, directs the speech, the choice of words, the accent, the extent of clarity or of obscurity, of disclosure or of concealment. The being of the speaker too is determined by that presence—his dispositions, his attitudes, his emotions. Even when he speaks to influence the other, he does so as already influenced by the latter. The writer is more free than the speaker; he writes more to determine the other than to be determined by the other. Powerful men prefer to issue written orders, their articulation or interpretation they would leave to their deputies. Government functions on paper, not on platforms. The spoken word invites resistance, the written word compels submission. You may ignore it altogether, but if you agree to read it, you have to read it carefully.

There are words of other kind than the words that compose orders, edicts, laws or business transactions. Words that one simply finds, words that one stumbles into, words they call revelatory or creative. These words are also recorded but the writers record them more for their own understanding than for that of others. Such words demand complete self-submission on the part of those who would understand them. These words evoke no resistance because they have no manipulating speakers. In every truth, these words are their own speakers.

There are, however, important distinctions to be made and appreciated.

A poet, to cite an example, may be seized by a rhythmic movement which may push aside the manipulator in him. The rhythmic movement will impel him to wait for the words that fit in with the movement and its music. He cannot manipulate his vocabulary for that purpose, that will offend the movement. The speech that he will finally come to utter will be the speech of the music, not of the man. There will be a distancing between him and the speech, between him the sociality that he ordinarily is and that speech of music.

In order to understand the meaning of that speech, words have to be studied not as ordinary constituents of sentences one may utter in ordinary transactions, the sentences one speaks in a given life context, but as parts of the musical movement. Apart from that meaning-less whole, these parts will not mean what they mean as parts of that rhythmic whole. They will reflect the meaning of speech acts outside the poetic sphere. It is indeed a crime to reduce a poem, a genuine poem, into a mere social document and study it as such. For no man whose being lies with others, as it ordinarily does, can utter that speech. You have to withdraw from others to understand it, you have to self-submit to it.

Occasions may arise when a thing before me may refuse to be a part of my world, neither the world I live in nor the world of my discourse, the world, say, of the physicist. It may disclose a darkness, nameless and measureless, threatening to engulf me and what I call the world. The fear of this devastating undoing seizes me to force me to resist its widening shadows, to pitch my entire being, now almost nameless and enmassed, against its onslaught and subdue it through the power of the name. If I succeed in the act, succeed in naming it, then the world will return, not, of course, the world I lived *in* and discoursed about, but the world in which each and every thing that I see is deep enough to swallow my old world and to throw up a name to create a new one.

The dread mystery of those things may prove too much for me and I may strive to forget them in my old pursuits and, if that becomes impossible, in my old pleasures and pastimes. If, on the contrary, I have the courage and the daring to allow myself to be swallowed by the waves of that darkness, allow myself to be undone by that darkness of unknowing, I shall become that darkness, that mystery, that unknowing. When I come out of that dark unknowing—as I must, for, to be redeemed I have to find that darkness and our common light as one[1]—, I shall come out *as* words. My being and the world's being and of what lies beyond me and the world too will come out as those words. They will not be mere human words. For [him] who will speak them they will be the Absolute itself, for the hearer his God, for the innocent his world—for that is what *nāda* is for a *yogin*—and for men of the world holy revelations or cultural documents or plain nonsense depending on their beliefs, attitudes and dispositions.

When objects turn dread abysms, they appear negations—of me, of my world, of my God. They appear negations only because I, who would not be supplanted by them, seek to negate them. When I allow myself to be negated by them, these negations, they reveal themselves as the real, the real in which the gap between the name and the named comes to be bridged. There remains no distancing between me and the world, between me and my god, between what I as an embodied being would call the real and the ideal. This happens, to put the matter in a different way, when I speak not as me but as the word. The word that I as me speak is spoken through the other but never becomes that other; the speaking word has no other because it itself is the other as it is me. And it has nothing beyond itself because it is the beyond too.

This word is the Vedic word, the word that speaks but is never spoken. It is the world and it is the god, it is the past and it is the future, the here and the beyond. Such is the language in which the Upaniṣads describe it. This its truth and its secret will not, however, be revealed unless and until one becomes one with it. If one treats revelation, Vedic or other, as a cultural document, one will reduce it to a collection of what are called mythical and magical formulas. To the *human* self it will appear only this much, a heap of beliefs, unfounded and untruthful, redeemed by an occasional, perhaps more than

1. The reader may forgive me for the active voice. True wisdom dawns on man when distinction between *samādhi* and wakefulness disappears, and also between Brahman and *māyā*. The point has received our constant attention in the preceding volumes.

occasional, poetic beauty and power. The man who swears in the name of humanism will not accept it as the disclosure of man's truth or the world's. For that he will turn to other discourses, perhaps to science. A man of such a conviction should, however, understand that even a work of great poetry would not, as we saw, be reduced to a cultural document, would not yield its meaning to one who understands language as obtaining only in human interactions, would not disclose itself even to one who has more sophisticated theories to offer. For language as the kind of poem we described reveals itself to be more than a social phenomenon, more than even sociality. As to the disclosure of the truth of the Vedic word to a man of this sort, the less said the better. To one, however, who self-submits to it, it will reveal itself not as a referential proposition or as a constitutive–constituted sociality but as the dwelling of man and his world, his reality and his ideals. That word alone is truth, that alone is the Absolute, not the word as the picture, for that latter is a fiction, the word without place or ontological ground. Also not the word that we, in our theoretical moods, would imagine as the constitutive principle of the world, for every phenomenon eludes it grasp.

To be the word that is the Absolute, we have to self-submit to that word, the word of revelation, the word, in the present context, of the Veda. And the first step towards this goal is to articulate, clearly and accurately, the sound and accent of that word. We are not to allow our own convenience to determine the sound of the word as we do in our ordinary speech. The Vedic word, or, for that matter, the word of any revelation, is not a medium of communication that it could be reduced to a mere equipment. Nor are the Vedic *mantras* propositions that their truth value could be tested empirically or their consistency logically. Nor do they contain constitutive language, language that could constitute new realities as they who chant their *mantras* as magic formulas would have us believe. We are to give up all these beliefs if we would know what these words are.

Paying attention to the *mantra* means isolating it from our daily speech; it must stand out alone and as all. Devotion to it would thus imply detachment from all other things, including one's own body. To get detached from the body, one must pay attention to the 'effort' that the vocal chords have to make to articulate a *mantra.* One has to pay heed to the breath, contemplate it, and also to the places of articulation of various sounds, how one place of articulation gives place to another in *sandhis,* euphonic combinations. Rules of *sandhis,* euphonic combinations, are not arbitrary rules; more often than not, they are expressive of the natural tendency of our vocal chords. The place of articulation and the quality of the sound, soft or hard, of the first letter of the second word and of the last letter of the first word often determine these rules of *sandhis.* In the days of the Vedas, when the written word had yet to be devised, the child learnt the rules of *sandhis* by paying attention to the vocal chords. The change of the place of articulation involved in *sandhis* was determined, he could see, by the vocal chords and so was the change in quality, change of the hard sound into the soft or *vice versa.* Even when writing had been devised, this learning of grammatical 'rules' from contemplation of one's breath and the vocal chords, from throat to lips, continued, for the emphasis remained focussed on the spoken word and not on the written word. So *śabdānuśāsana,* the discipline of grammar, was more an act of contemplation than of memory. It was this disposition, cultivated carefully in the child, the disposition of contemplation, that prepared him to contemplate, later on, the Vedic *mantra* or the word *aum* as if it were all that was or could be. When contemplation turned into a passive clearing, the word did become the all. That was the purpose behind paying meticulous attention to the pronunciation of the Vedic word.

Chapter 3

ŚB The Upaniṣad now proceeds to reveal the meditation relating to *saṃhitā,* joining together of letters.

1. **saha nau yaśaḥ, saha nau bramavarcasam, athātaḥ saṃhitāyā upaniṣadaṃ vyākhyāsyāmaḥ. pañcasvadhikaraṇeṣu, adhilokam adhijyautiṣam adhividyam adhiprajam adhyātmam, tā mahāsaṃhitā ity ācakṣate. athādhilokam. pṛthivī pūrvarūpam, dyauruttararūpam, ākāśaḥ saṃdhiḥ.**
2. **vāyuḥ saṃdhānam, ityadhilokam. athādhi-jyautiṣam. agniḥ pūrvarūpam, āditya uttararūpam, āpaḥ saṃdhiḥ, vaidyutaḥ saṃdhānam. ity adhijyautiṣam. athādhividyam. ācāryaḥ pūrvarūpam.**
3. **antevāsy uttararūpam, vidyā saṃdhiḥ, pravacanaṃ saṃdhānam ity adhividyam. athādhiprajam. mātā pūrvarūpam, pitottararūpam, prajā saṃdhiḥ, prajananaṃ saṃdhānam. ity adhiprajam.**
4. **athādhyātmam. adharā hanuḥ pūrvarūpam, uttarā hanur uttararūpam, vāk saṃdhiḥ, jihvā saṃdhānam. ity adhyātmam. itīmā mahā saṃhitāḥ. ya evam etā mahāsaṃhitā vyākhyātā veda saṃdhīyate prajayā paśubhiḥ, brahmavarcasenānnādyena suvargeṇa lokena.**

May glory be with us two, may the light of Brahman be with us two. Now shall we expound the meditation on juxtaposition under five heads—concerning the world, concerning the luminaries, concerning knowledge, concerning progeny, concerning the body. These, they say, are the great placings-together.

Now the meditation with regard to the world: the earth is the first letter, the heaven is the last letter and the sky is the meeting place (2) and vāyu, *air, is the connecting link. This is the meditation concerning the world. Now the meditation with regard to the shining ones.* Agni, *Fire, is the first letter, the sun is the last letter, water is the meeting place, and lightning is the connecting link. This is the meditation concerning the shining ones. Now the meditation with regard to knowledge. The teacher is the first letter, (3) the pupil is the last letter, knowledge is the meeting place and instruction is the connecting link. This is the meditation concerning knowledge. Now, the meditation with regard to progeny. Mother is the first letter, father is the last letter, progeny is the meeting place and procreation is the connecting link. This is the meditation concerning progeny. (4) Now, the meditation with regard to the body. The lower jaw is the first letter, the upper jaw is the last letter, speech is the meeting place and tongue the connecting link. This is the meditation with regard to the body.*

These are the great combinations. He who knows them as thus expounded becomes conjoined with progeny, with cattle, with the splendour of Brahman, with food, with the world of heaven.

ŚB May glory be with us two, with the pupil and the teacher as well. The glory which is prayed for is the one that full knowledge of the meditation on *saṃhitā* brings about. And the splendour of Brahman that this meditation lights up too may be with us two. This is the pupil's prayer. Only he can say this kind of prayer, away from the goal that he is. Not the teacher, the *ācārya,* for the *ācārya* is he who has already done what is to be done, has already attained what is to be attained.

Now, having given the injunction regarding the way the scriptures are to be studied, the Upaniṣad now proceeds to explain the meditation on *saṃhitā.* We shall, it says, explain the said meditation under five heads, explain it as related to five objects, objects of meditative knowledge. The Upaniṣad chooses to proceed this way because the intellect addicted to texts cannot easily be led to a disposition which is open to what the texts connote. It can, however, easily be led to meditation on *saṃhitā,* combination of letters, a mere step from the study of the words of a text.

Which are these five kinds of meditations? They are (1) the meditation concerning the world, (2) that concerning the shining beings, (3) that concerning knowledge, (4) that concerning progeny, and (5) that concerning the body. Knowers of the Vedas call these meditations 'great juxtapositions'. They designate them this way because these meditations are concerned with great things like the world and because they are also juxtapositions, *saṃhitās.*

Now is described the meditation concerning the world, the first among these five. The word *atha* indicates the order of the meditation in question in the series. The earth is the first form, the first letter. The implication is that wherever two letters coalesce in euphonic combination, one should think of the first letter as if it were the earth. The last form, the last letter, is heaven; sky, the intermediate region, is the meeting place, that is to say, the middle place between the two because it is here that the first form and the last come to coalesce.

Vāyu, air, is the *saṃdhāna*, the connecting link, that by which the coalescence comes to be. Thus has been described the meditation concerning the world.

The same way should be explained other meditations, from that relating to the shining beings to that relating to the body. He who knows this great combination, meditates on it—for 'to know' means 'to meditate' in the present context of meditation as will become evident later (1.6.2) where the *śruti* will say: 'Meditate, O Prācīnayogya!'—becomes conjoined with all that the Upaniṣad speaks of from progeny to heaven. He will be blessed with these fruits of the meditation in question.

When similar ideas succeed each other giving place to no others, then one may be said to do meditation. These ideas have to be scriptural and the object they are anchored to too should be scriptural. In the secular contexts too, the word 'meditation' carries this connotation of continuity. He who continuously waits on his *guru*, his teacher, or his king is said to meditate them, worship them. And he alone reaps the reward of this continuous worship. Here also the man given to continuous meditation reaps the reward of his meditation.

The words *iti* and *imāḥ* in the text refer to the meditations described earlier. The word *atha* preceding the name of every meditation in the series shows the order in which they are to be resorted to.

The meditation on *saṃhitā* may be summed up in the following table:

Pṛthivī Earth	*Antarikṣa* Interspace	*Dyu* Heaven	*Vāyu* air	the connecting link
Agni Fire	*Apas* Water	*Āditya* Sun	*Vidyuta* Lightning	- do -
Ācārya Teacher	*Vidyā* Knowledge	*Antevāsin* Pupil	*Pravacanam* Instruction	- do -
Mātṛ Mother	*Prajā* Progeny	*Pitṛ* Father	*Prajanam* Procreation	- do -
Adharā hanu Lower jaw	*Vāc* Speech	*Uttarā hanu* Upper jaw	*Jihvā* Tongue	- do -

Earth and heaven are not really opposites. There is a place where they meet as day and night meet in the evening or in the morning. Morning and evening, in fact, are nothing but the meeting of the day and the night. So *antarikṣa*, interspace, too is nothing but a name of the meeting of heaven and earth. *Pṛthivī*, earth, is an expanse of dense matter, the paradigm of the tangible, *dyu*, heaven, is all light, something one cannot touch. There is, however, air that partakes of the nature of both. One can feel its touch and yet it spreads out as does light. Its expansiveness is not the expansiveness of earth, but like the expansiveness of light, unrestricted, free and endless. Air 'moved', the Vedic man believed, freely from earth to heaven, it was all-pervasive. In air come to meet the tangibility of earth and the pervasiveness of heaven. Air is the presiding deity of the mid-space.

If man would attain to heaven, then he must become air, for air alone can lead one to heaven. In the yogic discipline, this is precisely what one is made to do. One must become breath to rise above the anus and the genitals, the organs that are earthly *par excellence,* and to reach the head, the counterpart of heaven in man.

Agni means the upleaping flame, *āditya* means the son of *Aditi,* the primal she-eater. *Āditya* is the all-absorbing sun, that giver of light and of life. How does destructive fire of earth turn into that blessed giver of life and light? Through lightning, that child of the water in the sky, of the rain laden clouds. Fire burns the earth, the symbol of frozen density, of inertness and lifelessness but only to release water, the symbol of life and its activity, a prisoner held within its confines, to turn it into clouds and itself into lightning, their child. On earth fire and water are antagonists, in the sky they are related through most intimate bonds, those obtaining between the mother and the child. This freedom and relationship come about only when fire releases water from the inert confines of earth through burning the latter. Until that happens, until the density of earth is consumed by fire, the reconciliation between fire and water, between life and its transcendental thrust, cannot come about. For the upleaping flame of fire symbolises precisely that, the transcendental thrust, and the earth resistance to this thrust. This fire in man, this transcendental thrust in him, is resisted by natural instincts, instincts that would tie him down to the earth, to the inert. This self-confining inertness has to be extinguished to let him move and live and see in fire, in destruction and death, the source of that life and that movement, the life and movement that the dark monsoon clouds symbolise. The inert in man has to die for this vision to dawn, the vision of the reconciliation between life and death, between what is and the negation of it. The moving clouds carry water and fire, carry them in harmony and as harmony and not in conflict as on earth. It is earth, that selfhood in man, that is the cause of conflict between him and the world, between that selfhood in him and the very elements that constitute his being. When man can encompass his mortality, as the clouds can the lightning, when he lives as a mortal, as a true mortal, when he breathes not merely the breath of life but also lives its cessation, then alone will he be absorbed in *Āditya,* the all absorbing sun, become one with it, and through this becoming one with it become the sustainer of life, life that so consistently eluded his grasp before. Meditation on the shining beings is meditation on fire, it is meditation on death, meditation that is redemptive *yajña,* sacrifice.

The third form of meditation, that concerning knowledge, consists of the *saṃhitā,* the coming together, of the teacher and the pupil. The teacher is the correlate of the earth and the pupil that of heaven and their meeting place is *vidyā,* knowledge, brought about by communicative discourse, by *pravacana,* instruction. It is to be noted that it is the teacher who is to reach out to the pupil as if the latter were his destination, his goal, his redemption. We are all familiar with the discourse through which the teacher passes his cognitive acquisitions on to the student, the discourse which is little better than a transaction, an exchange of ideational property as it were. In this kind of discourse, the teacher does not reach out to the student, does not flow out into him as if the latter were the end, the goal of his being and his life. The *pravacana,* the instruction, that brings about the meeting of the two in *vidyā,* in knowledge, is not the instruction that could be done through words as means. This flowing out into the other comes to be possible only when the teacher ceases to be the speaker of the word, when he, instead, becomes the word. The word does not come into being until it gets spoken to the other, the other is the very condition of its coming into being. The teacher as the word does not come into being until he has, so to say, flowed into the pupil, for it is in the pupil that he as the word can come to be himself. In other words, it is only when the teacher becomes the *śruti,* the word that is heard but cannot be spoken, the word of which there is a hearer but not a speaker, that he can impart *vidyā,* knowledge, to the student. The teacher dies into the word to possess the student, the passive recipient, the hearer, of the word. When the teacher dies and the student becomes passive, only then will knowledge dawn in the latter, knowledge that is redemption and not power.

One may well wonder what could be the significance of meditation on sexual relationship between man and woman. Notice how the Upaniṣad shifts the focus of our attention from the narcissistic relationship that obtains between man and woman as sexual creatures to their relationship as mortals when it equates man with father and woman with mother. When man and woman live as father and as mother respectively, they have already acknowledged their being as mortals; they live as and in their children, not as and in themselves as they would as creatures of sex. As a creature of sex woman would possess man through being possessed, as a mother, the counterpart of earth, woman would flow out into man as if the latter were her heaven, the place of her rest and the anchor of her being. For her being lies in her children and children need the protective care of their father, her husband. Her being, the being of the woman as mother, thus is anchored in man, the earner of bread. It is through children, and not through her sexual charms, that woman comes to relate to man, truly comes to relate to man. It is through this relationship that she comes to find herself as woman, woman as mother, woman as a mortal. As mother, as mother alone, can a woman find herself, find herself as wife. Modern world would equate the identity of woman more with the wife than with the mother, the Upaniṣads more with the mother than with the wife. As mother, woman lives as a mortal being-with-others, as wife she lives as a being-in-*itself* asleep to her mortality. Whose is the more authentic life, of the woman related or of the woman unrelated? And, more importantly, of the woman who lives as a mortal or of the woman who as a frozen individuality does not own up to her mortality? Let the reader dwell on this question. The question can be extended to man, too. He too can find his mortal identity as father, not as husband.

Last comes the meditation on the speech act. Perhaps, we in this our age need this meditation more than the others. We have become so used to speaking that we pay no heed to the process involved in the speech act. To contemplate a word being spoken, to perceive it being pronounced, to have a feel of its pronunciation, is to prepare oneself for opening out to the being of words, to acquire a disposition which finds words as real as oneself, to find them as ends and not as means. In a word, it is a preparation for cultivating the disposition that passively pays heed to a word to find it as the Absolute, the dwelling place of all that is. It is a preparation to find the word before one, the word contemplated, as *Aum*[1].

1. See Vol. 1 of this series pp. 266-272; 410-421; Vol. 2, consult index (under *aum*).

Chapter 4

1. **yaś chandasām ṛṣabho viśvarūpaḥ, chandobhyo'dhyamṛtāt saṃbabhūva, sa mendro medhayā spṛṇotu, amṛtasya deva dhārano bhūyāsam. śarīraṃ me vicarṣaṇam, jihvā me madhumattamā, karṇābhyāṃ bhūri viśruvam, brahmaṇah kośo'si medhayā pihitaḥ. śrutaṃ me gopāya, āvahantī vitanvānā.**

2. **kurvāṇā 'cīram ātmānaḥ, vāsāṃsi mama gāvaś ca, annapāne ca sarvadā. tato me śriyam āvaha. lomaśāṃ paśubhiḥ saha svāhā. āmāyantu brahamacāriṇaḥ svāhā, vimāyantu brahmacāriṇaḥ svāhā, pramāyantu brahmacāriṇaḥ svāhā, damāyantu brahmacāriṇaḥ svāhā, śamāyantu brahmacāriṇaḥ svāhā.**

May aum, *the most sublime of the Vedic syllables, the all-formed that sprang into being from hymns immortal, may that Lord supreme cheer me up with intelligence. May I, O Lord, be the wearer of immortality. May my body be fit, my tongue exceeding sweet, may my ears in abundance hear.*
Thou, O Aum, *art the sheath of Brahman covered and concealed by intelligence. Guard and protect what I have heard.*
Then bring unto me the prosperity that brings for me, ever and always, clothes and cows, food and drink, and animals woolly and nonwoolly. Bring me this prosperity that harbours no delay in doing this for me. Svāhā! *May come unto me from every side students of sacred knowledge.* Svāhā! *May they be sincere unto me.* Svāhā! *May they be blessed with knowledge true and holy.* Svāhā! *May they be self-controlled.* Svāhā! *May they be peaceful.* Svāhā!

ŚB These *mantras* reveal unto the man desirous of intelligence and of wealth how he should acquire them. The way to intelligence lies, the *śruti* tell us, through repetition of *mantras,* through sustained meditation on them, and the way to wealth through the act of sacrifice, of offering oblations to the sacred fire. 'May the Lord Supreme cheer me up with intelligence' and 'Then bring unto me the prosperity . . .' will speak for the truth of our remark.

Aum is among the Vedic words what a bull is in the midst of cows—prominent among them and sublime. The *śruti* calls it all-formed because it pervades *all* speech as another *śruti* text will instruct us (ChU 2.23.3):

> As leaves are permeated by a stalk so is all speech permeated by *aum.* Verily, the syllable *aum* is all this, verily, the syllable *aum* is all this.

The fact that *aum* pervades all speech and, for this reason, all this, all that is, establishes the superiority of *aum* over all other Vedic words. *Aum* is the object to be worshipped; for this reason, it is in the fitness of things that the *śruti* should highlight its pre-eminence through the image of a bull among the cows.

From the immortal hymns was born *aum,* born as the most sacred of all syllables. 'Immortal hymns' means the Vedas, for they, we know, are immortal. When Prajāpati, the Lord of Creation, desired to know what the most essential, the highest, truth of beings was, he meditated intently and fervently on the worlds, on the gods that shine, on the Vedas, on *vyāhṛti*-s, the sacred utterances that created heaven and earth and the world that lies between these two. To him thus engaged in *tapas,* in ardour, was revealed *aum,* the sacred syllable, as the essence finest of them all. The birth of *aum* was thus a revelation, a manifestation, not birth in the literal sense of the word. There can indeed be no real birth of the timeless and eternal which *aum* verily is.

May that *aum,* the prayer continues, that Lord who dispenses all that creatures desire and wish, cheer the student up, invigorate him, with intelligence, with wisdom. Strength in the form of wisdom is what is prayed for here.

And may *aum,* the god, make him wearer of immortality, of knowledge of Brahman that blesses the knower with immortality. The Upaniṣad is concerned with the revelation of Brahman. So immortality in the present context can mean only that [and not the immortality that holy acts and meditation can give, immortality in the form of life in heaven].

And may my body, the student continues, be fit and my tongue exceedingly sweet spoken and my ears hear in profusion the words of scriptures—may I be well instructed in them. In one word, the student prays that his body and senses become fit instruments for self-knowledge. To gain self-knowledge he prays for intelligence too.

And you, the student addresses *aum,* are the sheath of Brahman, the place of its realisation. For it is through *aum,* through contemplation of it, that Brahman is realised, it being the latter's *pratīka,* its symbol, its expression.

Intelligence, worldly intelligence, conceals *aum.* Men of the world, those endowed with common intelligence, cannot know what *aum* in truth is. [Therefore,] the student prays that *aum* protect what he has heard. Let his knowledge of the self, he implies, remain intact and all else [that is required for that knowledge], for hearing of scriptures culminates in self-knowledge. Let him attain to that knowledge, let him never forget it.

A man who would be endowed with intelligence should repeat these *mantras.*

In the text the word *bhūyāsam,* may I be, is used with reference to the person who says this prayer. The Upaniṣad does not use third person equivalent of it when the student prays for the strength of the body, etc. Accordingly, *bhūyāsam* may be converted into *bhūyat,* may it be, with reference to body, etc.

The syllable *aum* is eternal and so are the hymns out of which it is born. This syllable is all that is and also the lord of all that is, the dispenser of intelligence, of immortality, the protector and sustainer of the senses and the body, the shrine of Brahman, the Absolute. And yet it is veiled by intelligence.

For the worldly intelligence *aum* is a mere word among other words, but a word with, so to say, a disadvantage, for it is a name without a commonly recognised referent. Those who use words cannot find any ontological value in them except as constituents of a discourse or of daily conversation. So there appears, to people of this sort, something 'mystical' in the Upaniṣadic statement that would speak not only of the cosmotheandric dimensions of a single syllable but also of its being the ground of the cosmotheandric reality, of its being the Absolute itself.

How this single syllable comes to be all that is and the Absolute has received our attention in our study of the *Kaṭha Upaniṣad* and the *Māṇḍūkya Upaniṣad* and *Gauḍapāda Kārikā.*[1]

ŚB Now the *śruti* speaks of the *mantras* that are to accompany sacrificial offerings to the sacred fire. They are meant for the man who would be prosperous. He prays for the prosperity that brings him, ever and always, clothes and cows, food and drink, and so on, brings them about readily and without delay. And not only brings these but also increases them. But let this prosperity be mine, the man says, only when you, O *Aum,* have vouchsafed to me the wisdom I have prayed for. For prosperity without that wisdom only ruins a man.

And what kind of prosperity will he have ? The prosperity accompanied by woolly animals like goats and sheep as well as other animals.

The context shows that the deity addressed to in 'Then bring unto me the prosperity . . .' is the syllable *aum* itself. The word *svāhā* indicates the end of the *mantra* accompanying the offering.

And let students of sacred knowledge, to continue with the prayer, come unto me from every side. Let them be sincere, let them be blessed with right knowledge, let them be self-controlled and peaceful.

Grammatical notes: *Vitanvānā* derived from the root *tanu,* to increase, to expand; *acīram* is the Vedic form of *aciram,* without delay. *ā mā yantu* means *āyantu mām*: come to me from every side. The distancing of preposition *ā* from the verb *yantu* is a peculiarity of the Vedic syntax.

1. Vol. 1 & 2. See the indexes appended to these volumes.

Prosperity that will not ruin a man is the prosperity that comes about through prayer to the sacred syllable *aum*. Men seek prosperity through acts, straight or cunning. *Technê* is the weapon they would use against the slings of wayward *tüche.* The prosperity that comes about this way augments the selfhood of man, alienates him from the cosmic and divine dimensions of his being, will make him asleep to the truth about *aum,* to the truth about himself, about his self that is all and more than all. From death to death will he move, says the *śruti* about the man who seeks to find his place in the world through wealth earned through the action prompted by blind desire.

There is, the Upaniṣad says, another way to prosperity, the way that opens out before man when he attends to the word, when he leaves behind the cunning that insulted the word by degrading it into a means. The way opens out for man when a word, a single word, becomes the terrifying and awesome god for him, compelling his total surrender to its dread mystery. Prayer addressed to that word will not go waste. Nor will his offerings. They will bring him what he seeks. What he seeks will not, however, be for his own self; it will be for the use of others. In the text in question, the prayer for prosperity is immediately followed by prayer for students. The prosperity the teacher seeks is primarily meant for them. That is the kind of *praxis* the Upaniṣad preaches to bring about prosperity. Nature cannot, the Upaniṣad implies, but obey the call of such a man, the call of him who worships *aum,* a mere syllable, as the all and as the Absolute.

3. yaśo jane'sāni, svāhā! śreyān vasyo'sāni, svāhā! taṃ tvā bhaga praviśāni, svāhā! sa mā bhaga praviśa, svāhā! tasmin sahsra-śākhe nibhagāhaṃ tvayi mṛje, svāhā! yathā'paḥ pravatā yanti yathā māsā aharjaram evaṃ māṃ brahmacāriṇo dhātarāyantu sarvataḥ, svāhā! prativeśo'si pra mā pāhi pra mā padyasva.

May I be glorious among people, svāhā!
May I be superior to the richest, svāhā!
May I enter thee, O Gracious One, svāhā!
May you, O God, enter me, svāhā!
In thee of a thousand branches do I wash myself, svāhā!
As waters flow downwards, as months flow into the aharjara, *the year, so may come unto me, O Ordainer,*
students of sacred knowledge from every side, svāhā!

Refuge art thou [of the unhappy]
Shine forth unto me. Do thou come unto me.

ŚB May I be glorious among people, among whole multitudes of them. May I be superior to the richest, to him who excels the entire class of the wealthy. May I enter thee, O Gracious Lord, thee who art the very sheath of Brahman. And having entered thee become one with thee, one with thy self. And you too enter me, O Lord, so that you and me become one and single self. And in thee, O Gracious One, of a thousand branches do I wash myself of my sins.

'As waters flow downwards, as months into *aharjara,* the year ...' *Aharjara* means the year because it wears out (*jaryati*) people while itself changing day by day or because days get worn out in it, get comprehended in it. So as waters flow downwards and as months into the year, so, O Ordainer, may students of sacred knowledge come unto me from every side.

You are the refuge, the place of rest at hand for those who are devoted to you. In you, their place of rest, they can disburden themselves of their sins and the misery they cause. Do then shine forth unto me and come unto me: make me one with yourself as the metallic head of an arrow becomes one with its target when it is soaked in mercury.

In the present context of self-knowledge, the seeker of prosperity seeks it for the purpose of doing holy deeds so that the sins he committed in past lives may get undone. For self-knowledge will not shine forth until those sins become extinct.

> Knowledge arises in man when his sins have all faded away. As if in a mirror clean in the self will he see the self.
>
> Thus a text of traditional wisdom (*MB Śāntiparvan* 204.8).

The desire for glory reflects a culture different from our own. In the days of the Upaniṣads men of power and wealth were no doubt held in respect but not as much as were men blessed with spiritual insight. Theirs was a glory which neither a king could command nor a man of wealth. Wealth was sought for the purpose of performing holy deeds so that one could be purified of one's sinful inclinations inherited from past lives. The man in question desires wealth for the holy purpose of teaching.

Holy deeds like teaching and others were resorted to for the sake of self-purification so that man could come to know his self. This knowledge did not mean acquisition of ideas or learning. One had to drain oneself out of oneself to let the other become the self. Not without self-extinction could this happen. Self-knowledge meant only this much, the revelation of the other as the self. Hence the need for self-purification, for the extinction of the ego, of the I.

The seeker of fortune who would be a teacher does not seek to be a teacher of words. He prayss to the Word that he be the Word. It is as the Word that he will reveal self-knowledge to his students. To be the Word means to be the all, to [experience] the all as the self.

The image of the waters flowing downwards and of months into the year invokes the spirit of self-surrender towards the Word-become teacher. The Word undoes the student to make him one with It. Months have no being of their own, they are merely limbs of the year.

Chapter 5

ŚB The Upaniṣad first revealed the meditation on conjunction. Then followed the *mantras* for the seeker of intelligence and, then, for the seeker of prosperity. These *mantras* too subserve knowledge but only indirectly. The Upaniṣad now proceeds to present internal meditation of Brahman[1] as identified with utterances. This meditation of Brahman in the form of utterances leads to the state where one is the Lord of oneself.

1. bhūr bhuvaḥ suvar iti vā etās tisro vyāhṛtayaḥ. tāsām u ha smaitāṃ caturthīṃ māhācamasyaḥ pravedyate maha iti. tad brahma. sa ātmā. angāny anyā devatāḥ. bhūr iti vā ayaṃ lokaḥ. bhuva ity antarikṣam. suvar ity asau lokaḥ.

2. maha ity ādityaḥ. adityena vāva sarve lokā mahīyante. bhūr iti vā agniḥ. bhuva iti vāyuḥ. suvar ity ādityaḥ. maha iti candramāḥ. candramasā vāva sarvāṇi jyotīṃṣi mahīyante. bhūr iti vā ṛcaḥ bhuva iti sāmāni. suvar iti yajūṃṣi.

3. maha iti brahma. brahmaṇā vāva sarve vedā mahīyante. bhūr iti vai prāṇaḥ. bhuva ity apānaḥ. suvar iti vyānaḥ. maha ity annam. annena vāva sarve prāṇā mahīyante. tā vā etāś catasraś caturdhā. catasraś catasro vyāhṛtayaḥ. tā yo veda. sa veda brahma. sarva'smai devā balim āvahanti.

Bhūr! Bhuvas! Suvar! *These, verily, are the three utterances. There is the fourth too that Māhācasmasya came to know, namely,* Mahas. *That is Brahman, that is* ātman, *its limbs the other gods.* Bhūr, *verily, is this world,* bhuvas, *the interspace,* suvar, *the yonder world,* mahas, *sun the all-absorber. Through the all-absorbing sun do all the worlds flourish.* Bhūr, *verily is* agni, *the flaming deity,* bhuvas, vāyū, *the blowing deity,* suvar, *sun the all-absorbing deity,* mahas, *the* candramas, *the moon, the god that shines to soothe and delight. Through the soothing light,* candramas, *do all the lights flourish.*

---

1. Lower Brahman, *Hiraṇyagarbha,* the Golden Germ.

> Bhūr, *verily, is* ṛc-es, *the hymns of the* Ṛg Veda, bhuvas, sāmans, *the songs of the* Sāma Veda, suvar, yajus-es, *the* mantras *of the* Yajur Veda, mahas, *Brahman. Through Brahman indeed do all the Vedas flourish.* Bhūr, *indeed, is the outgoing breath,* bhuvas, *the incoming breath,* suvar, *the distributive breath,* mahas, *the food they eat. By food do all the breaths flourish.*
> *Verily, these four are fourfold; four, four are the utterances. He who knows these, knows Brahman. To him bring offerings all the shining ones.*

ŚB *Bhur, bhuvas, suvar*—these three utterances are celebrated [in the ritualistic portions of the Vedas]. The Upaniṣad here recalls these well known utterances. *Iti, etāḥ tisrāḥ,* these three, emphasise the point that these three utterances have already been mentioned in the ritualistic portion of the Vedas. *Vai,* verily, calls them up to one's memory. Among such utterances there is also the fourth one, *mahas.* It was Māhācamasya, son of Mahācamasya, who came to know this utterance. *Pravedyate* is in the present tense but when it is accompanied by the particles *u ha sma,* it carries the sense of the past tense. The mention of the name Māhācamasya is meant to remind the hearer of the text that *mahas* revealed itself on its own to a seer [that it is not a word of human origin but a word of revelation]. The fact that the name of the seer of the utterance has been mentioned here shows that remembrance of the name of the concerned seer is an integral part of the meditation on *vyāhṛti*-s, utterances.

This *vyāhṛti, mahas,* that the sage Māhācamasya saw is Brahman. For Brahman also is called *mahat* (great), a word which sounds very much like *mahas.* [Literally: For Brahman is *mahat* and this *vyāhṛti* too is *mahas.*] What else is this utterance? It is *ātman,* derived from the root *āp,* to pervade, to comprehend, to attain. This *vyāhṛti* is all-attaining. The other *vyāhṛtis*—the worlds, the gods, the Vedas and the breaths—can all be attained by *mahas,* the *ātman* in the forms [respectively] of the all-absorbing sun, the soothing light called *candramas* (moon), Brahman (*aum*) and *anna,* the food they eat. For this reason, other gods are only limbs of this *vyāhṛti.* The word *gods* here means these others, namely, the worlds, the deities, the Vedas and breaths. Since the worlds and other gods are the limbs of the *ātman* called *mahas,* these are said to flourish, to excel, by the varied forms of it, namely, the all-absorbing sun, the *candramas* and the like. For it is the *ātman* that makes the limbs grow and develop.

The word *mahanam* means growth, increase. Hence *mahīyante* means: they grow, develop, increase.

The first *vyāhṛti, bhūḥ,* is this world, *agni,* the upleaping flame, *Ṛg Veda* and *prāṇa,* breath. Other *vyāhṛti*-s alike have four forms each. *Mahas* is Brahman, that is, the syllable *aum;* except the syllable *aum* no other meaning of

Brahman is possible in the context in question, the context of words. Other points have already been explained.

These four *vyāhṛtis,* namely, *bhūr, bhuvas, suvar* and *mahas* are each fourfold, of four forms. Four in all, they individually are of four forms each. The Upaniṣad has already presented the *vyāhṛtis* each in its fourfold aspects. Its reiteration [through actual enumeration] of what it has already presented is meant to lay down the rule for their meditation [that each be meditated in its fourfold aspects and the four in their sixteen aspects]. He who knows these *vyāhṛtis* this way, verily, knows Brahman.

Śaṅkara's commentary on this chapter is not detailed enough nor is Sureśvara's *Vārtika* of much help. Nor, for that matter, is Vidyāraṇya. The Vedic symbolism elaborated in the description of the *vyāhṛtis* requires careful attention and calls for detailed analysis.

First, about the word itself. The word *vyāhṛti* is derived from the root *hṛ,* to speak. *Vyāhṛti* is the word that speaks but is not spoken. One is to meditate on *bhūr* until the word and the world become one. To be *bhūr* means to be the world, to go beyond the distinction between the name and the referent. The distinction will remain as long as the speaker remains. When the speaker dissolves into the word, he and the world will become one. When will this happen?

This happens when *agni,* the fierce consuming flame, the subjective counterpart of *bhūr,* earth, turns into *candramas,* the light that soothes and delights. *Agni* operates in man in the form of hunger. The light that soothes and delights assumes this fierce form when man becomes identified with the body. In order to appease this *agni,* he consumes the earth, alienates himself from and turns hostile to others. The flame that burns him can however turn redemptive if man offers himself to it instead of things other than himself. Self-restraint is the first kind of *tapas* that he must perform. When he has burnt his passions and his self-love, he rises above the earthly state to become ethereal. He becomes the dweller of *antarikṣa,* of the sky, whose presiding deity is *vāyu,* the blowing deity of air or wind. That which was the burning and consuming flame on earth turns into the freely moving air in the interspace. As long as man is self-centred, as long as he imagines himself as confined within the narrow walls of the body, the divine will appear fierce and destructive. When he offers himself to that fire as an oblation, man will not die into what is called nothingness, he will turn into air and freely move with it. He will lose his personal identity to become all others—one after the other. He will be all because he himself will be [a] nothing.

This self ever on the move, this everything that is nothing, this generosity that can move on to everything to be anything, this self without a character will eventually become all, will become *āditya,* the all-absorbing light. As the all-absorbing sun, he will inhabit *dyu,* the world of radiance. In this world, the subjective light will become one with the objective light; man will not remain man: he will become what he calls the cosmos and what he calls the gods. In other words, he will dwell as space and live as time. And that will mean the end of all hunger and all struggle; the light that consumed all will now turn into the soothing light of *candramas,* the benign form of the terrible *agni.* As *agni,* this fire burnt all, including man. When man burnt with *agni,* he became one with *agni* the all-absorber. What as the other was *agni* now becomes *āditya* the self, for as *āditya* he absorbs all into himself, finds all his own self. When all becomes one with the self, then all turns into the blissful *candramas,* the *soma,* the moon. The same *agni,* the same sun becomes the joyous light called the moon.

Those who worship earth have to live as sacrificial victims. That, in every truth, is the fate of mortal men. Their path to redemption lies through the flame of fire. Their words are the words of *ṛc-es,* the prayers of the *Ṛg Veda.* Men of earth will undo themselves if they use words as mere instruments of interpretation or communication. They will use them only to distort and dissimulate. If ever they wish to save themselves they will have to use words as prayer, prayer offered to the gods, each of which will turn into *viśvedevāḥ,* all the deities, as well as *viśvelokāḥ,* all the worlds provided these mortals flow out with their prayers. Let the flame of prayer do to man's narcissistic interpretations and his communications what the flame of fire does to his oblations and the flame of *tapas,* austerity, meditation, does to his desires. Let him sacrifice his anthropocentric meanings and understandings and pour out his soul in prayer. When the fire in the form of *ṛc-es* has released him from his individualistic confines, the time will have come for his prayers to change into ecstatic song, song that would almost wipe out the distinction between one who says the prayer and one to whom the prayer is addressed. Such a man will be drunk with joy, the man who pours his soul out in ecstasy. Whatever be his state, whatever be his place, the joy will not leave him. As every place is the home of air, so will it be his. He will become the inhabitant of *antarikṣa,* the sphere of air and his speech will be the songs of the *Sāma Veda,* the Veda of the exalted song.

The *Chāndogya Upaniṣad* reserves *antarikṣa,* interspace, for *yajur vidyā,* revelation in the form of sacrificial formulas and *dyu* for the *sāma-vidyā.* The *Taittirīya Upaniṣad,* an Upaniṣad of the *Yajur Veda,* reverses this order. For this Upaniṣad, *ṛg-vidyā* is the *vidyā,* knowledge, of the *bhūr, pṛthivī,* earth, *sāma-vidyā* is the *vidyā,* knowledge, of *antarikṣa,* interspace, and *yajur-vidyā* is the *vidyā,* knowledge, of *dyu,* heaven[1]. Mere joy of ecstasy, mere flowing out into all that is like airy currents, will not ensure freedom from earth, no permanent freedom that is, for as air can blow down so can man fall again from those ecstatic heights. When man has attained freedom from fixed identity, when he has the freedom ensured by self-negating ecstasy, he must resist the temptation of exulting in that joy. For exulting in it will mean the end of the joy and his fall into the miseries of the earth. He must realise that the joy he feels is still conditioned by his body, however vague his experience of the body might be in that mood, and that it is as fragile as the breath of his life is. If he lives as a genuine mortal, if he truly and experientially knows what mortality is, knows it in every breath that he breathes, he will not lay much store by his ecstasy and his joy. The ecstasy will be his anguish, his joy his pain. He will distance himself from this joy, this ecstasy as he will from sensuality and pride and will be a nothing, a void, a nonentity. He will, in one word, live as sacrifice, live the wisdom revealed in the form of *Yajur Veda.* When he lives as sacrifice he will truly die into the all-absorbing sun, will become that all-absorber, will not find anything other than himself. He will see all as himself, as his self as *āditya.* That will be the 'moment' of his entry into *dyu,* heaven, the radiant region of immortality.

Earth, interspace and heaven are merely three letters of *aum. A* is earth, *agni, ṛg-vidyā; u* is interspace, air, *sāma-vidyā; m* is *dyu,* heaven, sun the absorber, *yajur-vidyā.* When man has died into *āditya,* when he has become heaven and has sacrificed his consciousness into it and has, through this negation of himself, negated his heaven too, then he comes to know what *aum* or *mahas* or Brahman truly is. To know *aum* truly is to see as one earth, interspace and heaven, it is to have the vision of *samatvam,* of sameness, between fall and redemption, bondage and liberation, Brahman and *māyā.* This is precisely what it means to know the fourth, invisible, letter of *aum.* For a detailed description of the vision of *aum* and its implication, the reader should consult volume 2 of this work (*Māṇḍūkya Upaniṣad* and *Gauḍapāda Kārikā*).

ŚB *Objection: Mahas* has already been identified with Brahman and *ātman,* the Absolute and the self. The knower of *mahas* thus would be the knower of Brahman. How is it that the *śruti* now speaks of the knower of the four

1. The reader should remember that *ṛg-vidyā, yajur-vidyā* and *sāma-vidyā* refer to levels of revelation, not to the books called the Vedas. Each of Vedas contains the three levels of revelation. See Vol. I, pp. 412-19.

vyāhṛtis and the fourfold aspects of each of them as the knower of Brahman? Does it not thereby negate its own earlier statement?

Answer: The objection is misplaced. When the *śruti* speaks of the knowledge of Brahman in terms of the four *vyāhṛtis* and of the fourfold aspects of each of them, its purpose is to draw attention to the specific nature of Brahman and its attributes. These the *śruti* will describe presently when it will speak of its being realisable within the heart, possessed of mind, enriched with peace and so on. Merely the knowledge that *mahas* is Brahman is not enough. That is why the *śruti* speaks of Brahman as if it had not yet been revealed and proceeds to say that it is the knower of the four fourfold *vyāhṛtis* who knows Brahman and not merely the knower of *mahas*. The implication is that Brahman is to be known with all the attributes that the *śurti* is going to describe in the next section. There is thus no room for the objection you have raised.

This anticipation of what is to be described in the next chapter shows the thematic unity of the two chapters. For both relate to the same meditation. The *śruti* itself indicates this thematic unity, this sameness of meditation in its own words: 'He is established in fire as *bhūḥ*, earth' (Section 6). Moreover, the sixth chapter has no words of commandments, words like, 'Let him pay heed to,' 'Let him meditate' to call upon man to resort to another meditation. In the present section, 'He who knows thus knows Brahman' thus anticipates what is to be said in the section to follow; it points out the continuity of the self-same meditation. We have already pointed out the need of this continuity when we said that in insisting that the knower of the four fourfold *vyāhṛti-s* alone is the knower of Brahman, its purpose was to mention the specific attributes of Brahman to be meditated.

To him who meditates on Brahman this way, all the *devas*, the shining gods, bring oblations as do the limbs [the organs] to the body. For such a man attains to self-lordship.

Chapter 6

ŚB It has been said that other gods—namely, *bhūḥ, bhuvaḥ, suvaḥ* are limbs of Brahman, the *vyāhṛti mahas*. Of that Brahman which has these three for its limbs is now described the place of realisation. That place is the space within the heart. One has to contemplate that space as Brahman as one would contemplate a stone icon as Viṣṇu. When one contemplates the cavity of the heart this way, one realises it as having mind, immortality and other attributes. This realisation will be direct and immediate, as immediate as is the perception of a piece of myrobalan fruit placed in the palm of one's hand. The *śruti* has also to reveal the path to the vision of the all as the self. The chapter in question is commenced with this end in view.

1. sa ya eṣo'ntarhṛdaya ākāśaḥ, tasminn ayaṃ puruṣo manomayaḥ. amṛto hiraṇmayaḥ. antareṇa tāluke. ya eṣa stana ivālmbate, sendrayoniḥ. yatrāsau keśānto vivartate, vyapohya śīrṣakapāle. bhūr ity aganau pratitiṣṭhati. bhḥuva iti vāyau.

2. suvar ity āditye. maha iti brahmaṇi. āpnoti svarājyam, āpnoti manasaspatim, vākpatiś cakṣuṣpatiḥ, śrotrapatir vijñānapatiḥ. etat tato bhavati. ākāśaśarīraṃ brahma. satyātma prāṇārāmaṃ mana ānandam, śāntisamṛddham amṛtam. iti prācīnayogyopāssva.

Here in the space within the heart dwells the person one with the mind, bright and immortal. That which hangs down inbetween the palates like a teat is the birth place of Indra, the path that leads to Brahman. This path goes up to the head where the roots of the hair divide to burst through the two regions of the skull. He rests in Agni, *fire, as* bhūḥ, *earth, in* vāyu, air, *as* bhuvaḥ, *interspace, in* Āditya, *the sun the all-absorber, as* suvar, *in Brahman as* mahas. *He attains to self rule, he attains to the lord of the mind, the lord of speech, the lord of the eye, the lord of the ear, the lord of consciousness. This he becomes and more. He becomes Brahman whose body is space, who is of the nature of truth, whose delight is breath, whose mind is bliss, who is replete with peace, who is immortal. Thus do thou meditate, O Prācīnayogya, You of the Ancient Yoga.*

ŚB Syntactically, *saḥ,* he, relates to *ayaṃ puruṣaḥ,* this person, not to the intervening words. The heart is a lump of flesh of the shape of the white lotus. It is the seat of breath, opening out through many a nerve, with its stalk upwards and face downwards. One can easily see it in the dissected body of a sacrificial victim. Within this heart lies space, empty like the space within a vessel. In this space, familiar [to adepts in yoga], resides this *puruṣa,* this person. They call him *puruṣa* because he sleeps (*śayanāt*) in the city called the body or because all the worlds from the earth onwards are replete (*pūrṇa*) with his presence. That *puruṣa* is of the nature of *manas,* mind. *Manas* may be taken here as derived from the root *man,* to know. *Puruṣa* may be called of the nature of *manas,* because of the fact that it is realised through *manas,* knowledge. Another interpretation too should be in order. For *man,* the root from which *manas* is derived, also means *to think.* If the root is taken in this sense, then *manas* would be the internal organ [as against the sense organs], the organ of thinking. *Puruṣa* may then be called of the nature of *manas* in this sense because he takes himself as one with mind. Also because he is indicated by the mind, this bright and immortal person.

This Indra, this Lord whose nature the Upaniṣad has just described, the enlightened seers realise in the space within the heart, realise it as their very self. The Upaniṣad points out the path that leads to this person. There is a nerve, celebrated in the yogic scriptures, called *suṣumnā.* It passes upwards from the heart to the mid-region between the two palates and through that bit of flesh that hangs down like the nipple between these two palates. From there it stretches up to the crown of the head where the roots of the hair divide. There it passes out, breaking open the skull in the middle and dividing it into two regions [the right and the left]. This path of the nerve is the path that leads to Indra, to Brahman, to its real being.

The Upaniṣad describes the yogic path to self realisation. The crown of the head is the place of self realisation; of self realisation, not absorption in the self. When the yogic *agni,* the *kuṇḍalinī,* reaches this place, man transcends body consciousness and becomes the all-pervasive stillness. This is the meaning of breaking open the skull. The medieval saints of India called this passing out as passing out from the *piṇḍa* to the *brahmāṇḍa,* from the body to the cosmos. This transformation, this becoming the all, is only establishment in the self, not absorption in it. The journey further is, however, no journey, for human efforts and, for that matter, divine efforts can go no further. Man as the cosmos has to remain content with his being as the universal sacrifice, living with all and dying with all, killing with the killer and getting killed with the killed (to invoke the phraseology of the *Bhagavadgītā*). Participating in the joy and the agony of all, the cosmic man is cosmic nothing because he is everything. That is his glory and his humility.

ŚB The wise man thus realises, through the path of *suṣumnā,* the self as conditioned by mind. Transcending the confines of the body through the door in the head, he comes to be established in the *vyāhṛti bhūḥ,* that limb of the great Brahman called *agni,* the fire, that presiding deity of this world. He becomes, in other words, *agni* itself and, as *agni,* pervades the entire world, this world. Then does he get established in the second *vyāhṛti* called air [to pervade the intermediate region entire]. Next comes the stage of getting established in the *vyāhṛti* called *āditya,* the all-absorber. Lastly, he gets established in *mahas,* the fourth *vyārhṛti,* Brahman, to which the first three are related as parts are related to the whole.

Established in the first three as their self, himself becoming Brahman itself, he attains to sovereignty. As Brahman is the sovereign of the shining gods, its limbs, so he too becomes their sovereign. And as the gods, the limbs, bring offerings to Brahman, the limbed, so do they bring unto him too those offerings.

And he attains to the lord of the mind, to Brahman, who as the self of all is the lord of all minds and thinks through all minds. To that Brahman attains the wise man who follows the path of *suṣumnā.* And he attains to the lord of speech, each and every, of every eye and of every ear, of every cognition, every knowledge. As the self of all, he becomes possessed of the organs [sense organs and motor organs] of all that live and breathe.

Not only does he see with all eyes, hears with all ears and thinks with every mind. He becomes more than this; he becomes Brahman itself, the Brahman the Upaniṣad has been speaking about. This Brahman has the ether of space for its body, has a body subtle like the latter, has truth itself for its being, truth formed and formless. To it breath is delight and to breath is it delight. And for bliss it has the mind. [Unlike unto the creatures of the world] the mind brings it bliss, and only bliss. And peace is it and perfection. The perfection it has is the perfection of peace, enriched by it. One can attain to it through that alone, through peace alone. The compound *śānti-smṛddham,* peace-perfection carries this suggestion too. And by its very nature is it immortal.

It should be understood that these additional attributes pertain to the same Brahman as has been described as conditioned by the mind and so on. 'Thus do you, O Prācīnayogya, meditate on Brahman as conditioned by the mind and other attributes, Brahman as described above.' The commandment of the teacher brings forth the regard he has for this meditation. The term *meditation* has already been explained.

The yogic meditation leads one to the realisation of Brahman, but Brahman conditioned by the mind, not Brahman the unconditioned, the reality absolute. This conditioned Brahman is called lower Brahman or *Hiraṇyagarbha,* the Golden Germ. The term *mind* has been used here, the commentator says, in two senses: in the sense of knowledge, and, secondly, in the sense of thought. The individual is conditioned not merely by the mind but also by the body. To do away with the adjunct of the body means to do away with 'I am' consciousness and the consciousness of the other; it means end of the consciousness of the world of space. One should not, however, rush to the conclusion that *Hiraṇyagarbha* is pure temporality, for one cannot be conscious of temporal sequence without the 'I am' thought. In other words, only the individuated, embodied consciousness is aware of time. This means that without the world of space, without being placed in it, one cannot have experience of time.

What could then be the meaning of *manas,* mind? If what we call 'thought' is the connotation of the term, then thought may be said to be the attribute of the embodied, placed individual. But, mind it, the individual has thought as a trait, he is not one with it, it is not his self. Whereas Brahman as *Hiraṇyagarbha,* is one with thought. He is not [a] thinker but thought itself. But what is thought for him? In other words: what is thought for thought?

For us, thought is a succession of images, feelings, ideas, concepts, a flow, a process. I cannot, however, perceive this thought process unless I am different from it, stand apart from it to survey it. My very consciousness of thought shows that I am not thought, not the succession of thoughts that I take myself to be.

Hiraṇyagarbha, however, is thought itself because he is not conscious of thought process. For this reason, he is not really thought process because there is no thought process for what we call thought process. It is we, who assert ourselves as thougtht process, that find him one with thought or mind. Not that innocence, that thought that knows not that it is thought. He is also called one with knowledge. He is, that is to say, not the knower but only knowledge. And knowledge, without the knower, is not knowledge as we understand the term. To be a cognition, to be immersed in it, is to cease to be cognition. But all this is negative talk, an indication of the poverty of our thought and language. *Hiraṇyagarbha* is a nothing that sees with every eye, hears with every ear, speaks with every tongue, lives with and as every creature and dies with it. He lives the meanness of creatures and their generosities, their folly and their wisdom, their frivolous pleasures and their awful undoings.

The misery of our thinking is his joy because he lives as much our death as our life. The corpse is as much a joy for him as is a supple and youthful body. Our anxiety is his bliss, our foolish concerns his happy sports. And yet in himself he is all peace, immeasurable and without limit. This peace saves him from being what we call nothingness. As silence is not mere absence of sound, so this peace is not what we term nothingness. There is a plenitude about it, a still perfection, a stillness which is the goal of every movement, every event, every endeavour.

The eye, a god in the Upaniṣadic language, sees an object, an object situated in space and time. As an object in space it engages my desire and passion; as an item in temporal sequence, my theoretico-practical impulse. The object as such, the object in and for itself, is however not what my desire takes it to be or, for that matter, my theoretico-practical impulse. To find the object, I have to be purged of my desire and my theoretico-practical passion. To find it I have to pay my exclusive regard to it, to dwell in it and as it. If I succeed in doing that, I shall find the object, find it not merely an individual object but the very cosmos itself and more than the cosmos. For it will reveal depths of stillness in comparison with which the cosmos will be like a bubble floating on an ocean, depths which can swallow it all without producing even the semblance of a ripple on its placid surface. That stillness is this *Hiraṇyagarbha,* the nothing rich and profound. What the eye reveals is only an oblation which will be offered to this fire called *Hiraṇyagarbha,* this *yajña,* this sacrifice. For all phenomena, subjective as well objective, come into being to be food for this eater. This *yajña,* this sacrifice, that the universe is is a tragedy, grim and forbidding, for creatures of desire and cognitive passions that we are. Until we give up these miseries our tragedy will not relent. When these come to be replaced by the peaceful stillness that resides hidden in man, he will find, in, every truth, the world a *yajña,* the divine sacrifice, where creatures are born in glory and die in glory. In that *yajña,* to be replaced by the other is to find oneself.

All senses thus bring their objects as offerings to this holy fire. And not only objects but also themselves. For the body has to melt into that peace to be that peace. So has to melt into it the mind. The yogic practice leads one to the creator who himself is creation and what follows creation, destruction. With every thought is he born and with every thought does he die. Every thought, every moment of it, is that peaceful nonbeing, and every collapse of it. Thought reveals him in its undoing.

The path to *Hiraṇyagarbha* is marked by many a milestone. The first consists in becoming one with *agni,* the fire that burns in man in the form of hunger and sex passion. Let man burn with that fire; let him make offerings of his desire and himself in that fire and not of food and woman. Fasting and chastity are thus preludes to the yogic practice. When man burns with that fire, becomes that fire and does not seek to appease it through food and woman, he will find another flame light up in him, the flame of holy fire. It will burn bright and fierce in the region of the navel and will consume the passion that the anus and the genitals generate in man, the passion for food and sex. Mere fasting, however, will not be enough nor will be chastity. They are only steps towards noncovetousness and nonacquistiveness. The aim is to live insecure and defenceless, to live, that is to say, truly as a mortal. If man succeeds in living thus, he and the world will coalesce into harmony, provided he does so in serene calmness, not out of pride or vanity. The ego of the doer will prove to be his undoing.

Through food man seeks to save himself from death, through sex he would forget about it. Through the medium of the other body, he would feel himself replete with bodiness, with its thinginess, with the feeling of being a being, being an IS. In the larger context of life, this passion weaves the vistas of linear time, a time in which death is seen as merely a moment, not its undoer. This is how a man of family would look at death: not the end of time, whether linear or recurring but a moment in it. So do men of knowledge and men of action. Desire for knowledge and for social change, the theories we formulate and the practices we devise, spring, in a sense, from the sexual passion, are merely sublimation of it. For all these relate to our passion to sleep over the truth of our mortality.

If a man can live the fury of the passion of sex, can burn himself in it, then the other will not remain the other for him. The other is the ontological necessity for this passion. A deep narcissistic relationship obtains between him and that other. Only when he outlives this narcissistic fury, does man come alive as a genuine mortal, partaking in full the mortality of others. Only thus can he live for others and as others, a sharer of their fate and undoing. And those others will not be mere human others, they will include all creatures, of the earth, of the waters, of the sky. A man who can thus live for and as others, can live as a genuine mortal, alone will know how to love the world of space and be it. He will glimmer with the dawn, flow with the rivers, fly with the birds and low with the cows. He who lives as time will also know how to dwell as space. Living each moment, he will live as every thing, any thing that catches his eye. But only on certain lucid occasions, not always. For his selfhood is obstinate, his tragedy deep, too deep, indeed, for any attitudes or dispositions he may adopt or cultivate.

The path of yoga enables man to convert this fragile vision into a stable one. When man thus becomes the fire that consumes one, fire in the form of passion for food and sex, another fire comes to burn in him, the fire that burns in the regions of the navel as against the one that burnt in the regions of the anus and the genitals. This upleaping flame carries him to the domain of *vāyu,* of air in motion. The serene *yogin* moves with the air moving in him to become 'eventually' that very air. When he becomes the breath in him, he finds his body turn into a process, first a process of sensations, then a process of breath. There remains no feel of flesh nor of bones. An emptiness comes to reside in the body like that of the sky without, only a barely felt layer of skin dividing these two. When all consciousness melts into breath, then the *yogin* does not feel the presence of breath either. With the feel of breath gone, the feel of the skin too vanishes and the two spaces, that within and that without, merge to become one. This is the meaning of getting established in *bhuvaḥ,* in *antarikṣa,* in interspace.

From the domain of *bhuvaḥ* to that of *suvaḥ,* from the domain of *vāyu,* air, to the domain of *āditya,* the sun, from the region, to talk in microcosmic terms, stretching from the navel to the throat to that of the forehead, there is a path, the path of *suṣumnā.* The same path leads one to the world of *Hiraṇyagarbha,* to the door at the crown of the head, the door that opens out to the disembodied state of being. There resides the resort of all that is, their goal and their source. That is the end of *yoga,* indeed of all practice, of all seeking. This does not, however, mean that one cannot fall from this bliss, this joy. One can and does awake from this ecstasy to see how man–world harmony emanates from it to change into man–world duality and, eventually, into man and the world marked by cruel otherness. This insight into ecstasy and anguish, into the fragility of redemption and fall eventually undoes man and his god, his ecstasy and his anguish. For he knows that ecstasy will give place to anguish, as much as anguish will to ecstasy. With this insight into their inevitability, he will be indifferent to both, accepting his fall with the same tranquillity as his redemption. There is no way to attain to higher Brahman except the way of self-submission to this ebb and flow of bliss and pain. He who seeks higher Brahman will not find it but he who gives himself up to lower Brahman as if the latter were the Absolute Itself will find it transform itself into higher Brahman. The implied paradox should not be lost sight of. The paradox has received our attention in earlier volumes and will occupy us again in the sections to follow. The paradox is central to the teachings of the Upaniṣads.

Chapter 7

ŚB The *śruti* has revealed the Brahman to be worshipped in the form of *vyāhṛtis*. Of that very Brahman, it is now going to reveal another meditation, the meditation of the fivefolds beginning with *pṛthivī*, the vast expanse of earth. Because of the similarity of the number five, these groups of the five are equated with the metre *paṅkti*. For this reason of similarity, all that is comes to be identified with *paṅkti*. Sacrifice too is a *pāṅkta,* made of *paṅkti,* as a *śruti* text would bear out: 'Five feet has the metre *paṅkti* and so has a sacrifice five factors' (BṛU 1.4.17). Therefore, he who meditates on all from the cosmos to the individual as fivefold, meditates it as sacrifice. He who performs this meditative sacrifice attains to *Prajāpati* the fivefold. How all this is fivefold is now being stated.

The yogic way demands of the *yogin* that he burn himself out, for his body is the altar where burns the sacred fire to burn the dross in him. Those who cannot perform this sacrifice within are asked to perform the cosmic sacrifice the Upaniṣad is going to reveal. The equation of the cosmos with the *paṅkti* metre demands of the contemplator that he visualise the cosmos as a *chanda,* a rhythmic movement, and not an inert topography that his eyes reveal it to be. Let him join the ear to the eye, let him listen when he sees. For everything that he sees is a moment in the cosmic harmony, from earth to interspace to heaven, from gods to man to creatures that move or do not move. His eyes cannot see the whole; the invisible is the precondition of the being of the visible. He can, however, hear the cosmic harmony if he would only listen to the music of things. So let him focus his attention on the ears, have a feel of what they register when he looks at the vast expanse of earth, from the ground he sits on to the utmost bounds of the horizon. Let him look at the whole expanse, not at this or that thing and let him take in the vast dome of the sky, drink it in as it were. If he does this, he will find the sound of silence ring in him, a sound soft and thought-swallowing. If he gives himself up to that sound of silence, if he lets it swallow his thoughts, he will find the world, within and without, become one, single presence. The stars will shine as before and the clouds will float as they do but they will fail to arrest his attention, for that would be commanded by an overwhelming whole that the universe will become in that moment. Even his body will lose its independence; it will become an integral part of that whole, will be concretely experienced as such. That is what the Upaniṣad wants us to attain to when it asks us to be aware of the audible dimensions of the visible. This will, however, constitute the bare beginning of this meditation.

1. pṛthivy antarikṣaṃ dyaur diśo 'vāntar-diśāḥ; agnir vāyur ādityaś candramā nakṣatrāṇi; āpa oṣadhayo vanaspataya ākāśa ātmā; ity adhibhūtam.

athādhyātmam: prāṇo vyāno 'pāna udānaḥ samānaḥ. cakṣuḥ śrotraṃ mano vāk tvak. carma māṃsaṃ snāvāsthi majjā. etad adhividhāya ṛṣir avocat : pāṅktaṃ vā idaṃ sarvam. pāṅktenaiva pāṅktaṃ spṛṇotīti.

Earth, interspace, heaven, quarters and quarters intermediate; the flaming one, fire, the blowing one, air, the all-absorbing one, the sun, the moon that shines to soothe and delight, the stars, the glimmering lights on the move; waters, herbs, plants, sky, and the self.
Thus with regard to the [theo-] cosmic dimension.
Now with regard to the individual dimension:
The outgoing breath, the diffused breath, the incoming breath, the upward breath, the distributive breath; the eye, the ear, the mind, speech, touch; skin, flesh, muscles, bones, marrow.
Having ordained thus, the seer said, 'Fivefold, verily, is all this. With the fivefold indeed does one augment the fivefold.'

ŚB Earth, interspace, heaven, quarters and intermediate quarters constitute the fivefold world. Fire, air, the sun, the moon and the stars constitute the fivefold divinity. Water, herbs, plants, sky and the self constitute the fivefold sphere of objectivity. Since the context is of the objective sphere, the self [*ātman*] connotes *Virāj* here, *Virāj*, the Radiant Person, that has the cosmos for his body. 'The cosmic dimension' means 'theo-cosmic dimension', for not only the worlds but also the deities have been enumerated in these fivefolds.

Then are mentioned the three fivefolds with regard to the individual. Life breath and others form the fivefold air; the eye and others the group of five senses; skin and others the group of five constituents of the body. This exhausts the list of the fivefolds with regard to the individual and the external world.

Having ordained thus, having imagined thus, said the seer, that is to say, the Veda. Or it may be that some seer endowed with this vision might have said this. What did the Veda or the seer say? 'Fivefold, verily, is all this. With the fivefold indeed, fivefold relating to the individual, does one augment the external fivefolds, fills them up.' Augments and fills them up because of the similarity of the number five. The implication is that through the fivefold they are realised as one, that which is within and that which is without. Prajāpati, the lord of creation, does he become who knows all this as fivefold.

Śaṅkara's commentary is little better than a paraphrase and does not bring out, in any adequate terms, the meditative depth of this seemingly mythical and (to many) fanciful classification, though his introductory remarks do give, as we saw, a clue to a more detailed interpretation. As the first step towards this interpretation, we have to find out what the Upaniṣad means by the musical harmony that it says obtains in the world and its various regions. Those who live on earth as 'earth', confined to food and sex, are deaf to this music. There has to be the contemplative ability to stand apart from the natural man in us. The way lies through concentrating all one's attention on one's ears. He who has the capacity to listen to, who is alive to the message that the ears bring him, will find, before long, his attention all focussed on his open eyes. That is to say, he will not look at the things present before him as one normally does; he will look, so to say, at his eyes and eyes alone. In this disposition of distancing from the eyes, the objects of the world will be seen not *there* but within the eye, for all the space and all the objects in it will come to reside in the eye alone, there itself, rather here itself. The eye will be the world, the whole of it. This my distancing from the eye and the world's de-distancing from it will be accompanied with a soft, mellow hum in the ears. This is a mood or a state in which perception of particularities is simply out of question, for the perception of the whole, an immediate sense of its presence will make them recede from the focus of one's attention. In this state of deep calm the tumult of thoughts will subside to a remarkable degree: they will not distract one's attention from the breathless beauty of the eye and the soft tranquillity of the ear. It is in such blessed moments that one realises that there is indeed such a thing as the music of the spheres and of the *nāda* the *yogins* hear in their trance. For man then lives not just on the earth but also in the sky and what lies beyond the sky. In truth, the sky comes near you, so near indeed that you feel you have only to raise your arm to touch the moon and the stars. And, then, you do not know whether you are in the sky or the sky is in you. As for the body, you won't be able to place it anywhere, for all places come to be the body as it were. The earth and the sky and that which is beyond the sky become one and concentrated. So powerful and overwhelming is the sense of the whole. As for the quarters, one simply cannot place them or think of them. The east is here and the west is here, in this very eye. And what lies between the quarters too is in the eye. This is the meaning of the contemplation of the universe as a *chanda.* This music of the spheres is, however, audible only to those who can see their eyes and hear their ears, not those who see *with* their eyes and hear *with* their ears. To hear the music of the worlds is to see the universe as a whole in the eye, in this very eye of yours. What a redemptive liquidation of distinctions comes to be when man is seized by such holy visions!

For the earthly man, fire and air, the sun and the moon and the stars are mere natural phenomena. The universe consists of either balls of burning fire or expanses of rocks and deserts. The earth alone is the paradise in that vast nothingness. As the earth is the only place of joy for him, so the body alone is the means of attaining that joy. His entire *ekstatic* urge is oriented towards enjoying this sick joy. The *ekstatic* force in man was never throttled the way it has been in these our cruel times. In the times of Vedas there were men and women who allowed themselves to be led by this urge. They looked through and beyond the obvious, could feel that in fire, in air, in the sun and the moon and the stars too there was a rhythm and movement that transformed these phenomena into the moments in harmony, the moments of an ecstatic song.

Since the present context is the context of the song (of sacrifice we shall speak presently), the ear is not to be forgotten. The holy flame of fire is not to be contemplated merely as a visual phenomenon, the visual has to be contemplated as the audible too. To experience the harmony in the world, to experience it as the *chanda,* man has to know how to orchestrate his senses. The senses of the natural man work almost as independent agents, often in conflict with each other, taste and touch often dominating other senses. Most men cannot experience the beauty of the plant they consume or of the animal they slaughter nor of the women they think they love. Taste and touch often turn them blind and deaf. They cannot pause to smell the air they breathe as would a *yogin.* Nor can they experience the soothing touch that a puff of breeze can bring them. Unhappy sadists they live deprived and disinherited. The cause of this deprivation is the conflict that obtains among their senses. One has to harmonise the senses if one is to experience the beauty of the world and the spirit. The harmonisation of the eye and the ear that the Upaniṣad speaks of is only symbolic: the Upaniṣad wants man to harmonise all his senses.

Thus fire is to be contemplated with the attention focussed on the ear. The fire will then be seen to burn within the eye ball, revealing world-shattering dimensions that lie hidden in it, in the flame that one sees upleaping before one's eye. The contemplation of fire will also bring in, through its warmth, the sense of touch. When the eye and the ear and the touch experience, in harmony with each other, a flame of fire, the flaming one will turn into the blowing one, the *agni* into *vāyu,* and so will this body, an entity, turn into a flowing one, into process.

And so will the world. When all thus turns into process, from the body to the mountain to the cloud and the sky, the moment will not be far off when all will melt into what we, obsessed with self-affirmation, cannot but call nothingness but which the Upaniṣad calls *āditya,* the all-absorbing sun, the light which ceases to shine forth because all that it shone on has become one with it.

Higher than the all-absorbing sun is the state of bliss, symbolised by *candra,* the light that pleases and delights, the light called the moon. And higher than *candra* is the domain of *nakṣatras,* stars. The word is derived from the root *nakṣ,* to move. The sun as *āditya* absorbs all, the moon as *candra* delights all. This absorption and this bliss are, however, relational; they come to be in relation to something else. The sun comes to be *āditya* in relation to what it absorbs, the moon becomes a delight in relation to the eyes cast on it. The stars, on the contrary, twinkle on their own, they move on unrelated. Stars as *nakṣatras* symbolise consciousness unrelated, consciousness *absolutus.*

We were, however, talking about the senses. When the eye and the ear and the organ of touch operated in harmony, the body and the world, we saw, turned into a harmonic movement. There is, however, the nose, the organ of smell, to consider and also the organ of taste. When I smell in the flaming rhythmic movement, I shall find, before long, these two, the flame and me, merge into each other, I becoming the flame and the flame me. There will remain, then, no consciousness, consciousness as what is called intentionality. We shall become *āditya,* we two, the flame and me. *Āditya* will turn into *candra,* the all into bliss, when taste comes to join the eye, the ear, the touch and the smell. The region of the moving stars, the region of unrelated light, is, of course, beyond the region of the senses. But the way to it lies through the senses, the senses in unison. The ecstasy of the senses in unison culminates in consciousness the absolutus. That, in every truth, is the glory of the senses-in-harmony, of the ecstasy of their undoing.

The world of objects, too, has to be contemplated as the five-footed metre. The first foot is *āpaḥ,* waters. The juxtaposition of water with herbs and plants emphasises that an intimate relationship obtains among them. Not only among them but also with men's life. Water nurtures herbs and plants and the three nurture and sustain man. The harmonic unity that water, herbs, plants, the sky and *Virāj,* the cosmic self, make is remarkably brought forth in the paintings depicting Kṛṣṇa's, *rāsa-līlā,* his erotic sport, with *gopīs,* cowherdesses. The river Yamunā that flows bluish, the dark green verdure and trees on its banks, the dark blue sky above and the bluish Kṛṣṇa make one presence, one cosmotheandric presence. The water flowing in Yamunā, the nurture of plants and herbs, is not merely the life of *gopīs*, it is also the sky, the entire universe itself. It is also Kṛṣṇa, the delight and bliss of *gopīs,* their *candra.* Water on earth, water as man and god, as Kṛṣṇa, water as sky, water as plants and herbs is not only the life and being of every mortal, it is also his delight, his destination. Water is cosmotheandric being, is *Virāj*, water that I daily drink and bathe in.

The Upaniṣad also speaks about the fivefold of the eye, the ear, the mind, speech and touch. Of the concord of the eye and the ear (and also of touch) we have already spoken: it reveals harmony between the internal and the external, the subjective and the objective. The mind that ordinarily would understand and enjoy the things it perceives, turns, in those moments of quiet harmony, into a passive clearing, a void of openness with speech turning into speech of silence, like the soft hum that one hears in leafy glades and silent gorges, the hum that is there in breathless solitude. When the eye and the ear and thoughts and speech have mingled, so to say, into this quiet and silent music, when they are pervaded by it, the body becomes a void, empty of all solid content. All that remains of it is its outer layer, a bare feel of tactuality. Within the body, with in that layer of the skin, open out depths infinite and measureless, depths which are, in every truth, say the seers, the depths of the universe.

Contemplation of the body as consisting of the fivefold—skin, flesh, muscles, bones and marrow—leads to the disposition of *vairāgya,* of dispassion. The contemplation implies distancing from the body, from its passions and urges; it is a stepping out of it and out of the motion of its breath. Contemplation of five breaths indicates the yogic contemplation. The regulation of outgoing and incoming breaths leads to the release of *udāna,* the upward breath, culminating in *samāna,* the all-pervasive breath. The rousal of the upward breath is preceded by the cleaning up of the entire body with *vyāna,* the distributive breath. The process has received our detailed attention earlier. (notably in our discussion of the *Praśna Upaniṣad* in Volume 1).[1]

1. See pp. 374-409

Chapter 8

ŚB By now the Upaniṣad has described contemplation of Brahman in the form of *vyāhṛti*-s, mystical utterances. It has also described the contemplation of the same in the form of fivefoldedness. *Aum,* we know, is a constituent of every form of contemplation. For this reason, the *śruti* would enjoin upon us meditation on the syllable *aum.* Though a word, *aum* can lead one to the realisation of Brahman, higher as well as lower, depending on whether one meditates on it as higher Brahman or as lower Brahman. *Aum* is the symbol of the two forms of Brahman as an image is that of Viṣṇu, it is the support for contemplation of the two forms of Brahman as an image is a support for contemplation of that god. In support of this our contention, we have the word of the *śruti* itself :

> The higher and the lower Brahman, O Satyakāma, are but the word *aum.* With this support alone does the wise man attain either of the two. (PrU 5.2)

1. aum iti brahma. aum itīdaṃ sarvam. aum ity etad anukṛtir ha sma vā apyo śrāvayetyāśrāvayanti. aum iti sāmāni gāyanti. auṃ śom iti śastrāṇi śaṃsanti. aum ity adhvaryuḥ pratigaraṃ pratigṛṇāti. aum iti brahmā prasauti. aum ity agnihotram anujānāti. aum iti brāhmaṇaḥ pravakṣyann āha brahmopāpnavānīti. brahmaivopāpnoti.

Aum *is* Brahman. Aum *is all this.* Aum *is the word of compliance, for when they say, 'Recite,' they recite. With* aum *do they sing the* sāman *songs, with* aum śom *do they intonate the prayers. With* aum *does the officiating priest accept, with aum does the* Brahman *priest approve, with* aum *does he permit offering to the fire. With* aum *the Brahmin begins his recitation, saying, 'May I attain Brahman.' And attain it indeed does he.*

ŚB *Iti* in '*aum iti*', calls attention to the word '*aum*' [as distinguished from its meaning]. One should contemplate this word as if it were Brahman itself. For *aum* is all this. Since all that could be named is anchored to, is dependent on, the name, and since all speech is pervaded by *aum,* therefore all this is *aum* itself. This we have on the authority of another *śruti* text:

> As leaves are pervaded by fibres, so is speech pervaded by *aum. Aum* is all this. (ChU 2.23.3)

The rest of the passage is a tribute to the word *aum,* for *aum,* the word as such, is adorable.

Aum is the word of compliance. When reminded of one's duty, one says *aum* to indicate one's resolve to do it. There is an age old well established practice to use *aum* as a word of compliance. The utterance of *aum* indicates that the man in question consents to do whatever he has been asked to do, will go wherever he has been asked to go, will recite whatever he has been urged to recite.

Singers of *sāman*-chants sing their chants with *aum.* And those who say their prayers invoke *aum śom* to say their prayers. With *aum* does the officiating priest convey his acceptance, the Brahmin priest his approval, calls upon his assistant to commence a ceremony and makes announcement of its commencement. With *aum* does he give that permission.

With *aum* does a Brahmin begin his recitation of the Vedas, begins their study. He resorts to this way of study, study preceded by *aum,* in order to master the Vedas. For the meaning of the word *Brahman* in 'May I attain Brahman' is the *Vedas.* The word *Brahman* in 'May I attain Brahman' could also connote Brahman, the supreme self. In that case, he utters the word *aum* at the commencement of his study of the Vedas in order to attain to Brahman. And he does attain to Brahman through that syllable.

All those activities which people start with uttering the syllable *aum* do not fail to bear fruit. Therefore, it should be contemplated as Brahman itself. This is the gist of the passage.

The passage in question indicates that *aum* had already come to be regarded as a sacred syllable by the time the *Taittirīya Upaniṣad* came to be composed. This belies the belief, held by many in our times, that the word *aum* appears for the first time in the Upaniṣads alone and not earlier. The *Taittirīya Upaniṣad* states in explicit terms that *aum* was a part of holy rituals. The claim is well supported in, for example, the *Aitareya Brāhmaṇa* (1.12.1). It is necessary to quote some lines from this *Brāhmaṇa* to show how wide of the mark is the belief that considers *aum* as an Upaniṣadic word alone :

ukthaṃ vācīty āha śastvā catur akṣaram. om ukthaśā ity adhvaryuś caturakṣaram. tad aṣṭākṣaraṃ sampadyate. aṣṭākṣarā vai gāyatrī. gāyatrīm eva tad ubhyataḥ prātassavane 'cīkḷpatām. adhvaryo śoṃsāvom ity āhvayate madhyaṃdine ṣaḷakṣareṇa. śaṃsāmodaivom ity adhvaryuḥ pratigṛṇāti pañcākṣareṇa. tad ekādaśākṣaraṃ sampadyate. ekādaśākṣarā vai tṛṣṭup. tṛṣṭubham eva tat purastān madhyaṃ dine'cīkḷpatām. ukthaṃ vacīndrāyetyāha śastvā saptākṣram. om ukthaśā ity adhvaryuḥ catur akṣaram...!

adhvaryor śośomṣāvom ity āhvayate tṛtīyasavane spatākṣareṇa. śaṃśāmodaivom ityadhvaryuḥ pratigṛṇāti pañcākṣareṇa. tad dvādaśākṣraṃ sampadyate. dvādaśākṣarā vai jagatī. jagatīm eva tat purastāt tṛtīyasavane'cīkḷpatām. ukthaṃ vācīndrāya devebhya ity āha śastvaikādáśākṣaram. aum ity adhvaryur ekākṣaram...

The hymn has been recited, he says, having recited in syllables four. 'Aum, *yes, O reciter of hymns,' replies the* adhvaryu *priest in syllables four. This makes up eight syllables. Of eight syllables is the* gāyatrī *metre. The* gāyatrī *do they place on both the sides at the pressing of* soma *in the morning. 'Let us two,* aum, *O* Adhvaryu,*' says he in six syllables at noon. 'Let us,* aum, *recite, O you descended form gods,' replies the* adhvaryu *in syllables five. This makes up eleven syllables. The* triṣṭubh *has eleven syllables. The* triṣṭubh *do they place in front at the pressing at noon. 'The hymn has been uttered to Indra,' says he, having recited in seven syllables.* 'Aum, *yes, O reciter of hymns,' says the* adhvaryu, *in syllables four . . . . 'So let us two,* aum, *recite, O* Adhvaryu,*' he says in syllables seven at the third pressing. 'Let us recite,* aum, *O of divine origin,' says the* adhvaryu *in syllables five. This makes up twelve syllables. Of twelve syllables is the* jagatī. *The* jagatī *do they place in front at the third pressing. 'The hymn has been said to Indra and to the gods,' says he having recited in syllables eleven.* 'Aum, *yes,' says the* adhvaryu *in one syllable. . . .*

The passage shows how the *Aitareya Brāhmaṇa* uses the word *aum* in the senses enumerated by the *Taittirīya Upaniṣad.* The reader will bear with me for the clumsiness of certain expressions in the translation. This became inevitable because I wanted to retain the word *aum* to refute the unfounded belief that *aum* appears for the first time in the Upaniṣads alone. The word was already a sacred word for the priests when they gave their assent, their approval or complied with a request or order through uttering it. In the Upaniṣads this sacred word became the primordial icon or expression of Brahman the Absolute, not a word to be uttered but a word to be heard and self-submitted to. The practitioners of *yoga* say that they hear this syllable in their trance. The word gets transformed, they say, into Brahman when man dissolves his ego-personality into this immortal sound.

The Upaniṣad, however, implies that the word could not have been considered so sacred unless the ritualists had some inkling that it was the holiest of the holy words, that there was something primordial about its holiness[1]. It calls upon seekers of truth to meditate on that very word which the Vedas declare to be sacred and tradition holy. To attain to the highest goal, meditation on this sacred syllable is, the Upaniṣad declares, enough.

Cultures for which words are mere means of communication do not find anything sacred in them. For such cultures human beings and language are 'born' together. Some of their members may even go to the extent of imagining man without language. What kind of a world would non-linguistic man inhabit, men of this sort would not pause to consider. They evidently assume him inhabiting their 'real' world, that is to say, the world interpreted in terms linguistic and conceptual. They would not realise that prelinguistic man cannot be the inhabitant of *their* world, the world of linguistic beings. The Vedic culture by and large did not imagine man without language but it, unlike many a modern thinker, did believe that the word preceded man. The word that preceded man was not, however, the word that he could use or utter. When that word, the word that was more primordial than man, became the tool of man, it underwent a process of concealment. *Aum* is that primordial word but the *aum* that men utter as holy and sacred is only a concealed form of that primordial word. That word will, the Vedas say, reveal its true form if man contemplates its concealed form, its symbol and expression, as if it were the former, as if it were the sole reality. When the word is contemplated as the all, the contemplator losing sense of before and after, it will reveal itself as the all. *Aum* the name will become Brahman the named.

This contemplation is, however, possible only for those who are possessed of the sense of the sacredness of words, for those who know there are words more real than themselves, holier than the holiest of their thoughts. It is because of this awareness that they sanctify their promises and transactions through these words, even their interrelationships, their endeavours and their undertakings. To speak and hear the primordial word, even in its concealed form, means to be conscious of the reality unknown to man, unknown though not nonimmanent; to speak and hear it with regard to daily life transactions, worldly or ritualistic, is to bridge the gap between the secular and the sacred, the immediate and the remote. You feel the dread mystery of the word on your lips, mystery as deep as that of the world, as profound as that of life itself.

1. Cp AB 5.32 where *aum* is treated as the essence of the Vedas and the world.

Those who can only use words but are incapable of contemplating them find themselves at the mercy of words. Whatever they perceive or observe, think or talk about ever remains questionable, with the result that the act of interpretation becomes a never ending act, an act ultimately frustrating and nauseating. Language which itself is one with the real, with Brahman, comes to conceal Brahman, that is to say, itself. A word contemplated reveals itself as one with reality, as a tool it conceals the reality it is supposed to reveal. The tragic depth of this paradox has to be lived if one wants to know it in all its horror.

Interpretative language is constituted by the non-interpreted. The order, the meaning it would superimpose on to the non-interpreted is constantly disdained by the latter. The ordered forms of Apollo are too weak for the chaotic Dionysus. Even the beauty that art would find in life or create is a precarious, fragile beauty. The two gods do not get reconciled: neither in the *polis* nor in the tragic theatre. The two are pitted against each other at a more fundamental level than we realise, at a, one may say, darker level. Life has death for its constitutive other. In our pains and in our pleasures, in our contemplations and our praxis, we tend to forget this relationship, indeed do our best to sleep over it. When in certain moments of self illumination we see through our futile endeavours, we may summon the courage to contemplate the forces of our undoing. This contemplation, this clear eyed looking at, sometimes produces works of great art, wherein the truth of our chaos, of our darkness is not slept over but is allowed to reveal itself, is even provoked to reveal itself. In these moments of fierce creativity, moments when chaos rages in my eyes and in my ears death, I still sing of that chaos, that death and madnes, sing of them in triumphant humility, serene in the tumult, joyous in the pain. Still that singing, that serenity, that joy is an escape from my truth. All creativity is dependent on my organism which will disintegrate one day to expose the futility of my creativity. Dionysus refuses to be tamed by Apollo. Life remains, ever reamins, a joke of death.

Modern civilisation chose another path, the path not of reconciliation of Apollo and Dionysus as did the Greeks but the path of exclusive devotion to Apollo. We banished our mad men from our midst to the asylums, drove the irrational in us to nowhere and concerned ourselves with the rational, almost exclusively with it. Calculation took the place of vision, *techne* of endurance, praxis of contemplation, self-affirmation of self-submission. We lost the sense of sacredness of words, their awesome redemptive power because we thought only of using them, not contemplating them. There are no more holy words for us to bind us, to command our faith and our obedience.

When there remain no holy words to bind us to our promises and to our allegiance, we resort to written agreements and to legal bonds. These agreements and bonds are, however, distancing mediations; they relate men and women to each other through an inert and cruel otherness, which men and women would rather violate or evade than accept or honour. We who live in the culture of agreements and bonds should not lose sight of the implications it has for our life and attitudes. Agreements consist of interpretative words. Those who enter into them are supposed to bind themselves to the referents of those words. But the referents of interpretative words are always elusive, always un-identifiable. You cannot identify them simply because they are interpreted. Insensitive to this ambiguity men and women take the interpreted as the thing in itself. Words no longer command their allegiance because words as tools cannot; only words as revelations, as reality itself can command it. Things of the world, which men and women take to be reals in themselves, are no doubt creation of language but the language that creates them precedes men. Men of the world cannot know that creative language, their language is only a tool at the mercy of their passion for things. Slaves of things, insensitive to the holiness of words, these miserable creatures of greed are ready to destroy each other for the sake of their petty gains. Greed and fraud are the guiding force behind the culture of agreements and bonds.

Those who know, are sensitive to the life and being of words, alone can bind themselves to them. Words of this kind, words holy and divine, have no referents, they are the names as well as the named. Those who can feel the force of these words in their daily life, in their business, in their relationships, their strifes and struggles alone can contemplate these words and give themselves up to them. To them the words will reveal their truth and their being, which will be the truth of the world and its being. Cultures which do not feel the dread mystery of words are poor cultures; for them words never become transparent, never become truth and being.

When the Upaniṣad has pointed out the pervasiveness of *aum* through its pervasiveness in the life of the people, both holy and secular, it no longer feels the necessity of metaphysical arguments to establish its ontological pervasiveness. In Sanskrit alphabet, *aum* spans the entire range of articulation, from that done through the throat to that done through lips. So *aum* may be said to pervade the entire speech. And since speech is a constituent of all phenomena, *aum* may, some may contend, be said to be all phenomena. This would, however, mean sleeping over the ambiguity that obtains in phenomena. *Aum* as a sacred word is not, cannot, be all that is. For even a sacred word can be uttered. *Aum* becomes all when man gets immersed in *aum,* becomes one with it. Then alone will *aum* become the Absolute, will become *idaṃ sarvam,* all this. Not before. The nonreferential word alone is truth, the referential word is a concealment of it.

Chapter 9

ŚB The *śruti* has declared that one attains to sovereignty through knowledge alone. This might suggest to some that holy acts, whether ordained by the Vedas or sanctioned by tradition, are of no use. To ward off this suggestion the *śruti* points out, in the *mantras* to follow, how these acts contribute to the attainment of the goal of life.

1. **ṛtam ca svādhyāya-pravacane ca, satyaṃ ca svādhyāya-pravacane ca. tapaś ca svādhyāya-pravacane ca. damaś ca svādhyāya-pravacane ca. śamaś ca svādhyāya-pravacane ca. agnayaś ca svādhyāya-pravacane ca. agnihotraṃ ca svādhyāya-pravacane ca. athitayaś ca svādhyāya- pravacane ca. mānuṣaṃ ca svādhyāya-pravacane ca. prajā ca svādhyāya-pravacane ca. prajanaś ca svādhyāya-pravacane ca. prajātiś ca svādhyāya-pravacane ca. satyam iti satyavacā rāthītaraḥ. tapa iti taponityaḥ pauruśiṣṭiḥ. svādhyāya-pravacane eveti nāko maudgalyaḥ. tad dhi tapas tad dhi tapaḥ.**

The right as well as study and teaching, truth as well as study and teaching, austerity as well as study and teaching, restraint of senses as well as study and teaching, restraint of mind as well as study and teaching, fires as well as study and teaching, fire worship as well as study and teaching, guests as well as study and teaching, human—social—obligation as well as study and teaching, progeny as well as study and teaching, begetting as well as study and teaching, propagation as well as study and teaching. Truth alone is what counts. Thus Satyavacas, Rathītara's son. Penance alone counts. Thus Taponitya, Puruśiṣtis' son. Study and teaching alone count. Thus Nāka, Mudgala's son. For that alone is austerity, that alone is austerity.

ŚB *Ṛta,* the right, has already been explained. *Svādhyāya* means study of the Vedas, *pravacana,* their teaching or self recital. The right is to be practised and so are other duties as well as study and teaching. 'To be practised' may be understood as the complement of 'The right as well as study and teaching' and of the other succeeding phrases. *Truth* here means truthfulness or it may carry the same connotation as explained earlier. *Austerity* means bodily penance. *Dama* means restraint of the sense organs; *śama* restraint of the mind, its tranquillity. While committing himself to the right, to truth, to restraint of the senses and so on, let man lay the sacrificial fires and perform the fire worship. Nor should he forget that guests who come unknown and unannounced are to be honoured. He should also remember that he has social obligations which he should discharge as the occasion may require. And he is also to beget progeny. For this purpose, he should approach his wife at the time when she is likely to conceive. Propagation of the race requires that he procure a wife for his son to have a grandson.

A man who practices all these should also study and teach the Vedas with diligence. It is to bring home this point that the *śruti* mentions these two duties along with each and every other duty it enjoins upon man. The highest goal of life can be reached through understanding the Vedas and this understanding can be acquired only through their study. Their teaching or self-recital is imperative for their retention in one's memory and also for augmenting righteousness. For these reasons, it is necessary that one have due regard for the study of the Vedas and their teaching.

For the teacher Satyavacas, of the line of Rathītara, truthfulness alone is enjoined upon man, it alone is man's duty. Maybe his name is a descriptive one, the name Satyavacas, one who speaks the truth. It is, however, possible that the name may be merely a proper name without any figurative value. The name of puruśiṣṭi's son, Taponitya, may also be a suggestive name, meaning: one who is ever engaged in *tapas,* austerity. It is, however, possible that this, too, was his proper name. This teacher is of the view that *tapas,* austerity, [alone] is man's bounden duty. Whereas Nāka, Mudgala's son, believes that study and teaching should be practised. For they alone, he says, constitute *tapas,* austerity and, for this reason, should be resorted to.

Truth, austerity, study and teaching were mentioned earlier too in the passage in question as one's duties. Their reiteration through the invocation of the names of revered teachers shows the regard the *śruti* has for these.

Ṛta means, in the present context, not the ordered rhythm of the world process and its disruption but living in accordance with that rhythm and disruption. Man's life and the world's being are constituted by opposites. The wheel of time turns things into their opposites; so will it man. He who lives today will turn into inert earth tomorrow as certainly as day dies into night and night into day. Let man live ever open to the other, let him be a ready home for what he is not, what is other than him. Let him live his decay and his death even when he is strong and alive.

Let him live as a mortal each and every moment, with each and every breath as do the *yogins.* Thus will he live in tune with *ṛta,* the law. Thus will he live the right way.

And let him, this mortal, this *yogin,* study the Vedas with diligence. For even he who lives as a mortal in every breath he inhales and exhales, may become a victim of *hubris,* and, in the fashion of many a thinker and a poet, may turn his *ṛta* into the Absolute. Here the Vedas will lead him out of his temptations, for they will not rest contented until they compel him to become the *ṛta.* Not until he becomes the *ṛta,* forgets himself into it and forgets the *ṛta* itself, will the mortal attain to the goal. Not before this extinction of his self and of his world.

Teaching of the Vedas is an integral part of this self instruction, of this self extinction. A genuine mortal carries in his heart the agony of each and every other mortal. He alone is compassionate, he alone is the fellow sufferer. He teaches the Vedas not in the way of the learned but in the spirit of a co-sufferer, a starving man sharing his food with other starving men as it were. His words will not intimidate that other, nor persuade nor even inspire; they will only awaken and make him still.

Let his mind be still and his senses restrained lest they disrupt this wakefulness and this stillness. This state he will bring about through *tapas,* austerity. *Tapas* means, literally, burning. Let man burn in pain and in patience, let him live the pangs of needs and the torture of passions and those stabbing wounds of humiliations. Let him suffer them in patience and in humility if he is to step out of the senses and see how the world dwells in them. And let him step out of the mind to see his flesh and the elements that compose the world melt into events, into process, a continuity unaccompanied by thoughts.

Let this humility, this tranquil nothing, do the rituals and the duties he is called upon to do by life. Let him do them so that he remains a man among men, a copilgrim and cosufferer, not a whit superior to them. An extraordinary man must live as an ordinary man to protect his extraordinariness. While living in harmony with *ṛta,* speaking the truth, denying himself the pleasures that make him asleep to his mortal lot, let man live innocent of these and of the insights vouchsafed to him. For glory lies in humility, in openness and in opening out.

Marriage, procreation etc. should be understood in this context only. They are not imperatives.

Chapter 10

ŚB The *mantra* to follow is meant for self-recital. The section under study is devoted to self-knowledge; there is no other purpose it has in view. Given this context, self-recital of the *mantra* too is to be resorted to with the same end in view, namely, that of self-knowledge. The *śruti* gives us to understand that recital of the *mantras* leads to self-knowledge *through* purification of the mind.

1. ahaṃ vṛkṣasya rerivā. kīrtiḥ pṛṣṭhaṃ girer iva. ūrdhva-pavitro vājinīva svamṛtam asmi. draviṇaṃ savarcasam. sumedhā amṛtokṣitaḥ. iti triśaṅkor vedānuvacanam.

Mover am I of the Tree, my glory high as a mountain peak. With the pure One for my cause, I am as the immortal one that dwells in the sun, the courser. A shining treasure am I, blessedly wise, immortal, indestructible. Thus spake Triśaṅku when knowledge redemptive had come to dawn on him.

ŚB The transient world is like a tree which cannot but fall one day. I dwell in this world-tree to control it from within, to move it and impel it. My fame is high like a mountain peak. The pure one is my cause, the Supreme Brahman that can be realised through *jñāna,* through that opening out that knows its object by becoming ti. That pure on is my cause, of me who dwells in all as their self.

I am as the immortal one that dwells in the *savitṛ,* the form the sun assumes before its rise and after its setting. That invisible sun is *vājini,* i.e. *vājavati,* possessed of food. In that sun dwells, say *śrutis* and *smṛtis,* hundreds of them, Nectar, pure, beautiful and holy, dwells the real as the self or the self as it really is. That self, holy and pure, am I.

A shining treasure (to complete the sentence) am I, shining treasure that again is the real as the self or the self as it truly is. *The shining treasure* could also mean knowledge of Brahman, knowledge that reveals the self as it really is. Knowledge of Brahman is a treasure because it blesses one with the joy of liberation. If one accepts the latter interpretation, then one should read the sentence as follows: 'I have attained the shining treasure' instead of 'I am the shining treasure.'

And blessedly wise am I. Blessedly wise because this wisdom is all-knowing. I am all-knowing because I have the power to create the world, to sustain it and destroy it. Immortal, therefore, am I, indestructible and undecaying. Indestructible could also mean 'soaked with the waters of immortality' as a *Brāhmaṇa* text would say: "Soaked am I with the waters of immortality, *amṛtokṣito'ham.*"

This is the after-word of the seer Triśaṅku, a knower of Brahman, who had become one with Brahman. This he uttered after he had attained to the vision of the self as the sole reality. *Anuvacanam,* after-word, suggests this, the fact that he said these words after self-realisation. Like Vāmadeva, Triśanku too was all blessed, had achieved all that is to be achieved. This *mantra* proclaims that blessed state of his, this *mantra* that he 'saw' with the eyes of a seer. Of *ātma-vidyā,* self-knowledge, is it a revealer, this revelation vouchsafed to Triśanku. Its recitation, one may take it, leads to self-knowledge.

The preceding chapter dealt with the right and other sacred acts which a disinterested seeker of Brahman was called upon to perform. The present chapter relates to the revelatory word, the word that reveals itself after the revelation of *ātman.* This arrangement of the text shows that the desireless seeker of Brahman who performs all the obligatory acts commanded by the *śruti* and sanctioned by the *smṛti,* is blessed with the same revelation as was vouchsafed to the Vedic seers, the revelation relating to the self and all that follows from the realisation of the self.

The present *mantra* is indeed a revelation about revelation. The seer becomes one with the mover, the creator and sustainer of the world, the world transient and ephemeral. And yet this moving spirit of the moving world is not the *causa sui,* for he too has the Pure One for his cause. The creator finds his truth in someone other than what he finds himself to be, the Pure One interior and anterior to what he takes himself to be. Yet the glory of this seer, this creator and sustainer is unsurpassable, it is like the mountain peak, the highest point one could reach.

Beyond and above the peak there is no point to reach. The sky, of course, is there with the sun shining bright in it. There is, however, no way to reach that bright and luminous god. The summit alone could be reached but nothing beyond the summit. Not the sun of truth which shines as distant as before, making nonsense of the difference between the summit and the plains. How to reach the sun is the question, the momentous question.

When Dante saw the sun resting on the summit of the mountain before him, the sun that kept men on the straight path, he tried to reach it by scaling the mountain but failed in his endeavours. Human passions do not allow man to reach that height. Here the seer has scaled the mountain and reached the peak but only to find the sun, the Pure One, as distant as ever. The seer is of course related to that sun, that Pure One, as the effect is related to the cause, as the son to the father. However intimate the relationship, the cause remains the cause even when it has turned into the effect. Its being, its content is inexhaustible, no effect can fathom it or measure it. Though the finite is related to the infinite in terms most intimate and close, yet the infinite remains ever distant, ever unknown. That is the state of the *ṛṣi,* of that lonely dweller on the top. Yet in the same breath, in the same line, the seer finds the distance gone and himself one with 'the immortal one that dwells in the sun.' As long as the seer was the effect, the cause was beyond his reach, the pure one beyond the impure one that the seer was. When the impure one died, the pure one too ceased to be. The sun turned into the immortal person as the seer turned into him. In the sun, the courser, the immortal one dwells ever passive and still. The immortal one has no course to cover, so has the seer, as one with him, no destination to reach. He becomes that still point in the moving sun and the moving world. And it is that serene nothingness, that stillness that peals into the Vedic *mantra.* The *ṛṣi,* the seer, is neither its recipient nor its speaker. The speaker has died into it and the hearer has faded into it. The world rises out of that silence and the word speaks out of it. For us the worldlings, the world is a burden and the word, if we are faithfuls, the way out, the revelation. For the seer, the world, the word and he himself are one. While creating the world and speaking the word he ever remains the immortal one, the same immortal one that dwells in the sun. Between him and the sun, between him and creation there is no divide, no otherness. As the world he binds himself and as the word he frees himself. His is the cry and his the ecstasy, his the agony and his the joy. That verily is his glory, of him who would not choose between what they call fall and what they call redemption.

Chapter 11

ŚB The present chapter commences with a commandment for the aspirant to self-knowledge, for him who would realise the Absolute as the self, that he do certain acts and duties. Before the rise of this knowledge, man must, the commandment implies, do all the holy deeds the Vedas enjoin and the traditional wisdom calls upon man to do. For they will regenerate him, purify him and bless him, without much ado, with self-knowledge. That this indeed is the purpose of the commandment will be supported by the traditional wisdom and what the Upaniṣad will itself declare in its subsequent teachings. Thus we have, in this regard, the words of Manu to this effect:

> Through *tapas,* through ardour fervent, man burns out his sins, through *vidyā,* passive wisdom, he attains to immortality. (12.104)

And of this Upaniṣad itself:

> Through *tapas* do thou seek to know Brahman. (3.2–5)

Imperative, therefore, is it that he who wishes to be blessed with knowledge of the real-as-the-self, should do the holy acts. That these acts are imperatives is borne out by the fact that they are presented in the form of commandments, commandments of the teacher to the student. Violation of these commandments will, it is implied, pollute the student with sin.

There is, however, one point that should be taken note of regarding the place of holy acts. The Upaniṣad mentions the holy acts before it comes to speak about knowledge, not after. In truth, it makes it a point to emphasise their irrelevance after the dawn of self-knowledge. To cite but a few examples in this regard:

> When man finds in this invisible, this selfless, this inexpressible and nestless the state fearless, then he [too] becomes fearless. (2.7.1)
> Wherefrom returns speech finding nothing along with the mind, knowing that bliss of Brahman one fears not anything. (2.9.1)
> Not for him the remorse: Why did I not do the good? Why did I do the evil? (*Ibid*)

These quotations and many other words of revelatory wisdom as well as of traditional wisdom would show how holy acts bring about self-knowledge through undoing the sins man heaped up for himself in the past. When these sins have been undone, man will come to be blessed with self-knowledge as the *Īśa Upaniṣad* would bear out:

> Knowledge and ignorance, he who knows the two together, will cross death through ignorance and through knowledge shall he become immortal.

Earlier, in Chapter 9, too, the *śruti* invoked the holy deeds. But then its purpose was only to refute the view that would dismiss the holy deeds as of no consequence for the pilgrim to truth. Here the *śruti* emphasises the imperative nature of the holy deeds. These acts cause the rise of self-knowledge. Therefore, he who would aspire to it must perform them. That is the tenor of the chapter in question.

1. vedam anūcyācāryo'ntevāsinam anuśāsti: satyaṃ vad, dharmaṃ cara, svādhyāyān mā pramadaḥ. acāryāya priyaṃ dhanam āhṛtya prajātantuṃ mā vyavacchetsīḥ. satyān na pramadityavyam. dharmān na pramaditavyam. kuśalān na pramaditavyam. bhūtyai na pramaditavyam. svādhyāya-pravacanābhyāṃ na prama-ditavyam.

Having taught the Vedas, the teacher instructs the student: Speak the truth, do the right. Neglect not the study of the Vedas. Having offered to the teacher the gift dear unto him, cut not off the thread of progeny. Truth is not to be slept over, righteousness is not to be slept over. Welfare is not to be slept over. Prosperity is not to be slept over. Study is not to be slept over. Teaching is not to be slept over.

ŚB Having taught the student the words of the Vedas, their texts, the teacher now gives him commandments, instructs him about the meaning of those texts. Until he has enquired into the nature of *dharma*, of the obligatory holy acts, a student is not to leave the teacher's home even after learning the Vedic texts. 'Let him,' says the *Āpastamba-dharma-sūtra*, 'do the holy acts after duly understanding them.' (2.21.5)

What are those instructions? Let the student, says the teacher, speak the truth, what he comes to know from valid means of knowledge. That truth, the truth he has come to know from those means, should also be speakable, fit to be uttered. And let him do what is righteous, 'righteous' in a general sense, in the sense of what should be done in general, specific duties like truthfulness and others being mentioned separately. He is also not to neglect study of the Vedas, turning his mind to them. And let him bring, as a return for the knowledge he got, a gift for the teacher, a gift acceptable to him. When he has thus paid back the debt, let him take, with the teacher's permission, a suitable woman for his wife. Let him not cut off the thread of progeny, it is not proper that he do it. If, perchance, a son is not born unto him, let him not fail to perform the rite enjoined for the purpose. Let there be no laxity of effort on his part. This appears to be the meaning of the *śruti*. The justification for this inference may be found in the fact that while speaking of progeny (at 1.9), the *śruti* did not merely speak of begetting but of offspring, begetting and propagation.

Truth is not to be slept over, there should be no lapse in this regard. For the lapse would amount to falsehood. 'Sleeping over' or 'lapse' suggests that the *śruti* prohibits not mere intentional telling of lies but also inadvertent falsehood. If this had not been the intention of the *śruti*, it would have simply commanded man to refrain from lying, the command for vigilance in the matter would have been out of place. Similarly, one should not be forgetful about *dharma*, righteousness. *Dharma*, in the present context, connotes holy acts. One should not, the *śruti* says in effect, neglect the holy acts enjoined by the Vedas. One should see to it that one performs them. Nor should one neglect the acts that conduce to one's welfare, acts that protect one. Nor is prosperity to be slept over, acts that lead to prosperity. Nor is study of the Vedas to be neglected nor their teaching. These should be done without let or go.

It would be proper to keep in mind that these instructions and the others to follow are given to prepare the student for the revelation of the meaning of the sacred *words* already revealed to him. The Upaniṣad does not lay emphasis on scholarship and scholastic equipment. The Vedas do not reveal their sense and tenor to a mere scholar. They reveal themselves only to a man who is, to mention the first qualification, truthful. To open oneself out to the Veda, one has to open oneself out to fellow creatures. No consideration of one's interests, even of one's safety, are to be entertained in this regard. A truthful man is at once himself and others, he incorporates the other, the gaze of the other, into himself; he is *Vaiśvānara*, the Universal Person, in the making, that Radiant One who becomes nothing to become all. The next commandment relates to the performance of the holy deeds, those acts that enable man to participate in the meeting of the opposites, symbolised by evening, morning and noon. Such a man as has become the other, the other as man and the other as the world, should return to the words of the Vedas, should give himself up to them, linger on them and, concentrating all his mind upon them, should endeavour to become them, those holy words.

Thus equipped should he return home after giving to the teacher a gift of the latter's choice. The teacher cannot demand a fee from the student until he has taught him, over the years, all that he is to teach and the student has to learn. There can be no bargaining on this count. And the student too has to offer the teacher, now that his studies are over, whatever the latter demands of him. In giving education, the teacher has no right to demand, in giving fee the student has no right to hold back. The other's will invariably prevails. Thus equipped, the student, now a man, should return home.

The truth of rebirth will not dawn on man until he flows one with the rhythm of his breath. To prepare himself for this participation in the process of life and death, enacted every moment by the inflow and outflow of breath, the incoming breath dying to give rise to the outgoing breath and *vice versa*, man must live as a being-for-the-dead. For this purpose, let him marry a woman to perpetuate the thread of progeny, remembering all the time that he is but a link in a long line of generations. Let him make offerings to the dead ancestors, for they feed on them, what he offers them, as he will be fed, when he joins them in the world of the dead, what his descendents will offer him. The myth of forefathers and their world reveals man's being as anchored to them, his life here on earth being only a preparation for that life-in-death. Let him prepare himself for that life, the life dependent on his descendents' generosity and faith, by rearing a family. To feel one's affinity with the dead, to find the dead as one's relations, as near to one as are one's descendents, is to live as a mortal. To know and understand the Vedas man should be careful not to forget that his lot is a mortal lot.

The myth about the world of the dead, the world of one's ancestors, is woven to prepare man, as I said above, to live as a mortal. If man lives as a mortal, owns up to his mortality, he will become innocent enough to flow with the rhythm of breath, to be born and die with every breath. When man comes to live his death this way, only then will the truth of rebirth dawn upon him. Not through arguments, however ingenious or subtle. The untruth regarding the world of ancestors is indeed a holy untruth, for it reveals to man the truth of rebirth with all the tragedies and possibilities involved in the realisation of that truth. The Upaniṣads can speak, without any hesitation, about the two visions, that of the world of ancestors and that of rebirth, because they find no contradictions between the two, one being only a preparation for the other.

Welfare and prosperity are not to be neglected by a man dedicated this way to truthfulness, to holy rites and to the truth of his mortality. Welfare and prosperity often make one oblivious of the truth about life and death but if man sticks to truthfulness, can become others to contemplate himself from varied standpoints, and, more importantly, if he remembers that he is a mortal, then he will stick to the straight path, despite his prosperity and his riches.

Let him, enriched and impoverished this way, enriched in openness, humility and in innocence born out of the erosion of rigid concepts that participatory acts can effect, acts like fire worship, and impoverished of self-centredness and interpretative concepts, return to the texts of the Vedas. Let him attend to the sound and movement of their *mantras*, to pronunciation and etymologies of their words. To him thus equipped, with openness and scholarship, with innocence and self-submission, the Vedas will start speaking. Let him, then, impart that revelation to others, not with the ego of a teacher but with the humility of a bare medium. If he speaks as a medium, he will soon become one with the words he speaks to reside in the soul of the student. To this giver of himself unto the Vedas and unto the student, the Vedas will reveal themselves as they truly are, the Reality Absolute, that which scriptures call Brahman.

2. deva-pitṛ-kāryābhyāṃ na pramaditavyam. mātṛdevo bhava, pitṛdevo bhava, ācāryadevo bhava, atithidevo bhava. yāny anavadyāni karmāṇi tāni sevitavyāni. no itarāṇi. yāny asmākaṃ sucaritāni tāni tvyopāsyāni.

One is not to neglect the acts dedicated unto gods and unto fathers. Worship your mother as if she were a goddess and your father as if he were a god and so do you your teacher. And so the guest that comes to your home unknown and unannounced. And do the acts that no one can censure, not the ones that they can. And hold in respect the good deeds that we, the teachers, do.

ŚB And one should not neglect the acts dedicated to gods and to fathers, for it is one's duty to do them. And treat your mother as if she were a goddess, and your father as if he were a god and so do you your teacher. Like gods and goddesses should be worshipped they. And all those other acts that are free from blame and censure, acts that wise and good men do, should be done by you too: do them as if they were binding for you. Not the other acts, acts one could find faults with, even though wise and good men may be seen to do them. You are also to do the good deeds that we, the teachers, do, the deeds that accord with the teachings of scriptures. Only such deeds should you respect and do so that you may reap their reward in other worlds. Do them regularly, without fail and exception.

Man is not merely a living being, he is a dying being, a being whose origin and destiny is anchored to death. From nothingness are born beings and to nothingness do they return. That is the truth about *me*, not history, which is the disembodied, 'immortal' *cogito*'s truth, not my, a mortal being's truth. To worship aged parents, frail creatures crawling towards death, those who know and realise that their being and their destiny are not tied to this world—to worship these mortals means acknowledgement of one's being as anchored to death. It means resistance to the bewitching call of the 'they' in us or of the Cartesian Cogito in us.

To die as man is to be born as god. To be nothing means to be everything, to be all in everything, 'to be the ocean in a drop.' When man thus dies into cosmotheandric dimensions, let him not cease to live as man. Let him live and suffer as a man if he would not tempt pride and invite his fall. For he should remember that human self does not die easily even after the revelation. To neglect the debt that human birth has incurred for him would lead to false pride. Let man, therefore, own up his debts to those who shaped and fashioned his human self—to mother, to father and teacher. Let him also remember his debt to humanity at large which, unknown to him, has made him what he is. Let him pay back his debt to humanity when it comes to him in the form of an *atithi*, one without a date, comes to him unknown and unannounced.

And let him not be contemptuous of acts sanctified by tradition. To question the need of those acts is to rouse up the Narcissus in him. Rebels of this sort do not generally turn genuine way seekers. To live originally is to live in almost intolerable pain. The price is too heavy for most of us. The easier course for man is to honour the norms of behaviour cherished by tradition. Traditional morality makes the dull-witted vain but ennobles the insightfuls. These traditional norms too he should reject if they contradict revelation. For the man caught up in the vortex of the world, there is only one guide to his safety. And the guide is *śruti*, the word that speaks to man but is not, cannot be, spoken by him. Until that word reveals itself as sole reality, as Brahman the Absolute, let man repose his trust in it. For neither custom can be of avail to him nor tradition nor, in the final analysis, the ways of the good, nor his own reasoning powers.

3. no itarāṇi. ye ke cāsmac chreyāṃso brāhmaṇāh, tēṣāṃ tvayāsanena praśvasitavyam. śraddhayā deyam. aśraddhayā 'deyam. śriyā deyam. hriyā deyam. bhiyā deyam. saṃvidā deyam. atha yadi te karma-vicikitsā vā vṛtt-vicikitsā vā syāt.

4. ye tatra brāhmaṇāh saṃmarśinaḥ. yuktā āyuktāḥ. alūkṣā dharma-kāmāḥ syuḥ. yathā te tatra varteran, tathā tatra vartethāḥ. athābhyākhyā-teṣu. ye tatra brāhmaṇāh saṃmarśinah. yuktā

āyuktāḥ alūkṣā dharmakāmāḥ syuḥ. yathā te teṣu varteran tathā teṣu vartethāḥ. eṣa ādeṣaḥ. eṣa updeśaḥ. eṣa vedopaniṣat. etad anuśāsanam. evam upāsitavyam. evam u caitad upāsyam.

Not others. Whatever Brāhmaṇas *are superior unto us, you should offer them a seat to regain their breath, to refresh themselves.* [*Or. Whatever* brāhmaṇas *are superior unto us, breathe you not a word in their presence. Read:* teṣāṃ tvyāsane na praśvasitavyam].

With faith is one to give, not without faith.
In plenty should one give and with modesty.
With fear should one give and with empathy.
If ever doubts assail thee regarding an act or a custom,

4. *then see if there be thoughtful* brāhmaṇas *around thee, to holy acts given and to ethos dedicated, but given thus and dedicated out of choice; men who would not judge hard, men who love* dharma, *the law that sustains man and holds together the world. If there be* brāhmaṇas *of this kind, then do as they do in cases such.*

Now as to the accused: see if there be thoughtful brāhmaṇas *around thee, to holy acts given and to ethos dedicated, but given and dedicated out of choice; men who judge not hard, men who love* dharma, *the law that sustains man and holds together the world. If there be* brāhmaṇas *of this kind, then thou shalt judge as they would judge.*

This is the commandment, this the advice, this the secret of the Vedas, this the Lord's command. Thus shalt thou worship, thus indeed shalt thou worship it, ob-serve it.

ŚB You are not to do other acts, acts that do not accord with the teachings of scriptures even if you find your teachers do them.

There are men who have achieved eminence because of their status as teachers of the Vedas and the qualifications that go with that station. Such men are superior to us, have earned the kind of praise we could not, if men of this superior mettle, if they be men who are *brāhmaṇas,* those who know and speak the *śruti,* and are not of the class of men who possess and rule over dominions of the earth or of the class that owns wealth, —if men of this kind come to you, then honour them with seats so that they may regain their breath, refresh themselves from fatigue. Or, to follow the other reading, you are not to breathe a word in their presence, when you see them occupying an honoured seat to give a discourse in an assembly. Attempt only to grasp the meaning of their discourse.

And whatever is to be given, should be given with faith, not without faith. And in plenty and with modesty and with fear. And with a feeling of empathy as if you were giving it to a friend, to one who is verily you as the other.

If living this way, there arise, on occasions, doubts in your mind regarding acts enjoined by the Vedas or the tradition or regarding customary behaviour, then you, in that situation or that time, should observe the conduct of *brāhmaṇas*, of those who know and speak the Vedas; you should note the acts they are engaged in: men who are thoughtful, can think and discriminate, given to holy acts and dedicated to ethos but out of their own choice, not under the influence of others; men, moreover, who do not judge hard, are not of hard hearts, love *dharma*, the sustaining principle of the world, are desirous, that is, of the unseen results, results that accrue to a man of piety in the other world. In other words, men who have not lost their power of discrimination through desire. The acts these men of wisdom do, you too should do, the customs they follow, you too should follow.

In the same way should you behave towards a man suspected of questionable conduct as do the *brāhmaṇas* described above.

Tatra in '*ye tatra brāhmaṇāh saṃmarśinaḥ*' should be taken to relate, syntactically, to *yukta*.

This is [to attend to the meaning of the text] the *ādeśa*, commandment of the Vedas, this the *upadeśa*, advice, as would a father give to his son. This is *vedopaniṣat*, the secret of the Vedas, their sense and tenor. And this is the *anuśāsana*, the Lord's command, his word, or the command of all those considered authoritative. The latter interpretation seems more in order since the Lord's commandments is the same as the *ādeśa*, commandment, of the Vedas and that the Upaniṣad has already mentioned.

This being the case, all that has been mentioned should be worshipped thus, meditated thus. 'Indeed shalt thou worship' repeats the exhortation to impress upon man not to neglect this worship; the repetition highlights the importance of the instruction given here.

We saw earlier how the Upaniṣad asked man to follow *mores* and *ethos*, those unopposed to the teachings of the Vedas, but out of choice, not out of the force of habit or compulsions of respectability. When there is a doubt regarding the merit of a certain custom, then the ways of the wise are to be followed. Here too one is to do this out of free choice, not out of social pressure.

A man who follows custom not to build up a self image but out of free choice is a man who has deliberately chosen the path of participation in *ṛta*, the principle of harmony that holds together the world as well as society. Free choice falls to the lot of only that man who can transcend the narrow confines of his ego personality and flow out of himself to others, be they men or be they birds or beasts. Even things inanimate. Free choice can be exercised by only such a non-person. Only he can act as the others do because he can live as those others, can be those others.

And judge too should he not those around him, neither rashly nor hastily. A judge cannot live as others, cannot become them. Let him follow the judgement of those who have died into the word to become the Absolute and its revelation. Let his criteria of judgement be what the revealed word proclaims them to be. Let him not fabricate his own criteria, for they will be fashioned by sadistic and masochistic tendencies in him. Even when he follows the words of revelation in this regard, let him not judge others harshly. Let him place himself in the position of the accused before he passes a judgement on the latter's conduct.

This is the way to know the sense and tenor of the Vedas, the way of sacrifice of the ego and extinction of passions and pride and the tendency to formulate and to judge. He who has purged himself into innocence and openness through participatory acts, into self-submission to others through truthfulness and through immersion in the right ways of the world will alone be blessed with the Vedic vision.

To earn this vision, let him bow down only before men of wisdom, those who have dwelt in the words of the Vedas, have become one with them. And who speak the words of the Vedas not as men but as one with those words. That, I take it, is the meaning of *brāhmaṇa* in the present text, not a member of a particular caste. To accept the latter meaning would imply discarding the principle of 'free choice'. And let him not barter himself away to the rich and the powerful. Let him not be greedy but generous while giving away gifts. Let him not give those gifts out of vanity, self-righteousness or pride. Let him fear the impulse for charity when doing the acts of charity. One should remember that giver's pride can indeed be a very mean pride. In the presence of an unhappy man the ego of the saviour too is prone to assert itself in us, us who often forget that the tragedy of the man we pity is not merely his tragedy but ours too, his tragedy, is, in every truth, our tragedy in the making. What a mortal considers a happy fortune today will turn into his misery tomorrow. Common sense can visualise this as a possibility only; for the law of *karman,* however, this is inevitable. The world, according to this law, has no independent ontology, man and the world are not man and the world but man–world. If man nurtures the ego of the prosperous man today, his prosperity will not stay long with him. For the ego destroys his creative powers. When misery comes to visit him, this poor man will find himself utterly inadequate to it. There is, according to this law, nothing more ruinous for man than to exult in good fortune. Man's *placed* self is a miserable self, his unhappiness crushing and his happiness pathetic. Let him, therefore, the law implies, deanchor himself from every situational context and find that self which is *sarvam idam*, all that is.

ŚB To distinguish between *vidyā* and *karman*, between knowing the real through becoming it and the participatory act, we address ourselves to the following questions: Are holy acts alone capable of blessing man with liberation, with the highest good or they can do so only when they are supplemented with *vidyā*? Or, does one need to combine the two to reach that goal? Or does this knowledge need to be supplemented with holy, participatory acts, or will it alone do?

Let us first consider one of the possible answers to these questions, namely: Holy acts alone will do for the purpose. One needs, the answer assumes, to understand the entire Vedic revelation to qualify for doing these acts. 'The twice born,' says a text of traditional wisdom, 'should master the entire Vedic corpus along with their secret wisdom.' This means that mastery of the Vedas implies mastery over the Upaniṣads too, those secret portions of the Vedas concerned with self-knowledge. Everywhere we find [the argument runs] the knower of the Vedas alone qualified to perform the holy acts, in texts like, for example, the following: 'The knower sacrifices,' 'The knower officiates over the sacrifice.' Also: 'Performance follows knowledge.'

Thus many are there to contend that the whole Vedic revelation is oriented towards holy deeds; they constitute the Vedic purport. If holy deeds fail to bring about liberation for man, then the Vedas will be rendered useless.

Vedāntin: The contention is unacceptable on the simple ground that liberation is ever present, innate to one's nature. That which is caused by an action is not native to one's nature, is not permanent. This is a matter of common experience. No one can possibly accept the contention that holy acts can bring about eternal liberation. The contention runs counter to what the *śruti* declares in this regard:

> As here decays the world brought about by acts, so will the other won by holy deeds, too. (ChU 8.1.6)

This assertion by the *śruti* would be acceptable to reason too.

Objection: If man refrains from acts sinful and prohibited by the Vedas and from those meant to satisfy his specific desires, if, further, he accepts without question whatever 'destiny' unfolds before him—that result of the past deeds responsible for his present birth [result that cannot be avoided], and if he performs the obligatory acts enjoined by the Vedas, thereby avoiding the sin that accrues from their nonperformance, then liberation will follow on its own accord. There will be no need to add self-knowledge to the acts done this way.

Answer : This view too is not the right view. We have already refuted it (*vide* introduction). Our contention was that the argument does not take into account the acts that are yet to bear fruit; their after-effects cannot possibly be wiped out this way. These acts will give rise to other bodies. This is an established truth [for us who believe in the law of *karman*]. There is, as a matter of fact, no contradiction between obligatory acts and acts of this kind. The former cannot undo the latter to bring about liberation.

As to your contention that the man who knows the Vedas in entirety is a man of holy acts, for these acts constitute their purport, and, for this reason, are competent to cause liberation, the goal of life envisaged by the Vedas—to this contention of yours we have this to say: Your position is a false one. For apart from what one comes to know from *śravaṇa*, hearing of Vedic texts from a teacher, there is such a thing as *upāsanam*, dwelling near them, self-submitting to them, waiting upon them. Merely *śravaṇa* qualifies a man to do the holy deeds; he need not, for that purpose, dwell near the words he has heard and wait upon them. The Vedas, however, call upon man to do *upāsanam*, to open himself out to the words of the Vedas he has heard from a teacher—something quite different from listening to them. This contemplative opening out leads to liberation and is known [for this reason] as altogether a different thing from mere *śravaṇa*, hearing the words of the Vedas.

After calling upon man to listen to the revelatory texts from a teacher, the *śruti* goes on to enjoin him to think about that revelation and *nididhyāsana*, to do sustained meditation on the self. This injunction establishes the fact that *upāsanā*, contemplative opening out, is not the same thing as learning the texts through *śravaṇa*, through listening to them from the lips of a teacher.

My behaviour *vis-a-vis* the Vedas is the same as my behaviour *vis-a-vis* the world. The world I am born in is already an interpreted world. Here distinctions obtain in a bewildering variety, distinctions, to mention but a few, between me and my environment, between desire and fulfilment, between the idea and the reality. I seek to undo these distinctions either through eliminating one (*e.g.*, evil) for the sake of another (*e.g.*, good) or try to reconcile them (idea and reality, the real and the ideal). The gap, however, stays obstinate. So does the desire to undo or reconcile those distinctions.

To man, a creature of desire and, consequently, of action, the gap is unacceptable. He created civilisations to undo the gap but to no purpose. No theory could succeed in this matter and no practice. Dissatisfied with his own reinterpretations of the 'given' interpreted world, finding every reinterpretation rejected, some men turn to *śruti*, the word that originates not in man but from that from which proceeds the world. But even to this word this creature of desire and of action tends to respond in the way he responded to the already interpreted world. Distinctions obtain here too as they did in the world, distinctions between the is and the ought, between what is and what is sought. The end, however, is not the end of immediate desire, it is the end universal, the end that all nature seeks, from the inanimate to the animate. The alienated creature of desire, action and thought is made aware of the affinity between his seeking and the world's seeking and he is asked to direct his energy and desire not to personal seeking but to the seeking of the world. Let him bear with the earth and flow with the waters. Let him flow out of his narcissistic self into the world as the air would. And, lastly, he is asked to become the sky, that vast emptiness in which things are born to die and die to be born again without affecting it in the least. That, in every truth, should become he, an emptiness in which the entire world comes to dwell, in this little corporeal frame of his. This little body should have space enough to accommodate the entire world, moving and unmoving.

In this pilgrim's progress, where does interpretation end and passive meditation begin? The commentator says that mere *śravaṇa*, hearing or study of the Vedas, qualifies man for holy deeds alone. As long as his understanding is interpretative, action will remain, only the narcissistic action will give place to participatory action. Participatory acts will, however, slowly melt away the interpretative vision of means and ends and transform the doer of the acts of sacrifice into a creature of innocence. That will be the moment when the doer will turn contemplative, will do *upāsanā*, dwell near the things to become the things. When *upāsanā* turns into *nididhyāsana*, continuous dwelling in the object, that will be the moment of disclosure of the object, its revelation as the all.

The object in question may be a thing of the world or a word of the Veda. As man participates in the process of day and night or in the life and being of things, he starts 'floating' in the words of the Vedas. Instead of interpreting the text, he lets the text speak to him. If he self-submits to that speaking, the user of words will turn into the sharer of the word. Eventually, the sharer of the word will become the word and the word the all.

ŚB *Objection*: That means liberation is the result of acts aided by self-submissive meditation. Acts supplemented by meditation are capable of producing an effect other than what they can produce on their own. Poison and curds, to give an instance, cause, respectively, death and fever. But when poison has been sanctified with a *mantra*, it produces altogether a different effect. And so do the curds when mixed with sugar. In the same way, acts in combination with meditation can bring about liberation.

Answer: This cannot be true. We have already said whatever is brought about has a beginning [and liberation has no beginning]. Liberation brought about by holy acts–meditation combine cannot be liberation in the true sense of the term.

Objection: There is a scriptural word to the effect that once liberated, man does not return to the worldly mode of being (Cp. ChU 8.15.1). This would show that liberation is eternal, though brought about.

Answer: There is no point in invoking the word of the *śruti* to support an absurdity. The word of the *śruti* is only a revelatory word; it reveals the truth about things; it does not create what is not. Even a hundred *śruti* texts cannot establish that the eternal has a beginning or that what has a beginning is indestructible. This way we dispose of your view that holy acts–meditation combine can bring about liberation.

Objection: Suppose we say that holy acts–meditation combine remove *obstacles* in the way to liberation [and does not *produce* liberation].

Answer: No. For, we know that acts produce an altogether different kind of effect. They can produce that which was not there, can bring about a change in an already existing thing, can make it better than what it is, can help one in acquiring what one wishes to acquire. But liberation can neither be created, nor changed, nor improved upon nor acquired.

Objection: There are *śruti* texts that speak of the path that leads to liberation. We have, for example, the following words of the *śruti* (MuṇḍU 1.2.11; KaṭhaU 2.3.16.):

> But the reposeful knowers who dwell in the forest, to austerity given and faith and a beggar's life, through the door of the sun do they depart free from sin, to where dwells the immortal person, the imperishable self.
>
> A hundred and one are the nerves of the heart. Of them one goes out piercing the crown of the head. Going upward through that one attains to immortality. The others that branch out in various other directions lead one to death.

Don't these words show that liberation too can be acquired?

Answer: No. Brahman is all pervasive, nondifferent from those who would tread the path to liberation; it is the cause of even the all pervasive *ākāśa*, the ether of space. Conscious souls too are nondifferent from Brahman. [And since liberation is nothing else than realisation of Brahman as the self,] therefore, one cannot speak of liberation in terms of attainment or acquisition. The destination to be reached is always different from the traveller. Nor does it stand where the traveller stands. Going implies going to something different from oneself, not to that which is nondifferent from oneself. Nondifference of Brahman from one's self is, however, a well-known Vedic truth, for hundreds of *śruti* and *smṛti* texts speak of it. Thus the *Taittirīya Upaniṣad* (2.6.1):

> Having created it, he entered into it.

And the *Bhagavadgītā* (13.2)

> Know me, O you descendent of Bharata, the knower of the field, the self same knower in all of them. The knowledge that relates to the field and to the knower of the field alone, I say unto you, is knowledge true.

Objection: This conclusion of yours does not accord with the *śruti* texts that describe the paths the soul follows after death and those that speak of its divine glory. If liberation were unattainable, then not only the texts speaking about the paths of the soul would be rendered nonsensical but also texts like the following:

> One does he become, twofold does he become, threefold, sevenfold and also elevenfold. . . . (ChU 7.26.2)
>
> If he desires the world of fathers, fathers shall arise by a mere thought of his. . . .(ChU 8.2.1)
>
> There one moves about laughing, playing and rejoicing in the company of women or with chariots, remembering not the body he was born into. (ChU 8.12.3)

Answer: No. Passages like these relate not to liberation but to *kārya-brahman*, the manifest form of Brahman. It is only in relation to Brahman the effect that one can speak of chariots, women etc. not in relation to Brahman the cause. About the latter the *śruti* speaks in words like the following:

> Being alone, my friend, was all this at first, one only without a second (ChU 6.2.1).
>
> Where one sees nothing else, hears nothing else, knows nothing else (ChU 7.24.1).
>
> When all this has become the self, what will one perceive and by what? (BṛU 2.4.14; 4.5.15)

Moreover, *vidyā* and *karma*, [self-]knowledge and action, being opposed to each other, cannot go together. For [self-]knowledge has the real for its content, the real devoid of factors like the agent and the rest. Action, on the contrary, is impossible without these factors. So the two are opposites and cannot possibly be combined. You cannot simply imagine a thing with and without these distinct factors. Either it has these characteristics or it hasn't. Either of the two states of its being must be a false attribution. However, if one is to decide between these two states, between the state of doership in which distinctions obtain and the state of enlightenment in which they do not, then the former must be rejected as unreal. For that state of duality is set up by ignorance innate in every being.

> Where there is duality as it were, there one smells another, sees another, hears another . . . (BṛU 2.5.1);

> What indeed is here is there; what is there is again here. From death to death moves he who sees like difference here (KaṭhU 2.1.10);
>
> With the mind is this to be attained; here is no plurality whatsoever. From death to death goes he who here sees plurality as it were (KaṭhU 2.1.11, BṛU 4.4.19);
>
> Where one sees not the other, hears not the other, knows not the other, that is the infinite. But where one sees the other, hears the other, knows the other, that is the small, the finite (ChU 7.24.1);
>
> So whoever worships a god other than the self, thinking 'he is one and I another', he does not know (BṛU 1.4.10);
>
> But when he makes even a trite of distinction, there will be fear to smite him (TaitU 2.7.1).

Thus do hundreds of *śruti* texts speak of the unreality of duality. On the contrary, the reality of oneness the *śruti* affirms at so many places. To quote but a few texts in this connection:

> As one should it be realised, this constant being unknowable (BṛU 4.4.20);
>
> One only without a second (ChU 6.2.1);
>
> Brahman alone is all this (MuṇḍU 2.2.11);
>
> The self alone is all this (ChU 7.25.2).

When one cannot perceive distinctions that grammatical structures of language reflect, distinctions reflected in, *e.g.*, cases like the nominative, accusative, instrumental, dative and so on, one cannot conceive of the possibility of action. Thousands of *śruti* texts deny that consciousness of distinctions can obtain in the knowledge [that reveals the all as the self]. Hence the opposition between knowledge and action and the impossibility of their combination. Therefore, your earlier contention that act–knowledge combine can bring about liberation is unsustainable.

It is to be noted that Śaṅkara's remarks invoke the *śruti* to 'establish' the truth of self-knowledge (which alone is knowledge proper for him, knowledge of the other being ignorance) and the untruth of duality, the domain of action. He does not generally care to invoke reason except for hermeneutical purposes. We should not forget that reasoning is always hermeneutical. We are born in an already interpreted world. What we call reasoning is merely an interpretation of that interpretation, a series of interpretations of the received interpretation. Interpretation is *avidyā*, ignorance. It reflects our disposition to be, our passion to affirm ourselves. The interpreted world that I call the objective world is an objective correlate of this passion, the other of the affirmed *me*. Every discourse assumes this given interpretation, the interpretation that sets up our day-to-day world. These discourses occur 'within' this world.

The *śruti*, however, does not assume that world, for it has no speaker; it peals out when the interpreted world has ceased to be, when all has become the self. In the interpreted world the name and the named, the word and its referent, are dualities, constituting each other as the other of each other. The *śruti*, on the contrary, is the word without the world, the word that is the Absolute, is Brahman itself. The Vedas appear a collection of ordinary, familiar words to us. They do so because we are entrenched in the word–world duality. If we ever come to self–submit to these words, then the Vedas too will come to reveal themselves as Brahman. For they are not interpretations of the given interpretation. They are not words with the world as their constitutive other, they are words that *are* the world. We who rely on our reasoning power will only move from one interpretation to another interpretation, move so without an end. And that movement will be, in the words of the Upaniṣads, a movement from death to death.

ŚB *Objection* : Acts too are ordained by the *śruti*. If we accept your view, we will be acting against the teaching of the *śruti*. If the *śruti* makes man find all that is as his self through eradicating the sense of doership and other factors necessary for action, then it will be just like making one see a rope as a rope through eradicating its illusory perception as a serpent. In such a case, the *śruti* texts enjoining holy acts will be rendered meaningless. And that will mean contradiction between what the Vedas reveal by way of [self-] knowledge and what they reveal by way of holy acts. And enjoined indeed have been these acts by the Vedas. Since every part of the Vedas is authoritative, the kind of opposition you have sought to establish between self-knowledge and action is inadmissible.
Answer: Your criticism is not valid. The *śruti* has the one aim of making man reach the goal of life. And that goal is liberation of man from the recurring cycle of birth and death. And since the cause of this cycle is *avidyā*, false knowledge, knowledge of the other, the *śruti* has to eradicate this ignorance through knowledge of all as the self. For this reason, it is oriented towards revelation of [true] knowledge. Therefore, the *śruti* does not contradict itself [when for one man it enjoins that he strive for knowledge and for the other, the less advanced, it enjoins holy acts as preparation for that knowledge].
Objection: But what about the *śruti* texts that speak of the reality of the agent and other factors involved in action? Surely, what you say cannot but contradict them [and violate the authority of the *śruti*].
Answer: People of the world are born to find these factors as facts of their experience. The *śruti* provisionally accepts these facts as facts and enjoins

Vedic acts upon seekers of liberation and those who are anxious to reap some rewards from holy acts. The purpose is to cleanse the seekers of liberation of the stain of accumulated sins, accumulated in this and past lives, and enable those desirous of the fruit of their deeds find that fruit. The commandments about acts thus assume the reality of the factors of action, not that the *śruti* is concerned with establishing the reality of those factors.

Knowledge of all as the self will not dawn on man until he remains weighed down by those accumulated sins. With their cessation alone will arise that knowledge. With that arising will cease ignorance. With its cessation will follow the cessation absolute of *saṃsāra,* that continuous motion from death to death.

Moreover, he who sees something other than the self alone has desire for that other. And he who desires has to act. And to taste the fruit of his actions, he will have to take a body etc. To be embodied, of course, is the same thing as to be thrown into the worldly state of being, with its fore births and after births. The seer of the self as one and the sole reality, on the contrary, sees no objects. For this reason, he has no desire. One cannot possibly desire one's own self because the self is not the other. Therefore, liberation, that abiding in the self, ensues on its own for him. Knowledge of all as the self and action thus do not go together. Knowledge alone is enough for liberation; it does not need the support of holy acts.

Of course, obligatory acts enjoined in the Vedas are not to be dismissed as useless. For they undo the sins accumulated in the past, sins that lie dormant in one but will show their results in future lives. Undoing of these sins gives rise to that state of being where all becomes the self, the state of knowledge true. For this very purpose of purification, the *śruti* has, in the present section, called upon man to do certain deeds. This point we have already made. The *śruti* texts that command man to do holy deeds do not thus run counter to those that speak of the self as the single and sole reality. This should prove that knowledge of all as the self *alone* can bestow the highest good on man.

Objection: Since, as you say, holy acts lead to the dawn of realisation of the self as the single and sole reality, there is no place for stages of life other than that of the householder. For holy acts are enjoined only for him [not for the student, the forest dweller and the renunciate]. There can thus be only one stage of life [not four]. And this would accord with such Vedic commandments as call upon man to worship the holy fire all his life.

Answer: *Agni-hotra,* fire worship, and other rites enjoined for the householder are not the only acts that purify man. There are also chastity, penance, truthfulness, control of mind and of senses, nonviolence and others. These acts, as everyone knows, are meant to be performed in the other stages of life. Along with concentration and meditation, these acts are the most effective in giving rise to the vision of all as the self. This the Upaniṣad will itself affirm later on in the following words:

> Through austerity do thou seek to know Brahman (3.2–5).

Moreover, there may be some who are born pure and may be blessed with the vision of all as the self even before they enter the householder's life. Such men have already done the holy deeds in their past lives. When the very purpose of holy deeds—birth of self-knowledge—has already been served, a householder's life will be no use to them. One becomes a householder only to do the holy deeds, not otherwise.

Other considerations could also prompt one to become a householder: to be blessed with a son to win back this world; to resort to holy deeds to win the worlds of fathers and to meditation to win the world of gods. The knower of Brahman, however, has nothing to do with these worlds, all his desires having been spent out. For he perceives only one world, the ever present world of the self where no desire can possibly arise. Such a man can find no purpose in any acts whatsoever. How will he, then, be inclined towards them? If even a householder ever comes to be blessed with self-knowledge, he too will give up all acts. For, with the ripening of this knowledge, he will find no purpose in them. The *śruti* gives an indication of his state when it speaks about Yājñavalkya who says to his wife: 'Verily, my dear, go forth from this place now shall I.'

Objection: What you say does not seem to be true. The *śruti*, you know, addresses itself more to the formulation of holy deeds than to *ātmajñāna*, revelation of the self. Acts like the fire worship, for example, occupy the *śruti* more than *ātmajñāna*. Requiring many a means, these acts require great effort too. Chastity and austerity and other acts enjoined for other stages do not require as many means. The householder is expected to do these acts, too, in addition to the ones especially enjoined for him. Keeping in view the heavy load of duties that a householder has to carry, is it not improper to say that each of the other stages are as purificatory as the householder's stage, as if one could exercise a choice between this stage and others?

Answer: Some men inherit favours from their past lives. For this reason, there arises no need for them to do the onerous duties enjoined on the householder for his purification. True is it that the *śruti* speaks at greater length about holy acts than about self-knowledge. This fact does not, however, violate what we have said [that holy acts are a preparation for self-knowledge]. Even the fireworship performed in earlier lives is helpful in this regard. So are chastity and other acts. They are all helpful in the rise of the vision of the all as the self. It is because they have done these deeds in their past lives that some men are seen to inherit dispassion from their very birth. Others engaged in acts, have no such dispassion. They dislike self-knowledge, are prejudiced against it. This being the case, those who are born dispassionate owing to the after effects of the holy deeds done by them in their past lives should opt for other stages of life, other than that of the householder [for the latter can do them no further good].

There are reasons why the *śruti* should elaborate holy acts in details. There is the fact of the multiplicity of the acts themselves and of the innumerable results they give rise to, results like children, heaven, glory of holiness and so on. There is also the additional factor of the people's desire for these results;

they ever pray for this thing or that. Given these facts, it is but right that the *śruti* should be more elaborate in the matter of holy acts than in that of self-knowledge.

There is this further reason why the *śruti* dwells on acts more than on self-knowledge. These acts give rise to, we said earlier, the vision of the self as the all. It is but proper that means should receive more attention than ends.
Objection: Vision of the all as the self comes to be possible through holy acts alone. Given this fact, there is no need to undertake any other endeavour. Sins done in the past lives alone stand in the way of this vision, which arises as soon as one has undone them through holy deeds. There remains then no need to care for anything else than the holy deeds. Effort expended on learning the Upaniṣads will be a futile effort.
Answer : There is no fixed rule that only holy acts can give rise to the vision by undoing the sins incurred in the past lives, those obstructions, and not the Lord's grace or means like ardent penance or yogic meditation. Love for creatures and self-restraint in the form of chastity etc. can equally help bring about the vision. As for hearing the Upaniṣadic texts from a seer of truth, thinking about their teachings and sustained dwelling on their words, these constitute direct and immediate causes of enlightenment. So one need not rush to the conclusion that the householder alone qualifies for enlightenment and not the student, the forest dweller or the renunciate. The need for these other stages of life is obvious enough. We conclude, therefore, that realisation of all as the self alone can lead one to the attainment of the highest goal of life.

The last paragraphs of the commentary demand careful consideration. Man's life has no beginning. The chain of his births has been as long as the chain of causes and effects called the world. All these countless lives he did actions without a count, good as well as bad, under the promptings of desire and passion. A heavy load of retribution awaits him, a load more than he can carry, more than what a god can carry. His deeds have been countless and his rewards and punishments too have been countless and will be countless. He cannot possibly exhaust the inexhaustible. His piety cannot undo that past, human endeavour is hopelessly inadequate for the human condition. For that condition is preconditioned by beginningless past. Whether that past is in the form of past births or in the form of past history is only a secondary point. There is of course a difference between the two views regarding the ontological status of the world. The doctrine of rebirth envisages man and the world as man–world duality, the other view envisages the world, the humanly interpreted world, as existing independently of man, though it is, as I said, a world interpreted in human terms and human language. Therein lies the weakness of the latter view. There is, of course, another chilling truth, the truth that our human world is constituted by a prehuman world too, that it existed before man appeared on the scene. Though how it looked before the arrival of man, what things inhabited it and what beings, the advocates of the second view do not pause to think about seriously. Did distinctions like present, past and future exist then or those like the precept and the percept, the name and the named, the ideal and the real, distinctions without which we cannot talk about our world, any world? If ever there was a prehuman world, then prehuman beings were also there to constitute it and to be constituted by it. And since we do find man a rather late comer, our world is constituted by a past that was prehuman. It is the precondition of man–world duality that it be constituted by a prehuman past.

Man is thus burdened by a past that is only partly human but predominantly animal and inert. For as we find the arrival of man rather late so we find the arrival of life too as rather late. How to undo that past, the sinful, the bestial, the inert? No human endeavour can lift this burden off man because that endeavour itself is conditioned by the sin, the beast, the stone. Freedom is denied man from his birth by his very birth. The *śruti* has revealed to him participatory acts that undo the forbidding past by undoing the entity called man, by making him flow out of the confines of his self and its beastly and inert dimensions into the life of things. This way he can shed off his burden, not by his pathetic efforts.

Only as a householder can man do these participatory acts. His house is situated at a village, a village on the earth. He must live as a part of the village and of the earth, must know what he owes to others in the village and to the earth. There is also his past, his parents and his forebearers. To that past too he must be grateful. Man, in other words, should live as being-with-others and a being-on-the-earth. More importantly, he should live as a being wedded to death, a being fragile and mortal. He should also remember that there is the sky above him and the sun and the moon and the stars. Themselves unapproachable, the sky and the sun, the moon and the stars ever approach him to protect and sustain him and his home, the earth. He will find that his being is not merely human and earthly but also a partaker of these etherial sustainers, that what he deems to be a mere human identity is truly a cosmotheandric identity, the home at once of man, of the earth, of the sky and the sun, the moon and the stars. It is as this meek, generous and nonconspicuous identity, which in truth is no identity, that he becomes eligible for the vision of all as the self. For this self is not a mere confluence of the earth, the sky and man; man is, in this vision, the cosmos and the cosmos is man, is, in truth, more than the cosmos, he is the unknown and unknowable. It is all one, this peaceful chaos, this elating death. This is how man dies into himself through holy, participatory deeds. The householder's way is the way of this participation in the life of man, of earth, of sky and, above all, in death.

This participation in the world cannot truly take place without participation in the prehuman world. This means that man, while owning up to the past of the world, has to own up to his correlates in that past, namely, animals and stones. He has to be stones and animals to imagine that world and to own it up. If the past of my world constitutes my present, human world, then I have to be the subjective counterpart of that world. I was the stone, I was the animal and I shall be god as surely as I am man. There can be no world without me, me as an inert thing, me as an animal, me as man or me as god. The doctrine of rebirth acknowledges this constitutive role of me. It also acknowledges that what this me comes to be depends on what its world is. I and the world constitute a duality. There will of course be other humans to constitute my human personality, for a human world can be perceived only by a human-with-other-humans. And, needless to add, by man with other species constituting his species. These *mes,* are, however, false *mes* and so are their worlds. When the me and the others and the world become one, when all becomes the self and the self becomes the all, only then does man come to be truly himself and the world to be truly itself. Participatory acts lead man to this vision, through participation in the stone, in animals, in gods. No man can know, the Vedas imply, the truth of rebirth until he has done this act of participation, this supreme act of the supreme sacrifice.

There is another way, that of the Lord's grace, but a way that is not truly a *way* but a gift, for grace falls upon man 'from above'. The destination comes to man to own him up, not that he moves up to it. This is the portion cut out for the unhappy, the insulted and the humiliated, for those who have no place in the village, on the earth, under the sky, for whom the world passes by without noticing them. To such beings alone the grace comes to turn their tortures into ecstasies, man into god. Such men need not do the holy deeds nor sing their prayers nor do contemplation. For the deeds will be done for them, their prayers sung, their meditations accomplished. They must endure all to become all.

True to the spirit of the *Bhagavadgītā*, Śaṅkara here undermines not only mechanical ceremonial piety but also, by implication, the caste system itself. The priests, time and again, forgot the spirit of Vedic rites, the spirit of participation, and reduced them into soulless exercises. For their greed, they made it appear as if these rites were indispensable for man's salvation. The tradition of the seers rejected the claims of priests with contempt with the result that the Vedic rites virtually disappeared from the daily life of the people of India to be replaced by *bhakti,* devotion to the Lord, and yogic practice. It is these two, in addition to moral virtues and service of the poor and the needy, that were given pride of place in the teachings of medieval saints and those who followed them. Vedic deeds are only one of the ways to self purification and that too only when they are done in the right way, done as participatory acts. Mechanical performance of these acts cannot purify any one.

There are other souls, stern and uncompromising, men of principles and determination, contemptuous of every frailty, every failing. Such men can be a terror for the world, they often are. Men of this sort seldom seek self-knowledge, their awesome energies are often spent in 'reforming' the world, if not in conquering it. And these reforms seldom fail in ruining the world. For such 'makers' of history, too, there is a way. The way consists of stern discipline for themselves and compassion and forbearance for others. Theirs is the way of penance saved from sadistic–masochistic distortions through this care and concern for others. Self-deception is, however, a treacherous enemy. Therefore, yogic meditation is a must for bringing to consciousness unconscious tendencies and extinguishing them not through a determined penance but through understanding the deep tragedy of life. Without this understanding, the *yogin* cannot possibly flow with the flow of breath to die, ultimately, in revelation. The self righteous man has to die into the righteous man, the righteous man into a man of understanding, understanding of the truth of the inevitability of suffering, the understanding giving him enough of calm and serenity to die into breath, bare breath. What the *yogin* attains through discipline, the unhappy man may find through the very depth of his suffering provided he endures it with the calmness which only a few are blessed with.

Poets float in language. They feel the presence of words as ordinary people feel the presence of things. It is not that words lose all their referential value for poets but they feel the presence of things in and through words, for a poet can hardly be said to know what he has to say until he has said it. A philosopher too is a creature of discourse, he too would know truth in and through language but he feels the presence of nonlinguistic reality more than he feels the presence of words. That is why he invents conceptual words, universals and terms. He thinks these terms reflect truth more transparently than the words that come to him spontaneously. He is not a finder of words but their maker. The language that a philosopher thus fabricates becomes more important for him than things. He may not agree to the view that for him this particular language is the reality; he may insist that his words and terms do have a referential load but to reach the referent will be as difficult for him as forms, *eidos*, are for a Platonist. His dilemma is that he cannot accept language as the sole reality and yet cannot go beyond it. If some philosophers in our century have been rash enough to accept language as the sole reality, they have not been able to explain why they give priority to concept-words over words that describe a concrete, individual or unique situation. The dilemma of a philosopher in the modern sense of the term is that he has to be a sort of a Platonist even while decrying Platonism. Yet this attempt to reach out to the world of truth, the referent of his language, is doomed to failure — as long as, that is, the remains a philosopher. He remains confined within his discourse, he discourse remains his reality, even when it is other-referential.

A science enthusiast may—there was a time when they did—make the claim that in science at least language becomes subservient to truth. The scientist's theory laden observation, however, gives a lie to this claim, for even he would rearrange the world of concrete experience in accord with his words, his discourse—as far as he can. If poets float in language, then philosophers may be said to exult in it and scientists would make it a determinant. Thus man would, through various discourses, make himself independent of his situational context. Few are there who can live on earth as its inmates, the majority lives only to manipulate it or to vandalise it or, if nothing else, to reinterpret it. Man's varied attempts to be independent do not succeed because language cannot free itself of its referential burden. A linguistic being that he is, man cannot but find himself confronted with the other, the referent. Language is constituted by the beyond, the beyond is immanent in it.

The beyond cannot be comprehended but it cannot, at the same time, be overlooked. All that man comes to know is the interpreted but the so-called interpreted disowns interpretation, ever and always. The other persists ineliminable, rejecting all interpretations as adventitious to it. There seems no way out of this impasse, this tragedy. For let us not forget that the tragedy of our life is woven by this *other*, this incomprehensible *other* that dwells in our words as other than words, mocking at every attempt by man to relate to it as a presence to a presence. With each attempt to comprehend and master it, it turns more mysterious, more fearful, more intimidating and dangerous. One has only to cast a look at the chemist's report about what constitutes the air we breathe, the water we drink and the earth we walk on to know what mystery lies in the obvious, what danger and what destruction.

Is there a word which is also its referent, a word which is the world? When I do not use words, do not make instruments of them but hear the word to become it, then the word, the world and me become one. That word, the dwelling of all that is, is the word as *śruti.* It is called *śruti,* the Heard, because (he) who speaks it speaks it *as* the word, not as its speaker. To him who hears it, it is only a word, to the speaker, the speaker who speaks it as one with it, it is his self. That speaker is not really what we understand by the term 'speaker', he is the word itself, the word that is truth itself, is the self or Brahman itself. The sage who speaks it comes to hear it only when the man rises up in him again, when he wakes up from his *samādhi.* So it ever remains the Heard, whether the hearer is the man resurrected in the sage or his *antevāsin,* his disciple. When the seer speaks it, he is dead as speaker, as man.

It is only when man and the word become one that man becomes the all and so does the word. It is man as the all that speaks the word that is the all. And he who self-submits to this word will also become the all if he becomes the word that is the *śruti.* That is the way open for those who would free the word from its referentiality, those who would self-submit to *śruti* as if it were the Absolute. It is for this reason that the commentator gives primary place to hearing and meditation on *śruti* for self realisation, not to holy acts.

Chapter 12

ŚB Now an invocation is being sung for the removal of the obstacles that may stand in the way of revelation of the real as the self.

1. **aum! śaṃ no mitraś śaṃ varuṇaḥ, śaṃ no bhavatv aryamā, śaṃ na indro bṛhaspatiḥ, śaṃ no viṣṇur uru-karmaḥ, namo brahmaṇe, namas te vāyo tvam eva pratyakṣaṃ brahmāsi, tvām eva pratyakṣaṃ brahmāvādiṣam, ṛtam avādiṣam, satyam avādiṣam, tan māmāvīt, tad vaktāram āvīt, āvīn mām, āvīd vaktāram. auṃ śāntiḥ, śāntiḥ, śāntiḥ.**

Aum! May Mitra be propitious unto us,
May Varuṇa and so be Aryaman
And Indra and Bṛhaspati
And Viṣṇu, the far striding.
Adoration to Brahman!
Adoration to thee, Vāyu!
Thou indeed art Brahman *the visible!*
Thee have I proclaimed Brahman *the visible!*
Thee have I called ṛta
and thee the truth!
That has protected me
and him that speaks.
That has protected me and the speaker!
Aum! peaceful be the world and the elements,
peaceful the heavens and the gods
peaceful the creatures that live and move.

ŚB The peace chant has already been explained (1.1).

Part 2

Brahmāṇanda Vallī

Chapter 1

ŚB Towards the end of Part 1, a peace chant was sung for the removal of the obstacles that may stand in the way of revelation of the real as the self, the revelation described earlier. Now is being sung another peace chant for the sake of removing the obstacles in the way of the revelation about to be described.

1. aum̥ saha nāv avatu, saha nau bhunaktu, saha vīryam̥ karvāvahai, tejasvi nāv adhītam astu mā vidviṣāvahai. aum! śāntiḥ śāntiḥ śāntiḥ.

Aum! *May* [*he*] *protect us both, may* [*he*] *nourish us both, may we acquire strength together, may what we have studied be illuminating. May we not hate each other.* Aum! *Peace, peace, peace.*

ŚB May he protect us both, the teacher and the student. May he nourish us both. May we acquire strength together, strength born out of *vidyā*, self-knowledge and what follows it. Let what we, we who are full of light, have studied well be illuminating, reveal what it is about, its referent. May we not hate each other, the teacher the student and the student the teacher. The student and the teacher may come to hate each other because of some unwitting lapse on the part of either of the two. To prevent this hate, this prayer (lit. 'benediction') is said: 'May we not hate each other.'

Why '*śānti*', peace, is repeated three times has already been explained. [It is a prayer for the end of cosmotheandric ills].

This peace chant is also sung to remove all that may stand between man and what the *śruti* is going to speak unto him. Let man be blessed with the vision of all as the self. That verily is the theme of this prayer. For that vision alone can lead man to beatitude.

Meditation relating to *saṃhitā*, joining together of letters, has already been revealed along with others, meditations that go well with holy acts (1.3). Afterwards was revealed the purely mental meditation of the conditioned Self. This meditation was done through meditation on *vyāhṛtis*. The meditation made one lord of oneself (1.6.2) but only this much, it and the earlier meditations could not free one from the cycle of birth and death. For the seed, the cause, of bondage is not destroyed through them. The present section is oriented towards the destruction of that seed, the seed of ignorance which brings to creatures miseries, each and every. The destruction of that seed comes to be possible through the vision of the self denuded of all distinctions, distinctions falsely attributed to it through the superimposition of conditioning adjuncts. This part of the Upaniṣad seeks to help man have that emancipatory vision.

The purpose of *vidyā*, the vision of the all as the self, is the cessation of ignorance, that knowledge of the other. For it is only when [one] ceases to know the other that he will cease to be reborn. This the Upaniṣad will affirm [at 2.9] where it will say that the man of *vidyā*, the man who *knows* [who knows all as the self] has nothing whatever to fear. As long as *avidyā*, that knowledge of the other persists in man, there can be neither freedom from fear for him nor from the torments that virtue and vice inflict upon their doer. For that *avidyā* is the cause of the worldly mode of being, that unending cycle of births and deaths. That mode of being, that cycle, will cease only when one knows Brahman, that self of all [in each]. With that knowledge alone will it cease absolutely.

At the very beginning of this section, the Upaniṣad itself tells us what its purpose is and what is the relation of that purpose to the life of man. 'The knower of Brahman attains the supreme' verily states that purpose. It is in the fitness of things that this purpose and this relation should be so stated. For only when one knows these two, one will care to pay heed to what the *śruti* reveals, will listen to it, will try to grasp what it says, will interiorise it and will dwell on, be absorbed in, it. It is only when one has thus given oneself up to the words of the *śruti* that one comes to be blessed with knowledge, comes to see all as his self. Other texts of the *śruti* too advise man to the same effect: that he listen to what the *śruti* says about the self, think over it and meditate it (BṛU 2.4.5., 4.5.6).

1. auṃ brahma-vid āpnoti param. tad eśa'bhiyuktā. satyaṃ jñānam anantaṃ brahma. yo veda nihitaṃ guhāyāṃ parame vyoman, so'śnute sarvān kāmān saha brahmaṇā vipaściteti.

tasmād vā etasmād ātmana ākāśaḥ saṃbhūtaḥ. ākāśād vāyuḥ. vāyor agniḥ. agner āpaḥ. adbhyaḥ pṛthivī. pṛthivyā ośadhayaḥ. ośadhībhyo'nnam, annāt puruṣaḥ. sa vā eṣa puruṣo 'nnarasamayaḥ. tasyedam eva śiraḥ. ayaṃ dakṣiṇaḥ pakṣaḥ. ayam uttaraḥ pakṣaḥ. ayam ātmā. idaṃ pucchaṃ pratiṣṭhā. tad apy eṣa śloko bhavati.

Aum! *The knower of Brahman attains the supreme.*
About this is quoted the sacred verse.
Brahman is truth, knowledge and infinity.
Hidden in the heart who knows him, in the heaven highest,
obtains he all that one could desire,
obtains them all together along with Brahman the wise.

From that [Brahman], from this ātman, *originated the ether of space, from the ether of space air, from air fire, from fire waters, from waters earth, from earth plants, from plants food, from food the person. This is truly the person that consists of the essence of food. Of him this indeed is the head, this his southern side, this his northern side, this his self, this tail [the lower part] his support. As to that, there is this* śloka, *this verse:*

ŚB Brahman, the characteristics of which the Upaniṣad will describe presently, is called 'brahman' because it is superlatively great. [The meaning of the root *bṛh* from which the word is derived being 'to grow', 'to swell'.] The knower of Brahman, that supremely great, attains to the supreme, the absolutely highest. That *supreme,* that *absolutely highest,* cannot be anything else than Brahman itself. For, one cannot possibly know one thing and attain another. Another *śruti* text makes this point unambiguously clear how the knower of Brahman becomes Brahman. 'Verily, does he become Brahman,' says it among other things, 'who knows that supreme Brahman. (MuṇḍU 3.2.9)

Objection: Brahman, the Upaniṣad will say, pervades all and is the self of all. For this reason, it is not something one can attain or reach. One can attain another, one limited being an other limited being. This is a matter of common observation. Brahman, however, is unlimited and is the self of all. It makes little sense, therefore, to speak of its attainment as if it were something limited and other than one's self.

Answer: There is nothing wrong if the Upaniṣad speaks in this vein.

Objection: How?

Answer: What are called attainment or nonattainment of Brahman relate, respectively, to its revelation or nonrevelation. The being that has come to live in the world is, ontologically speaking, nothing else than Brahman itself. Yet he believes himself to be, and is attached to, the physical and other sheaths, sheaths limited and external to his self and composed of material elements, gross and subtle. His condition is similar to that of the man who is so engrossed in counting others that he forgets to count himself, the very person to supply the missing number, and the most proximate. The embodied being misses his real self like this counter. He believes himself to be what he is not, what is other than his true self—sheaths from the one consisting of food to that consisting of bliss. 'I am,' he would assert, 'none other than these not-selves, these sheaths, physical and others.' Such is the spell that *avidyā*, primal ignorance that makes one confound the self with the not-self, casts on him. This way Brahman, which verily is one's own self, remains unattained for him.

That Brahman, that self of all, the *śruti* reveals through its teaching. When man gives himself up to that teaching, he attains the wisdom that reveals that self of all as his own very self. This revelation, this disclosure may legitimately be called 'attainment of Brahman'. Once again, the story of the ten persons who had swum across a river is in order. Each one counted the others but not himself thereby remaining one short of the requisite number of the swimmers. They may be said to have 'attained' to themselves when someone enlightened them about the omission. The same is the case with the worldlings who live oblivious of their true self.

'The knower of Brahman attains the supreme' sums up in brief the entire purport of Part 2 of this Upaniṣad. The Upaniṣad quotes a sacred verse in order to determine the true nature of Brahman through a definition capable of setting forth its intrinsic nature as distinguished from all else. The statement 'The knower of Brahman attains the supreme' does show forth, in an aphoristic way, that Brahman should be known but it does not determine its charcteristic features. Nor does it specify in precise terms what this knowledge of Brahman is. The *ṛg-mantra* ['Brahman is truth, knowledge and infinity . . .'] is invoked to speak of those characteristics and specify what that knowledge is. This knowledge, the *mantra* will disclose, is nothing else than realisation of Brahman as nondifferent from [our] true inner self. It will also state that the result that follows from *brahma-vidyā*, knowledge of Brahman—namely, the attainment of the supreme—is nothing else than to become the self of all, the self that is Brahman the transcendental, Brahman beyond all worldly attributes.

With regard to this statement of the *Brāhmaṇa* part of the Upaniṣad, the statement 'The knower of Brahman attains the supreme,' is quoted this *ṛg-mantra*: *satyaṃ jñānam anantaṃ brahma*, Brahman is truth, knowledge and infinity. [The sentence as it stands has no verb. In such cases, the last word should be understood as the subject and the earlier words as predicates. This is the rule. Śaṅkara, however, invokes substantial matters to justify this syntax]. The statement aims at defining Brahman. 'Brahman' is the substantive and 'truth', 'knowledge' and 'infinity' predicate specific attributes of it. 'Brahman' is the substantive because the Upaniṣad has sought to present it in'The knower of Brahman attains the supreme' as the thing to be known. As such, Brahman forms the subject of the discourse. Since Brahman thus is primarily sought to be presented [in the said statement] as knowable, it should be understood as the substantive. For the reason that Brahman and *satyaṃ jñānam anantam*, truth, knowledge, infinity, are related to each other as substantive and attributes, the nouns forming the latter set have the same case endings and stand in apposition to one another. Qualified by these three epithets, Brahman gets marked out from all other substantives. This way does Brahman get known, for a thing gets known only when it is distinguished from everything else. We know, for example, a particular lotus when we distinguish it from other lotuses by marking out its shade of colour, its size and its smell from those of other lotuses, and say, 'The lotus that is blue, large and sweet smelling.'

You come to know a thing when you know it as unique and different from all else. What we ordinarily know of things fails, however, to meet this criterion. Our knowledge consists of universals and categories and as such conceals the thing before us. How to reach the object, how to let it reveal itself to us is the question. The question, however, becomes the despair of every kind of discourse. Many seek to escape from this despair by taking refuge in the idea that reality is ever and always linguistically constituted and the very thought of it as denuded of linguistic interpretation is a contradiction in terms. To know a thing, this view says in effect, is to interpret it, interpret it in terms of universals. This is a view quite in fashion in our times. *The Taittirīya Upaniṣad* leads us to the object itself. It does not discard language for the purpose. Rather it invokes it to lead one beyond it. That is the magic of the Upaniṣadic 'discourse'.

ŚB *Doubt* : Specification of a substantive implies exclusion of certain attributes. 'Blue lotus' and 'red lotus', for example, exclude other colours that could characterise some other lotuses. A qualified can meaningfully admit a qualifier only if it could be differentiated from other qualifieds belonging to the same class, admitting the possibility of being qualified by other qualifiers. A single thing with no class to get placed in, cannot have meaningful attributes because they cannot be differentiated from other attributes specifying other members of the class. Like the sun, Brahman too is all alone. There are no other Brahmans from which it could be distinguished as a blue lotus can be from lotuses of other colours.

Concepts are constituted by otherness, are made intelligible by it. You require other individuals to perceive an individual, other classes to conceive a class, whether the class in question is the class of substantives or of attributes. To predicate something of a thing is to depredicate something else of it. Negation constitutes universals. Interpreted world is thus is a world of plurality. The single and sole reality that the Vedānta calls *Brahman* thus becomes, interpretatively speaking, unintelligible.

ŚB *Answer*: Your objection is not valid. For the attributes of *satyaṃ jñānam anantam* are intended to make a definition of Brahman. Since they define Brahman more than qualify it, your objection has no force in the present context.
Opponent: How will you distinguish between definition–defined category from qualifier–qualified category.

Answer: A qualifier distinguishes a qualified from other qualifieds of the same class, while a definition distinguishes the defined from everything else. The definition of *ākāśa*—'that which gives space'—, for example, distinguishes it from everything else [from phenomena falling under the class *elements* and from all that falls outside that class]. The statement—Brahman is truth, knowledge and infinity—belongs, we have already said, to the category of definition [and, for this reason, is not open to the objection you have raised].

'Truth', 'consciousness' and 'infinity' do not relate to each other because [as the syntax and other factors noted above show] they relate to something other than themselves. To the substantive Brahman they relate, each one of them, independently of others. We could thus paraphrase the statement in question this way: Brahman is truth, Brahman is consciousness, Brahman is infinity.

That is said to be *satya*, truth, which does not deviate from what it has been ascertained to be. That is said to be *asatya*, untruth, which deviates from what it has been ascertained to be. All modifications, all mutations, are, therefore, *asatya*, unreal. This is what the *śruti* teaches us.

> All modifications originate in speech, are mere names, the reality is nothing but clay (Chu 6.1.4).

Thus does the *śruti* hold existence alone to be the truth. Therefore, the definition 'Brahman is truth' distinguishes Brahman from all that is subject to modifications.

To reach the truth, man is not to invoke theories of correspondence, coherence, practicality and the like. Before he seeks to find refuge in theories like these, he must find out what is the truth he seeks. Enquiry into the nature of truth, mere asking the question, 'What is truth?', puts into question the reality of what man perceives and experiences. Does not mere asking this question show that man does not feel at home in the world of change and death? The inhabitant of the so called lived world tries to sleep over the truth of change and death through food and sex. When the attempt does not succeed, he tries to forget them through action. The desire for food and sex invests the natural and human world with truth and reality, the passion for action invests time with these, with truth and reality. This way the world of space, time and human relationships are sought to be made our saviours from the fate that awaits us, from our destiny to be reduced to nothingness. That fate is, however, inexorable, compelling man to fabricate more sophisticated weapons against it. Thus the myths of social progress, of linear time and its teleological thrust are woven to transform man, a helpless individual, into a moment in history, an end into a mere means. As the seeker of food and sex, he was the end, as the doer he ends up as a means. The theory of correspondence gives man a pride of place, it places him at the centre of the world, not, of course, as a living individual but as an abstraction, as the cogito of the Cartesian kind. The theory of coherence reduces him into a moment in relationships, and theories of praxis into a moment in history. Those who find these theories as mere myths, invented by our hunger for safety and power, find it hard to save man's life from consumer culture, from being a creature of tentativeness, from meaningless pleasures which turn out to be little else than meaningless despair. Man thus allows himself to be reduced to an abstraction, a means, a contextuality, an embodiment of despair only to escape from his mortality. Not to be is what frightens him the most. He seeks being ever and always, in his pleasures, his relationships, his theories and his practices.

Be-ing, however, eludes man as long as he is man. He remains a creature of disinheritance, and his world marked by every sign of absence. That is the portion of a being who affirms himself, is burdened with the passion to be an 'I am'. As long as he remains burdened with the thought of 'I am', he remains a perpetual displacement, a constant disowning until death comes to put an end to his misery. The misery, however, does not end with death; it, the Upaniṣads say, renews itself in the form of other births and other deaths. The misery will end when 'I am' comes to die. With the death of 'I am', the world ceases to be the other, it becomes the self. The all as the self is Brahman, the truth absolute.

When man comes to define this All-as-the-self, he can define it only in contrast to his own existential condition. 'I am' lives in the domain of death, this Innocence appears to be a state of life. Eternity, immortality, truth absolute are some of the names given to this state. Let not the conceptualist in us forget, however, that this immortality is attained through death, the death of what I consider to constitute 'I am'. And that implies death of all my concepts, including those of 'truth', of 'eternity', 'immortality', 'truth absolute' and the like.

ŚB From this [saying of the *śruti*, viz., that clay alone is truth] it may follow that Brahman is the material cause of the world. And since a material cause is a thing, it can be a factor of an action [as clay is in the action involving the production of a pot]. This would reduce Brahman to an insentient thing like clay. Hence the next term in the definition, *jñānam*. The term means knowledge, consciousness. Brahman, it should be noted, is *knowledge*, not the knower. As an attribute of Brahman, along with truth and infinity, knowledge can carry no subject-ive connotations, cannot mean 'the knower'. A knower cannot possibly be truth and infinity. A knower is subject to change and modification and cannot, for this very reason, be truth. Nor can he be infinity. Infinite is that to which nothing else sets limits, divides it (the infinite) from itself (the thing in question). The knower, however, is delimited by what it knows and by knowledge. Brahman as knower could not, therefore, be called infinity. We have the authority of the *Chāndogya Upaniṣad* to support our interpretation, which says: 'Where one knows not the other, that is the infinite. Where one knows the other that is the small, the finite' (ChU 7.24.1).

A cause can be a material cause, it can also be an efficient cause. As the material cause of the world, as the stuff the world is made of, Brahman has no other to set limits to it. The world is not different from Brahman to set limits to it, as a pot, to invoke the image used in the *Chāndogya Upaniṣad*, is not different from the clay it is made of. The world is only an appearance of Brahman, a facet of it. But what about the efficient cause, *kāraka-hetu*? Efficient causes are doers like men and women, they are not creators. They work upon materials, things other than themselves. As doers, they are conditioned by the other, the inert other. Men and women, the doers, however, proclaim themselves as conscious, sentient beings, these creatures whose being is conditioned by what they claim to know, who are a part of the world they think they know, know as other than themselves. Dependent upon the world, parts, so to say, of it, they would be independent of the world.

The doer, however, is not consciousness, the doer is an object among objects, a thing among things, inert like them, 'like clay'. A knower also is not consciousness. A knower is, according to commonsense, one who knows something and knows that he knows something. He is, in other words, not one who sets limits to the world but is a part of the world, a known among the knowns. The real, true, knower is not, however, a part of the world, not a part of the field he knows, he is the knower of the field—to invoke the language of the *Bhagavadgītā*. That means he is not, cannot be, what is ordinarily termed the knower. He is bare consciousness, he is knowledge, not, truly speaking, the knower. However, if knowledge is the limit of the world, then the world too is its limit. Could, then, Brahman, which is knowledge, be called infinity? The answer to this question requires further deliberation on *knowledge* and *truth*. Brahman, the bare consciousness, the knower that does not know that it is the knower, to begin the deliberation, does not know that it knows the world. To know a thing, one has also to 'know' oneself, to be, that is to say, conscious of oneself, to reduce oneself to a thing among things. One who knows that there is such a thing as the world finds oneself a part of the world, its creature. One becomes *alpa*, the little. Brahman as consciousness does not, therefore, know that it is consciousness. To define Brahman as knowledge, therefore, implies denying the epithet as it is commonly understood. In the same breath, the Upaniṣad denies what it affirms, recants what it attributes to Brahman.

Sat, we already know, is that which has been ascertained to be ever itself. This definition excludes all that one could know, all that constitutes what is called in the Vedāntic tradition 'the field of knowables'. For whatever is known is known in and through thought process and is, for this very reason, ever changing. Even the knower does not remain untouched by the knowing process, the knower as the knowable. If *sat* is that which ever remains itself, then we can neither know it as an object nor imagine it. Brahman as *is* cannot, therefore, be imagined or known as a phenomenon can be. The IS however is the ground of the intelligibility, of the possibility of all phenomena. For nothing can be cognised, not even change and process, without *sat*, for isness, permanence, is the constitutive other of all that we know or could know. We have elaborated this point time and again.

Sat and *cit* thus depredicate all that one could think of Brahman, of the self. There remains the third attribution of *anantam*, infinity. But Śaṅkara has not yet finished with the elaboration of *cit*, knowledge or consciousness.

ŚB *Objection*: The quotation you cited above—viz., 'Where one knows not the other. . .' specifically denies knowledge of the other in the self. The denial affirms, implicitly, self-knowledge in the self.
Answer: This conclusion of yours is unwarranted. The sentence in question seeks to define the infinite. There is the fact of life that in all perception or knowledge there occurs the subject–object divide. [Consequently, all that one can come to know has to be small, finite.] Taking its stand on this fact of life, the *śruti* defines *infinite* as that in which obtains no perception or knowledge of itself and the divide that perception or knowledge implies. This way the *śruti* makes us know the infinite. 'The other' in the sentence connotes the content of what is cognised or perceived. The sentence thus denies in the *ātman* the process [of knowing]. For in the absence of the subject–object divide in the self, there can be no possibility of knowledge *in* the self. If the self could *know* itself, as you contend, if it could become an object to be known, there would remain no knower to know it. Since you have already, through your contention, reduced it to a knowable, you cannot then think of the self as the knower.
Objection: The self could well be both the knower and the known.
Answer: The *ātman* is not a whole composed of parts that it could simultaneously be both the knower and the known. The indivisible cannot admit of this possibility. Besides, if one could cognise the *ātman* as an object among objects, there would be no need for scriptures to instruct seekers about it. No instruction will be worth while about an object as veridical as a pot, for example.

Hence Brahman cannot be the knower, for this will contradict its infinity. Nor can Brahman the knower be bare existence, which, according to another *śruti* text (ChU 6.8.7), it is. For these reasons, *jñāna* carries, in the present context, the connotation of knowledge alone. The other two terms, namely, 'truth' and 'infinity', that occur in the definition rule out other connotations [like that of the knower, for example] of the term. The attribution of *jñāna* to Brahman, therefore, negates of Brahman the attribute of the agent and other factors of action and also of nonconsciousness which one associates with inert things like clay.

'Brahman is knowledge' may suggest the finitude of Brahman, for knowledge, as commonly understood, is limited and is of the limited. To ward off this understanding about Brahman, the *śruti* resorts to another attribution, that of infinity.

Objection: Terms like 'truth' are not used in this scriptural description to predicate of Brahman what these terms normally connote; they are used only to negate such attributions to Brahman as those of untruth, of nonconsciousness and of finitude. There is, we know, no way of knowing Brahman other than what scriptures tell us about it, for Brahman is not an object of common observation, as, for example, a lotus is. This being the case, we find ourselves landed in *śūnyatā*, nothingness. Are we not hearing a 'proposition' like the following: 'Behold a son of a barren woman going away after a bath in the waters of a mirage, wearing a crown of sky flowers and carrying a bow made of the horns of a rabbit?'

Brahman admits of no predicate terms with positive meanings. All that we are told is that Brahman is not this, not this. The result is, the critic says, that we are left with nothing else than the term 'Brahman', a bare subject-term, with no meaning, no referential value. It comes to have sense only, he implies, in relation to predicate terms. Predicate terms alone, he would say, have referential value.

When we talk about a thing which does not lie within the sphere of common observation, we should talk, the opponent would say further, in terms which are acceptable to common sense. Percipients have concepts and ideas which work well, or tolerably well, in the world revealed to us. These ideas, he would say, are rooted in reality and have, for this reason, validity. The criterion of truth, for the opponent, is empirical knowledge.

For the majority of people, the real is the observable and the interpretable. Brahman as the all is neither observable nor interpretable. The observable and the interpretable are always limited, limited by the other. The limited is the transient. The transient is not what we mortals seek as truth. The stability that we perceive in phenomena is barely enough to make them cognisable. It is the tragedy of us mortals that we seek our being in that fake stability.

This fake stability of phenomena is not, however, without an ontological ground. That we can interpret the noninterpretable, cognise the noncognisable, analyse the unanalysable, conceive integral wholes where there cannot be intergal wholes shows that these appearances are informed by the stable, by being, these existents by existence. This stable being, this existence, this *sat* cannot, however, be cognised unless and until 'existents' are there to steal our gaze and attention and absorption. If we ever come to be absorbed in the thing before us, absorbed completely without a sense of the before and after, if the thing in question becomes the single and sole reality for us, it will melt out to reveal the existence in it, reveal the dispenser of its identity, its *ātmadā*, giver of the self. The definition of Brahman as *sat* seeks to do precisely this. It makes one pause at the bare subject, at bare *this*, divested of all predicates. What is nonsensical or meaningless for a thinker, represented by the objector above, is the revealer of truth for the dispassionate and the innocent. Let one allow oneself to be divested of all thoughts, all predicate terms. Let there remain only the bare *this* if you are observing or only a word, say *aum*, if you are thinking. If you ever come to be aware of only the *this* or *aum*, if you ever come to be blessed with so much of *ignorance*, you will not have to wait for long to see the *this* turn into all and the word into Brahman.

The second defining principle is knowledge. Brahman is not the knower but knowledge. As Brahman is existence alone and not an existent, so it is knowledge alone, not the knower. It is indeed hard to formulate in what are called intelligible terms what bare knowledge or bare consciousness is. As bare existence seems nothingness to most of us, so bare consciousness too seems nothingness to most of us. There are many in our times who would do away with the term 'consciousness' and replace it with language. For language as relationality reveals, according to these thinkers, our true ontology, the ontology as relationality. Consciousness smacks of independent ontology and, for this reason, distorts, does not picture accurately, our being as relationalities. The contention that consciousness too is a relation, a duality constituted by its object, shows consciousness as informed by language, as little else than language. It is, therefore, useless, they argue, to retain the term.

The equation of consciousness with language is, however, unwarranted. To dissociate consciousness from all relations and raise it to an independent real is to commit, of course, the Cartesian mistake but to reduce it to relationality too will not do, it too will be a distortion. [Even language, we shall see, resists this equation.] Consciousness, when *looked at*, reveals two facets: one consisting of thought, ideas, images, feelings—succeeding each other without interruption, and the other as observation, noticing of these phenomena and their succession. Thoughts, ideas, etc.—mental phenomena—are not the elemental givens, they are constructs, wholes, cognisable wholes, even the seemingly smallest among them are made of up of parts. The atomic constituents of these moments, the so called 'ultimate atomic facts' are simply not available to experience, for the minutest experientiable or conceivable moment is already a construct. Thoughts thus are not consciousness as they are generally assumed to be. They are objects of consciousness but seem so proximate to it as to appear one with it. Consciousness is not thoughts but awareness of these thoughts, their knowledge. These thoughts appear to be consciousness, these mental phenomena, in relation to their objects. When looked at in and for themselves, these phenomena, these thoughts, turn out to be a succession, a stream with no observable *necessary* relation obtaining among them. This looking at them, this observation, however, notices only these phenomena, these thoughts, not the fact of observation itself, not that which subsists unchanged in the midst of these succeeding thoughts, that which can notice and remember what precedes and what succeeds. Blindess to this awareness, awareness that observes the succession but itself is not a part of the succession, destroys our faith in the world constituted by intelligible relationships. This is what happened, as is well known, in the case of Hume. His scepticism was a challenge which philosophers found difficult to meet.

The discoveries of science, however, continued unaffected by scepticism, discoveries that found the world a complex of relations. If philosophy failed to notice these relations, so much the worse for philosophy. From this threat of being declared an irrelevance, philosophy tried to save itself by replacing consciousness with language. Language was found to be the paradigm of relationships; it promised to free philosophy from the prison of sceptical idealism. The cost, however, was rather high, too high, in fact. My toothache is not *my* toothache but toothache as such. This is how medical science would look at it. Though toothache may be an intersubjective phenomenon, my experience of toothache remains my experience. When I feel the pain, you, no doubt, know that I am suffering, the doctor too understands it but neither you nor the doctor can, at this moment, *experience* my pain. The burden of experience is there to account for, the burden of being the sufferer. Why is it that when I live the pain, the pain of 'they', it becomes *my* pain. I am a category, a bundle of categories, conceivable and common. I cannot, however, live these common categories until I convert them into mine, in truth, into *me*, a me who is not 'they'. Do away with these thoughts, these thoughts of 'they', I as an individual will cease to be. But how is it that I cannot live these thoughts without turning them into me, into an isolated me? What is there in me that I can turn them into mine? And not merely mine but me?

The burden of being a me, of being an individuality, cannot really be wished away. Even the most 'inauthentic' person, the very embodiment of they, lives the they as me. This self, this me, cannot be reduced to relationality. Language as an intersubjective phenomenon—some would say, language as intersubjectivity—at once constituting men and women and being constituted by them, cannot really encompass this me, cannot, in one word, reduce it to relationality. The heavy load of individuality remains there for every one to bear and carry; everyone has to bear it though some may choose to bear it with lucid understanding, others, most of them, including, as it would seem, some philosophers, without that understanding. It is noteworthy that when philosophy was trying, in England, to replace consciousness with language, literature was becoming more 'conscious' of consciousness. Witness the rise, in England, of the stream of consciousness novel. When man is sought to be reduced to relationality, the more sensitive among his kind feel all the more the presence of consciousness. You cannot possibly undo it for the sake of science and its achievements. The more you seek to lay stress on man's communality, the more acute becomes his sense of loneliness. So acute does it become at moments that consciousness becomes *the* reality for certain men.

Consciousness thus refuses to be eliminated, not only, be it understood, existentially but also conceptually. Thoughts are, no doubt, relationalities, they are linguistically constituted. But they are not really me, not consciousness. A thought experiences neither itself nor other thoughts. Nor are thoughts givens, have reality in and for themselves. Every thought is a constituted thought, every moment of it. What constitutes these thoughts does not belong to them, nor memory which enables one to recognise them nor anticipation which, along with *memory*, makes of them moments in a chain, a succession. Consciousness of thoughts is, of course, there and also of their succession. It is linked to thoughts as their being but is itself not thoughts. This consciousness, however, escapes the notice of many a thinker, so powerful is the fascination of thoughts for man, so firm is their hold over him. But it *shows forth* in the words of such thinkers, even in the words of the thinkers that deny it. Hume was such a thinker and so, I think, was Descartes for whom too the self is only thoughts, despite the seeming drift of his argument to the contrary. If Descartes had been a little more consistent, he would have landed at the concept of mind as a succession of thoughts as did Hume. If man is only thinking, then he can be nothing else than a succession of thoughts. The inconsistency in Descartes, however, shows forth a sensitivity in him which Hume lacked: Descartes was conscious of the observer of thoughts, Hume, despite his words, was not. This observer Descartes could not possibly equate with thoughts but the fact is that he did it. The result was that he enunciated a theory of the *Cogito*, the common, immortal thinker that could not possibly be. A contradiction through and through, this *Cogito* became the creator of our modern scientific civilisation. Absurdities can be lived, the inconceivable can be turned into an existential reality! Such is the power of *avidyā*!

How to arrive at this consciousness, this witness, this *kṣetrajña*, the knower of the field? One arrives at it when one becomes passive enough not to think. For the majority of thinkers today, this will be blankness, nothingness, as it was for our objector above. But those who can distance themselves from thoughts do not come to be nothing but something else:

> She could be herself, by herself. And that was what now she often felt the need of—to think, well, not even to think. To be silent, to be alone. All the being and the doing, expansive, glittering, vocal, evaporated; and one shrunk, with a sense of solemnity, to being oneself, a wedge-shaped core of darkness, something invisible to others. Although she continued to knit, and sat upright, it was thus that she felt herself; and this self having shed its attachments was free for the strangest adventures. When life sank down for a moment, the range of experience seemed limitless. And to everybody there was always this sense of unlimited resources, she supposed; one after another, she, Lily, Augustus, Carmichael, must feel, our apparitions, the things you know us by, are merely childish. Beneath it is all dark, it is all spreading, it is unfathomably deep; but now and again we rise to the surface and that what you know us by. Her horizons seemed to her to be limitless. There were all the places she had not seen; the Indian plains; she felt herself pushing aside the thick leather curtain of a church in Rome. This core of darkness could go anywhere, for no one saw it. They could not stop it, she thought exulting. There was freedom, there was peace, there was, most welcome of all, a summoning together, a resting on a platform of stability. Not as oneself did one find rest ever, in her experience (she accomplished here something dexterous,

> with her needle), but as a wedge of darkness. Losing personality, one lost the fret, the hurry, the stir; and there rose to her lips always some exclamation of triumph over life when things came together in this peace, this rest, this eternity, and pausing here she looked to meet that stroke of the lighthouse, the long steady stroke, the last of the three, which was her stroke, for watching them in this mood always at this hour one could not help attaching oneself to one thing especially of the things one saw; and this thing, the long steady stroke, was her strike. Often she found herself sitting and looking, sitting and looking, with her work in her hands until she became the thing she looked at—that light for example.[1]

What many a philosopher, with a self complacent confidence, would call nothingness reveals itself as something radically different, as sheer plenitude of being, as a state in which Mrs Ramsay ('she') 'could be herself, by herself'. This 'herself' is not, of course, the independent thinking self, the 'I think' of a Descartes but something else, 'a wedge-shaped core of darkness, something invisible to others'. This darkness reveals itself as the self of man when he sheds what may be called his self as a sociality, a communality, an intersubjectivity. When Mrs Ramsay's surface self, her human self comes to be usurped by this 'core of darkness', she wants to, tries to, think but cannot. For her being as relationality, 'being . . . expansive', evaporates and so does her being 'vocal', communicative, and being 'glittering', vain and self proclaiming. And so does doing, the subtle passion that would not allow one to be oneself, by oneself. When thus the self known to me and known to others, the self they call *Mitsein* or *Dasein*, melts away, only then the wedge-shaped darkness, the inbeing invisible to me and to others reveals itself. In this absence-of-mood, Mrs Ramsay's ordinary routine of duties continues unhampered, the invisible peace is not rude enough to disrupt the self visible to others, but she knows that her active self, the self relational, is not really her own self. Her true self is the other one, silent, anonymous, unobtrusive, all pervasive. What we call our self, what others call our self is a mere apparition, something childish. And the paradox is that in losing myself I not only find myself but the world too. For that wedge of darkness seems to contain, Mrs Ramsay finds, the horizons of the world she has never explored, could never explore. Here was all peace, all reality, the whole world, the coming to rest of time into eternity. This nothing was

1. Woolf, Virginia: *To the Lighthouse.*

all full, all fulfilment. Becoming this nothingness, she becomes any thing, this stroke of the lighthouse, this ray of light. This is what Mrs Ramsay comes to find when she has lost herself, this stability, this allness.

And yet there is a witness of this darkness, there is a consciousness of this peace, this coming to rest of what we call our human, relational knowledge. Consciousness stands apart, unobtrusively, inconspicuously, from this luminous, this revelatory darkness, this all inclusive nothingness. As there is consciousness to experience the darkness of sleep, so there is consciousness to experience this darkness, consciousness more anonymous than even this darkness into which 'life sank down for a moment.' This wedge of darkness is visible at least to this consciousness but the latter is not visible even to itself.

Brahman is this consciousness. Mrs Ramsay finds life an unhappy affair, a fret, a hurry, a stir. She, who could be this wedge of darkness, would arrest the cruel flow of time. She would not like her children to grow into clever adults. Her children, however, grow, inevitably grow to suffer and to die. Mrs Ramsay herself dies unhappy and in despair. The mother in her—that paradigm of existential relationality—would not hear the voices of the sea, of death. As the peaceful and stable core of her being becomes visible to her when her human, surface self is suspended, so the voices of the sea too become audible to her when human voices are silent. There is a close relationship between death and this wedge of darkness, this she welcomes, that she does not. In the darkness, the knower remains to know and to feel, in death the knower does not remain, it is swallowed by darkness. Mrs Ramsay would not take this final plunge, she would enjoy darkness but she would not be darkness. And because the knower in her remains to enjoy the darkness, it remains too to assert and to suffer. The knower has to die to become what the Upaniṣad calls *jñāna*, knowledge, bare consciousness purged of the knower. This consciousness is not the consciousness that we know, consciousness related to an object or objects. The Upanis.ad calls this innocence consciousness because that is the ultimate interiority for us, the last veil that is revelation itself.

When the fretful fever of life comes to rest, the world changes into all-inclusive darkness, into *śūnya* and man into a bare passive witness of it. This witness turns, before long, into the active doer to turn back again into the state of passivity. This ebbing and flowing continues. Man welcomes the passive state, the state that reveals the world as darkness but not the active state, that of the mortal. There is the third state which also he does not welcome, the state of death. That death

Mrs Ramsay fears more than she fears what we ordinarily call life. The Upaniṣads call upon man to welcome that death, invite him to die before his physical death. Let him die even as the knower of darkness. He can die as the knower either through fading into darkness or through withdrawing from it. Not to think about darkness but to be still, absolutely still, so still indeed as not to, not to be able to, notice that darkness, not to speak of dwelling on it in the fashion of Mrs Ramsay. That moment of utter passivity is the moment when the knower dies into knowledge. And so does the darkness. That is the moment when all becomes the self, the self with no other to set limit to it, the self that is infinity. One can describe the external landscape, the landscape of memory and of mind, even the dark interiority within us can be described. But not knowledge with no other to sustain it, neither the world nor thoughts nor darkness. We are so much, so deeply, inflicted with intentionality that we cannot imagine consciousness without the other, be it even the darkness of sleep. Our destiny is, however, linked to, tied to death, to absolute nothingness. We can become death only if we become innocent of every other, even of darkness, of peace and of stability. Only a Naciketas, the not-knower, can become *jñāna*, he who goes to Yama, to Death, before he dies. Gauḍapāda tells us in a few verses what one is to do to be stillness absolute:

> With measures proper should one restrain the mind when desires distract it and pleasures and when it lies submerged, all peaceful, in sleep. For as is desire so is sleep.
>
> Let man never forget all is misery. Remembering this misery, let him keep apart from desires and from pleasures. The born shall he not perceive when he remembers ever that all is unborn.
>
> When sleep comes to overwhelm the mind, let him wake it up, when pleasures distract it, let him calm it down. Let him know it to be stained dull with passion [when it is neither asleep nor distracted]. Let him not disturb it when it has attained the state of sameness.
>
> Let him not succumb to the joy of sameness, let him stay unattached, in wisdom. If the mind, steadfast, ever tends to move out, let him strive to make it retain itself.
>
> When the mind is not lost in sleep nor distracted by passion, when, motionless, it stays non-phenomenalised, then it becomes Brahman itself, the Absolute itself.[1]

1. *Gauḍapāda Kārikā* 3.42-46.

Even when the fever of life, the peace of darkness and death become one, let not man enjoy the bliss of this vision. Let the enjoyer die in him and the knower, let these die absolutely. That will be the moment when man will turn into knowledge. After he has attained this state of equanimity, his own endevours will come to cease. Knowledge will turn into truth on its own, provided he dies into stillness.

ŚB *Answer.* The definition does not land one into *śūnyatā*, into nothingness [in the literal sense of the term] as you allege. Words like truth, knowledge and infinity are used, in the present context, as defining terms. That, verily, is their primary function here, attributive terms though they be. We have already made this point earlier. Now there is no point in attempting a definition of a nonexisting substance. The *śruti* invokes these terms not to establish Brahman as nothingness but to affirm its reality. Its very attempt to define it in these terms shows, we believe, that the *śruti* takes it to be real. Even as attributive terms, *satya, jñāna* and *ananta,* truth, knowledge and infinity cannot exclude *asatya, ajñāna* and *antam,* untruth, ignorance and finitude without retaining their own connotations. As meaningless words, they cannot possibly distinguish their own referent from those of other terms. Only as sensible terms could these terms help one distinguish their referent Brahman from other substantives possessing opposite attributes. Besides, even the word 'brahman' has its own meaning [to convey in positive terms what it is, infinite being].

The fact of the matter, however, is that only infinity, among the three terms, connotes it meaning *via* negation. It negates finitude of Brahman. The other two define it on their own. They are terms with positive connotations, both truth and knowledge.

Objection: 'From that Brahman, from this *ātman,* originated the ether of space' (TaitU 2.1). In this text, 'brahman' and '*ātman*' are used as synonymous terms. From this it would follow that Brahman is the self of the knower. At 2.8.5 too, this Upaniṣad will equate the two, Brahman and the self, when it will speak of the attainment of Brahman as the attainment of the blissful self. Moreover, at 2.6.1, it will recount how Brahman created the individual being and entered his body as living being. All these quotations show that Brahman constitutes the ontology of the knowing being, it is the being of that being, its reality.

This would prove Brahman as the knower, this fact that Brahman is the self. For the self, we know, is of the nature of the knower. The very words of the *śruti* about Brahman, 'He desired. . .' (TaitU 2.6.1) show Brahman to be the knower, for he who desires is one who knows. Therefore, to say Brahman is mere knowledge is not a proper way to speak about it.

Besides, Brahman as knowledge cannot redeem itself from impermanence and dependence. For knowledge is only the noun form of the root 'to know', is derived from it and as such reflects the sense of activity associated with the verbal root. Abstract nouns *reflect* only various senses of the verbal roots in accordance with their cases. The word *jñāna*, too, reflects the meaning of its verbal root *jñā*, to know. As a mere abstract name for the process of knowing, *jñāna* is itself a process, is transitory; as a name, a linguistic factor, it is conditioned by other linguistic factors. Transitory and other-dependent, it cannot be Brahman.

Platonism, the objector implies, is bewitched by language. Abstract nouns have no referential value, they are mere convenient communicatives, fabricated on the analogies of things. When we forget this motive of communicative ease behind their formulations, we tend to think that these abstractions are not mere abstractions but names of entities. Communicative ease, of course, implies communication to oneself too. We are so used to thinking in terms of entities, that we often formulate events, processes, acts in terms of entity-like abstractions. This habit of mankind, born out of fear of mortality, creates the illusion of realities corresponding to these 'names'.

ŚB *Answer*: Your objection is not a valid one. Knowledge is one with Brahman, is itself Brahman. To equate knowledge with activity [for this is what your argument implies: that 'knowledge' is only a naming word used in place of a doing word and not an entity] is an act of false attribution. The self itself is knowledge, knowledge is not something separate from it. Knowledge is thus eternal. But there is *buddhi*, the intellect, that conditioning adjunct of the self. It manifests itself in the form of sense objects, gets transformed into them when it, this conditioning adjunct, itself gets conditioned by sense gates. Even before these manifestations of the intellect become fully manifest, even when they are in the process of emerging as sense objects, these sense-objects-to-be are objects of knowledge as the self, even as manifestations-to-be. And when they fully emerge as objects of the senses, they are pervaded by that knowledge. So what they call knowledge, knowledge bearing the root-meaning of 'to know', is only an appearance of knowledge. Nondiscriminating people, who cannot distinguish between knowledge and its reflection in what is called the knowing process, imagine these transient appearances as the attributes of the self.

Śaṅkara concedes the point of the opponent that 'knowledge' as commonly understood is only a naming word instead of a doing word. He, however, joins issue with the opponent regarding the nature of knowledge itself. Knowledge does not, he argues, belong to the realm of sensations or what is called mental stuff. It is interior to both. Common sense, of course, equates knowledge with a kind of sense and mind activity. My perception, it says, is a cognitive process and so is my thinking. Process cannot, however, be cognitive, the organising involved in the knowing process shows forth a factor outside the process. Knowledge is what we call consciousness; the sense–mind complex, cannot, therefore, be consciousness. Consciousness is only superimposed onto it to lend it the appearance of consciousness.

There is a kind of idealism reflected in Śaṅkara's language. That it is not subjectivism will be clear to those who have the patience to go through my analysis of *Gauḍapāda Kārikā* and Śaṅkara's commentary thereon. I do not propose to repeat the ideas discussed in details in the second volume.

ŚB Brahman's knowledge is not different from Brahman, it is one with Brahman. As you cannot distinguish light from the sun or heat from fire, you cannot distinguish knowledge from Brahman. That knowledge has no cause other than itself, for it is by nature eternal. Time in which things endure and space in which they exist are one with Brahman, are indistinguishable from it. It is also their cause, of time as well as of space. And subtler is it than the subtle. For these reasons, there is nothing that it cannot know, nothing that can remain unknowable to it, neither the subtle nor the screened, neither the far [nor the near], neither that which has been nor that which is nor that which will be. Brahman is, for this reason, called the omniscient.

Man is a knower, has the ego of a knower. For this reason, his knowledge is small and his ignorance without limits. Inexhaustible is the depth of this ignorance and the mystery of things it confronts. Brahman, on the contrary, is only knowledge, it has no ego of the knower. This knowledge, therefore, has no limits. Let man too shed his ego of the knower, let him be innocent of his knowledge, he too will become omniscient. He will be omniscient because he will not violate the infinitude of the spatial world as he now does as a knower. Nor will he stand as a knower of time to divide it into present, past and future. The present moment will be eternity for him and the present object infinity. It matters not whether the thing in question, the thing he contemplates, is a thing in the world, or a word resounding in his ears or a thought passing in his mind. He will know all because each thing will be the all. When man thus dies as a knower to become knowledge, he becomes Brahman the All. The knower is ever and always ignorant. So is the god of popular imagination, the god supposed to know all that we do not know. To such a god things do not reveal their Godhood.

ŚB The Sacred Word too describes Brahman this way. Thus *Śvetāśvatara Upaniṣad* (3.19):

> He walks afast without feet, he touches without hands,
> he sees without eyes and hears without ears.

> Knoweth he the knowable, of him is not the knower;
> him did they call the person, the primal and the great.

And also the *Bṛhadāraṇyaka Upaniṣad* (4.3.30.):

> No end is there to the knower's knowing, for immortal does it abide without a second.

Brahman thus is not different from the knower's own being. Nor does this knowledge depend on sense organs and other instruments [of that semblance that in common parlance is termed 'knowledge']. For these reasons, even though of the nature of knowledge, Brahman is eternal. Since this knowledge is not an act, it is not to be connoted by the root *jñā*, to know.

The apparent inconsistencies should be resolved and reconciled. The words of the *mantras* quoted from the two Upaniṣads equate, virtually or explicitly, Brahman with the knower. This knower, however, does not depend on the instruments of knowing, senses and the like. In the *Bhagavadgītā*, too, the Lord is equated with the knower, the knower of the field, *kṣetrajña* (*vide* Chapter 13). Śaṅkara, following the lead of the *mantras* quoted in the commentary, first equates the self with the knower and, then, towards the end of the paragraph again comes to speak of Brahman as knowledge.

This inconsistency is, however, not a real inconsistency. What we ordinarily call a knower is always a placed, contextual being; he knows something through something else, through the instruments of knowledge. Do away with the instrument, he ceases to be the knower. The *Śvetāśvatara Upaniṣad* recants its attribution of knower to Brahman the moment it takes away the instruments of knowing. It also says, as does the *Bhagavadgītā,* that Brahman ever remains the knower but never becomes the known. This effectively undoes 'the knower' it attributes to Brahman, undoes the knower who knows himself to be the knower. The *Bṛhadāraṇyaka Upaniṣad* also not only attributes, in the quotation above, 'the knower' to Brahman but also the act of knowing, but these attributions it recants in the same breath when it denies the presence of the second, of the other. With the denial of the second, of the other, denial of knowledge also ensues. Does it mean that even 'knowledge' is a false attribution like the knower? *The Taittirīya Upaniṣad* will, we shall find, recant this attribution as much as the two Upaniṣads quoted do the knower. In the commentary to follow Śaṅkara is going to do precisely this.

ŚB For this reason, for the reason that knowledge is not an act, Brahman cannot be called the *knower,* the agent of knowing. Nor can it, for this very reason, be called *knowledge.* The word *jñāna,* knowledge, only indicates

Brahman, it does not designate Brahman. For the word refers only to the appearance of knowledge and to an attribute of the determinating faculty, the intellect. The word in question cannot designate Brahman because it has no class or other factors which could render possible its articulation in words. Similarly, the word *satya*, truth, too, can only indicate Brahman, not designate it. It cannot designate it because no distinctions obtain in Brahman, it is in its nature to be devoid of them. So when 'truth' is attributed to Brahman, it is only external existence or being as such, existence as a generality devoid of existents, which is attributed to it. For that is the meaning or the referent of the word *sat*, of truth. The word truth in 'Brahman is truth' denoting this way bare existence as such can only indicate Brahman. Brahman cannot really be denoted by this word, by *satya*, truth.

Passages like these show how even commentaries required a *milieu*, a teacher–pupil tradition, to be fully intelligible. I have rendered the translation, in accordance with the practice adopted in this work, somewhat freely. Still the ideas expressed in these words require careful attention.

What does, to come to the first point, Śaṅkara mean when he says that words *jñāna*, knowledge, and *satya*, truth, can only indicate Brahman, not designate it? *Knowledge* is only a false attribution but an attribution that eventually cancels itself out. Every man/woman imagines himself/herself a knower. These creatures that know are constituted by what they know as much as they constitute what they know. The other by which they are constituted refuses, by the very reason that it constitutes them, to be encompassed by their knowledge. Their knowledge thus ever remains ignorance, a mere promise that can never fulfil itself. True knowledge comes to be only when the other ceases to be the other, when it becomes the self. But can this disclosure of all as the self be called knowledge, this innocence, this nonawareness of the other? Disclosure of all as the self cancels out knowledge as it is ordinarily understood. This innocence of the other the Upaniṣads term *vidyā*, true knowledge, this undoer of all knowledge.

Propositional or communicative knowledge is informed by universals, qualities, motion, etc. Naming a thing means putting it in a complex of relationships, relationships with other things, similar or dissimilar, with what constitutes it and what it constitutes, with befores and afters, relations spatial, temporal, causal, teleological and others constituting the linguistically determined world, the world we would make the object of our knowledge. We forget in our ambition that this world is a condition of our knowledge and of our being: we forget that we who seek to know the world are only a relation among relations and, for this very reason, we cannot know the world in truth, the very framework in which our knowledge is only a moment. When after many a shock of disillusionment man does come to have this understanding, his passion for knowledge comes to an end. A mood of serenity, a state of deeply passive awareness comes to dwell in him. It is in this state of serene passivity that man becomes aware of consciousness as such, consciousness that knows but knows not that it knows. This consciousness, this peace, silent and passive, alone becomes his self, his personality having been set aside. When this passivity becomes more profound it becomes spacious enough to accommodate what appeared as the world to him who was once a man. It is to this great and spacious peace, this blissful nothingness that the all becomes the self, so immediately and so intimately indeed that one would not like to profane even a recollection of it by naming it as *ātman* or Brahman. Bare consciousness which seems an absurdity as a concept comes to be an awful, overwhelming presence when man becomes innocent.

What is called Brahman as knowledge occupies only a stage, a resting place as it were, in this pilgrimage. It shines forth when man becomes a passivity, a peace of innocence, shines forth as interior to the senses, the mind, to the intellect. This peace, however, is not peace to and for itself, neither is it consciousness to and for itself but only to a man who recollects it after he has come out of it and is, for this reason, adventitious to it, not one with it. For him alone it is consciousness, for the refallen. When he comes eventually to die finally into it, it will cease to be either peace or consciousness, either *śūnya* or the *ātman*. Consciousness as stillness, as passivity thus only indicates Brahman, the Real, but is not the Real. It is an icon of Being, the last and final icon, but not Being itself.

As most of us confuse thoughts, images and feelings with consciousness, so do we confuse existence with existents, bare existence with things and objects. Our external world is peopled, we find, with existents, existents related to one another in a highly complex way. This is how we look at the world as body-selves. When in certain contemplative states a distancing takes place from the body, the latter manifests itself as not an entity but a sense process. When the contemplative consciousness flows with this sense process as one with it, then the process turns into stillness, into *sat*, into bare existence. With this death of the body into this stillness, the other of the body, the world too turns, first, into process and then into stillness, into *sat*, into existence.

For an analytical thinker, 'the real thing' of the man of the world is an entity–process, sense–concept duality, with the problem of its existence in space and time added to it. How sensations and concepts come to coalesce is a problem for him, and how this coalescence turns into a thing in time and space is a still more ticklish question that defies an intelligible answer. Invocation of language to perform the miracle is futile because language itself is a process–entity duality. How an interpretation comes to be a thing is *the* mystery for every thinking man.

Phenomena in themselves are, conceptually speaking, inconceivable. One cannot call them permanent or impermanent, processes or entities. They are, in and for themselves, inconceivable, including language. They are not existents, things that exist, yet they seem to be. What is it that lends them being and intelligibility? That dispenser is *sat*, existence. That dispenser is called existence only because it lends being to phenomena, phenomena that cannot *be* still appear to *be*, that are inconceivable yet appear to exist as solid realities. It is in relation to phenomena that *sat* or existence makes sense. What is precisely that which we term existence we do not know. All that we can say about it is that we have to postulate it as the ground, the inbeing of interpretations we call phenomena. The ground as ground we can neither perceive nor think about nor interpret nor imagine. Our truth as existence can only indicate that ground, that Real, it cannot denote it or desginate it. This does not however mean that what we cannot think, perceive, interpret or imagine can never reveal itself to us. It does reveal itself to us when we become true passive openings. But then existence does not remain existence, does not appear something that could correspond to our concept of existence or could be interpreted in its terms. Its presence overwhelms us, undoes us, us and our world and all the concepts in terms of which we think and perceive.

ŚB The juxtaposition of *truth, knowledge* and *infinity* results in qualification of one with the other. Thus qualifying and qualified by each other, these words no longer retain their normal referential value *vis-a-vis* Brahman. Arranged in this syntactical order, they can only define Brahman [distinguish it from all that falls within the field of knowledge]. Hence the unspeakability of Brahman, as the following *śruti* texts will would reveal:

> Wherefrom speech returns without finding anything along with the mind (TaiU 2.4.1). . .
> . . . in the unuttered, in the homeless (TaitU 2.7.1)

There can be no proposition about Brahman as there can be about observable things, e.g., the proposition: '[this is] a blue lotus.'

To give a *lakṣaṇa*, definition, of a thing is to highlight its uniqueness, its individuality. When we point out *viśeṣaṇa*-s, attributes, of a thing, we only highlight its class, not its unique individuality. That is the distinction which Śaṅkara makes between *lakṣaṇa* and *viśeṣaṇa*, between a definition and a qualifier. In our discourses, we do not ordinarily go beyond *viśeṣaṇa*, our knowledge of things stops at the universal. The proper name we give to things or persons remains a mere label, totally adventitious to the thing or the individual in question, never coming to inform it or him as does, so we believe, the common name. We do not, however, know a thing, cannot be said to know it unless and until we have found the name proper to it, uniquely proper to it. Our theories and investigations are endless and falsifiable because we deal only in universals and not in genuine proper names, proper names that are inseparable from the thing in question. When I have really and truly found the name of this leaf before me, my investigation will end. That, alas, does not happen to us who are so proud of the power of our speech. My aspiration as a speaking being, however, is to find the true name, the name proper of each and every thing:

> *Hier* ist des *Säglichen* Zeit, hier seine Heimat. Sprich und bekenn.[1]

This moment, this moment that I live, is the time for the sayable. Here is its homeland. Let me speak and bear witness to it. I cannot, however, bear witness to a thing before me unless I experience its unique being and find its own, unique name. The unique name is what poets seek but fail to find. Other discoursers are content with common names: they are happy to talk *about* the thing before them, it never occurs to them to speak to it and bear witness to it.

There is a famous *sūkta* in the *Ṛg Veda* (10.71) which could save us from our insensitiveness to the word. We must pay heed to it in order to respond meaningfully to the language of the Upaniṣad and to be awake to the sacredness of *vāc*, speech, which our philosophies so often tend to trivialise.

1. bṛhaspate prathamaṃ vāco agraṃ
yat prairata nāmadheyaṃ dadhānāḥ,
yad eṣāṃ śreṣṭhaṃ yad ariprам āsīt
preṇā tad eṣāṃ nihitaṃ guhāviḥ.

1. Ninth Elegy, Rilke.

When seers, O Lord of the Holy Word, gave names to things, that was the first beginning of the word. That which was noble, that which was pure and hidden in their hearts, that did they reveal through their love.

Men care to name only those things that they love, others they merely categorise and classify. The word comes into being through this act of naming, naming the noble, the pure, the sacred hidden in their hearts. Before this naming through love, living speech is not born: it remains an inert tool neither holy nor divine.

2. saktum iva tita-unā punanto
yatra dhīrā manasā vācam akrata,
atrā sakhāyaḥ sakhyāni jānate
bhadraiṣāṃ lakṣmīr nihatādhi vāci.

They created the word through their mind, those seers,
sifting it as they would sift the corn with a sieve.
Thus do the same-named know the same name.
A blessed seal on their speech is set.

Only the pure and loving mind can create speech, and the mind overpowered by a mystery within. Purity and love and mystery are not, however, enough. The words would come contaminated with other words, words born not out of love but repeated through habit, words not issuing from mystery but from convention. These dead words should be sifted out. The sifting out will become possible only when the conventional man has been sifted out, not before. Only he who is holy and pure in the presence of a mystery holy and pure can utter the sacred word, the word that lives and gives life.

And only such a man can recognise *his* name, his own name in others, can recognise the sameness of their names and, thereby, the sameness of their life and being. Can there be such a name as can be uniquely yours as well as uniquely of others, of each and every one of them? Common names are merely common, they do not become uniquely mine and yours. I can manipulate them but I cannot *be* them. Nor can you. The speech of only such a man is blessed as can bear his name as uniquely his name and, at the same time, as uniquely yours and of each and every one. What is that word, the blessed and holy?

3. yajñena vācaḥ padvīyam āyan
tām anvavindann ṛṣiṣu praviṣṭām,

tām ābhṛtyā vyadadhuḥ purutrā
tāṃ sapta rebhā abhi saṃ navante.

They followed with sacrifice the path of the word
and found her entered within the seers.
They brought her forth to reveal it to many.
In concert sing her the seven singers.

The Word dwells within the heart of the seers, not on the tongue of man as the world mistakenly believes. And the seer within whom the word abides is he who has found the word that is mine and yours, the universal that is the individual and the individual that is the universal. That word, the Vedas tell us, is the imperishable word that is all this, *sarvam idam.* This word, the dwelling place of all, the seers reveal to the world in the form of revelatory words, in the form of *śruti,* the Heard. In this *vāc,* this revelatory speech, the Word reveals itself. Those who chant these words with their entire being will find the Word, in each and every one of them.

The seven singers are the seven stars of the Great Bear. They symbolise the two eyes, the two ears, the two nostrils and the mouth. When the word resounds, to anticipate the Upaniṣads, in the crown of the head, the senses lose their narcissistic desires and get tuned to the Word. It is in this Word that the divide between the universal and the individual becomes reconciled. In our human speech the divide remains unhealed.

4. uta tvaḥ paśyan na dadarśa vācam
uta tvaḥ sṛṇvan na śṛṇoty enām
uto tvasmai tanvaṃ vi sasre,
jāyeva patya uśatī suvāsāḥ.

Yet there is one who, while seeing, sees not the Word
and there is another who, though hearing, hears her not.
But there is one to whom she reveals her body
as a fair-robed bride in desire to her lord.

When senses are oriented towards the external world, they fail to experience the Word. To those in whom the seven stars located in the face revolve around the eternal pole star—the resounding Word—to such men the Word reveals its real form. The simile of the fair robed bride reveals that the Word as *praṇava,* as the roaring thunder, is not the real form of the Word, as the fair robes are not the body of the bride. The real body, its truth and reality, will she reveal when to the fully devoted man it comes to be gracious. The final revelation is a gift and blessing, not an achievement.

5. uta tvaṃ sakhye sthira-pītam āhur
nainaṃ hinvanty api vājineṣu,
adhenvā carati māyayaiṣa vācaṃ
śuśruvāṃ aphalām apuṣpām.

One they call ever-soaked in same-naming;
unemulated he discerns as the Word would discern.
The other moves among sterile delusions,
the word he heard bears no fruit, no blossom.

This is a most difficult verse. I, following *Uṇādisūtra* 4.138 translate *sakhyam* as same-naming [*sakhi sama samānaṃ khyāyate*]. *Hinvanti* I interpret, with Sāyaṇa, as *anugacchanti*, emulate. *Vājineṣu* I interpret with Yāska as *vāgjñeyeṣu*, meanings which the Word alone can understand. He who has found the universal that is his own, uniquely his own, name, and his own proper name as the universal, alone finds the divide between the word and its referent bridged. Those who do not have this vision, do not know the Word, at once the universal and the individual, the common and the proper, deal only with the appearance of the Word, with what they choose to call language. This language will never lead them to truth, for it will ever be inflicted with the divide between the universal and the individual, the name and the named, the common and the proper.

Māyayā I interpret, following Yāska, as *pratirūpayā*. Language is only a picture, not reality.

What is that state where the universal becomes the individual, the common the proper and *vice versa*? When I try to seek my own, proper, being I find it to be the all. *The Taittirīya Upaniṣad*, while isolating Brahman from everything else, while defining it, comes, at last, to equate it with infinity. Similarly, when I try to find my own name, my own unique name, the name which is me, I find that name to be the name of the all, the name which is the all. That name the Vedas call *vāc*, the Word, the *akṣara*, the Word Imperishable, or (later on) *aum*. They also call it Brahman, for that too is one of the meanings of 'brahman', the Word. As the world proceeds from Brahman to return to it, so speech originates from the Word to return to it. When speech loses its distinctions to become the Word, the divide between the word and its referent is bridged. For the Word is not different from its

Referent. This point has received our attention in the second volume.[1] It should be remembered that the title of this *sūkta* is *jñāna*, knowledge.

6. yas tityāja sacividaṃ sakhāyaṃ
na tasya vācy api bhāgo asti.
yad īṃ śṛṇoty alakaṃ śṛṇoti
nahi praveda sukṛtasya panthām.

No share of the word shall fall to his lot
who has abandoned the same-named aware of the bond.
Whatsoever he hears, he hears in vain.
Of holy deeds he knows not the path.

I prefer the nonfelicitous 'the same-named' instead of the smooth 'friend'. *Saci* I render as 'bond'. The word is an indeclinable meaning *together. Sacivida* would mean: one who knows how one is existentially bonded, tied with others. One is united to others because one shares with them the same name and, for this reason, the same being. For sharing of the name means sharing one's being, one's ontology: it does not mean membership of a class, where the class, though an abstraction, has ontological precedence over me because it has a name, a constitutive name and I have none, my proper name being a convenient label, not my constitutive principle.

If I abandon a co-sharer of my my name and of my being, the Word would disclaim me, disinherit me. Whatever I shall hear will be a vain, foolish noise, adventitious to my being, my life. And I shall lose the way of holy deeds. Holy deeds for the Vedas are deeds that make one a participant in the world, make one an inmate of the earth, of the sky and of heaven. If one does not care for the Name that is the name at once of all and of each, if one sleeps over this Name, one cannot truly be a holy man, for one becomes holy only when one lives an inmate of this earth and lives a sharer of the life of all—from that of inert earth to herbs to beasts to man to gods. The Word will withdraw its soul from the speech of the man who abandons the same-named.

7. akṣaṇvantaḥ karṇavantaḥ sakhāyo
manojaveṣvasamā babhūvuḥ,
ādaghnāsa upakakṣāsa u tve
hṛdā iva snātvā u tve dadṛśre.

1. See pp. 266 ff.

Beings bearing the same name are gifted alike in eyes and ears. Yet they are not alike in quickness of mind. Some look like tanks that reach up to mouth and shoulders, others like lakes deep enough to bathe in.

8. hṛdā taṣṭeṣu manaso javeṣu
yad brāhmaṇāḥ saṃyajante sakhāyaḥ,
atrāha tvaṃ vi jahur vedyābhir
oha-brahmāṇo vi carantyu tve.

When blessed with names alike, Brahmins sacrifice with the insight their heart has fashioned; they leave one far behind by what they know. While others merely stray away, the boastful ones.

These two verses show that even when the vision of sameness, of *samatvam,* has been vouchsafed to men, their participation in it is not alike. That depends on how quickly they respond to it and let themselves be suffused with it. 'Quickness of mind' here connotes their openness; it connotes, as this verse itself would say, sacrifice of the ego-self which lives as unreal abstraction, the sacrifice, that is, of the false name, the category. Those who do not sacrifice with insight are left behind by *jñāna,* knowledge of the Word. As for Brahmins who are merely men of learning, they are spurned by the Word. Their learning of the Vedas is of little use.

9. ime ye nārvāṅ na paraścaranti
na brāhmaṇāso na sutekarāsaḥ,
ta ete vācam abhi padya pāpayā
sirīstantaraṃ tanvate aprajajñayaḥ.

Those who move neither backward nor forward,
who know not Brahman or press not soma,
in sinfulness do they attain to the Word.
Ignorant, they weave a thread out of water.

The thread that man is to weave is the thread that holds together all the constituents of the world. The Vedas call that thread *ṛta,* the Upaniṣads *virāj.* Does this mean that man is not merely to discover that thread but has to participate in its creation? The *ṛta* has no being apart from the beings of the world. It is only when creatures self-submit to their sacrificial roles that *ṛta* comes to be. When they do not live as sacrificial victims, the *ṛta* turns into the Law, forbidding and killing. So man must weave the thread actively, must move forward and backward. When he has thus participated in the goings on of the universe, he attains to Brahman or, at least, drinks at the fount of *soma*, attains to the drunken state of *avyakta*, the innocent source of all that is and could be. If he does not participate in the sacrifice that the world is, he will not know the Word. What he calls speech will only be a sinful acquisition, not the Word that is life and being but the word that atrophies the living into abstractions, degrades being into death. And this speech will only be an instrument, not the adorable Word that is at once *satyam, jñānam anantam*, truth, knowledge and infinity. Whatever this ignorant man knows will not be the Word. Futile will be his endeavours and vain.

10. sarve nandanti yaśasāgatena
sabhāsāhena sakhyā sakhāyaḥ,
kilbiṣasprit pituṣaṇir hy eṣām
araṃ hito bhavati vājināya.

All the same-named rejoice when cometh unto them the same-named glorious, the conqueror of assembly, the deliverer from sin, the giver of food. Placed in the body, he is fit for the heroic deed.

Those who have found the Word that pervades each as full and also all as full rejoice when it comes to own them up. It delivers them from sin that goes with language and its distinctions and transforms assembly into itself. It transforms, to use the language of the Upaniṣads, diversity into the sole self. And it, the Word, is the provider of food too. For the knower of the Word, *soma* is the food; the ecstatic joy of the *avyakta*, of the unmanifest, alone is their life. That *soma*, that joy, is placed in the body. He who has drunk deep at that fount alone is a participant in the redemptive sacrifice, the sacrifice about which the Veda will speak in the *mantra* to follow.

11. ṛcāṃ tvaḥ poṣamāste pupuṣvān
gāyatraṃ tvo gāyati sakvarīṣu,
brahmā tvo vadati jātavidyāṃ
yajñasya mātrāṃ vi mimīta u tvaḥ.

One man nurtures the ṛc*-es reciting them,*
another sings the holy song in sakvarī *metre.*
One, the brahman, *reveals the wisdom of what has come to be.*
And one measures out the measure of sacrifice.

How is man to perform the act of sacrifice? The answer to this question one finds symbolically reflected in the duties of the four priests. The word for the priest is *ṛtvij*, one who sacrifices at the proper time. Sacrifice is not merely a human act, but an act in tune with what is going on in the universe. Only that man can qualify to be a priest who can act as a participant in the world process. If one sacrifices in order to fulfil a mere personal desire, one does not perform an act of sacrifice, one does violence to what has come to be.

The first priest is the *hotṛ*, the offerer of oblations. As his oblations feed the fire, so his recitation of the *ṛc*-es, the verses of the *Ṛg Veda*, nurtures as it were the *ṛc*-es. He feeds them, nurtures them with the oblations of his thoughts, his feelings, his desires. The fire is *jāta-vedas*, the knower of all that has come to be. The *Ṛg Veda* too is that fire. When man pours himself into this fire, the *Ṛg Veda*, he too turns into *jāta-vedas*, the god that knows all that has come to be.

When desire has been burnt up and man has become the fire, the *hotṛ* turns into *udgātṛ*, the offerer into the ecstatic singer, the singer of the exalted song. The *Ṛg Veda*, the *Chāndogya Upaniṣad* tells us, is the wisdom of earth. The *vāc* as *ṛc* is the *vāc* as *agni*, the mediating god. One has to sacrifice oneself into this fire, this redemptive speech of earth, to be transformed into god. When man as *hotṛ* has sacrificed himself into *ṛc*, the *ṛc* turns into *udgītha*, the song exalted. The *ṛc* is uttered in the language of the earth, the language that men understand and communicate with. The *udgītha* is *sāman*, the form speech assumes in *dyu*, in heaven. It is language as *aum*. Thus does the *Chāndogya Upaniṣad* instruct us:

> **aum iti etad akṣaram udgītham upasīta (1.1.1) . . . puruṣasya vāg raso vāca ṛg rasaḥ, ṛcaḥ sāma rasaḥ, sāmana udgītho rasaḥ (1.1.2).**
>
> *This imperishable word,* aum, *is* udgītha, *the song exalted. One should meditate it.*
> *The Word is the essence of man; of the Word the* ṛc, *the hymn of the* Ṛg Veda, *is the essence; of* ṛc *the* sāman, *the song of the* Sāma Veda; *of* sāman *the* udgītha, *the song exalted.*

The language that men speak to each other is not the true *vāc* but only a *pratirūpa* of it, a semblance of it. If man really wants to know the true face of the word, then let him immerse himself in the words of the Vedas. When he comes to be fully absorbed in those words, absorbed to the extent of becoming one with them, the *ṛc*-es will turn into *sāmans* and *sāmans* will, eventually, turn into *udgītha, praṇava,* the roaring thunder. That will be the moment when man, as *udgītha*, will speak of the truth of all that has come to be. For *aum, praṇava*, is all that is, all that was and all that ever will be (to adopt the language of the Upaniṣads). Man as *brahman* priest, the priest one with the Word, is the finder and revealer of the wisdom of all that has come to be. That indeed is the *vidyā* revealed in *Atharva Veda*, the Veda of Fire, of *jātavedas*, the knower of all that has come to be.

Sacrifice, the *Ṛg Veda* tells us (1.64.39), is the centre of *bhuvana*, of the world, and the altar, the *antaḥ*, the end, the outermost bound, of *pṛthivī*, earth. *Pṛthivī*, derived from the root *pṛth*, to extend, is itself the extended one, so extended indeed that one does not know its limits. To know the limits of earth, of *pṛthivī*, you do not have to undertake the hopeless task of measuring it, for the earth is as it were extension itself. But the altar, this altar (*iyam vedī*) is the end of the extended, the limit of the measureless. Here the *pṛthivī*, the extended, ends and so does extension, the concept. The act of sacrifice, the centre of the *vedī*, the altar that is the end of the world, is the centre of *bhuvana*, of the world, of all that has come to be. It is the centre of the world because all extensionality has come to end here. The centre is indeed measureless, you cannot pinpoint it *pṛthivyā*, in terms of extension. This centre is the circumference too. The fourth priest, *adhvaryu*, measures the measureless. The *adhvaryu* is the priest of *Yajur Veda*, the wisdom of sacrifice. He is also the layer of *soma* sacrifice. One drunk in *soma* knows this altar as infinity, and this sacrifice as the all. He alone knows what infinity is, he who has drunk the drink of immortality through self-immolation.

This is *jñāna*, this is knowledge, according to *Ṛg Veda*. When you seek the real name of a thing, the name that really and truly belongs to it, when you seek the name proper to it, you will end up in infinity, you will become infinity. Man is born a common name. The proper name is not gifted to him, he has to find it. That truly is his sacred duty, finding the genuine proper name. And find it he shall provided he is prepared to surrender his speech to revelation, his *vāc* to *śruti*. The word he speaks is not the real word, it is only a delusion; the word he hears, the word which no one speaks, is the real word. It is the real word because in it the divide between the word and its referent is bridged.

This should make clear why search for the *lakṣaṇa* of Brahman, its definition, ends up in cessation of all speech. The world today does not respond favourably to the Vedas when they tell us that truth is beyond speech. What the Vedas mean to say is that the truth of speech is beyond what *we* call speech. To find that truth you do not have to go beyond words but only to surrender to words. Not, of course, to words that you speak but to the words that speak to you. Great poets, we have often remarked, know the power of words, the words that speak to man, speak to him when he is silent and in stillness. The poetic word is not, however, *śruti* because man hears it as man, he does not become the word and speak as the word, audible to others but not to himself. This word alone is the redemptive word, the word that is man's self. In that word the distinction between the word and reality comes to end. As long as man remains a speaker, his word will remain false and his world an illusion.

ŚB [Hidden in *guhā*, mystery, who knows him,
in the highest heaven, together he obtains all desires
with Brahman the wise . . .][1]

He who knows him, Brahman as explained above, explained as truth, knowledge and infinity. *Hidden,* existing, in *guhā*. *Guhā* is derived from the root *guh,* to hide, to conceal. In the intellect lie hidden knowledge, the knowable and the knower. So *guhā* could mean *buddhi,* the intellect. The intellect could be called *guhā* also because in it lie hidden two human objectives, namely, enjoyment and liberation. The highest heaven means the ether of space within the intellect. This ether of space within the intellect is called the unmanifest. And it is called the highest heaven because it lies near the imperishable Brahman. 'In this imperishable, O Gārgī,' the *śruti* assures us, 'the ether of space is woven like warp and woof' (BṛU 3.8.11). It is, however, possible that *guhā* and the highest heaven may be apposites. In that case, the space unmanifest itself would be the *guhā,* the mystery. For it is in the unmanifest space that all things lie hidden in the three dimensions of time. They remain ever absorbed in it because it is their cause and also because it is more subtle than those things. In that unmanifest space lies hidden Brahman, the Absolute.

In the present context, it makes better sense to interpret *the highest heaven* as the ether of space within the heart. We should remember that the *śruti* here wishes to present that heaven as the object of knowledge, that is to say, of meditation. In that respect, the ether of space within the heart would be a more appropriate translation of the term than the unmanifest. That the ether of space within the heart is indeed the highest heaven is known to everyone who has heard these words of the *Chāndogya Upaniṣad*:

> The ether of space which is outside the person is the ether of space which is within the person and this ether of space which is within the person is the ether of space which is within the heart (ChU 3.12.7-9)

1. To rephrase the translation of the *mantra* a little in tune with *ŚB*.

In that ether of space within the heart resides the cave, the *buddhi* or the intellect. And in this cave lies hidden Brahman. Through the functioning of the intellect can it be clearly experienced. In no other way is Brahman related to any particular time or space [that one could perceive it as one could perceive an ordinary object]; it is all pervasive and devoid of distinctions.

The commentary explains the Vedic vision in a very terse way. The cosmos without is present in all its fullness in the empty space within the body. And this cosmo-anthropo space is present in the space within the heart. That is the highest heaven, this little space within the heart. In that heaven, in that all-in-each resides the intellect, the determinating faculty. One cannot know the secret, the truth of the intellect as long as the world exists as the outer space, as long as it does not come to reside in the tiny space within the heart. It is that secret, hidden dimension of the intellect, the dimension that has in it all that the world is, all that man is, that can reveal all as the self, and the self as Brahman, the Absolute. This intellect is the centre of all that is. That which the Vedas term as *yajña,* sacrifice, is this *buddhi,* this intellect and what they term as *vedī,* altar, is this body. One is the centre of the world, the other, its utmost bound.

How does *buddhi* reveal Brahman through its functioning? Not through concepts. These can determine only spatial–temporal phenomena. It reveals Brahman as sacrifice, as consciousness that is innocent of itself. It reveals Brahman because it itself is Brahman. For what is Brahman if not the mortal world innocent of itself? As conceptual activity, the intellect can reveal Brahman as merely the witness of thoughts and concepts, as the knower of the field, provided man is alert enough to distinguish between thoughts and their observer, their knower, which many philosophers are not. But this revelation does not reveal the true nature of the knower as the all, as Brahman the Absolute. For that revelation, *buddhi* has to become utter passivity, bare consciousness, bare knowledge, it has to become innocence itself.

ŚB What does the man, who knows Brahman this way, come to obtain? He obtains, the *śruti* says, all his desires, enjoys all that is to be enjoyed, all without exception. He does not enjoy those pleasures as you and I would enjoy them—one after another, now the birth of a son, now heaven. He enjoys them all together, simultaneously, concentrated in one single moment. A single perception of his encompasses all of them, perception that shines eternal like the light of the sun, perception which is inseparable from Brahman, from what we called truth, knowledge and infinity '. . . with Brahman the wise' has this implication.

Passages like these are apt to be dismissed in our times as mere mystical effusions. There is, many of us feel, no moment into which has been distilled all that the world could give us, a moment which contains within itself all time and all space. Could there be a perception, moreover, a single perception which could encompass that moment, that eternity and infinity? If there is one, that perception will also be that moment, it too will be eternal, infinite.

To the seekers of infinite knowledge, infinite in the Faustian sense of the term, to those who would master and understand the world, the very thought of such a moment and such a perception will be an absurdity. These seekers can only think about a moment, can survey it and measure it, they cannot live it. If they ever come to live a moment, if they ever become a moment, a single moment, they will find it the home of all, they will find it all. They will find their perception of this moment coalesce with it, melt into it. This coalescence they will find to be Brahman, that truth, knowledge and infinity. There is no mysticism in all this for those who have the simplicity to live a moment; for them, this will be lucidity itself. Only for the restless manipulators this lucid vision will be a mystery, even worse than a mystery: mysticism or plain nonsense. Such is the arrogance of the clever and the curious.

ŚB As Brahman itself does the knower of Brahman obtain all his desires simultaneously, not as the conditioned self which is born to die and dies to be born again. This self which is related to the real self as the image of the sun reflected in water is related to the sun, creatures of the world mistake as their self. As a self conditioned [by the adjuncts of the intellect, desires and volitions and of the organs, those of sense and action], a worldly being obtains his desires as dependent on his deeds, good and bad, and on his organs, the eye and the like. This way, he can obtain his desires not simultaneously but only one after another. That is not the way a knower of Brahman obtains his desires. He obtains them the way described above–obtains them simultaneously, all together. He obtains them this way because he finds himself as the eternal Brahman, the Absolute that knows all, pervades all and is the self of all, Brahman which does not have to depend on good and bad actions to obtain its end, or on organs like the eye and the ear.

The *śruti* calls that Brahman 'the wise'. 'The wise' means 'the omniscient'. Wisdom means omniscience. As that Brahman the omniscient, the knower of Brahman obtains his desires. The word *iti* in the text denotes the conclusion of the *mantra.*

The knowledge we have is rounded and conditioned by ignorance; it reveals our ignorance, highlights the problematic nature of each and every phenomenon. Omniscience is not an awesome and forbidding acquisition. The knower of Brahman does not know all as we know the few, he knows each as the all, the ripple, to invoke an Indian image, as the river, the ant, to invoke another, as the hill. This is his omniscience, not what the faithfuls attribute to their God.

And since he knows each as the all, therefore each moment is his fulfilment absolute. There is nothing beyond the moment that he could desire or seek, that is the eternal for him and that the infinite, the very perfection of plenitude, its fullness and his fulfilment.

ŚB 'The knower of Brahman attains the supreme.' This brief statement occurring in the ritualistic portion of the Vedas, this *Brāhmaṇ*-ic statement, sums up, with an aphoristic brevity, the purport of the entire part (2) of the Upaniṣad. The *mantra*—'Brahman is truth . . . desires'—explains, again briefly, this *brāhmaṇ*-ic aphorism. The statement, however, demands detailed elaboration. The rest of this chapter is oriented to this very end and may be taken as a gloss on what the *mantra* has said.

The *mantra* begins with defining Brahman as truth, knowledge and infinity. The text elaborates this definition. Infinity [to take up the last term first] can be spoken of in three ways. There is the infinity of space and of time; there could also be such a thing as the infinity of a thing. The ether of space could be said to exemplify the infinity of space; one cannot possibly think of any limit, any horizon of it. But one cannot think of this infinity as infinity in terms of time, one cannot speak of it as eternity. Nor can it be equated with the infinity of a *thing*. It cannot be spoken of as such because the ether of space is an effect, is sprung from a cause. Brahman, however, is infinite in terms of time as well, for it is not an effect as the ether of space is. Only an effect is circumscribed by time, and Brahman is not an effect. For this reason, it is infinite in terms of time, too.

And so is it infinite as a *thing* too. It is infinite as a thing because there is no other to it. Things set limits to each other because of their difference from each other. Cognition of a thing implies decognition of [an] already cognised thing[s]. The cognised thing thus sets limits to the decognised. When one, to illustrate the point, cognises a horse one decognises what one cognised before, a cow. The concept of the horse is the point where the concept of the cow comes to end. Therefore, the cow is a finite being, a being with a limit. All distinct things thus set limits to each other. But no distinctions obtain in Brahman. Therefore, as a thing, a substance, too it is infinite.

Time and space are not things but constitute the Place of things. They seem infinite because one cannot perceive them as one can perceive a thing, these existential homes of all things. You can perceive the sky but not its horizons, its utmost limits, you can experience time but neither its beginning nor its end. Space seems infinite and time endless and beginningless, yet infinite space is limited by the past and the future times; it does not coextend with them. There is always a before and after to our spatial world. Moreover, this infinite world gives no indication of its being self-existent, its past haunts it and its future beckons it, ever and always. It exists, ever and always, as an effect, like each and everything in it. Its cause is untraceable, but is always there to make its presence felt by its very absence. An ontological deprivation is the characteristic mark of our world. This effect cannot coincide with the infinity of time, its past and its future.

That the 'infinity' of time too is limited by the 'infinity' of space is too patent a fact to need a mention: The past and the future are limited by the present which, I have often argued, coincides with the spatial world. . . Space and time thus seem 'infinite' to our cognition, which can grasp only a limited part of them. What we cognise can only be a finite thing. When we cognise it, all other things collapse into an undifferentiated mass as it were, everything outside the field of our observation. So cognition of a thing or things puts an end to the cognition of other things. What could, then, be the meaning of the phrase: infinity of a thing when everything is limited, finite? The so-called totality of things, including the ether of space, is flanked, so to say, with the past and the future. Time and space are not infinite in themselves; they are imagined infinite because they constitute the framework of our experience, its assumed background. The unknowability of this background is equated with infinity. Brahman is not infinite in the sense in which the Place is, Brahman is infinite as *this,* as the object of our experience, as *vastu,* as thing. A thing reveals its infinitude, turns into Brahman, when it is attended to in and for itself, divorced from its fake Place, the so-called infinities of time and space. Brahman is the thing in itself, not the thing in itself of epistemology but of ontology. You find it here within the field of phenomena as the thing before you but as the thing unrelated and in itself. This thing, the bare thing is the genuine infinity, each and every thing. Here in one moment resides eternity, in one atom infinity. The infinity of time and of space dwell here, in the moment, in the atom. It is the infinity of a thing that is real infinity, time and space are merely its shadows.

ŚB How is Brahman nondifferent from each and every thing? Because it is the cause of each and everything. Brahman is the cause of every thing starting from time and the ether of space.
Objection: If Brahman is the cause of the world, then it is limited in relation to its effect, the world. This means its finitude as a thing.
Answer: No, for the effect is unreal. The effect has really no being without the cause. It cannot, therefore, supplant the cognition of the cause. 'Modifications

originating from speech are mere names. Clay alone is real' (ChU 6.1.4); and similarly, 'Existence alone is real '(ChU 6.2.1). Thus do we learn from another *śruti* text.

Since Brahman is the cause of the ether of space, therefore, it is infinite, infinite in terms of space, in terms of spatiality. The infinity of the ether of space is well-known, infinity in terms of space. The infinity of the self, which is the cause of the ether of space, is therefore evident, its infinity in terms of spatiality. For the all-pervasive *ākāśa,* ether of space, cannot conceivably be born out of that which is not all-pervasive. Hence the spatial infinity of Brahman is total and absolute. And since Brahman is never an effect but only *the* cause, its temporal infinity is also in evidence. And so is its infinity as a thing, for all things are Brahman itself, there being nothing different from it. Therefore, Brahman is truth the absolute.

Since the Upaniṣad is going to speak about Brahman as the cause of the world, Śaṅkara invokes the *Sāṅkhya* theory of *satkāryayāda,* to establish the ontological nondifference of the cause from the effect. The effect he, however, terms as unreal. How is the cause, then, present in the world which is unreal? Śaṅkara's favourite image of the serpent and the rope will help explain the point. The rope is the material cause of the snake-appearance, it remains present in the 'effect' as its content. 'This' in 'This is a snake' is the rope onto which the snake-appearance somehow gets superimposed. In the absence of the rope-cognition, the act of superimposition is impossible. So in every cognition, there are two elements: the pure cognitive element and the interpretative element. The interpretative element has time and space as what may be called its structural correlates, and things, phenomena, as what may be called its textural correlates. Both the structure and the texture are superimposed onto what pure cognition reveals. Time and space and things constitute the snake in our paradigm and rope the correlate of pure cognition. Purge your cognition of this structure and texture and look at the thing before you, look at it to the extent of becoming it, and [you] will [find] the thing become the infinite, sucking you into itself. These are but poor words! For neither will you be there nor will be the finding. The real infinity resides in the flower that blooms and withers in your garden, it belongs to the blade of grass that grows underneath it, not to the vast expanse of the world nor to time endless and beginningless.

ŚB 'From that [Brahman], this *ātman,* originated the ether of space. . .' 'From that' refers to what the original *brahma-vākya, Brāhmaṇic* sentence, aphoristically stated, namely, Brahman. 'This' in '. . .this *ātman* . . . 'refers to Brahman as subsequently defined in the sentence constituting the *mantra.*

From that Brahman, which earlier the *brahma-vākya* aphorismised and which, later, the *mantra* defined as truth, knowledge and infinity—from that Brahman, from *this* Brahman, this *ātman* was born the ether of space. The word *ātman*, 'the self', has Brahman alone for its referent. For that alone is the *ātman*, the self, of all as one could learn from these words from another *śruti* text, 'That is truth, he the self' (ChU 6.8-16). Brahman, the Absolute, thus is the self [of each and every being, living or inert]. From that Brahman of the *brahma-vākya* and this Brahman defined in the *mantra*, Brahman which is the self [of all in each] was born the ether of space.

Ākāśa, the ether of space, is that which has sound for its quality and provides space to all corporeal things. From that *ākāśa*, from that ether of space, was born *vāyu*, air of two qualities, one of touch, its own and the second of sound, which it inherits from its cause, the ether of space. In the text 'was born' is not explicitly mentioned but is understood. From air was born *agni*, fire, of three qualities, one of colour, its own, and the other two it inherits from the ether of space and air, its predecessors in evolution. From *agni*, fire, was born water of four qualities, that of taste, its own, and the three qualities of its predecessors. And from water was born earth of five qualities—smell, its own, and the four of its four predecessors. From earth were born herbs, from herbs food, from food, transformed into semen, was born person with head, hand and feet, person endowed with a material form [called the body].

The myth of creation is similar to that given in the *Praśna Upaniṣad* and the commentary too is written in the vein of the commentary on that myth. That the world is born out of the *śūnya*, the emptiness that is *ākāśa*, makes one pause and contemplate that vast and infinite emptiness. We who are addicted to think of things, of their causes and effects, are not sensitive to the awful horizons of the world. They seem too distant, too unreal to interest us. But this emptiness is the home of the world and also of man. The Upaniṣads say that this infinite nothingness is not indifferent to man, it speaks to him as sound, resounds for him in the emptiness of the ear. How can one hear that sound which can suck man into the cosmos, make him one with the cosmos? The commentary provides the answer. There is the sensation of touch in man and there is its correlate in the world in the form of *vāyu*, air. There is also the visual sensation and its correlate fire, with colour for its quality. And there is taste in man and there is water in the world as its correlate. And there is smell in man and its correlate earth.

As these elements have emerged out of emptiness, so has man. He is not an independent individual but an individual who is also the cosmos. His senses have their life and being in the world. This he has to realise. And realise this he can provided he gives up his conceptual thinking and his self-centred interests and pursuits. How should he realise, then, that he and this earth are not what he takes them to be, each the other of the other? Let him, the answer is, pay attention to concrete experience of smell, let him watch the breath he inhales and exhales. If he is calm enough to allow himself to be inhaled and exhaled, he will find his body and its other, the world, turn liquid as it were, he will find stable, solid things become moving events. He will, in one word, find earth turn into water, the fifth element into the fourth. This experience will not be a cold experience. The liquid man will *taste* this liquidity, his and of the world. He will experience it as *madhu*, honey, as *soma*, that milk of heaven. The ecstasy and joy of this melting into water is brought out well in Panikkar's translation of the following verses from the *Ṛg Veda* (8.48.3–6)[1]

3. We have drunk the Soma and become immortal!
We have attained the light, we have found the gods!
What can the malice of mortal man
or his spite, O Immortal, do to us now?

4. Bless the heart, O Life-Drop, which has received you,
as a father his son, or a friend his friend.
Wise soma, whose voice we hear from afar,
prolong our days that we may live.

5. These glorious drops are my health and salvation:
they strengthen my joints as thongs do a cart.
May these droplets guard my foot lest it stumble
and chase from my body all manner of ills.

6. Make me shine brightly like fire produced by friction.
Illumine us, make us ever more prosperous.
Enthused by you, Soma, I find myself rich!
Enter within us for our well being.

The fluid watery world does not admit of distinctions that freeze and confine; it is a world flowing free and unhindered, man becoming the cosmos and divinity (verse 3) and the cosmos becoming man—'father', 'friend' (verse 4). Yet there is a sense of being bound, being not really free. The fetters are not, however, restrictive; they enable this anthropocosmic being to move on as would a chariot joined whole. *Soma* is at once freedom giving and law enforcing. It is the *ṛta* that one

1. *The Vedic Experience,* Delhi, India, 1994, pp. 367-68.

becomes conscious of when one has melted out of the inert confines of the body. And this *ṛta*, this binding, is harmony itself: The 'bound' chariot alone can move, not the unbound, the disintegrated. The prayer at the end of the verse is a prayer for continuation of this vision of harmony lest one slip back to the lame-footed existence of earthly life, where all movement is toilsome, painful and frustrating.

The shadows of the fall loom large on this freedom. Water cannot really and truly rise above the earth. The ecstasy must mature into insight, *soma* into *agni*. The bright flame is to be sought in the water itself, for here indeed will he be reborn as water was born out of *agni* when the world was born. In the return journey, the father will become the child, *apāṃ napāta* (cp. RV 2.35). But where are the two sticks to produce the fire by friction (cp. RV 10.5.1-2)? The two sticks are indeed there in the waters, in the watery mode of being. Within man, the two sticks are the outgoing breath and the incoming breath, one hot and the other cold. On the earth, the two sticks are the day and the night, the bright fortnight and the dark fortnight, six months of summer and the six months of winter. The watery man flows as one to become the other. Not for him is choice or preference.[1] He who lives as a constant pilgrim will find every step his home and every moment his moment. He who can flow this way and has the peace to dwell on each moment as if it were *the* moment will find the flame leap up into life. The flame will burn bright and live whenever the pilgrim becomes the moment. The altar where this holy flame will burn is the navel. It is at that moment that the watery world will shine as *dyu*, as light divine.

Fire provides form and shape to things. It burns and shines dependent on earth and water. Since it burns and shines so dependent, its flame may well die back into earth and water. This is precisely what happens frequently to *agni*, to this god born out of the waters, *apām napāta*. Agni has to be redeemed from waters, its flame kept alive and eternal. That, however, is not possible because it is parasitical on earthly and watery oblations, on rice, barley, butter and other things (cp. RV 10.51. 8-9). How to make this god rise above earth and water?

The answer is: When the flame leaps up within man, let him burn with it to be burnt out with it. What will remain of the watery man–world when *agni* has burnt it away, of this anthropocosmic being? The earth will burn into smoke, the water will evaporate and the fire will burn out. Earth–water–fire will be transformed into air. Blowing every-

1. Vide Volume I 358-373.

where, air has no altar, unlike *agni*. So the flame cannot burn eternal because it has to change into air. The Vedic vision of air has been admirably summed up by Panikkar:

> What is said of the Wind could easily be said of the Spirit. The Wind collects, enraptures, and takes away in his chariot towards the celestial heights those who are caught in his blowing, bringing them together. . . This same wind is connected with primordial waters, is called the first born, and yet is said to be of unknown origin; for nobody knows where it goes and where it comes from: it wanders free, is heard but not seen, is invisible, can only be felt, experienced, sensed, without being comprehended or understood.[1]

The air is also omnipresent. That means it carries all that has come to be towards celestial regions. This all-pervasive principle is present in the world as the transcendental principle. Air thus is what later on came to be called the *sattva guṇa* in its purest form. As fire this principle of transcendence is mixed with *rajas* and *tamas*, with water and earth, as air it is *sattva* alone. When fire has burnt away earth and evaporated water, it turns into air. And since there remains nowhere from which wind could now blow and to which it could blow, it comes to be absorbed in *ākāśa*, emptiness denuded of all contents.

With *sattva* thus absorbed into it, *ākāśa* becomes the sole reality, without a before and without an after. They call it *śūnya*, emptiness, a void that, they find and say, resonates with *nāda* or sound. There are others whose sense of the presence of the *śūnya* is so deep and immediate that they find that sound too disappears into *ākāśa*, the sky. This happens, they say, when breath comes to be still and suspended, the blessed moment when *ākāśa* turns into Brahman.

A few are there that hear the echoes of *ākāśa* only fitfully. Their mortal agony and woe not allowing them to linger long on them. They seek the path straight of *brahma-jñāna*, enlightenment. The joy of pilgrimage is not for them.

The account of the birth of the elements have these and other experiential dimensions. One would commit a serious mistake if one were to equate it with what may be called a realistic or naturalistic account. The Upaniṣads do not contain what are called scientific propositions.

ŚB *This truly is the person that consists of the essence of food.* The essence of food has transformed itself into him. The seed that sprouts into man consists of

1. *The Vedic Experience*, Delhi, India, 1994, p.131

semen, the splendour that emerges out of all parts of the human body. This splendour, this seed, is informed by a potentiality for human shape. He who is born out of it is also of the same human shape. That is the law prevailing among all classes of being: the fathered assumes the form and shape of him who fathers [and of her who bears].

Doubt: All creatures are transformations of the essence of food and are, likewise, descendents of Brahman. Why should man alone, then, be singled out?

Answer: Because of his pre-eminence, pre-eminence he has earned on account of his eligibility for the holy deeds and contemplation of the gods. Man fulfils the conditions for that eligibility for the reason that he has the ability to know and practice what the Vedas command him to know and practice and also because he feels the want and the force of that want which will tolerate no indifference on his part. 'In man alone did the *ātman* manifest itself the most. He alone is gifted most with knowledge superior; he alone speaks the known and perceives the known. The events of the morrow he knows and the worlds, higher and lower. With the mortal he seeks the immortal. Thus is he gifted. The knowledge that creatures other than man have is restricted to only hunger and thirst' (AiĀ 2.3.2.5). Thus does another *śruti* text speak about the pre-eminence of man.

That man the *śruti* would carry near Brahman, the interiority among interiorities, through wisdom, the content and tenor of the present section. But such is the disposition of his intellect that it would take distinctions as the self, distinctions that assume the form of externalities, distinctions that are not the self, are other than the self. The intellect disposed this way cannot, all of a sudden and without the support of a distinct object, be made to cognise the interior of the interiors, the self that dwells within man. It will not give up its anchors, will not be contentless—not suddenly. Therefore, the *śruti* provides it with an anchor, a support to orient it towards interiority. This support is the body itself, the body visible to each and every being. The *śruti* makes us imagine it, this body, as the analogue of the self, to lead the intellect into it. To enable children to perceive the new moon, they often ask them to focus their vision on a branch of a tall tree that happens to stand before them. The shift from the high branch to the new moon then becomes an easy affair. Similar is the case with this resorting to the body as a symbol of the self.

Of him this indeed is the head. Of him, the person who consists of the essence of food, this indeed is the head, the head known to every body. The *śruti* will invoke the imagery of the head even when it will speak of the noncorporeal sheaths of the self, beginning with the sheath of breath. Lest someone reduce 'the head' of the food-self too into a figurative image, the *śruti* emphasises the point that this very head, the head perceived by all, is the head of the food-self, this corporeal head itself. Similar is the case with sides and other parts. This right arm is his southern side and this left arm is his northern side. We are supposed to imagine the person facing the east. *This his self. This* here refers to the middle portion of his limbs, to his trunk. That *this* indeed refers to the middle portion, we learn from another *śruti* text too, which says: of these limbs the middle portion is the self (AiU 3.5.4). The part of the body below the navel is the tail, the support. This part keeps the body stable. Hence the attribution: 'the support'. This part is called the tail because it hangs down [as it were from the middle portion] as does the tail of a cow.

The symbolism invoked in the case of the other sheaths of the self, from that of breath-sheath onwards, follows the symbolism of the food-self. As molten copper poured into a crucible assumes the form of an image, so will other sheaths assume a concrete shape when described in its imagistic symbolism.

As to that, bearing on what the *brāhmaṇa* says, there is this verse, this *mantra,* which reveals the nature of the self consisting of food.

How to lead man from the senses and the sensed to the nonsensuous, the interior of the interiors, is the question. Can one, by choice and deliberation, bracket out the body and the material world. In such *epoche* possible? No Cartesian meditation can chant away these existential anchors of consciousness. You have to accept the truth and reality of these others, these constitutive others of consciousness if you accept consciousness as something real and existent. So the way to the innermost core of being lies through meditation of and on the corporeal, on the presence before you, this body born out of food. And you have to contemplate it, limb by limb, keep it before you as a concrete, immediate fact. This indeed is the head of this food-self, this mass of flesh and bones, this home of the eyes, of the ears, of the mouth and the tongue. This is how you are to commence your contemplation of the body, with contemplation of the head. Look at this head as a fact, look at it as you find it, without asking questions, without a theoretical framework. Let your contemplation be such that the content of perception replace your thinking, the head of flesh and bone overpower your mind. In the same way you are to feel and perceive and be possessed by your left arm and your right arm and by the thingy weight of your trunk, with all the discomforts and the disorders of your stomach, its filth, its fat, its embarrassing weight or its beauty if you choose to see it when young. Be this flesh, this ungainly flesh that you would rather cover and conceal. Disclose it before you and feel how the lower portion of your body hangs down as if it were more of an appendage than your self. For you feel your self residing in the trunk and the genitals and the anus, not in the legs that seem to lie on its fringes as it were. These parts seem to be mine but they don't seem to be me. Some feeling of distance is there, they do not seem to constitute the centre of my being. Functionally they are vital and indispensable but not constitutively. In the body too there are distances, the margins and the centre, the me and the they.

Let the distant toes too be contemplated, the defecating anus, the tortuous genitals, the burdensome belly and the guardian arms, the right and the left. Let them be contemplated and lived. And the eyes and the ears and the organs of taste and smell. When you contemplate these limbs and organs, you will find yourself step out of the body as it were, you will find yourself distance yourself from it. This is the strange paradox of this contemplation. But of this presently. In the meantime we have to look at other things before we find this meditation consummated.

Chapter 2

1. **annād vai prajāḥ prajāyante. yāḥ kāśca pṛthivīṃ śritāḥ, atho annenaiva jīvanti, athainad api yanty antataḥ. annaṃ hi bhūtānāṃ jyeṣṭham. tasmāt sarvauṣadham ucyate. sarvaṃ vai te'nnam āpnuvanti ye'nnaṃ brahmopāsate. annaṃ hi bhūtānāṃ jyeṣṭham. tasmāt sarvauṣadham ucyate. annād bhūtāni jāyante. jātāny annena vardhante. adyate'tti ca bhūtāni. tasmād annaṃ tad ucyata iti. tasmād vā etasmād annarasamayād anyo'ntara ātmā prāṇamayaḥ. tenaiṣa pūrṇaḥ. sa vā eṣa puruṣavidha eva. tasya puruṣavidhatām anvayaṃ puruṣavidhaḥ. tasya prāṇa eva śiraḥ. vyāno dakṣiṇaḥ pakṣaḥ apāna uttaraḥ pakṣaḥ. ākāśa ātmā. pṛthivī pucchaṃ pratiṣṭhā. tad apy eṣa śloko bhavati.**

From food indeed are creatures born, whatever creatures dwell on earth. And by food do they live and unto it alone do they finally return. Food alone is the elder among bhūtāni, *among those that have come to be. Therefore do they call it the cure for all. Verily do they obtain all food who worship food as Brahman. Truly, food is the elder among* bhūtāni. *Therefore would they call it the cure for all. From food are born beings, by food do they grow, those who have come to be born. Those that have come to be eat it and them does it eat. Therefore do they call it* annam, *the eaten [that eats].*

Verily, other than this self that consists of the essence of food and within it dwells the self that consists of breath. By that self is replete this self. And like it, that other too has the form of a person. According unto that form is this form of a person. Of this the outgoing breath is the head, the diffused breath the right side, the incoming breath the left side, the ether of space the self, the earth the tail, the support. With regard to this, there is this verse:

ŚB From food, from the food turned into its essence, are born creatures, those that move and those that do not. *Vai*, indeed, reminds man that he remember this fact. Whatever creatures dwell on earth, they all without distinction are indeed born out of food. And by food do they live after birth, by it do they sustain their breath, their life, by it alone do they grow. And unto it, unto food, alone do they return, into it do they get merged. They get merged into it finally when their life process comes to end.

Api in '*api yanti*' has the connotation of 'towards'. At the end of their life, creatures, the word suggests, move *towards* food to get merged in it.

Why this process of emerging from and merging in food? Because food is the elder among creatures, the first born among them. All other creatures, from those that consist of food to others, have food as their cause. Therefore, from food are all other creatures born, on it do they live and into it do they merge. Since food is the origin, the end and the sustaining principle of creatures, therefore do they call it *sarva-auṣadham*, the cure for all. Food puts to rest every malady of the body.

What do they gain who meditate on food as Brahman? Verily do they obtain, the *śruti* says, all food, those who worship the aforesaid food as Brahman, worship it as their origin, their being and their end. When they worship food this way, they find it Brahman itself.

Materialism as a doctrine, as an ideology, is not acceptable to the Upaniṣads. Not so the worship of, the meditation on matter. What does my observation show what I call the *me* to be? A creature sprung from earth, sustained by it and destined to die back into it. The earth, matter, food precede me ontologically speaking; my being, I find, is anchored to them. This is what my theory-free[1], unsophisticated, observation reveals to me. Matter is at the beginning, matter is in the middle, matter is at the end. *Arché* alone is *télos* and what I consider the tension between the two is also the same. The Upaniṣadic view thus runs counter to the Greek view which puts beast at the beginning, gods at the end and man in the middle. Or, desert at the beginning, heaven at the end and *polis* in the middle. It also runs counter to the Judeo-Christian vision of hell–purgatory–heaven or Satan–man–God. Greek tragedy, with some exceptions—*vide* Sophocles' Theban plays—found their *télos* unattainable, whereas Judeo–Christian tradition has hopes of redemption. However, both look at the end as other than the beginning or the middle. [This summing up cannot, however, ignore exceptions]. The Upaniṣadic meditation[2] does not ask man to strive for 'perfection', does not ask him to attain to heaven. It does not even tell man, as Dante did, that hell and purgatory will turn into heaven when man reaches heaven. It asks man to rest content with his present

1. Relatively speaking.
2. Meditation on food.

findings, the result of his unsophisticated observation. The materialistic vision this observation yields is enough for his redemption.

Born from matter, man is destined to remain matter, to remain food. I choose to call myself 'eater' and the matter other than me 'food'. But I eat food only to be food and remain food. For what I eat today—this earth—will one day eat me. Creaturs of dust that are dust will, however, make distinctions, between this dust that they call *me* and that dust which they call *it.* Dust will insult other dust, kill other dust to possess dust. The dust called 'me' has, in my view, privileged ontology. The Upaniṣadic meditation calls upon man to change this attitude; it calls upon man to look at himself as others will look at him, as earth will 'look' at him. As others are food and fodder for his vanities and ambitions, so is he for others. As earth is food for him, so is he food for it. If he comes to look at himself as the other, as earth, he will become the other, the earth. As me, he will be spurned by others and earth, as food he will be all, for all are food.

This 'materialistic' vision then turns into the vision of the world as sacrifice, as *yajña,* where every being, every creature is an oblation. Creatures know that this indeed is their fate but they would believe it to be true in the case of others, not with regard to themselves, not truly. That is their *avidyā,* their ignorance. Once they shift the focus of their vision a little to include themselves in it, they will be blessed with *vidyā,* with *gnosis,* with knowledge. For wisdom is nothing else than the realisation that the eater too is the eaten, the sacrificer the victim.

In other words, knowledge means realisation of the body-self as the food-self, to realise the body, the ever hungry body, as food. When man looks at the body as food, he steps out of its blind urges and wants, steps out of it as if to look at it from a distance. This me, this eater, will then turn into it, into food, into an inert this. In this state of distancing, of detachment from the body, man turns into [mere and bare] breath. He will rise from the navel to die in the atmosphere to rise again there to die again at the navel. His life will ever turn into death and his death into life, one becoming the other and the other one.

Thus will the food-self become the breath-self, the self as victim, the self as innocence. For the breath-self alone is the genuine innocent self, ever becoming the other, it has no fight with the other. Human self, as the food-self, can at best be the victim self, the tragic self, not the innocent self, not until it dies into breath to become breath.

ŚB How does contemplation of food as the self lead to the attainment of all food? The *śruti* gives the following answer to this question. Food is the elder among beings, it came into being before them all. This fact, the fact that it was the first-born, makes of it the panacea, the cure for all. There can thus be no question that the person who meditates on all food as the self will obtain all food.

Clever people of all ages, not only of ours, will dismiss these words of the Upaniṣad as no more than 'enthusiastic' effusions. The words of the commentator too will not change their opinion because they turn out to be a mere paraphrase of the Upaniṣadic saying. We must therefore meditate these words with care, for passing 'thoughts' in the *śruti* often turn out to be profound truths when they are paid the homage of careful attention. To contemplate all food as the self means to contemplate the inert other as the living me and the living me as the inert other. The paradox of this form of materialism is that it invests the other with life, with *my* life. To be the object of the other's look has, no doubt, masochistic ramifications; it may also mean surrender of one's individuality to the other, the act of Sartrean bad faith. This happens because the look remains informed by the same narcissism as was the look that reified the other. The vision of food as the self is, on the contrary, informed by a profound humility: here I and the other acquire equal status. The freezing narcissism that generates sadistic and masochistic tendencies is radically disrupted in this *ec*-centric vision, *ec*-centric because in this vision, there is no centre, neither me nor the other, nor the world. *Ec*-centricity alone becomes the centre, the *it* changing into *me*, *me* into the *it*, *I* into the *other*, the *other* into *me*. When I speak to you about the other, you and I often tend to reduce the other into an *it*. Even God meets this fate, God of discourse. But as food you and I will equate the other with us, even the inert other.

In this state of being, it will not occur to me to enunciate the doctrine: All is matter. When tree and stone, man and beast have disrupted me and, as a consequence, disrupted themselves, there remains no me to articulate a theoretical position and no *matter* to be the content of that theory. Language as interpretative tool too will become, in the process, the victim of this disruption, for it too will, like me, become food. When I use words, make them my tools, they too will use me, reduce me to their tools, make me their bonded prisoner. As user of words, I find myself constituted by them; they seem to have ontological priority over me. For whatever I find and experience, I find them as the constituting or, at least, the sustaining principles of what I call 'me'. When I come to know this truth about language and me, its interpretation, when I know how we two are food to each other, how we constitute and are constituted by each other, then the word will reveal its *deinon* character, its holiness dread and awesome. It will command my attention and my homage. Not for me will then be theories to formulate, defend and criticise.

This radical disruption of me and the world and of language unfolds a vision of everything as everything else. This vision is a panacea because it places man on the way to the liquidation of his personal identity, that cause of every malady. It erodes the concept and what goes with it, independent ontologies.

ŚB *From food are born beings, by food do they grow. . .* The repetition of the sentence with which this chapter commenced indicates the end, the conclusion of the meditation of food as Brahman. Now, the *śruti* proceeds to explain [in effect] the etymology of the word *anna,* food. *Anna* is that which those that have come to be—creatures—eat and which itself eats them. As consumed by all beings and as consuming all beings, food is called *anna.*

The word *iti* indicates the conclusion of what the *śruti* has to reveal about the self consisting of food.

The ambiguity of the term *anna* should be kept in mind. Whether or not *anna,* the eaten, can, grammatically speaking, be equated with the eater—he who *atti,* eats, the fact remains that food has this ambiguous character about it. This fact is a tragedy for *centric* creatures, creatures who deceive themselves into believing that they are independent realities. Those whose centres have been disrupted, who can become the other to experience themselves as food, those who have shed their false selfhood, find in this tragedy their redemption. They alone have the vision of the food-self who are aware of the ambiguity that the eater is the eaten and the eaten eater.

ŚB There is the innermost self called Brahman interior to all the 'selves' ranging from the one composed of food to the one composed of bliss. These 'selves' are like sheaths and the true, real, self is like a sword. These selves are the creations of ignorance, of *avidyā.* The *śruti* seeks to eliminate these sheaths to reveal Brahman as our inbeing, our inself, as one would eliminate a number of husks from the grain *kodrava* to extract rice from it. The removal of the *kośas,* sheaths, is possible through *vidyā,* wisdom. The *śruti* commences this process of elimination through wisdom with the words:

> Verily, other than this self that consists of food, and within it dwells the self that consists of breath. . . .

Different from this self the *śruti* has revealed to us, the self that consists of the essence of food, different from this body that is both the eater and the eaten, and within it, dwells another self consisting of breath, of air—

predominantly constituted by it. Like the self constituted by the essence of food, the body that is the eater and the eaten, this self too is falsely imagined as the real self. The self constituted by the essence of food is replete with this self as bellows are with air. This self also has the form of a person with limbs like head and sides.

This form is not, however, native to it as is the person-form of the self consisting of the essence of food, the person-form which everyone can see and perceive. According unto that form of the self consisting of the essence of food is the person-form of the breath-self. It is as it were an image of that form like the image forged in a crucible. The 'selves' to follow too will have this [symbolic] likeness, each will be a 'man' as the one preceding it is a 'man'. Likewise, the preceding one will be replete with the succeeding one.

And how is the breath-self too 'man', has the form of a man? Of this self constituted by breath, the outgoing breath is the head. The breath-self, this modification of air, has, for one of its functions, exhaling through mouth and the nostrils. This function the *śruti* prompts us to imagine as the head. Other forms of breath too are imagined as the limbs of the breath-person on the authority of the *śruti*. Thus *vyāna*, the diffused breath, is the right side, *apāna*, the incoming breath, the left side. The ether of space is the self. Here, in this context of *breath* process, the ether of space connotes *samāna*, the distributive breath operating in the ether of space. The distributive breath operates in the middle portion of the body, the other breaths in the peripheries. Therefore is it compared to *ātman*, the self. The Vedas, we know, allot this status to the mid-placed as is evident from this saying of the *śruti*, 'The middle of these limbs is the self' (AiĀ 3.5.4).

The earth is the tail, the support of the breath-self. The earth here means the presiding deity of earth. That the presiding deity of earth sustains the breath within the body through stabilising it will be borne out by the following text:

> The sun is the external breath; it rises up bestowing favour on the breath in the eye. The deity [of] earth vouchsafes favours to the downward breath of a person by attracting it, holding it; that which is the intermediate space [is = favours] the distributive breath; the air [is = favours] the diffused breath. (PrU 3.8)

If this had not been the case, if the deity of the earth had not favoured the downward breath by holding it, the body would have flown upwards by the force of the upward breath or would have fallen down because of its weight. Therefore, the deity of the earth is the tail, the support of the self composed of breath. With regard to this, to the self composed of breath, there is this verse:

The breath self will reveal its form, its anthropomorphic form only to him who has become aware of his body-self as the food-self, as the eater–eaten polarity. When man thus freely flows into what for him is an inert thing, an object of consumption or use, when he can lend all his life and being to it, only then will he know himself from the being-point of the other, the other which will have, at this moment, become the I to flow back to me, me who will have then become the inert other. To be as the other of oneself, to be the food-self, is to open up deeper dimensions in oneself. As I said above, this looking at one's human person as *this*, as an it, involves living as identical with the breath-self. There remains, for such a man, only this interiority to fall back upon when the human person has gone out to become a thing among things. When this happens, man becomes life–death duality. As food-self one becomes the other, the lifeless other to endow it with one's life, as breath-self one becomes death to find in it the source of life.

This breath-self is not an empty thought but is a living person in its own way. The head of man is the dwelling place of seven seers, the altar where burn the seven flames of the senses. The outgoing breath feeds these flames, keeps them burning. Those who practise *yoga*, those in whom the flame of the Vedic *Agni*, Fire, burns and shines, daily see how the incoming breath makes the flame rise up and how it reaches the head to feed the senses to orient them inwards. So let us not in our haste reject this symbol as a mere fancy. The sides too are the two yogic nerves, *iḍā* and *piṅgalā*. The left side is called the incoming breath because it is, according to the yogic tradition, the cool nerve, with the moon for its symbol. The right side is the hot nerve, with the sun for its symbol. The *samāna* is equated with the middle of the body because its sphere of operation is the intermediate region between the navel and the throat. *Apāna* is the downward breath, the force that keeps man glued to earth, to the anus and the genitals, through hunger and thirst.

These breaths that work in different and contrary directions in the natural man, come to be integrated in the breath-self. When a man who has attained to this peace, this calm, looks within himself, he finds his body as *one* emptiness, from the anus to the head; as one *ākāśa* which admits of no other predicate than that of peace. If man summons up the courage to plunge into this abyss, he will find even the outer layers of the skin melting into it. The body then will appear to assume truly infinite proportions: one can see no end to this peace, no shore to set limit to it. That is the grandeur of this infinite 'ignorance', this darkness.

When such a man opens his eyes, he finds it difficult to draw the distinction between the external and the internal. Such distinctions seem too arbitrary to arrest and merit his attention. Man no longer rudely intrudes into the world to be a limit to it. The vast space of the world extends unhindered into him.

Chapter 3

1. **prāṇam devā anu prāṇanti, manuṣyāḥ paśavaś ca ye. prāṇo hi bhūtānām āyuḥ. tasmāt sarvāyuṣam ucyate. sarvam eva ta āyur yanti ye prāṇaṃ brahmopāsate. prāṇo hi bhūtānām āyuḥ. tasmāt sarvāyuṣam ucyata iti. tasyaiṣa eva śārīra ātmā yaḥ pūrvasya. tasmādvā estasmāt prāṇamayād anyo'ntar ātmā manomayaḥ. tenaiṣa pūrṇaḥ. sa vā eṣa puruṣa-vidha eva. tasya puruṣavidhatām anvayaṃ puruṣavidhaḥ. tasya yajur eva śiraḥ, ṛg dakṣiṇḥ pakṣaḥ. sāmottaraḥ pakṣaḥ. ādeśa ātmā. atharvāṅgirasaḥ pucchaṃ pratiṣṭhā. tad apy eṣa śloko bhavati.**

The gods breathe after breath, so do men and so do animals. For breath is their life, of those that have come to be. Hence is it called of all the life. Full life do they attain who meditate on breath as Brahman. Breath is the life of beings. Hence do they call it the life of all.

Of the preceding one this indeed is the śārīra ātman, *the self with a body. Other than this self that consists of breath, and within it, dwells the self that consists of mind. By that other self is replete this self. And like it that other too has the form of a person. Like unto that form [of the breath-self] is this form of the person [of the mind-self]. Of it* Yajur Veda *is the head,* Ṛg Veda *the right side,* Sāma Veda *the left side, the instruction the trunk and revelations vouched unto Atharvāṅgirases the tail, the support.*

ŚB As one with breath do *Agni* and other gods breathe, as one with air operating as breath in them, whose power it is to set in motion the process of breathing. It is, in one word, by identifying themselves with breath the air that they do the act of breathing, the process that makes them active. Since the Upaniṣad is speaking, in the present context, in terms of the microcosm, the gods may be understood as the sense-organs which function as followers of the chief breath, the breath in the mouth. Men and beasts too acquire the power to be active from breath the air.

It is, thus, not merely the food-self, the self limited and confined, that bestows selves, identities, on living beings, men and others, but also the breath-self, the self common to all of them, pervading each and every body. That self that dwells within the food-self also makes men and other creatures creatures-with-selves. In the same way, all creatures come to acquire their identities through the 'selves', through the sheaths, beginning from the one consisting of mind up to the one consisting of bliss, each preceding one pervaded by the succeeding one, the grosser by the subtler. These 'selves' are made up of elements like *ākāśa* and others and are [unreal appearances] set up by ignorance. As creatures acquire their identities from these five sheaths so do they acquire from the all-self too, the self that exists beyond these sheaths, the cause spontaneous of *ākāśa* and other elements, the self eternal, unchanging and all-pervading, the self the Upaniṣad has defined as truth, knowledge and infinity. That, that self alone is the true self of all has also been stated, implicitly, through these words.

Some literal minded students, missing the tenor of the commentator's words, have sometimes wondered why the revered commentator has equated the sheaths with selves, when there is only one true self. The answer to this objection is not far to seek if we have the innocence and the imagination to live these sheaths, which we can live only as our selves. When I am engaged in the affairs of the world, I live as the body-self. I live, in these moments, as the body and since I live as the body I am not, in those moments, conscious of the body. To be conscious of the body means to discard it as the self and turn it into an object, into food. Contemplation of this food, of the body as an it and not me, is possible when I live as breath. Instead of body, breath becomes my self. The food-self has a name and a form, it has, as the commentator says, limits and confines but not the breath-self which is another name for anonymity and the anonymous has no confines. Air blows *eachwhere* and everywhere; it is all-pervasive.

It is when man becomes the breath-self that what was the food-self turns into food-sheath, something exterior to this self, concealing it. Of this self, the self as breath we have already spoken as the person, of the limbs that constituted this person. What once was a body now turns into emptiness, eventually melting into the emptiness without, the pot-space into the great space. First the emptiness within seems confined by a thin, barely felt, layer of the skin as it were. A time comes when even this layer melts away, putting an end to all sense of limits with regard to the body, to this self consisting of breath, of air, this life of all, *sarvāyuṣam*. Of course, this self too will turn into sheath when the meditator steps into the mind-'self'. Of this we shall have occasion to speak presently.

ŚB The gods, the senses, the *śruti* says, breathe after breath. What is it that makes them do so? Breath, the answer is, is the life of those who have come to be, to live. 'As long as,' another Upaniṣad says, 'breath dwells in this body as long will last life in it' (KauU 3.2). For this reason, the *Taittirīya Upaniṣad* calls breath 'life of all', *sarvāyuṣam* being another word for *sarvāyuḥ*, life of all. Life deserts man the moment breath deserts him. Therefore, breath is acknowledged to be the life of all.

Those who have dissociated their self from this exteriority, this confined 'self', this 'self' consisting of food and meditate on this interiority, his nonconfined self consisting of breath as Brahman, attain to full life in this world, do not die before they have lived the span ordained [by their *prārabdha karmans*, the acts that are responsible for the coming to be of their present birth]. They do not die a sudden, untimely or accidental death. 'Full life', famous in the Upaniṣads—e.g., the *Chāndogya Upaniṣad* 2.11-20, 4.11-13—should be taken to mean a life span of a hundred years.

One should resort to this meditation, the giver of full life, in this way: I am *prāṇa*, the breath, the life of all that have come to be, the source of their life, therefore, their life.

Why should meditation on breath bless man with the full term of life? Because: '*prāṇa*, breath, is the life of beings. Hence do they call it the life of all.' The *śruti* repeats these words in order to highlight what result that meditation can bring to man. For man shares in the very qualities that he worships Brahman as endowed with.

The breath-self is the self of the preceding food-self. It has the latter for its body, as its dwelling.

The self as the body is the eater-self, the self as food is the eater–eaten duality, the self as breath is the self as life. Creatures do not live by food, the Upaniṣads say, but through and as breath. How life and breath are synonymous, we can know by looking at the process of breathing. It is a movement towards the death of the outgoing breath to the birth, out of that death, of the incoming breath and *vice versa.* Breath is the life–death *rhythm,* not a struggle of life against death. What we call life is a perversion of this rhythm, being a mere conflict and a futile effort. When body appears as food, the eater as the eaten, then life turns into sacrifice, a promise, though not a realisation, of life in death. The food self is only the sacrificial victim, the Lamb going to the cross, tortured and humiliated, not yet the life that will resurrect out of this sacrifice. The sacrificial victim is innocent and humble, willing but weak. The last words of Jesus, 'O God, why hast thou forsaken me?' could be the words of the food self. The breath self is not tortured, not in despair because it knows life as bi-polar, as life–death polarity or, more accurately speaking, as birth–life–death trinity. This life which is not that negative anxious life, that despairing struggle against death which most men and women merely cling to but never, even for a moment, come to live, is the despair of may a sensitive soul, which cannot even dream of it in full, not to speak of living it in full. We should turn to the muse, and not to our reasoning powers, to know what that life, that soul, that self is, the self the Upaniṣad calls the breath-self.

In Xanadu did Kubla Khan
A stately pleasure-dome decree:
Where Alph, the sacred river, ran
Through caverns measureless to man
    Down to a sunless sea.

So twice five miles of fertile ground
With walls and towers were girdled round:
And there were gardens bright with sinuous rills,
Where blossomed many an incense-bearing tree;
And here were forests ancient as the hills,
Enfolding sunny spots of greenery.

The lines belong to S.T. Coleridge's *Kubla Khan*, which Coleridge calls a fragment but which, on analysis, shows itself, in every way, a complete poem. An eastern king, Kubla Khan, a despot, commands a pleasure dome to be built at a spot where the river of life flows. The name of the sacred river is Alph, the reminder of the first letter of the alphabet, Persian, Arabic and Greek. There is something of the look of the primordial, of the first, of the beginning about life. What precedes the sacred river has being and reality but reality, as the poem will unfold, so eerie and forbidding and fearful that man would equate the beginning with the beginning of life itself. As the first letter of the alphabet symbolises the beginning of intelligibility and communicativeness to man, so the beginning of life seems to him the beginning of being itself. So at least would man believe.

This is what Kubla Khan believes with regard to the sacred river, denying it its mystery and the turmoil it caused when it burst out into the open. The river passes 'Through caverns measureless to man' into a 'sunless sea'—into death. The measureless caverns should warn man against reducing life to the measurable but the name the river carries would induce man to measure it, determinate it and its nature, and when that has been done, to regulate it. The river that runs through caverns measureless to man is made to pass, through the decree of a despot, through measured distance, 'twice five miles', mastered space—

'with walls and towers girdled round', chosen landscape—'fertile ground'—and is subjected to manipulative engineering to render the space beautiful, in tune with the aesthetic sense of man. The wild, however, remains to encircle this paradise and threaten it with extinction. Man's attempt to make earth habitable and beautiful is not very successful, '. . . forest ancient as the hills' continue to enfold 'sunny spots of greenery'.

That is the way of men: to control and tame and make their world less forbidding, the place through which their life flows, life as Alph, life as what they understand of it. Beneath the intelligible layers, however, lurk dangerous dimensions:

> But oh! that deep romantic chasm which slanted
> Down the green hill athwart a cedar cover!
> A savage place! as holy and enchanted
> As e'er beneath a waning moon was haunted
> By woman wailing for her demon-lover!
> And from this chasm, with ceaseless turmoil seething
> As if this earth in fast thick pants were breathing,
> A mighty fountain momently was forced:

The source from which the river originates is a 'savage place', also 'holy and enchanted'. It is a place of deprivation, of inconsolable despair. It speaks of man's aspiration for the unattainable, 'the demon lover'. The demon lover has deserted the woman he loved, making her distraught with the anguish of separation. Meanwhile, time, the waning moon, is wasting her away but nothing will make her forget the demon, her world turning savage and fearful without him. Such is the fate of man, that born deprivation and disinheritance. What he has lost he cannot recover, yet he cannot forget the loss, the disinheritance. To live this deprivation is well nigh impossible for man, for the pain is unbearable and the savagery of the place inhuman: 'Huge fragments vaulted like rebounding hail' where the fountain 'was forced' or like 'chaffy grain beneath the thresher's flail'.

The moment of realisation, realisation of our loss, is an unbearable moment for most of us. We would rather forget our lost paradise and try to convert our poor world into a sort of another paradise in the fashion of Kubla Khan. But the strategy would not work, for life would run only a short while, 'twice five miles' through the environs of the pleasure dome, to sink finally 'into a lifeless ocean'. In this process of destruction, civilisations themselves make their contributions, they themselves destroy their achievements through decadence, through wars, through sheer weariness. 'Ancestral voices prophesying war' highlights the suicidal strain in every civilisation, the projector of ideals. Man creates civilisation to forget his loss but civilisations themselves would make him remember it when they turn self-destructive.

The shadow of the dome of pleasure
Floated midway on the waves;
Where was heard the mingled measure
From the fountain and the caves.
It was a miracle of rare device,
A sunny pleasure-dome with caves of ice!

The river of life is a birth–life–death trivalence. Life a ten mile affair, birth mysterious and fearful and death dark and unknown. Yet in this little life, man would create a pleasure dome, a device that will ring with the voice from the fountain and from the caves, from the domains of birth and of death. What we term knowledge, arts and science are no doubt miracles of rare device, for they embody in them the irreconciliables, the polar opposites, especially the primal opposites of life and death. We dream of heaven where the divide will be healed, we create history to reach a goal, a land we have promised to ourselves, we create works of art to embody those polarities, the reality and the dream, me and my other and life and death. Sometimes we dream of man as more than a mortal, a cosmotheandric being like Achilles. But all these devices, rare and miraculous though they be, are brittle like Kubla's dome and speak of a civilisations's decadence, not its strength. We know the dome is a *pleasure* dome, not the product of a vision but of a 'decree'. Philosophies and visions that would reconcile life and death *consciously* are artificial and unreal. Our sense of their artificiality alone redeems them from superficiality. Therein precisely lies the strength of a poem like the *Iliad*; it has the insight to disown even the divine vision, the vision of man's cosmotheandric dimensions.[1]

Yet man's life is impossible without the polarity of the unattainable. It is the presence of this polarity that makes our little life meaningful and our unhappy world 'holy and enchanted'. If the unattainable fails to inspire man, man will degenerate into beast and his civilisation into wild nature, a point the Greeks understood quite lucidly with their vision of man as god–man–beast trivalence. The vision was deeply tragic, this vision of man as divided between god and beast. The vision of food self is this tragic vision, but a tragic vision redeemed by

1. Vide Vol. I, pp. 47-52.

acceptance. It is the vision of man as a willing sacrificial victim, a tragic vision with redemptive possibilities.

Kubla Khan is a poem aspiring for this vision, and what is beyond this vision: it aspires for a vision of the reconciliation of birth, life and death.

A damsel with a dulcimer
In a vision once I saw:
It was an Abyssinian maid,
And on her dulcimer she played,
Singing of Mount Abora.
Could I revive within me
Her symphony and song,
To such a deep delight 'twould win me,
That with music loud and long,
I would build that dome in air,
That sunny dome! those caves of ice!
And all who heard should see them there,
And all should cry, Beware! Beware!
His flashing eyes, his floating hair!
Weave a circle round him thrice,
And close your eyes with holy dread,
For he on honey-dew hath fed,
And drunk the milk of Paradise.

The vision, these words imply, is attainable only in a dream, not in 'actual' life. Even the pleasure-dome of Kubla Khan is shown to have been built in a dream. And therein too indirectly. For the poet did not see the dome in his dream, he only saw a quixotic Abyssinian maid singing about it. What he heard in the dream he has described in vivid details, transforming the audible into the visual through the force of his words. With all his artistic talent, the poet has not, however, been able to revive the music, the song of the maid; his song remains only a poor imitation of it. If he had really revived that song, that symphony, he would have built the dome 'in air', would have woven an etherial vision, not an earthly one as did Kubla. His dome would not have been a brittle artifice subject to ravages of time and wars, it would have been a transcendental truth, a truth which neither sight could discover nor thought.

Coleridge's insights are truly startling. Men and women cannot perceive the truth they seek, they can perceive only the speaker of truth, the inspired speaker who articulates his vision in ecstasy. The act of utterance alone guarantees the truth of what he utters, he who is an utterer without being one for himself. Such an utterer, who utters without knowing that he utters, is a person who is dead as a person, has become an inhabitant of the other world even when, to all appearances, he lives as an inhabitant of the world of mortals. He inspires a holy dread in mortals because his body embodies not the familiar man but the mysterious, the awesome, the unknown. Only he who has, like Odysseus, visited the world of the dead, can know the secret unknown to mortals that would cling to life. Only he can reconcile life and death, not men like Kubla Khan or the poet himself. Our Upaniṣad would concur with the poet on this point. It is only when man dies into breath to become breath, when he knows the secret of life and of death, when he knows how life becomes death and death life that he becomes the *yogin*, the prophet, the *deinon*, the mediator, *Agni* the glowing one. Such a man alone *lives*, lives fully because he lives death.

Śaṅkara equates 'full life' with a life spanning a hundred years. The drift of the passage does not seem to lend support to his interpretation. 'Full life' has qualitative connotations here rather than quantitative. A man who lives as breath finds enough in a single moment not to care for the length of his life.

ŚB *'Other than this self that consists of breath and within it....'* This sentence and its sequence have already been explained. Other than this breath-self is the inner self that consists of mind. Mind is the internal organ of the nature of thoughts—of volition, doubt, etc. Just as the first sheath consisted of food, so does this sheath consist of mind. It is the inner self of the self consisting of breath. Of this self, *yajus* is the head. *Yajus* is the *mantra* with no fixed number of syllables and feet and no fixed length of lines. Sayings of this kind are called *yajus*-es. *Yajus* is the head of this person because of its importance. The importance lies in its direct use in a sacrifice. When an oblation is offered, it is the *yajus* that is uttered along with *svāhā*, hail.

We may dispense with explanations of this kind and accept the symbolism of the person on the authority of the Upaniṣad itself.

Yajus is the state of mind, a mode, a process of it produced in one when one hears a *mantra* of the *Yajur Veda.* This state has, for its content, letters words and sentences of those *mantras* and the place of their articulation, the effort involved in that articulation and the sound produced and its intonation. This state is merely the thought of these, given to them. It is characterised by what the ears and other organs indicate as *yajus.* Similar is the case with *ṛg* and *sāma mantras.*

Śaṅkara's explanation is not very successful in explaining the texture of symbolism the *śruti* weaves before us. He has not succeeded in explaining the *puruṣa* symbolism of the text, though he has shown us the way how to understand the mind as the Veda. We shall, first, attend to this equation of mind with the Veda.

Obviously, the mind-self is not constituted by the mind that we know of. This mind-self manifests itself when, first, the body has been seen as what it is, food, and, secondly, when the food vision has been deepened into breath vision, the vision of life in death and death in life. In this passive openness, man becomes qualified to hear the speaking Word, to become the fit recipient of *vidyā*, wisdom, called the Veda. The first Veda is the Veda of the *yajus*-es, of the sacrificial formulas, the Veda that constitutes the head of the self consisting of mind. When the teacher utters the *mantras*, the student hears them, the fit student, not like us who would know the drift of the entire sentence, are anxious to rush to the meaning of the whole of it. He is peaceful enough to pay heed to and get absorbed in every letter, every word and every sentence. For him, the part is as important as the whole, the 'non-meaningful' letter as significant as the entire 'meaningful' text. Such a listener as attends to each and every syllable as much as to the entire sentence, becomes free from communicative and cultural contexts and situations. A desituated being, he resorts to no interpretations. And since he has already stepped out of his body as the breath self, he 'perceives' the place of articulation of each and every syllable he utters, the breathing effort he makes and the sound the articulation produces and the intonation of the utterance. Whether he hears the *mantra* or speaks it, he gets so immersed in it that he becomes the *mantra*. This is the mind-self, where thought becomes the word, the speaker *vāc*, speech, and the hearer the *śruti*, the word heard.

The self consisting of mind then is that state of being in which the word immerses into the mind and the mind into the word, a coalescence of the senses/motor organs and the mind. The food self that was transformed into the breath self, the mortal individual into *Virāj*, the Cosmic Person, now becomes *Hiraṇyagarbha*, the creator. The head of this person is the *Yajur Veda*, the Veda of sacrifice. The seven flames that burn in the head give up their consuming passions and turn into sacrificial flames, ready and willing to extinguish themselves when the dross in man has been burnt up. *Yajur Veda* is the head of this person because sacrifice is the first and foremost precondition for the transformation of the cosmic self into the creator-self. *Virāj* has the word for his anchor; when the sacrificial spirit has burnt away this anchor, when the already innocent breath becomes so innocent as to be totally deplaced, he turns into *Hiraṇyagarbha*, into the Word, the Word that is the creator.

It should be noted that only the natural man finds the world as the other. For the food self, man–world turns into sacrifice. At the level of the breath-self, man becomes *Virāj,* the divinity that is all that is. At the level of the mind-self, man–world–divinity turns into the Word the creator, the Word which to the natural man appears as the Veda. Of this person as the Word, the *Ṛg Veda* is the right side and the *Sāma Veda* the left side, the hymns of prayer the right side and the ecstatic song the left side.

To be the Word, man must pray to the unknown, must invoke and self-submit to it. No sacrifice is complete or authentic without this spirit of self-surrender to the unknown and the unknowable. Sacrifice to the known and the knowable often turns into manipulation, it is like human love which is never fully sincere and never fully authentic. Man must pay attention to the call of the beyond if he would be the Word, must feel the depth of his and the world's deprivation, the poverty of all that he knows and can know. And he must feel this with his entire being, not on its peripheries. The prayer he says to the unknown must rise into ecstasy, must kill the man who feels the deprivation and the poverty. To lift up the prayer and be the prayer is to forget the deprivation and the poverty, to turn the misery into the joy, the anguished prayer into the joyous song. The ecstasy will change him into the Word. This attainment of the Word, this becoming one with the Word some call death of the Word. There remains no distancing from the Word to know it. Man becomes the Word to become the creator of the world.

ŚB Mental repetition of *mantras* becomes a possibility when they assume the forms of states of mind. For only of these states can there possibly be mental repetition. If *mantras* remain mere external phenomena, their mental repetition will not be possible: they cannot be repeated *in* the mind because they are external to it as things like a pot are. The Vedas, however, often ask man, in the case of most sacrifices, to supplement sacrificial acts with *mantra*-meditation. [This means that turning the *mantra* into a mental state is a must for performance of many a holy act].

Objection: One could do sustained meditation on a *mantra* by repeating the memory, the thought, of its syllables.

Answer: This would amount to robbing the word *japa* of its primary, literal meaning. 'Let him repeat three times,' says the *śruti* enjoining meditation on *ṛg mantras*, 'the first verse and three times the last.' To repeat memory of the syllables of the *mantras* would mean sacrificing the primary meaning of these words which clearly call upon man to repeat the *mantras* themselves and not their memory, their thought. Therefore, what is called the *mantra* of the *Yajur Veda* is merely the self in the form of consciousness, consciousness without a beginning and without an end, but consciousness conditioned by and residing in a mental state. This would also prove the eternity of the Vedas. If the Vedas too were mere objects as are visual forms or sounds, they too would be transient as are these forms and sounds. That cannot possibly be the right thing to say about the Vedas.

> Where all the Vedas become one, that verily is the *ātman* stationed in the mind.

This *śruti* that speaks of the identity of the eternal self and *Ṛg* and other Vedas will be meaningful only if the eternity of the latter is established. The Vedic hymns too speak to the same effect:

> He who does not know the eternal syllable of the Vedas, the highest place where all the gods dwell, what will he do with the Vedas? Only they who know it sit here in peaceful assembly. (RV 1.164.39)

'Instruction' here refers to the *Brāhmaṇa* portion of the Vedas. For that is the portion that instructs mankind about their specific duties. And what Atharvāṅgirasa saw, what was revealed unto him by way of *mantras* and *brāhmaṇas,* are the tail, the support of this person. They are the support because they reveal the acts that lead to the growth and strengthening [of the body and of the mind] and to peace.

Regarding this, the sheath consisting of mind, there is this verse that reveals its nature. This sentence should be construed in accordance with the explanation given earlier.

This is an extremely terse account of the self consisting of the mind. This self is not to be equated with the mind as we ordinarily understand the term. The mind here is equated with the Vedas, the Vedas not as texts but as the state of mind they produce when one passively gives oneself up to them. This passive giving up comes to be possible when one becomes the *mantras,* becomes and lives as each and every sentence, every word, even every syllable, when one lives the sound, its intonation, even the effort of the speaker while speaking them. Mind is the spoken *mantra* lived in all its parts and facets. One has to live the hymn, the song and the prose sentence. It is relatively easier for man to participate in prayer. For prayer is existentially rooted in man. It is a cry of and from the human condition towards the cosmos, towards heaven and beyond man. But of and *from* man. Song also one can live, for song humanises heaven through its human syllable and human rhythm. It is human celebration of the negation of man, an ecstasy on his undoing. Sacrificial formulas man would equate with his duty, with commandments binding on him but coming from a source external to him. How to live the commandment is a question the pious cannot understand, not even imagine. They feel its awesome binding power but not its grace, its proximity. It is only he who has owned up to his mortality, who lives it, can feel and see the gracious mien of the commandment that calls upon man to sacrifice himself. To live as a martyr, without being conscious of one's being one, is to live the *yajus*, to change what was a sacrificial formula into sacrificial love. Thus the innocent sacrificial victim alone can be the *Yajur Veda*. The prayer can uplift man, the song bless him, but only the *yajus* can kill him into the act of sacrifice.

This person with the *yajus* for his head and the hymn and the song for his arms is sustained and nurtured by the *Atharva Veda*, the wisdom that burns. For *atharva* is derived from *athar*, fire. *Aṅgiras*, too, means the luminous, the glowing one. No man can really become the Veda the person unless and until he offers his human ontologies into the sacred fire—the transcendental principle that sustains our life, our human life, and saves us from inertness, prevents our sinking into dead matter. Even when man has become the prayer and the song and the act of sacrifice, let him remain alert and alive to the call of the beyond, let him not sink back into self-complacency. For there will be moments when the actor in him will assert himself and the singer and the man of prayer, replacing the formula of sacrifice, the song and the hymn. What shall he do then? He shall attend to the holy deeds described in the *Brāhmaṇa* portion, the trunk of the Veda the person. Let him do the holy deeds, as does the ordinary man, with care and humility. Only then will he 'formulate' the act through doing it, will recognise it as such after the deed has been done. As the genuine man of prayer will know what he said as prayer from others, as the singer will know the content of his song from others, so will the man who lives the commandment. He may also recall it from memory but the recalled commandment may not be fully dependable. A follower alone can turn him into a prophet, he who lives in his house, the *antevāsin*.

Veda as the self conditioned by the mental process:

When the sound, the intonation, the syllable, the word come to occupy the mind of man, when man becomes the *mantra*, each part of it, then the sense of the before and the after comes to cease and the *mantra* continues to repeat itself. You do not, in that state, *remember* the *mantra*, for remembering will mean that you are not the *mantra* but someone different form it: you remember it as something heard in the past. This distancing comes to end when you become the *mantra*; the latter no longer remains a thought that you could recall, it becomes you and you it. It comes to pass, this state, when you repeat, all attention, the *mantra* until the time comes when it repeats itself on its own, you flowing with this continuum serene and calm, so serene and calm that a single syllable of the *mantra* will absorb you into itself, fully absorb you into itself. That is the moment, the Upaniṣads say, of revelation, revelation of the syllable in question as the all. The syllable is the mind, the syllable attended to exclusively but spontaneously, it is the self because it reveals itself as such to the soul that selfsubmits to it. Mind one with a syllable is mind the all.

The mind as the word is, however, not the self in itself but the self conditioned by the mind, the self as *Virāj*, the Cosmic self and the self as *Hiraṇyagarbha*, the self as the creator. Interpretation of the words of the Vedas is meaningful only if it leads to self-submission to them. If an interpretation leads to other interpretations, it will not reveal the mind as the Word, the Word which is the creator of the world, the world which is the Word.

Chapter 4

1. yato vāco nirvartante, aprāpya manasā saha. ānandaṃ brahmaṇo vidvān, na vibheti kadācaneti. tasyaiṣa eva śārīra ātmā yaḥ pūrvasya. tasmād vā etasmān manomayād anyo'ntara ātmā vijñānamayas tenaiṣa pūrṇaḥ. sa vā eṣa puruṣavidha eva. tasya puruṣavidhatām anvayaṃ puruṣavidhaḥ. tasya śradhaiva śiraḥ. ṛtaṃ dakṣiṇḥ pakṣaḥ. satyam uttaraḥ pakṣaḥ. yoga ātmā. mahaḥ pucchaṃ pratiṣṭhā. tad apy eṣa śloko bhavati.

Wherefrom returns the word along with mind finding it not, knowing that, the Brahman blissful, man fears not at any time. Of the preceding one this indeed is the self with a body. Other than this self that consists of mind, and dwelling within it, is the self consisting of knowledge. With that is this replete. And like it has that too the form of a person. Like unto this form is that form. Faith is its head, the ṛta *its right side, the truth the left,* yoga *the trunk,* mahat *the tail, the support. With regard to that, this is the verse:*

ŚB 'Wherefrom returns the word along with the mind finding it not, knowing that, the Brahman blissful, man fears not at anytime'. Of that preceding one, of the sheath consisting of breath, this indeed is the self with a body dwelling within it, dwelling within the body consisting of breath. And what is it that dwells within it? This self consisting of mind. 'Other than this . . .' should be construed as before. The self other than and dwelling within the mind-self is the self consisting of knowledge.

It has already been said that the self consisting of mind is the self consisting of the Veda. Knowledge consists of that state of the intellect that has come to be certain about the meaning of the Vedas. This certitude is, of course, the trait of the internal organ. The self consisting of knowledge consists of this knowledge: it is constituted by cognitions that are determinative, cognitions that are authoritative. One undertakes holy acts of sacrifice etc. only after ascertaining their nature from knowledge arising from right sources. This fact the *śruti* will confirm in the next *mantra.*

In the man blessed with certain and determinate knowledge, arises, first of all, faith regarding the acts he is obliged to do. That faith indeed is the head of this body analogous to the head [of the preceding selves, its sheaths]. Faith is the head because it is the first among all duties, precedes them all.

Ṛta and truth have already been explained [*vide* 1.1]. Yoga, conjunction, concentration, is the self like the self—the trunk. The man who has concentration as his self has, for his limbs, faith, *ṛta* and truth, 'limbs' fit to acquire for him true knowledge. Therefore, concentration or yoga is the *ātman*, the self—the trunk—of the self consisting of knowledge. *Mahaḥ* is its tail, its support.

Mahaḥ is the principle called *mahat*, the first born. Thus does another *śruti*, the *Bṛhadāraṇyaka Upaniṣad*, tell us: 'He who knows this *mahat*, great, the adorable, the first born' (5.4.1). This principle, this Great, is the tail, the support of this person because it is his cause, his source. For the cause is the support of the effect as is the earth of trees and herbs. The principle *mahat* is the cause of all the cognitions of the intellect. For this reason, it is called the support of the self consisting of knowledge.

'With regard to that, this is the verse' should be explained as earlier. Just as there are verses to reveal the selves consisting of food, of breath and of mind, the selves this *brāhmaṇa* has explained, similarly there is a verse to reveal the self consisting of knowledge too.

The commentary is too cryptic for the modern reader and requires detailed analysis to be fully intelligible.

First of all, we have to understand what is that self or what is that sheath—for the self of one is the sheath of the other—that speech cannot find nor what is called *manas*, object-oriented consciousness. It is the self of food-self and the sheath of the mind-self, the self–sheath consisting of breath. Speech and mind can reveal the interpreted world but not the breath-self, for that is their self and, as their self, is beyond their reach. I need not mention that by mind I mean, as I have said, object-oriented consciousness and not the mind-self, the self as the Word. Of mind as object-oriented consciousness the breath self is the self but not the mind-self, the self as the Word. When I act, to come back to our explanation, I act as the body-self, when I distance myself from the body-self to contemplate it, I become breath. Breath, at that moment, remains undeterminated. There is no fear in this self because there is no other for it, no interpreted world and its uninterpreted but interpretable, so to say, horizons.

The self of the self consisting of mind, of the self as the Word, is the self consisting of knowledge. No interpretation of the Veda can be the final interpretation, for the Veda admits of endless number of interpretations as does an ordinary phenomenon. As a *noemesis* it is inexhaustible. When does one come to be certain, finally certain, about its meaning? When our knowledge, one could answer, itself becomes its means. All interpretative knowledge depends on means, means like perception, inference, observation, etc. As long as knowledge of the Vedas depends on these means, it remains uncertain, falsifiable, open to doubt and question. It is only when I becomes the Vedic word that I come to know it, really and truly. The Vedic Word reveals its meaning only to one who has become it, not to him who listens to it, analyses it, interprets it. Knowledge of the Veda is thus self-revelatory. It manifests itself, to adapt the Upaniṣadic language, through itself and to itself. This seeming mysticism is a simple revelation to the innocent self-submissive soul.

Of this person, the person as knowledge, faith is the head, faith in what is to be done. What does one do when one becomes the knowledge that reveals itself by itself? Śaṅkara seems to suggest ritualistic piety as the result of faith. Faith, however, has many levels. For him who has heard the final 'interpretation' of the Veda from a seer, for him who does not have the direct knowledge born out of itself, faith will merely mean faith in the commandments of the Vedas. But he who has become the commandment has only one duty to do: to remain the commandment. If he slides back into the lower state of being, the state in which he becomes conscious of the commandment, then his duty will be to do the participatory acts. His authoritative knowledge will result in piety. But, if he has become the knowledge that is final, then what kind of duty does he have?

He who has become the commandment will obey it without the knowledge that he obeys it. The ego of the doer will be dead in him, the true prophet. Men of the world become self-righteous when they try to be righteous. Not those who perceive themselves as food: their piety is born out of their sense of shared tragedy, not out of narcissistic self-esteem. Those who have become the Word will do righteous deeds out of compassion—when, that is to say, they step out of their blissful oblivion. To neither will knowledge as certainty be vouchsafed, only to one who has become the commandment will it be vouchsafed. To him alone the Word will reveal itself as all, as all the gods, all the possibilities of things. When this knowledge dawns on men, when earth, interspace and heaven come to reside in a single syllable, then all interpretations will cease and all pursuits. This does not, however, mean that this state could never slide back to its sheaths, one after the other. The temptations of self-celebration are there to ensure the fall, especially the temptation to denigrate all propositional knowledge. This denigration will mean self-assertion and that will mean fall from certain knowledge to uncertain knowledge, from revelation to thought. This he should avoid through faith in the redemptive power of the vision of all in each, of all in one syllable. Let him not degrade his vision into propositional knowledge. Let him remember that denigration of propositional knowledge itself is propositional knowledge.

Faith indeed is the head of this person. He must resort to it, remain anchored to it. For the *śruti* is his guide even at this state. *Ṛta* the commentator takes for the law, the sense of right planted in one's mind regarding one's duty in accord with the teachings of scriptures. That law, the clear and doubt-free sense of right, is the gift of the wind god to man. We saw, in our discussion of the *ṛta* at 1.1, how it is closely related to the yogic practice. It is when man rises above food and sex, earth and water, and becomes the wind-god that he comes to know for certain what *ṛta* is, that transcendental thrust that keeps the world moving towards. . . . I cannot add 'towards its goal' because the goal is not far away, it is here as well as there. To know *ṛta* means to see the goal at every step, in every moment, in every state. It is to live in utmost peace, to live certain that all one needs will be found here and now. For the man of the world, *ṛta* is the stern law of the world, forbidding, external, abstract. For the seer of the food-self, it is the law of mortality, for the breath-self it is the vision of life in death and death in life, for the mind-self *ṛta* transforms itself into a vision of coalescence of the word and reality.

If perchance one cannot stay long in this vision and the fever of thoughts and the noise of the senses come to inflict one, then let one, the Upaniṣad instructs, accept this lapse with humility and still respect the word. Let one respect it, in that state of lapse, in the form of truthfulness. When, that is to say, submission to the word becomes impossible, let man submit to others through truthfulness. Through this faith in others will he sustain himself as knowledge.

Truthful speech is sacred speech. For the truthful word is the sanctified word, something you honour, respect and worship. A truthful man never insults speech by reducing it into an instrument. It commands him, holds his life and death in its power. To such a man *vāc* reveals its truth, truth which is beyond the reach of the *vāc* fallen into an instrument. Our knowledge is ignorance because here *vāc* has fallen into degradation and we, who degrade it, into death. Truthfulness redeems speech from this slavery and us from our death.

Faith, *ṛta* and truthfulness lead man to concentration, concentration on a single object. That single object becomes, for such a man, the reality. When man can stay thus on one object, he is not then far away from the revelation of the truth, the reality of the object. That reality will be *Vaiśvānara*, cosmotheandric being. Such a man will see in the object all the world and all the gods. That will be *jñāna*, knowledge 'certain' and 'definite.'

The tail, the support, of this person will be *mahat*, the great. Śaṅkara refers to *Bṛhadāraṇyaka Upaniṣad* for an explanation of *mahat*. The passage in question (5.4.1) equates *mahat* with *Prajāpati* whom the preceding passage (5.3.1) equates with *hṛdaya* (heart). *Hṛdaya,* the passage explains, consists of three syllables: *hṛ,* to bring, *da* (from *dā*), to give and *ya* to go (from the root *in*). When the senses and the organs do not enjoy their objects but bring them, offer them to *hṛdaya,* when, likewise, they give away, sacrifice, their powers, powers to cognise and to do, to *hṛdaya,* then will man go to heaven. The imagery unmistakably points towards the yogic practice. When man gives up his desires and passions and also his cognitions and doership, then does he become the serene witness of breath, that which is brought to him—the incoming breath—and that which he is made to give—the outgoing breath. This serene witness of the two currents of breath falls asleep to his body, the moment their motion comes to a standstill. This being without breath is *Hiraṇyagarbha* or *Prajāpati,* this *hṛdaya,* this still point of the process of breath. That point is the source of the world and of the subjectivity bearing witness to that world.

Before this knowledge as certainty comes to rise in man, before, that is to say, he knows the meaning of the word by becoming the word, or a thing by becoming the thing, there is a tentative certainty available to him, certainty in the form of faith. To have this tentative certainty, he has to study the Vedas by the valid means of knowledge. This study has to be supplemented by faith—in the Veda as well as in the teacher. This tentative certainty cannot, however, reveal the truth about things; it can only lead man to participatory acts. These participatory acts, however, will turn him into an openness in which the Vedic Word will come to dwell in him to reveal itself. Those who are born as such openness need not do the participatory acts; they will be possessed by the Word the moment they hear it.

Chapter 5

1. vijñānaṃ yajñaṃ tanute. karmāṇi tanute'pi ca.
vijñānaṃ devāḥ sarve. brahma jyeṣṭham upāsate.
vijñānaṃ brahma ced veda. tasmāc cen na
pramādyati. śarīre pāpmano hitvā. sarvān kāmān
samaśnuta iti. tasyaiṣa eva śārīra ātmā yaḥ
pūrvasya. tasmād vā etasmād vijñānamayād
anyo'antara ātmānandamayaḥ. tenaiṣa pūrṇaḥ.
sa vā eṣa puruṣavidha eva. tasya puruṣavidhatām
anvyaṃ puruṣavidhaḥ. tasya priyam eva śiraḥ.
modo dakṣiṇaḥ pakṣaḥ. pramoda uttaraḥ pakṣaḥ.
ānanda ātmā. brahma pucchaṃ pratiṣṭhā. tad
apy eṣa śloko bhavati.

Knowledge spreads out the sacrifice and also the deeds holy. knowledge worship all the gods, knowledge the Brahman eldest. If a man knows Brahman as knowledge and is not neglectful of it, verily in the body will he leave all his sins behind, attaining all that he could desire. Of the preceding ātman *is this the* śārīra ātman, *of that self is this the self emnodied.*

Verily, other than and within the self consisting of knowledge is the self consisting of bliss. By that one is replete this one. This, verily, has the form of a person. As this one has the form of a person, the other one too has the form of a person. Joy verily is his head, delight his right side, rapture the left side and bliss his self. Brahman is the tail, the support. As to that, there is this verse:

ŚB Knowledge spreads out the sacrifice. A man endowed with knowledge alone performs it with faith, with the spirit of self-submission to the law and with truthfulness. For this reason, the *śruti* attributes performance of the sacrifice to knowledge. Holy acts too does it spread out. Since all that is, is the doing of knowledge, therefore right it is to equate the self made of knowledge with Brahman. All the gods, Indra and others, worship knowledge as Brahman the eldest. *The eldest* because it is the first born or because it is the precondition of every act. Worship here connotes meditation through self-identification. Gods worship it identifying themselves with Brahman consisting of knowledge. Glorious and full of knowledge do they become through this worship of Brahman the *mahat*, of *Hiraṇyagarbha.*

If a man knows Brahman as knowledge, he will leave behind all his sins in the body and attain all that he could desire. Mere knowledge of that Brahman is not, however, enough. He should also not be heedless towards it. This neglect becomes a possibility when one thinks of external not-selves as the self. This thought would make man fall from the thought of his being one with Brahman consisting of knowledge. To ward off this possibility, the text warns man not to be heedless towards this state of being wherein he finds himself one with Brahman as knowledge. Let him dwell as one with Brahman as knowledge. Let him not fall back into the states of being where he will find for his self the food and other sheaths.

If he thus remains one with knowledge-self, what will happen to him? He will leave behind his sins in the body. All sins are the result of 'I am the body'-thought. This body-ego decays and dies when one becomes one with the knowledge-Brahman. With the decay of the cause, the effect, the sins, too will decay. No shadow can remain once the umbrella has been folded. The man who has become one with knowledge-Brahman will this way leave behind all his sins in the body, that breeding ground of all sins when man comes to identify himself with it, when he turns into the body-ego. With knowledge-Brahman as his self, man attains, with all his sins gone, all desirables, enjoys them in full. For it is there, in the knowledge-self, that these obtain.

Of the preceding self consisting of mind is this the self embodied, dwelling in the body consisting of mind—this self that consists of knowledge. '. . . other than and within the self. . .' has already been explained. The word *ānandamaya*, consisting of bliss, refers to the conditioned self, not to the real self. The suffix *maya* (consisting of) would support this interpretation. And so will the context, which is concerned, we know, with material conditioned selves like the food-self. The bliss-self is one of them. The suffix *maya* [to dwell a little on the formation of the word *ānanda-maya*] suggests modification. Thus *ānandamaya* means one that is a modification of, composed of, bliss as *annamaya* means one that is a modification of, made of, food. Thus the self consisting of bliss should be understood as the self conditioned.

That the bliss-self is the conditioned self is also borne out by the fact that the *Taittirīya Upaniṣad* will speak of it in terms of attaining it (2.8). One can attain only to the conditioned self, which is, in every truth, the not-self. One hears the Vedas speak of the attainment of the self made of bliss in the same vein as one would speak of the attainment of the self made of food. As to the real self, its attainment is out of question. Neither the present context will countenance its possibility nor will the nature of the real self. The self cannot possibly attain itself, there being no division in the self to make its attainment possible. Brahman, let it not be forgotten, is nothing else than the very self of one who would attain it.

Moreover, the symbolism of the person cannot apply to the real, nonconditioned self. The Upaniṣad has already described the nature of this self. It is the cause of the ether of space and other elements and is not an effect among effects that one could think of it in terms of being composed of limbs like the head etc. The Upaniṣads explicitly deny distinctive attributes in the self to rule out the application of the symbolism in question to it. To quote just a few lines from them: 'When man finds in this invisible, this selfless, this inexpressible and nestless the state fearless . . .'(TaiU 2.7.1); 'Neither gross nor atomic' (BṛU 3.8.8); 'The self has been described as "Not this, not this"' (BṛU 3.9.26).

Moreover, the *mantra* the Upaniṣad will presently quote will have no relevance if the self made of bliss is equated with the real self. The *mantra* in question will say: Untruth shall he become who knows Brahman as untruth. Now, there is no possibility of one imagining the bliss-self as nonexistent. This self is perceived directly as composed of limbs like head and others—joy for its head, delight and rapture for its arms and so on. It is only the real self that people imagine as nonexistent. Besides, the Upaniṣad [to set all doubts at rest] describes Brahman as the tail, the support of the bliss-self—i.e. describes it as other than the bliss-self. Now this description would make no sense if the bliss-self were the unconditioned self. The *ānandamaya,* the self consisting of bliss, thus falls in the category of effects, it is not the self supreme.

Bliss is the fruit of holy acts and meditation. The bliss-self is made of that bliss, is a modification of it. It is, as the *śruti* would say, interior to the self made of knowledge, the self that brings about sacrifices and holy deeds. The fruit of sacrifice and holy acts is meant for the enjoyer. And the enjoyer is interior to the doer. For this reason, the bliss-self is interior to all the preceding selves, its sheaths. Moreover, one resorts to meditation and holy acts for the sake of joy, delight or bliss. Joy, delight, rapture and bliss that holy deeds and meditation give rise to are proximate to the self. Hence it is perfectly in order to affirm their interiority to the knowledge-self. One has only to invoke dream experience to see how the bliss-self, forged by the impressions of joy, etc., is dependent on the knowledge-self.

The vision of the redemptive possibilities of the eater–eaten self reveals the breath-self, the self as continuous sacrifice. The self as sacrifice, as breath leads to the vision of the self as the Word. This vision culminates in *vijñāna,* knowledge free from doubt. This knowledge can only be, as we saw, innocent immersion in an object, a word, a *mantra* or in breath-current. This immersion culminates in the realisation that consciousness being one with an object, a word, etc. is itself an obstacle in the way to the realisation of the object, the word concerned, as the self. This realisation slowly makes man give up the ego of the meditator. He barely lives, enjoying and suffering whatever life may bring to him in its uncertain course. This sufferer and enjoyer is the bliss-self, interior to all the earlier sheaths, this culmination of knowledge as *yoga.* As an individual he owns up fully to his mortality, would not prefer the peace of meditation or the joy of holiness to the misery of daily life and its trivial vexations. He will move from one to the other without question, without regrets.

How can this self be the self made of bliss? Life brings to man both misery and happiness and he who accepts both will end up in living as misery and as happiness. To live as misery, one could reply, is to transcend misery. There can be no misery for a man who has the humility to become misery. Every state becomes joy and ecstasy for him, for the man who can identify himself with every state. This state is called *ānandamaya*, the state made of bliss, because pain is the 'gift' and the curse of the other and joy that of the self. Nothing can wear the face of the other for the *humility* that lives mortality and does not fight against it.

Joy is, as I have said, a state of *samatvam*, of sameness. Would it make any sense to the reader if I said that it is a state in which the eyes *hear* and the ears *see* and taste and touch and smell too lose their distinct identities and functions? When the senses feel and see the same 'thing' only then does 'man' (if it is legitimate to speak of that everything–nothing as man) come to 'know' what joy is. That alone is the state of harmony, true and genuine, this blurring of distinctions. In that blessed moment, thoughts of desire come to cease and so do determinate cognitions. The eyes do not see, the ears do not hear, the nose ceases to breathe and the tongue to taste. Sitting the body does not feel the touch of things. There remain no things, no thoughts. But how full and rich is this joy, this blind and unfeeling nothingness! Its depth, its expansiveness, its richness one can feel only when one comes out of it, out of this blind and deaf joy that can swallow all the earth and all the sky. *Ānanda* is the richness of death, the joy of being undone, the all-destructive dance of the benign god of death, of Śiva.

There is, however, the possibility of fall from this state. The possibility of fall is there because this state is only consciousness of *samatvam*, of sameness, not *samatvam* itself. And consciousness is always fragile, be it the consciousness of *samatvam*. To be liberated man must die as this ecstasy, this joy.

ŚB Of this person made of bliss the head is the joy one experiences when one sees one's son or other things one loves. This joy is compared to the head because this kind of joy is the highest joy vouchsafed to worldlings. Delight is the happy feeling one experiences when one gets the thing one loves. When this happy feeling reaches its acme, it becomes rapture. *Ānanda*, happiness in general, is the trunk of the limbs called joy, delight and rapture. It is their trunk because it permeates them all.

Ānanda, bliss, is another name for the supreme Brahman, the Absolute. It is the Absolute that expresses itself in the form of the particular state of the mind that emerges when noble deeds done in past lives present before one a son, a friend or a thing one loves and desires. At such a moment, joy emerges because the mind flows out to the object, giving up *tamas*, the tendency that would keep it frozen in inertness. The mind, in this state, becomes *prasanna*, placid and tranquil, though what brings about this placidity, namely, the son and the like, are adventitious to it. This joy or happiness people know as object-related. This state of the mind cannot, however, stay for long. For the holy deeds that bring it about are unstable and so is the joy they give rise to. This joy will, however, increase in both quantity and quality if one resorts to austerity, meditation, chastity and faith, means that destroy *tamas*, the dark force that keeps the mind narcissistically inert, and purify it of all stains. The purification frees the mind from its passions and restores its tranquillity proprotionately: as much the purification, so much the freedom and the placidity. This point the Upaniṣad itself will make (at 2.7.1) in these words: 'Of the essences is this the essence. Blissful will he become who has found this essence. For this alone makes them happy.' And so does another Upaniṣad: 'On a particle of this very bliss subsist other beings' (BṛU 4.3.32). The *Taittirīya Upaniṣad* will also tell us how bliss will increase hundredfold with every successive state of being in proportion to coming to rest of desire.

However, if one were to keep in mind the state of the realisation of the Supreme Brahman, then one would find Brahman transcending this self made of bliss of varied grades, from the lower to the higher. That Brahman about which the Upaniṣad has been speaking, which it has defined in terms of truth, knowledge and infinity, is the tail, the support of this self made of bliss. The five sheaths, from that made of food to that made of bliss, have been presented with only one end in view, *viz.*, to facilitate the realisation of that Brahman, their interiority, of all of them, the dispenser of their respective identities. That alone is the support of the self made of bliss, that Brahman the nondual, that cessation of all duality set up by *avidyā*, false knowledge. That nondual Brahman is its support because oneness is the culmination of the *ānandamaya*, of the self made of bliss, its end. That tail, that support of the *ānandamaya* does, therefore, exist, that One, that nondual Brahman, that end of duality set up by ignorance. As to this fact, here is a verse:

Bliss is the expression of Brahman, from the human bliss to the divine bliss, bliss contaminated with desire and bliss purified of it. The bliss contaminated with desire is vitiated with duality; the *other* that gives pleasure also causes pain. There is anxiety when it is there, there is pain when it is not. Bliss purified of desire too is not fully purified, it being the anchor of the last infirmity, the infirmity that would not accept the truth of death. Even disinterested contemplation is an expression of the desire to be. Bliss cannot be true bliss unless it becomes me and me it. This oneness one cannot call bliss, it would be superficial to designate it so. For that is Brahman, that oneness, that death of bliss and me.

Chapter 6

1. **asann eva sa bhavati, asad brahmeti veda cet. asti brahmeti ced veda, santam enaṃ tato vidur iti. tasyaiṣa eva śārīra ātmā yaḥ pūrvasya. athāto 'nupraśnāḥ. utāvidvān amuṃ lokaṃ pretya kaṣcana gacchatī 3. āho vidvān amuṃ lokaṃ pretya kaścit samaśnutā 3 u. so'kāmayata. bahu syāṃ prajāyeyeti. sa tapo 'tapyata. sa tapas taptvā idaṃ sarvam asṛjata yad idaṃ kiṃca. tat sṛṣṭvā tad evānuprāviśat. tad anupraviśya sac ca tyac cābhavat. niruktaṃ cāniruktaṃ ca. nilayanaṃ cānilayanaṃ ca vijñānaṃ cāvijñānaṃ ca. satyaṃ cānṛtaṃ ca satyam abhavat. yadidaṃ kiṃca. tat satyam ity ācakṣate. tad apy eṣa śloko bhavati.**

Nonbeing does he himself become who knows Brahman as nonbeing. They know him to be *who knows Brahman to be. That which is the bodily self of the former is indeed the bodily self of this.*
Now the supplementary questions:
Does anyone who does not know also go after death to the other world? Or does only he who knows attain the other world after death?
He desired, 'Would that I could be many. Let me procreate.' He concentrated with fervour. And, having concentratede, created all this, all that is. Having created it, he entered into it. And having entered it, he became that which is and that which is not, that which is said and that which is not said, that which is the base and that which is not the base, that which is knowledge and that which is nonknowledge, that which is truth and that which is falsehood. All that is here became the truth. That they call the truth. As to this, there is this verse:

ŚB If a man knows Brahman as nonbeing, as nonexistent, he himself becomes nonbeing, something nonexistent. As untruth remains unrelated to the true goal of human life, so he too remains unrelated to it. As opposed to him, if a man knows Brahman to *be*, Brahman which, though devoid of all distinctions, is yet the ground of all diversities [or thoughts] and the source of all activities—if a man knows this Brahman to *be*, then they know him too to *be*, those who know Brahman.

Why do people entertain doubts as to the existence of Brahman? Because, we reply, Brahman is beyond empirical truth. The determinating faculty, the intellect, is so saturated with the thought of the reality of empirical things, things that have their origin in speech, that it denies even the existence of what is not distinct enough for practice. Whatever it can distinguish, use or deal with (*vyavahāra*) is given the status of the real—a pot, for example; whatever it can't, is relegated to the sphere of fiction [a son of a barren woman, for example]. Since Brahman is not an object among other objects, the intellect cannot distinguish it from those other objects and cannot, consequently, render it into an object of its practice. Therefore, doubts are raised as to its existence. Hence the words of the Upaniṣad to ward off such doubts: 'They know him to *be* who knows Brahman to *be*.'

What happens to him who knows Brahman this way? Knowers of Brahman know him to be existing, know him to be attained to the absolute truth. For he has become one with Brahman, he who knows Brahman as *sat*, as being. Because of this knowledge of Brahman as being, he too becomes like Brahman itself, worthy to be known.

On the contrary, nonbeing does he become who knows Brahman as nonbeing. Such a man will find, through lack of faith, the path to truth, the path consisting of the system of castes and stages of life and other factors, as no path as it will not lead him to Brahman. Therefore do they call this man who does not believe in the existence of Brahman a man devoid of being, of righteousness. Opposed to such a man is the man who knows Brahman as being. He, through faith, apprehends rightly the path to truth, the path consisting of the system of castes and stages of life and other factors, the path that leads one to the realisation of Brahman. For this reason, good persons call this man on the right path the righteous man. The gist of this saying is: Brahman should be taken as being, as existing.

The system of castes and stages of life has been a much abused system and has evoked protests and revolts since ancient times in the form of Buddhism, Jainism, the *bhakti*[1] movement, especially its *nirguṇa*[2] current, and, of course, the social reforms and movements that arose in India before she became independent and the political upheavals after the independence. No one, no one with any sense of justice or objectivity, can deny the justice behind these protests and revolts. But mere protests and revolts do not work unless age old systems are creatively reformed. Manu and Śaṅkara have often been

1. The movement that emphasised the importance of devotion to God as against ritualistic piety as a means for self-realisation. The movement became very popular during the Muslim rule.
2. The current that emphasised devotion to the unconditioned Brahman.

criticised in recent and past times as perpetuaters of the exploitative caste system. I will not deny that many interpreters and preachers of *advaita* have made of Śaṅkara a defender of their interests. We have had occasions to review Śaṅkara's views of the duties entrusted to the members of the four castes and the high moral tone and tenor of those duties.[1] The present passage too exposes, to an extent, the hasty nature of the charges laid at his door. The phrase 'hasty nature', of course, needs some qualifications.

First of all, let us see how far Śaṅkara's position can be defended. We should not forget that *varṇas,* castes and *āśramas,* stages, together constitute the system or the path, as Śaṅkara would term it, and not merely *varṇas.* The implication is that unless men observe the conduct laid down for the stages of life, they cannot observe the rules laid down for the various castes. The system of caste will degenerate into a mean and exploitative system, if it is not redeemed by the system of *āśramas,* stages of life. The duties of members of different castes at different stages of life need not detain us here. They have been enumerated by Manu and, to an extent, by Śaṅkara.[2] The implications of this social structure should, however, be firmly kept in mind before rushing to conclusions.

The Greeks, we know, found man a being that lived among others as constituted by and constituting them. The *polis* was the ontological place, the ground of man; beyond it lay the desert, the home not of man but of beasts. The desert and the *polis* were opposites for the Greeks, for most of them with the exception of a few like the wise Sophocles.[3] The Indians, on the contrary, interiorised the forest into the *grāma,* the village or the *nagara,* the city, interiorised it so thoroughly that the capital city extended, so to say, to it. For the forest was not merely the home of birds and beasts but also of *ṛṣis,* seers. Virtually three fourths of a noble *āryan*'s life was spent in the forest—as a student, as a forest dweller and as a renunciate. The civilisation that interiorises the forest to such a degree is a civilisation that, in a sense, disowns itself; it does not find itself pitted against wild nature, rather it extends itself into that nature. The Real Man, *sat puruṣa,* lives among birds and beasts to shower his blessings; he does not inflict injury on them. It is in the midst of trees, birds and beasts that he instructs his students to live as participants of *ṛta,* the law informing the world process, and of elements, recognising in plants, birds and beasts the

1. *Vide* Volume I pp. 241-47.
2. *Manusmṛti*: Ch. 2-6, 7, 8, 9, 10. Śaṅkara at B.G.13.
3. Vide: *The Theban Plays, esp. Oedipus at Colonus.*

same life that sets his own blood and breath in motion. What the student is made to learn, the householder is made to remember and the hermit and the renunciate are expected to realise through their patience, their humility and their insight. Civilisation is thus not looked at as opposed to nature, as its controller and tamer, but as its extension, its step towards the divine through the human.

Phenomenal reality thus does not remain mere man and nature, not even man and nature and god, it becomes man-cosmos-divinity. This cosmotheandric reality set aflame the imagination of poets like Bhāsa, Kālidāsa and Bhavabhūti. Their poetry is replete with celebration of this reality. The Upaniṣadic insight, however, finds it as informed by death. As the shield of Achilles, symbolising the cosmotheandric dimension of the hero's self, could not console him when the deep sense of the tragedy of mortal life dawned on him, similarly, the sublime Vedic vision of the cosmotheandric person could not console a Naciketas, a Nārada, a Satyakāma. This vision must, the Upaniṣads warn, culminate in vision of all as the self. Man must die into cosmos and man–cosmos into the self, passing through many a stage of self-immolation.

If man does not keep this goal of self-extinction in mind, then his righteousness will turn into self-righteousness, his heroism into self-glory, his generosity into acquisitiveness, his service into servitude. Selfishness, vanity, cruelty and hypocricy breed profusely under caste system when it does not remain true to *āśrama* system. Unrest and destruction will be the inevitable lot of a society which forgets the goal and keeps up the form. Hindu society, unfortunately, has been the victim of this suicidal hypocrisy. It has retained the caste system but has forgotten the *āśramas*. It forgot that the leafy forest alone could save this participatory system and became cruel, exploitative, even brutal.

It must be said to the credit of Śaṅkara that he always keeps the *āśrama* system in mind when he speaks about the caste system. There are, however, occasions when his clear eyed vision gets blurred with prejudice. Witness what he does to the passage which describes the birth of Satyakāma in the *Chāndogya Upaniṣad*. It is difficult for him to accept that the child of a fallen woman could also be admitted into the Brahmanical order by the sage Gautama and, by implication, by the *śruti*. For the *śruti*, it is obvious, the criterion for judging whether one is a Brahmin or not lies in his life and conduct and not in his birth. In this respect, Śaṅkara is not always true to the teachings of the *śruti*.

ŚB This self dwells in the body made of knowledge, this self made of bliss. One can have no doubt regarding its existence. Of the existence of Brahman alone there can be doubt because of the fact that it has no attributes. Also because it is common to all phenomena. For the reason that Brahman's existence is open to doubt, the disciple, to whom these words have been spoken, has some supplementary questions to ask, questions arising out of what the teacher has said.

Brahman is the cause of all that is, from the ether of space to earth. As the material cause of the world, Brahman is the common constitutive principle of each and every being. Could it be that even an ignorant man can attain to Brahman after death [as *e.g.*, pots return to earth, their material cause, when they are *broken*]? Hence the question: Does anyone, who does not know, also go after death to the other world? 'The other world' connotes here the supreme self. The word *cana* in the text connotes 'also'. 'Go' connotes 'attain to'. The question should also be understood to imply the alternative : . . . or does he not go?. The student, mind it, is asking supplementary question*s*, not *a* question.

The other two questions relate to one who knows, to the wise man. If the ignorant man cannot return to Brahman after death, to the material cause he shares with others, perhaps the wise man too might share his fate. This kind of doubt may arise regarding the destiny of the wise man. Hence the question about the fate of the wise man: 'Or does only he who knows attain the other world after death?'

[Some grammatical notes:] *U*, occurring at the end of this question, should be transferred from that position and *ta* should be borrowed from *uta* occurring at the beginning of the preceding question. These two should be combined to form *uta*. The student should be assumed to commence his question with this word *uta* [to make the construction accord with the normal grammatical form]. The form *samaśnutā* should be construed as follows. The original expression is *samaśnute,* attains to. When it is followed by *u*, it assumes the form *samaśnutay u* to become *samasnutā u*—*e* becoming *ay* when followed by *u, y* being dropped and *a* lengthened into the *pluta ā 3.*

The wise man attains the other world. The other question implicit in this question is: Or does he too, like the unwise man, not attain it?

Or, it may be there are only these two questions relating to the wise man and the unwise man. The plural refers to other questions implied in the teaching. The first of such questions relate to the existence or nonexistence of Brahman arising from the words of the text: *Nonbeing does he become who knows Brahman as nonbeing. They know him to be who knows Brahman to be.* These words give rise to doubt regarding existence or nonexistence of Brahman leading, by implication, to the said first question. The impartiality of Brahman leads to the second of such questions, the question relating to its attainment or otherwise by the nonenlightened. Since, further, Brahman is equal to all, there arises the same question with regard to the enlightened as to the unenlightened: Does he, or does he not, attain it? This could be the third supplementary question.

The text to follow will answer these questions. First, it takes up the question regarding the existence or nonexistence of Brahman. The Upaniṣad, we know, spoke of Brahman as truth, knowledge and infinity. Now, what does the term *truth* precisely mean? The Upaniṣad implicitly answers this question by affirming the existence of Brahman. By affirming its existence, it affirms Brahman's truth. Truth and existence are thus one for the *śruti*, as another text will affirm: Existence alone is truth (*vide* ChU 6.2.2). Thus once one has affirmed the existence of Brahman, one has affirmed its truth too. If one wants confirmation of this equation from the text, one has only to pay heed to its words and the drift of their meaning. 'That they call the truth' (2.6.1); '... if this ether of space, this bliss, were not there' (2.7.1) amply support the equation.

Doubts, however, arise regarding the existence of Brahman. And for good reasons. Whatever exists is an object of perception: it is perceived as a distinct entity, *e. g.*, a pot. That which is not, is also not perceived, *e.g.*, the horns of a hare. Brahman, too, is not an object of perception. Therefore, for the reason one cannot perceive it as a distinct object, it is, one may say, nonexistent.

This reasoning is, we reply, not applicable to Brahman. Brahman as the cause of all that is, from the ether of space to earth, cannot be called nonexistent. In view of the fact that we can perceive all that has evolved out of Brahman, all that has come to be from the ether of space downwards, we cannot possibly question the existence of Brahman, their cause. The experience of the world shows that from which something has arisen is something real, something existent. If the pot exists, then clay must, if the plant, then the seed. Since the phenomena of the world have arisen from Brahman, therefore Brahman cannot but exist; their being is a testimony to its being.

From the nonexistent no effect can be born. No one has ever seen an effect being born out of a cause that was never there. If effects like names and forms had been born from a nonexistent source, they would have been without distinct identities and would not have been perceived as names and forms. But the fact of the matter is that they are perceived. Therefore, Brahman, the dispenser of their identities, cannot but exist, cannot but be real. If phenomena sprung from a nonexistent cause could at all be perceived, then they would be perceived as informed by nonbeing. But they are not perceived as so informed. In view of this fact, the existence of Brahman cannot be questioned. 'How can,' asks another *śruti* text, 'that which is can come to be born out of that which is not' (ChU 6.2.2)? The logical impossibility of the existent being born out of the nonexistent is highlighted by this text. Therefore, the only position that one can sustain with reason is the one that admits of the existence of Brahman.

Objection: If that is the case, if Brahman is a cause like other causes, like, *e.g.*, clay and seed, then it too will be, like them, insentient [the insentient cause of the insentient world].

Answer: No, for the *śruti* speaks of him as desirous of creation. One with desire is not considered nonconscious in the world. That Brahman is all-knowing we

have already said. And as all-knowing, he can well be desiring.
Objection: A desiring Brahman is like you and me, frustrated and unfulfilled.
Answer: No, his desires do not enslave him as they do creatures of the world, creatures who are made to act under the compulsive force of desire and other defects. Brahman acts freely, not under the influence of desire. What kind of desires does he have? Of the nature of truth and knowledge. And pure because they are one with him. They do not, for this reason, compel him to act. Rather he impels them so that creatures of the world may reap the rewards of their deeds. Brahman thus is free of desire even when desiring. He has no desire to fulfil, that ever-fulfilled.

For a contemporary reader, the drift of the argument may appear an odd mixture of 'philosophical stuff' and 'theological speculation'. That perception is always of the distinct particular, implying differentiation and identification, he may readily concede. But a percept is not merely an individual among other individuals of the same and other classes but is also a pre-absence duality. This fact makes one, as I argued in Volume II[1], seek its ontology in its cause and its effect, in what constitutes it and what it constitutes. Our theoretico-practical disposition towards the percept never allows it to become a presence. We can feel the presence of an object only when we discard this disposition. When the object becomes a presence, only then it turns into Brahman.

A distinct entity is the ontological correlate of our theoretico-practical disposition. Brahman as presence cannot fit in the chain of cause and effect as do the phenomena revealed to this disposition. It does not meet the criterion of truth possible for the disposition in question. Presence is truth itself; it does not need a criterion to be judged as such because it needs no percipient to be perceived as such. Presence reveals itself when man sheds his theoretico-practical disposition, when, that is to say, he sheds himself.

There is the desire of Brahman to consider, an awesome myth. We creatures of desire and of action find the world attuned, to an extent, to our needs, our desires and our actions. This other will not become our slave but it consents to respond, to a point, to our efforts, theoretical as well as practical. We are indeed not its masters but we are undoubtedly its children. Its sky is our sky, its air our air, its waters our waters and its earth our earth. They compose us, uphold us, destroy us. We share in the stuff the world is made of as much as other phenomena, in fact more than those phenomena. And we partake of

1. pp. 197-201; see also Index (Vol. II): 'cause' and 'effect'.

its cause too as much as the world, our common ontological disinheritance being such that we cannot do and cannot be without that cause. So we have to assume creation as a fact, as a truth. The beginningless world is not what we seek and need, our need is the plenitude of being, its abundance, its, to use the Vedic word, fullness (*pūrṇatva*). The Absolute has to be assumed as the material cause of the world. We feel and find ourselves real, that is, existent, our world too as real. To talk of me and of the world as nonexistent is to talk in contradictions. And since I exist and the world exists, its creator too, I have to believe, exists. He creates us and, for us, the world, the place where we can live as creatures of desire and action, the home where we can never feel at home. We do not feel at home in the world because we as 'placed' beings, as *Daseins*, do not come fully to be and neither does our world. Yet we cannot say that I am not nor can I say that the world is not. There is, however, something lacking in our reality and of the world, our being is always on probation as it were. The lack in us, our ontological poverty, speaks of the fullness we seek. Our life, it is true, is a seeking, it is not a fulfilment, but it is also a promise of fulfilment. This is the advaitic position. Those who dismiss *advaita* as a philosophy that denies all reality to the world are hopelessly confused or misinformed about it. Man has only to open himself to the moment before him to find it full, *pūrṇa*.

To dwell a little on the desire of Brahman; his desire is for knowledge and for truth. His knowledge is not different from him nor is his truth. To be other than, to be alienated from, their knowledge and their truth is the lot of mortals, not of their goal, the immortal Brahman. When does one find that goal wherein one's knowledge turns into one's self and one's truth? When one abides in the object before one, dwells in it as one with it. This abiding, this dwelling in the object frees the object from the chain of cause and effect and their observer from the sense of before and after, from imperfection, from mortality. It turns the object, the knower and knowledge into one moment, the moment they call Brahman. Since we find ourselves creatures and not, truly speaking, *beings*—for we never really come to *be*—Brahman remains our creator for us, our perpetual creator. But [for him] we are his being, his truth, his *ātman*, his self. We who are prisoners of doership and concepts find it hard to imagine Brahman this way, the creator that is creation, the knower that is knowledge, the moment that is eternal. But if we try to live our time and our space, we may become knowledge, knowledge that is truth and truth that is infinity. Our only hope is that Brahman, our being, ever impels us to have this knowledge, this abiding in the object. We feel that impelling force in our pain, in our tragedies, in our mortality. To live the pain and the agony, to be the pain and the agony is our redemption, our *mokṣa*, our liberation. To seek to find meaning in our pain, to look beyond it, is to be bound, is to move from death to death.

Our Brahman, the Absolute that is *our* ontological need, has to be a desiring Absolute. He has to be a creator because we are creatures. The redeeming thing about his desire is that it is not a desire for the other. We can call otherness an illusion because in certain lucid moods we do find it falling away from us, the moods we cherish as moods of release, of freedom, moods in which we do not find ourselves impelled or compelled, impelling or compelling. That state we call the state of our freedom, our release from the cruel chain of causation that constitutes our unhappy world. This Brahman, this Absolute as the Creator is, however, *our* Brahman, the Brahman we need and aspire for. What is Brahman for itself, we do not know, cannot know. We can strive to attain only this conditioned Brahman, conditioned by our state of being, we cannot think beyond him. They say, those who have died into it or him (for gender is irrelevant in his/its case), that once man gives himself up to this conditioned Brahman, when one becomes it, it turns into the Absolute Brahman.

ŚB Brahman is free also because his desires are not means-dependent. Desires of all others are other-oriented and other-dependent. These creatures have to submit to ordainers like the Law and resort to means like the body and the senses to accomplish what they desire. Their desires thus make of these creatures other-dependents. Not so the desires of Brahman. They are nothing but the self [and so are their objects]. He submits to no Law for their fulfilment nor does he resort to any means.

This fact the *śruti* states in these words: *He desired. He* refers to the *ātman* from whom originated *ākāśa,* the ether of space. *He* desired that he should be many. How could one be many without entering something else? The answer to this question is contained in: *Let me procreate,* let me be born. Brahman does not become many by becoming something else as a man may be said to become many through the birth of his children. He becomes many through the manifestation of names and forms lying unmanifest in him. When names and forms lying unmanifest in the self are made manifest, their ontological status as the *ātman* remains inviolate. And so remains as Brahman the status of time and space, the *loci* of their manifestation. In every state of their manifestation, they remain the self and their *loci,* time and space, remain Brahman. Brahman's becoming the many is only this manifestation of names and forms. In no other way can the becoming many of the partless Brahman become intelligible nor its becoming the finite. The ether of space becomes divided and delimited through adventitious factors, *e.g.*, pots and the like. Likewise is the 'division' of the self into many.

Names and forms and their existential contexts, the spatio-temporal world ever remain what they, in truth, are, the self or Brahman. They retain their status as the self or the Absolute, whether they become manifest or remain unmanifest. One should not infer from the phraseology of the commentary that names and forms are the self but time and space, the world as such, their so-called ontological place, is Brahman. For to know a name as the self is to find it as the Absolute, as the all. Thus what is called *māyā*—the sum total of names and forms—is nothing else than Brahman, creation or no creation. If, however, the manifold appearance of Brahman is taken as a fact, then names and forms have to be taken as adventitious to Brahman: it is they that make one reality appear as many. If one wishes to reconcile this apparent inconsistency, understand this paradox, one has to attend to the ether of space. I say: attend to. For the ether of space is the first mien, expression, the *pratīka* of Brahman and partakes of its nature. This mien of Brahman is one and indivisible. Yet there are jars within it that seem to divide it. One can say these jars are adventitious to the indivisible ether of space and that their division of the ether of space is not real division; it is a mere appearance of division. What is the ontology of these jars that seem to violate the inviolate infinity of the ether of space? These jars are spatialities existing within the ether of space. The moment I attend to a jar, come to dwell in it to become it, the jar turns into the Absolute, absorbing within it me and the ether of space. Brahman and *māyā* remain different when I do not attend to a name or a form, *māyā* turns into Brahman when I become a name, a single name or a single form. [For Brahman], names and forms are, ever and always, no others, they are, to use the Vedāntic terminology, the *ātman*, the self. So are his desirables, knowledge and truth. They do not divide the ontological innocence that he is from him, as they divide us, his disinherited children. His knowledge is, as I said, abiding in the object and his truth the self that abiding in the object will turn it into. No distancing from the ideal is possible for the innocent as no attainment of it is possible for creatures, as long as they remain creatures. When, however, the latter cease to be creatures, when, that is, there remain no befores and no afters for them, then these desituated beings turn into Brahman, into truth, into knowledge, into infinity.

ŚB There can be no possibility of the existence of a thing as the not-self, as something other than the self. No duration of time can distance it from the self nor extension of space. Be it subtle or disconnected or remote, be it a thing past or a thing future, it has no being of its own. In all states of their being, names and forms exist informed by Brahman. But only they derive their being from Brahman [not Brahman its from them]. Brahman is not a partaker of their nature. But think away Brahman and you think away these names and forms. For this reason, they are said to be identical with Brahman. These two conditioning adjuncts, viz., names and forms, however, render Brahman into [a] participant in empirical process consisting of names like the knower, the known and knowledge and the like and the referents of these names.

People not familiar with the Vedāntic teaching are apt to be puzzled by these words. In the preceding paragraph phenomena of the world, names and forms as they are called, were declared as one with the self. Here the emphasis is on their unreality. Conceptually speaking, names and forms are neither one with Brahman nor should they be considered as such. As experiential phenomena, experiential in the propositional sense, names and forms can reveal only their ontological poverty, not their richness. They are infirm and uncertain ontologies, not firm and certain truths. They reveal their truth as all only to the person who is impoverished of concepts and, more importantly, of desires. Only to the soul who cannot think in terms of before and after, whom a passing feeling or a small, unnoticeable thing can absorb all into itself can find names and forms as Brahman. Theoretical Vedāntins should never commit the mistake of thinking themselves as Brahman. Like most mortals, they are so remote from being that they could be called nonbeings. It is only those who know themselves as nonbeings, experience themselves as nonbeings, will find themselves as the all. Not those who conceptually assert themselves as the all. As a mortal should live as a mortal to find immortality in his mortality, so a conceptualist should live as unreality to find his reality, find his untruth as truth. This is the paradox that most religions recognise. The Upaniṣads are no exception to it.

ŚB Suffused with desire this way, he performed *tapas*, austerity. *Tapas* means, in the present context, knowledge. This we can learn from another *śruti* text, 'Whose knowledge is this *tapas*' (MuṇḍU 1.1.8). He whose desire is ever fulfilled can perform no other *tapas* than the *tapas* in the form of knowledge. So 'He performed *tapas*' can only mean that the *ātman* contemplated (*alocanā*) the process of creation of the world it was about to create.

Having performed this *tapas* of contemplation, he created this entire world prompted by and in accordance with the acts, desires, dispositions, etc. of creatures, created it as he had experienced it and as do creatures, in every state, experience it—i.e. constituted by time, space, names and forms. *All this* in the text implies that Brahman created all that is there, without exception.

And what did he do after he had created the world? He entered it, says the *śruti*. In what form did he enter the world he had created? In the form of the creator himself or some other? We should consider this question and decide which of these two alternatives will meet the requirements of reasonableness.

The suffix *ktvā* in *tat sṛṣṭvā tad evānuprāviśat*—having created it, he entered it—would suggest that it was the creator himself that entered the world.

The passage makes, one could observe, rather a strange reading. Time and space, names and forms are said to have a kind of objective reality as it were. For the creator perceives them as such and so do creatures. Yet we have been told time and again that for the creator the world is nothing else than his self. How to reconcile this apparent inconsistency? The answer is to be sought in what prompts the creator to create the world. He creates it in accordance with the deeds and dispositions of creatures of the previous world cycle. The creator becomes those creatures, each and every, and creates their world, of each and every creature. He sees it as each and every creature would see it. Therein lies his glory—to become each and every creature and partake of their ignorance and their bondage and sufferings, and yet to remain innocent of that ignorance, that bondage and that suffering.

ŚB *Objection*: This cannot possibly be the right answer. Brahman is the material cause of the world as clay is that of a jar. The world, the effect, cannot therefore be different from Brahman, the cause. The cause itself has transformed itself into the effect. How can the cause, then, enter the effect over again when the latter comes into being? This entry would make it look as if the cause were something different from its effect. Clay does not *enter* into a pot except in the sense that it gets transformed into the pot.

Pseudo Vedāntin: The self enters the world assuming a form different from its own, as clay 'enters' a pot not in its own form but in the form of dust. The *śruti* too would lend support to this view. It says: 'Having entered in the form of this living being. . .' (ChU 6.3.2).

Objection: This is not a right kind of suggestion. Lumps of clay are many; they are wholes composed of parts. They can be reduced to powder to transform them into a pot. Moreover, dust is not all-present: there are many places bereft of it to make it possible for it to 'enter' those places. [The pot is one such 'place']. But Brahman is one and sole reality. Being one, Brahman, the self of all, is not a composite whole made of parts. It has nowhere to enter. Therefore, all talk about its entry makes no sense.

Pseudo Vedāntin: How would Brahman enter the world, then? That he did enter the world should be acceptable to reason since the *śruti* speaks to that effect.

Opponent: If you would make this entry acceptable to reason, then you have to envisage Brahman as composed of parts. As a composite whole in the form of a living soul he enters names and forms as would a hand a mouth. What would you say to this suggestion?

Vadāntin: I say this suggestion makes no sense to me. Brahman could be envisaged to enter a place if there were one devoid of his presence. But there is no such place. When Brahman transforms himself into effect, he suffuses that effect of names and forms with himself. Apart from the world of names and forms, there is no other world, a world devoid of the presence of the self, which Brahman could enter in the form of *jīva*, the individual soul.

Opponent: What if that living being should enter the cause itself?

Pseudo Vedāntin: Then he will cease to be a living being as a pot will when it mingles with clay, its cause. The words of the *śruti*, 'having created it, he entered into it' would not, in any case, countenance this supposition of yours.

Opponent: Suppose I say that one effect entered into another effect? All that the text in question implies is that the individual soul, an effect, entered into name and form, another effect.

Vedāntin: This suggestion too is unsustainable because it implies a contradiction in terms. One effect, a pot, cannot enter another effect, another pot. Moreover, this suggestion is out of step with the *śruti* texts that speak of their distinction. There are texts that reaffirm this distinction between the living soul and the effect—names and forms. Your suggestion will run counter to all of them. Besides, this merger of the soul into names and forms will also imply the impossibility of its release. For that which one would be freed from, one would not merge into. A thief would not be the fetters.

Pseudo-Vedāntin: Suppose this transformation of Brahman has two forms, external and internal. Suppose that the self-same cause, Brahman, gets transformed into the body the [external] base and into the inner soul that resorts to that base?

Objection: I can't suppose this. For only that which is external to something can enter that thing. Not that which dwells internal in it. The term 'to enter' connotes the externality of the entrant. Witness the usage, *e.g.*, in: 'He built the house and entered it.'

Pseudo-Vedāntin: The entry may here mean like that of the sun into water; it may mean mere reflection.

Vedāntin: No. For Brahman is not a shape with limits set to it that one could imagine of its reflection. Only a finite shape can get reflected in some other, transparent, thing as, for example, the sun in water. But not the self. It has no shape and no limits, this all-pervasive cause of the ether of space itself. There can be no reflector to reflect the self at a place where it is not, which is distant from it. Your analogy of reflection cannot, therefore, work.

Opponent: This would rule out the possibility of entry altogether. For we can think of no other form of 'entry' to defend the text, 'He created it and entered into that very thing.' The *śruti* alone is our guide to the knowledge of things supersensuous. This statement, however, has failed to enlighten us and this despite all our efforts to interpret it. We, therefore, regret to say that since we find it devoid of all meaning, we have no option but to reject it as of no use.

Vadāntin: No, you need not rush to this conclusion, for the statement in question has a different meaning to convey than the ones you have envisaged. How out of context you talk! If you keep the context in mind, you will find that the Upaniṣad has an altogether different meaning to impart through this sentence. That meaning one should remember. 'The knower of Brahman attains to the supreme ' (2.1.1), 'Brahman is truth, knowledge and infinity' (2.1.1), 'Hidden in the heart, who knows him, in the highest heaven' (2.1.1) would reveal that it is the knowledge of Brahman that the Upaniṣad seeks to impart and that precisely is the context in question. It is for imparting that knowledge that the effects, beginning from the one consisting of the ether of space to the one consisting of food were described and it is for that very purpose that the present [chapter/topic] has been commenced. There it was revealed how different from the food self was the breath-self dwelling in it, and how the mind self dwells in the breath self and the knowledge self in the mind self. This way one was led to the secret place of the intellect, its cavity. It was there, within that cavity, that the self made of bliss was shown, the self distinct from other selves.

This self made of bliss then serves as a pointer to the self [of all], the point where the swell of bliss comes to culminate, the self that is Brahman itself, that thought-less support of all thoughts, the not-modified base of all modifications—the tail of the bliss-self to be known in the secret place, in the cavity of the intellect. It is for this purpose of realisation of Brahman in the secret place that the myth of its entry has been woven. For nowhere else can it be cognised, this being without distinct attributes. An [attributeless] entity can be known only when it comes to be related to distinctly identifiable entities, as the bodiless monster Rāhu comes to be known when, at the time of the eclipse, it comes to swallow up distinct entities, the sun and the moon. In the same way, the attributeless Brahman comes to be known in relation to the distinctly identifiable entity called the cavity of the internal organ, the intellect. That relation makes it known. Lying proximate to it, the internal organ reveals the attributeless Brahman.

Śaṅkara reiterates here his oft-repeated view that the self gets cognised in and through mental ideas. One has only to step out of them to look at them to find the self. This looking at ideas, thoughts and images should, however, be done in utter passivity. All theoretical temptations should be resisted. Let not the watcher assert that there is an observer of the flow of thoughts distinct from them. That would mean stopping at the sign and not finding the thing. This dangerous pitfall he should avoid. If he can attain to this humility, a revelatory moment may come to him, a single moment to arrest him, to undo him and itself. That moment will be the moment of realisation.

ŚB Thus does that primal cause of sky, air and fire, water and earth enter as it were the effect he has transformed himself into, enter the secret place called the intellect to appear as the seer, the hearer, the thinker, the knower—to appear thus conditioned by these forms [by the activities of the mind]. That, in every truth, is its 'entry'. And since the effect is there, its cause, Brahman, too is there. And since Brahman is there, it should be known as 'It is'.

Lodged in the intellect, Brahman as self can be experienced there as conditioned by the activities of the mind, not as it is. A conceptualist can experience it only as a kind of continuity in the midst of the diversity of thoughts succeeding each other. This continuity he may term the soul, the unity of apperception, the self and so on. This soul he finds to be so mixed up with thoughts that he cannot really identity it, isolate it from them. Mind and soul, thoughts and the self would thus appear to him as a kind of ambiguity, not identifiable existents. The soul would appear the seer, the hearer, the thinker, the knower, would appear conditioned by the activities of the mind. To assert the existence of the soul would, however, lead to many insoluble problems. This way, the way of conceptual analysis, you cannot find the self, the Upaniṣad would say. The conceptualist has to live the myth of creation of the world and the self's entry into it to find it the truth. Interpretation of the myth will be of no help in finding the self. The myth says that the primal being, Brahman, has transformed itself into the world to dwell in it; it has also transformed itself into me to dwell in me. This less than a speck, this me, is equally the all, as the world, equally a speck, is the all. I truly exceed myself as the world exceeds itself. I exceed myself because the all exists in me, the all is me and yet not me, as it is the world and yet not the world. The dweller sets limits to the dwelling, to my all-ness and the world's all-ness. I am that and yet not that, that all who dwells in me as smaller than me. For to set limits to my all-ness and the world's all-ness he has to become smaller than me and the world to dwell in me and the world. The myth thus invokes distinctions of greatness and smallness, of transcendence and immanence but only to undo them.

If I live this myth, I will live as the observer of thoughts and not as thoughts. I will not think about what and who I am because that would mean to live as thoughts. I will just be the observer, the silent, unassertive, unnamed observer, the bare witness of what as a thinking and doing being I deemed myself to be. I shall this way become the dweller within me, the witness of the act of seeing in me, of hearing and of knowing. I shall become the dweller after discarding the dwelling, my individuality, after discarding all thinking. If I retain thinking, I shall either say that I am a thinker or merely thinking. Either way I shall be talking, as Nāgārjuna and Candrakīrti would say, nonsense. For thinker and thinking would not consent to part company from each other, these unidentifiables, these absurdities would persist in nurturing and consuming each other. The truth that the myth is will not thus reveal itself to thinkers but only to those who can live as *the* dweller, bare dweller. This dweller that seems an absurdity to thought will reveal itself as the all when man can live as one with it, live as it without questioning what it is and who it is.

ŚB What did Brahman do when he had thus entered its own creation? He became that which is and that which is not, he became the formed and the not-formed. The formed and the not-formed abide in the self unnamed and unshaped. It is the self dwelling in them that manifests these. But even when they become manifest, these phenomena called 'formed' and 'not-formed' abide inseparable from the self, these spatio-temporal phenomena. For this reason, it is said that the self became these.

The commentator retains the mythical element and the mythical style of the *śruti.* The world lay in the self unnamed and unshaped and the self dwelt in the unnamed and unshaped world. It is the self in which the world abided unshaped and unnamed and which abided in that world that gave it diverse names and shapes. This act of naming and shaping did not, however, imply a fall. For the world is still the god that it was. Before this manifestation, the world lay in the god but not as fully him. As the unmanifest it was not the self, as the manifest is not the self. Yet it was not different from the self as the manifest too is not different from it. Identity and difference do not make sense when we come to talk of the truth of our being. We have to live this contradiction, the truth of our simultaneous inheritance and disinheritance. I am all and yet I am nothing. This is my truth and the truth of my god, of my creator, the truth of identity–alienation. The redemptive aspect of this tragic paradox is that it is my nothingness that makes me one with all. I have only to own it up to be one with all. That is the difference between man and god. God owns up to his nothingness, man would not. The manifest world is oriented to render me into nothingness. This tragedy of mine has a divine aspect to redeem it. The redemption lies in my realisation that it is as nothing that I can be all, more than all. Truly, one has to die into life, into godhood. If I self-submit to the process of life, the process that leads towards my death, if I own up to my mortality, I will become nothing in due course, after a long probation. I can however choose to be nothing here and now by becoming the bare witness, bereft of all thoughts and images. The path of endurance will converge eventually with the path of negation, the Buddhist way with the Upaniṣadic revelation, the path of *karman,* action, with that of *jñāna,* knowledge as the *Bhagavadgītā* would term them.

ŚB And he became the said and the unsaid. One 'says' a thing [articulates it propositionally], when one isolates a phenomenon from those belonging and not belonging to its class and places it in time and space thereby rendering it articulable as: 'This is that.' The unsaid is the opposite of the said. The said and the unsaid are only qualifiers of the formed and the unformed. As 'which is' and 'which is not' are the descriptive terms used for the perceptible and the nonperceptible, similarly are the base and the not-base. *Nilaya,* literally, net, the base, is a constitutive principle of the formed. The not-base is the defining principle of the not-formed.

'That which is not', 'the unsaid' and the 'not-base' relate to the formless as its defining principles. Despite this, they belong to the sphere of the manifest. The Vedas refer to them as post-creation occurrences. 'That which is not' is the same as the 'not-said'—like breath etc.—and, also, the 'not-base'. These qualifiers, defining principles of the unformed belong to the sphere of the manifest.

The interpreted world does not exhaust the manifest, the world manifested to us. For 'that which is not', 'the unsaid' and the 'not based' as much inform this world as 'that which is', 'the said' and 'the base'. Every thing in the world, no matter how complex the terms in which it is interpreted, has dimensions which are inexhaustibly inarticulate. The truth of the matter is that it is the inarticulate depth of phenomena that perpetuates and keeps going the act of interpretation on the part of humanity. No interpretations and no cultural dispositions behind those interpretations can, however, fully articulate those depths. A time comes when this inexhaustibility questions not merely interpretations but also their cultural assumptions. This questioning or rejection of cultural dispositions renders their replacement inevitable. This way, the 'progress of knowledge' in the view of one culture becomes a relic of the past, a curiosity for another. The inarticulate, the opaque in things ultimately brings about the decline of every civilisation. 'Forms of life', they say, are responsible for interpretations but they also, through this act of interpretation, provoke the uninterpreted dimensions to force changes in forms of life, changes that many a time assume radical proportions. Of that which, we are told, one cannot talk, one should be silent. One would like to qualify this undoubtedly sage advice with the remark that it is precisely because one cannot talk that one is compelled to talk, modifying the earlier 'truths', even replacing them. There is, however, no thing, even the most insignificant, which does not mock at our interpretations and our forms of life. Our interpreted world is only a thin layer of the uninterpreted unmanifest. If one were to take Wittgenstein's words with the seriousness they deserve (the seriousness which Wittgenstein himself, I am compelled to say, did not display), one would have to stop the act of interpreting itself. Yes, if we do want the depths to disclose themselves, we have to stop our talk. Mortals can only wait for their disclosure, they cannot superimpose their own dispositions on to them. The latter they will reject with furious vengeance.

ŚB '. . . he became . . . that which is knowledge and that which is nonknowledge, that which is truth and that which is falsehood. . . .' Knowledge here means consciousness, nonknowledge means the nonconscious, things like stones, etc. Truth here does not mean truth absolute, it means empirical truth alone. For that is the context in question. The absolute truth is nothing else than Brahman. Here the *śruti* is concerned only with things empirical. From that point of view, water will be considered a truth whereas its appearance in a mirage would not be. This truth, the truth as water, will thus be dependent on the untruth of its appearance in a mirage. Nontruth is the opposite of this truth. That absolute truth became all this. And what is that absolute truth? That the absolute truth is Brahman itself we know from the fact that the Upaniṣad started this chapter with the definition of Brahman in such terms as truth, knowledge and infinity.

Brahman 'the truth' became all that is—from that which is to that which is not, from that which is with form to that which is not formed—became all that is there without exception, all modifications, each and every. There is no name and no form which could exist without him. It is for this reason that knowers of Brahman call him truth.

The truths of our life are anchored to our untruths. Let us not be dismissive of our dreams and our illusions, our mistakes and our errors, those unmistakable testimonials of our knowledge, our insight and our truth. I wonder if man can ever accept a discovery as truth which does not have the mien of an illusion about it, a kind of eerie strangeness, an atmosphere of the unbelievable. All of our 'true' truths are miraculous truths, not the commonplace truths. Miraculous truths disclose themselves when man learns to live with the irrational without and the mad within. If he has the courage to ask the strange and threatening, 'Who are you?', he becomes a genius. If he welcomes it, invites it to possess him, he becomes a seer, a seer of Brahman.

The epithet of truth is ascribed to what is called Brahman in relation to the world. Since he became the world and since there is nothing in the world without him, he is the dispenser of truth to the world and its phenomena. For this dispensation of truth to the world he is called truth. Not that he is truth, even 'the truth absolute'. Truth and untruth belong to the world and he is the truth of both, what we term truth and what we term untruth. Our truths are desertions, even our untruths are so. They are anchored to what exceeds in them, transgresses their bounds and limits. That excess in them, their being and their life, we call truth and life. Our untruth is thus responsible for this superimposition of 'truth' onto Brahman. Even the word *brahman* is a superimposition, for this also has reference to his/its swelling into the world.

Brahman thus is the truth in and of *māyā;* it/he is not truth opposed to falsehood, a category of our thought.

ŚB [It may be recalled that] it was to settle the supplementary question regarding the existence or nonexistence of Brahman that the *śruti* commenced its account of creation with the words: 'He desired, "Would that I could be many." ' That Brahman created, in accordance with that desire, effects characterised by *is* and *is not,* being and nonbeing, effects like the ether of space and others. After creating them, he entered them to turn into diverse forms of perceiver, hearer, thinker, knower [and so on]. Thus Brahman, that cause of the ether of space and other constituent elements of the world, came to stay in the effects he had turned into and lay hidden in the supreme space within the secret place, the cavity of the heart. In that secret place can Brahman be experienced: through the distinct ideas of the intellect that shine forth, manifest themselves, there. The purport of the account thus is to make man know that Brahman *is,* that he exists.

With regard to this, with regard to what this *brāhmaṇa* says, is the following verse, the following *mantra.* As in five the preceding chapters each devoted to the revelation of each of the five sheaths—from that made of food to the one made of bliss—, so is this verse to reveal the existence of Brahman through its effect, the creation it has transformed itself into.

Chapter 7

1. **asad vā idam agra āsīt. tato vai sad ajāyata. tad ātmānaṃ svayam akuruta. tasmāt tat sukṛtam ucayata iti. yad vai tat sukṛtaṃ raso vai saḥ. rasaṃ hy evāyaṃ labdhvānandī bhavati. ko hy evānyāt kaḥ prāṇyād yad eṣa ākāśa ānando na syāt. eṣa hy evānandayāti. yadā hy evaiṣa etasminn adṛśye'nātmye 'nirukte 'nilayane 'bhayaṃ pratiṣṭhām vindate. atha so 'bhayam gato bhavati. yadā hy evaiṣa etasminn udaram antaraṃ kurute. atha tasya bhayaṃ bhavati. tattveva bhayaṃ viduṣo manvānasya. tad apy eṣa śloko bhavati.**

Untruth indeed was all this in the beginning. From that indeed was born truth. Itself did that make itself. Hence 'the well made' do they call it. That which is the well made, that verily is the essence. Blissful does he become who but finds the essence. Who indeed could breathe in and who indeed could breathe out if this bliss were not in space? This alone gives bliss, this essence. When man finds in this invisible, this selfless, this inexpressible and nestless the state fearless, then he [too] becomes fearless. But when he makes even a trite of distinction, there will be fear to smite him. Unto the man who will be wise unto himself that indeed will be his fear, that very Brahman. With regard to this, there is this verse:

ŚB *Untruth indeed was all this in the beginning.* Untruth means that which contrasts with the manifest distinctions of names and forms. It is Brahman, the nonmanifest. 'Untruth' should not be taken to mean 'nonexistence' in the absolute sense of the term. For from untruth absolute, no truth can ever be born. *This* refers to the manifest moving world constituted by names and forms. In the beginning, before creation, this world was Brahman, the referent of 'untruth'. From that untruth was born truth, that *viśeṣa*, that particular entity with diversified names and forms.

I prefer to translate *viśeṣa* as 'a particular'. For that is what the Upaniṣad takes the all to be. The all is a *this* for the Upaniṣad, a particular that encompasses the universal 'all' in it. For the inmate man, the world exceeds the bounds of *this*, but for him who has stepped out of the all and out of thought, the correlate of the all, the world comes to acquire a limit, a finitude. For he finds a peaceful void in him, a void, a depth that admits of no articulation, which is infinite because it is nothing and all–absorbing. *All* is too small in comparison with that excess of being or death of being. Or of truth. From that nothingness, that untruth, that nonbeing is born this little world, this all, this all that comes to reside in its entirety in this my body, the body turned, in that state, into nothingness. Lest conceptualists should confuse that plenitude of nothingness with the concept of 'nothingness', Śaṅkara equates it with Brahman, the Absolute. Nothingness, untruth, nonbeing—the referent of the concepts 'nothingness', 'untruth', 'nonbeing'—belongs to the interpreted world, to the world of names and forms as the commentator said at 2.6. Truth and untruth belong to our world. Characterisation of Brahman, the ultimate reality, as *brahman*, as being or nonbeing is our conceptual compulsion. The deep silence within, the peace and the void, disdains all such distinctions.

ŚB Is, then, this effect, this truth, different from that cause, that untruth as the son is from his father? No, says the *śruti*. For the referent of 'untruth' made only itself, created only itself. Therefore is it called the well-made, the self-creator. That Brahman is the creator of itself is a well received thought in the world. This is so because Brahman is the cause of all.

Since Brahman itself made all as the self of all, therefore it is holy. For this reason of its being holy this way, it is also called *kāranaṃ sukṛtam*, cause the meritorious. The world recognises that cause as *sukṛta* which bears fruit, is fruitful, and all that follows from this relationship of fruitfulness obtaining between the cause and the effect it gives rise to. Brahman could neither be recognised cause the meritorious nor the cause that creates itself if it were not cause the conscious. Since Brahman is recognised as *sukṛta*, one has to accept that Brahman *is*.

Two points emerge from this part of the commentary: (1) that Brahman as nonbeing sacrifices itself into itself, that this act of self-sacrifice alone is the holy act; (2) that this truth is universally recognised and that this recognition establishes the reality, the truth of Brahman.

Is there any truth in these claims?

Our chosen ends are other than ourselves. There is one end, only one end, which is our destiny and not our choice, the end in the form of death, the end we would avoid. Since we avoid that end, our other ends turn into ambitions and vanities, to realise which we would turn things and beings other than ourselves into means, that is to say, into victims. This way our actions turn narcissistic and destructive despite appearances to the contrary. The only noble way is the way of the mortal. Brahman died into us to be itself, to be the sacrificial deed; we have to participate in that deed to die back into life, life that is not the *other* of death.

This truth is the universal truth of all revelations. This is not our truth, of us who would turn our mortality into history and reduce all beings into victims to bring about the so-called ends of history, be they final or tentative. And since this is not our truth, we remain evil and destructive in our life, collective as well as individual. There is no logical necessity about this truth, there is only existential necessity. We who would not live as mortals will live in vain because we will die unreconciled to our death and our civilisations will fail us because they will bring ruin to us through their sustained effort to historicise our mortality. This is the truth of our destiny.

This truth, the truth of the tragedy of the clever and the truth of the redemption of the innocent, shows forth the truth, the reality, of Brahman, that home of the plenitude of nothingness, of untruth, of self-sacrifice. For that is the end of our life, our goal, the goal that changes into death the moment we would preserve ourselves against our destiny. The inevitability of death is the proof of the existence of Brahman. All holiness, all nobility, all purity lies in meek acceptance of that destiny, all evil in disowning it.

ŚB Brahman *is* because of this further reason of its being of the nature of *rasa*. That which is *sukṛta*, cause of itself or cause the meritorious, is verily *rasa*. *Rasa* is that which brings about satisfaction, causes bliss. For this reason people give the name *rasa* to things sweet or sour. When man finds this *rasa*, he feels happy. Human experience does not countenance happiness arising from untruth. There is, however, a bliss, the bliss of Brahman, which knowers of Brahman experience. Men of this sort have no external means to depend upon, cherish no desire and undertake no efforts. Yet they seem to be happy like those who have all the external joys at their command. Brahman alone is their happiness. Their happiness speaks of the reality of Brahman, its cause. As *rasa* causes happiness of the men of the world so does Brahman that of men of wisdom.

The sight of a blessed seer would perhaps provide the best proof of the existence of Brahman. No thinking can replace that proof, no reasoning, no imagination. The seer is the true testimony to the existence of Brahman. He who has come across a genuine seer can easily dispense with other aids in order to be convinced of the truth of the *untruth*.

ŚB The motion of breath and other activities too reveals that Brahman is a reality. There is a motion of breath that compels the body of man and other living beings to exhale and the motion that compels it to inhale. In the same way, the body and the sense organs are seen to do other breathing, sense and motor activities, are seen to do so as parts of an integrated whole. This integration into a whole of the diverse parts for a given purpose is not possible without consciousness, consciousness that integrates the diverse parts of the body into an integrated whole but is itself not a part of that whole. Nowhere can one find an instance of this kind of integration in the absence of consciousness.

The same point the *śruti* makes when it declares: Who indeed could breathe in and who indeed could breathe out if in space—if in the supreme space, that hidden place where resides the intellect—were not this bliss? The fact that there are breathing and other functions of the body, the senses and the motor organs, speaks for the existence of Brahman, their final cause. There is also the fact that what creatures deem happiness is also its creation. When they feel happy as a result of their good deeds, it is the supreme self that dispenses this happiness to them. But creatures in their ignorance would imagine the self, the self which is bliss itself, as finite things [and attribute the bliss of the self to those things. Nevertheless Brahman *is*, it is present in things as bliss].

Besides, there is the fearlessness of the wise and the fear of the unwise. They too proclaim that Brahman is. The wise man lives without fear because he lives with the Real as his support, the unwise man cannot give up fear because he lives with the unreal as his support.

We must take another look at the words of the Upaniṣad to make an assessment of Śaṅkara's commentary. The untruth, the Upaniṣad says, became the truth, the not-made the well-made. The well-made is the essence, the source of joy, the impeller of all life functions. None could live, none could breathe if this bliss was not there in space, in atmosphere. Creatures live to breathe in this essence, this joy.

The language of the *mantra* is loaded with bold and extraordinary paradoxes radically changing the meaning of words commonly in use. Thus 'untruth' comes to be severely qualified by 'beginning' and 'truth' by 'untruth' and *vice versa*. Similarly 'cause' and 'effect' lose their conventional sense when the cause is said to produce itself. The well made is only that where the cause 'makes' itself into effect. The effect which is different from the cause is ill made. In our state of, to use the language of the Upaniṣads, bondage, we make what is different from us, we never transform ourselves into our creation. Therefore, our creations are ill made. Sometimes, we do get a glimpse of what is this 'making' ourselves when we come to produce a work of art. The work becomes great to the extent it is genuinely mine. A poem is not an assemblage of words which I utter out of semiological compulsions but because it embodies *my* words, words which are uniquely mine. The world is well made because it embodies the self of the creator, is his self itself. There is no otherness in it to distance it from him. The world is the essence of the creator because it is well made, because it is his self. Similarly, I shall find the essence of things only when I find them not others but my very self. This essence, this self is bliss, this is life, this is breath. Where this self is not, there bliss is not, there is only misery, there is only fear. But this self is invisible, for what is visible is the other, this self is also selfless, for there is no identifiable characteristic that one could find in it. Hence it is inexpressible. It is also nestless, homeless, base-less. Only the other has a base, an existential context, not this untruth, the truth of truth. To a man who is wise unto himself, that truth changes into the world, the place of otherness, of fear. For a thinker can only think of the other, there is no self for him.

The language has an immediacy about it, it is a chant that desituates the situated being, man. The world is well made, to recall the image once again, is anchored to the not-made, to untruth; it is itself that unmade, that untruth. That is the essence of the world, the fact of its being anchored to the unmade, to the untruth. To know this is to be in bliss. The atmosphere breathes this joy and creatures of the world live to drink in this joy. To experience this joy, one has to experience the truth as untruth, to experience the world as 'well made'. An atmosphere of untruth, of not-being broods over solid things. One can experience it when one finds, in a mood of stillness, oneself and one's world melting away as it were. A still nothingness manifests itself within the body to spread out to the whole of it and the world. How peaceful is that melting out, that unmaking, how deeply joyous! In this state or mood, one readily allows oneself to be undone, for in that undoing one feels the choking other that the solid world is melt away with oneself. All turns into harmony of nothingness, life melts into death and death comes to embrace life.

This may sound 'all too positive' to some in comparison with Śaṅkara's commentary and its chilling matter of fact style, only a step this side of scholastic pedantry. I offer no apologies for the style. There is however one point that the reader should remember. Śaṅkara who is seen here so painstakingly (some may say: tediously) arguing about the existence of Brahman can, as a matter of fact does, frequently recant this kind of argument. That Brahman *is* is, Śaṅkara would say, an important truth for a *mandabuddhiḥ*, one with a dull intellect, whereas it is a triviality for the genuine seeker for whom distinctions like *is* and *is not* are unreal distinctions. Our commentator can speak with as much ease to the dull witted, can speak as them and like them, as he can speak to the disillusioned and the anguished or to the sage and serious contemplators. His pendantry, therefore, is, in a very profound sense, deeply ironical. It disowns the high browish style as much as the latter disowns it. By such chameleon like style he disowns all styles, all discourse.

This kind of style is necessary only for those who are too much given to thought, it is necessary to release them from their conceptual addictions. This is not necessary for those who can feel the presence of a benign emptiness within. It is that emptiness that lends to the world an atmosphere of dreaminess, a kind of saving unreality. One has only to plunge into that nothingness within to find bliss in the very air that one breathes, in all that one sees and hears. When that nothingness recedes and the sense of reality returns to the world, the joy, the bliss does not altogether disappear, one finds it lingering in the things around one, in the sky, the waters, the mountains, in men, birds and beasts. Even the after-trace of the void blesses with joy our dreary world.

The ebb and flow of this mood shows the source of our joy in 'nothingness'. Even our ordinary joy is rooted in nothingness. I enjoy a thing by interiorising it, through denying it, to the extent possible for enjoyment, its reality. It is in the untruth of things that our joy lies. This joy, however, is suicidal because it is not accompanied by our own unmaking. The joy that is our essence, our life and our being will not be ours until we undo ourselves, until we undo the things through undoing ourselves. It is in my untruth that my joy lies, only secondarily in the untruth of things.

ŚB How Brahman causes fearlessness to rise in man, the *śruti* now proceeds to tell us. When, the *śruti* explains, the man on the path to truth finds the state fearless in this invisible, selfless, inexpressible and nestless Brahman, then he himself also attains to that state of fearlessness. The visible, anything that can be perceived, is a deviant. To be a phenomenon, to be perceived, is the very trait of the deviant. The invisible is the nondeviating, the ever-itself. The selfless means the bodiless. Brahman is bodiless because it is invisible. And because it is bodiless, it is inexpressible. The particular alone can be expressed and the particular is a deviant. Brahman, the source of all deviants, does not deviate from itself and is, for this reason, inexpressible. And since it is of this nature, it is nestless, without a support.

'Invisible, selfless, inexpressible, nestless' thus describes Brahman as transcending all the attributes that one could associate with an effect. In that Brahman one comes to be stable without fear, comes to be one with it. The word *abhayam*, fearlessly, is used adverbially to qualify the verb *vindate*, to find.

One may also read *abhyam* as the feminine *abhyām* to qualify the noun *pratiṣṭhām*, stability. The sentence then would read: In that Brahman one finds the support fearless or the state fearless. When man comes to find that state, he will find no diversity, that cause of fear that primal ignorance has brought into being.

The passage throws up thoughts in almost enigmatic phrases. The visible, it says, is a deviation from truth, from its real being, its nature. To be visible is the very nature of a deviant. Every perceived phenomenon is a fall, a deprivation, it tells a tale of its having been something else. The visible, it says further, is a particular and a particular alone is expressible. It is not that particulars, linguistically interpreted or determined particulars, alone are ontological deprivations, universals too share the same fate. And so too names. Not only percepts belong to the sphere of *doxa* but also *eidos*, Platonic forms. Language has to redeem itself into the Word, individuals and universals into the essence called the self, in order to be themselves, in order to cease to be deviants.

The visible phenomena are deviants because they never come to be themselves. This truth was recognised by Plato. Phenomena ever remain distanced from themselves. Universals are ever themselves but they are only frozen identities, not living truths, the moment they come to be alive they cease to be themselves. That is the unhappy irony of life; to come to be at the cost of life. Phenomena never come *to be themselves*, *eidos* never *come to be*. One is only an appearance of being itself, the other is the death of itself. Our tragedy is that we cannot even choose between deprivation and death, our life and our death; our life, our deprivation, has to end in death. What Plato termed as the world of *eidos*, the world of truth, knowledge, beauty and Good was only death's kingdom. How to make it alive, how to turn our death into life is a question the founder of Western philosophy did not really attend to despite the fact that he called philosophy meditation on death. And despite the fact that his mentor, Socrates, had found the secret of life in death. How else could he request Crito to offer a cock to the god of health for restoring, at long last, his health?

The way to knowledge and freedom from fear lies not through rational contemplation, as Plato would say, but through 'untruth'. We are not to discover forms as the informing principles of things, they are not the life of things but the death of things. We are to seek life by undoing ourselves, by becoming untruth through undoing the forms that constitute our identities. When I have undone the form 'man' in me, then the forms of things around me too will be undone. When the untruth in me has swallowed up the truth of all that is, of me and of my world, only then shall my fear disappear, not before. In untruth alone the conflict between me and my world will be composed, not in mastering things nor in contemplating the linguistic universals constituting their identities. I need not dwell on the distinction between concepts and language in the present context, it has already received our attention.[1]

ŚB When man comes to be established in his own nature, he sees no other, hears no other, knows no other. The other causes fear to its other, the self cannot possibly cause fear to itself. Therefore, the self alone is the cause of fearlessness. There are knowers of Brahman who live without fear even in the presence of things which one would rather fear. Now this could not be possible if there were no Brahman to redeem creatures from their fears. Freedom from fear of the knowers of Brahman is a proof of the existence of the cause of their fearlessness, the existence, that is, of Brahman.

When does the man on the path attain to the state of fearlessness? When he does not perceive the other, does not, the *śruti* says in effect, perceive distinctions in the self. In the state of ignorance, however, one afflicted by ignorance perceives objects set up by ignorance, perceives them as one with eyes afflicted with the disease called *timir* would perceive the second moon. When he thus perceives the other and creates in the self, in this Brahman, even a trite of difference, makes even a bit of a hole in it, then fear comes to seize him. Fear thus comes to seize the [embodied] self because of the fact that it sees differences. To see difference is to be in fear, even a little of it will cause that to rise. This way for the not-knowing, the self alone causes fear in the self.

The Upaniṣad states this very fact, the fact that for the 'wise' man, who sees differences, Brahman itself becomes his fear. For such a wise man sees himself as one, a creature subject to birth and death, and Brahman as other, as God. That very Brahman perceived as the other, as God, becomes his fear, of him who but sees a trite of difference, who would not see Brahman as one and sole reality. Therefore, the wise man who does not see the self as one and without differences is not, with all his wisdom, a [truly] wise man.

One who deems himself destructible will fear the very sight of the cause of his destruction. The nondestructible alone can be the cause of destruction. If there were no nondestructible cause of destruction, there would arise no fear among the destructibles as a result of their perception of it. But the whole world lives in fear. This fear of the world shows that there is a cause of it, the indestructible cause of destruction the world fears. Expressive of this thought, there is this verse:

One proof of the existence of Brahman is the fearlessness of the seers of Brahman, the seers who see no other, whose nomenclature as 'seers'

1. Our discussion on this question lies seattered in Vols. I & II. See, however, Volume II, pp. 213-17.

is a very negation of the word 'seer'. The true seer is one who does not see, those who see are, in every truth, blind, men of the world that would confuse blindness with sight. The absence of fear in such seers shows forth the existence of Brahman, is an inarticulate though positive proof of its existence. For a thinker, who would be rigorous, this kind of thinking, the thinking that draws such inferences, is an exercise in naivety that could appeal to the faithfuls but not to one who would know and understand things in terms rational and communicative. Such 'rigorous' thinkers forget the historical roots of their own mode of thinking, they do not see the moment of the birth of rigorous philosophy. That moment is the moment of the death of Socrates which Plato describes in words so vivid and in words so immediate in appeal as to constitute an absolute literary masterpiece. Yet what the literary genius in Plato saw so lucidly, the philosopher in him could not comprehend. I may be excused if I say that Plato's philosophy is an exercise in grand misinterpretation of the vision of the artist in him, and those who would allow themselves to be guided by Plato the interpreter of that vision are, in every truth, 'partakers' of the same blindness. We obviously need a relook at the passage to justify these comments.

> Now the hour of sunset was near, for a good deal of time had passed while he was within. When he came out, he sat down with us again after his bath, but not much was said. Soon the jailor, who was the servant of the Eleven, entered and stood by him, saying:—To you, Socretes, whom I know to be the noblest and gentlest and best of all who ever came to this place, I will not impute the angry feeling of other men, who rage and swear at me, when, in obedience to the authorities, I bid them drink the poison—indeed, I am sure that you will not be angry with me; for others, as you are aware, and not I, are to blame. And so fare you well, and try to bear lightly what must needs be—you know my errand. Then bursting into tears he turned away and went out.
>
> Socrates looked at him and said: I return your good wishes, and will do as you bid. Then turning to us, he said. How charming the man is: since I have been in prison he has always been coming to see me, and at times he would talk to me, and was as good to me as could be, and now see how generously he sorrows on my account. We must do as he says, Crito; and therefore let the cup be brought, if the poison is prepared: if not, let the attendant prepare some.
>
> Yet, said Crito, the sun is still upon the hill-tops, and I know that

many a one has taken the draught late, and after the announcement has been made to him, he has eaten and drunk, and enjoyed the society of his beloved: do not hurry—there is time enough.

Socrates said: Yes, Crito, and they of whom you speak are right in so acting, for they think that they will be gainers by the delay; but I am right in not following their example, for I do not think that I should gain anything by drinking the poison a little later; I should only be ridiculous in my own eyes for sparing and saving a life which is already forfeit. Please then to do as I say, and not to refuse me.

Crito made a sign to the servant, who was standing by; and he went out, and having been absent for some time, returned with the jailer carrying the cup of poison. Socrates said: You, my good friend, who are experienced in these matters, shall give me directions how I am to proceed. The man answered: You have only to walk about until your legs are heavy, and then to lie down, and the poison will act. At the same time he handed the cup to Socrates, who in the easiest and gentlest manner, without the least fear or change of colour or feature, looking at the man with all his eyes, Echecrates, as his manner was, took the cup and said: What do you say about making a libation out of this cup to any god? May I or not? The man answered: We only prepare, Socrates, just so much as is enough. I understand, he said: but I may and must ask the gods to prosper my journey from this to the other world—even so—and so be it according to my prayer. Then raising the cup to his lips, quite readily and cheerfully he drank off the poison. And hitherto most of us had been able to control our sorrow; but now when we saw him drinking and saw too that he had finished the draught, we could no longer forbear, and in spite of myself my own tears were flowing fast; so that I covered my face and wept, not for him, but at the thought of my own calamity in having to part from such a friend. Nor was I the first; for Crito, when he found himself unable to restrain his tears, had got up, and I followed: and at that moment, Apollodorus, who had been weeping all the time, broke out in a loud and passionate cry which made cowards of us all. Socrates alone retained his calmness: What is this strange outcry? He said. I sent away the women mainly in order that they might not misbehave in this way, for I have been told that a man should die in peace. Be quiet then, and have patience. When we heard his words we were ashamed, and refrained our tears; and he walked about until, as he said, his legs began to fail, and then he lay on his back, according to directions, until the man who gave

> him the poison now and then looked at his feet and legs; and after a while he pressed his foot hard, and asked him if he could feel; and he said, No: and then his leg, and so upwards and upwards, and showed us that he was cold and stiff. And he felt them himself, and said: When the poison reaches the heart, that will be the end. He was beginning to grow cold about the groin, when he uncovered his face, for he had covered himself up, and said—they were his last words—he said: Crito, I owe a cock to Asclepsius; will you remember to pay the debt? The debt shall be paid, said Crito; is there anything else? There was no answer to this question, but in a minute or two a movement was heard, and the attendants uncovered him: his eyes were set, and Crito closed his eyes and mouth.
>
> Such was the end, Echecrates, of our friend; concerning whom I may truly say, that of all men of his time whom I have known, he was the wisest and justest and best.[1]

The decree of the Eleven is that the condemned prisoner is to die at the time of the sunset. There is the element of the inexorable and inevitable about sunset, so is about death, whether of the condemned or the noncondemned. Even when men have seen the writing on the wall, whether by an edict of the *polis* or by fate, they would not accept the verdict. They would prolong their little life and its little pleasures for a few, pathetic moments, so totally meaningless death seems to them. Not, however, for the likes of Socrates. He has had a bath before the hour fixed for his death, the hour of sunset, the ceremonial bath that women were to give his body after his death, has, in a way, performed his own funeral rites. Socrates is already dead, dead as man, has already set, the man in him, before the sun has set. [He has preponed his death as others would postpone it.] The jailer, however, does not recognise the awesome implication of the bath and treats him as he would treat a living man, though 'the noblest and gentlest and best of all who ever came to this place,' expecting a magnanimous spirit from him which he could not expect from other men. He finds his lot hard, even the hardened jailer, and weeps for him.

Dead to himself, Socrates is not dead to others and to their feelings. There is no concern left in him for himself; he can, therefore, spare all concern for others. '. . . how generously he sorrows on my account. We must do as the says, Crito . . .' embodies his response to jailer's anguish. He would take the poison to save as it were the jailer from

1. *The Phaedo*: Jowett's translation.

his pain and anguish. This is something that Crito, his friend though he be, fails to understand and asks Socrates, as he would ask any other man, to postpone his death for a few more moments as if those moments alone had meaning and not the inevitable death, the end of all who have come to be. The gentle Socrates has to remind him, almost sternly, of the ridiculousness of his request. One who could feel so deeply for the jailer has not even a passing regret to spare for himself, not even a nostalgic feeling for his long life. He almost pleads to Crito to let the cup be prepared immediately, makes him understand that he would do him a favour as it were if he conceded his request. '. . . as it were' because it is, one feels, a blasphemy to speak about such a presence in such rudely human terms.

The cup contains something holy for Socrates, something he could offer to the gods, the drink of release, the panacea, the cure of *the* malady among maladies, the malady we, the poor worldlings, miscall life. When he takes the cup from the servant, he shows neither fear like ordinary mortals nor the exaltation of the martyr, neither pain nor ecstacy. He drinks the poison as a man would drink water and follows the instructions of the servant as a patient would of a doctor. And he looks at the working of the poison with a detachment which none else present could command. Only when he knows that he has time barely enough to utter a sentence that he asks Crito to release him from his debt to Asclepsius, the god of health. At long last, the god has freed him from his seventy year old disease. The offering made, there would remain no more duty for him to do.

It is noteworthy that Plato who has seen so much in Socrates, I mean the artist in Plato, fails to realise what he has seen. In the last paragraph of the dialogue, he speaks in the vein of the jailer. As for the jailer, Socrates was 'the noblest, gentlest and best of all who ever came to this place,' for Plato, Socrates was 'the wisest, justest and best.' The jailer sought, yearned for, in Socrates's presence, nobility, gentleness and goodness, traits he lacked in view of the harsh and unfeeling nature of his profession. The philosopher sought wisdom, justice and goodness. The noble and gentle philosopher felt the need of goodness as much as the not so noble and not so gentle jailer. Socrates was their common ideal, the very embodiment of the form of the Good as it were. For neither was he 'untruth,' because neither could reconcile himself to his mortality, his death.

The personality of Socrates was undoutedly a miracle for Plato, a miracle that turned an aristocrat into a philosopher. He was an enigma for him, a *deinon* in comparison with whom the Homeric gods appear too frail and too human. The sense of wonder he felt in the presence of Socrates he perhaps best describes in the words he attributes to Crito in the dialogue bearing the latter's name for its title:

Socrates: Why have you come at this hour, Crito? It must be quite early?

Crito: Yes certainly.

Socrates: What is the exact time?

Crito: The dawn is breaking.

Socrates: I wonder that the keeper of the prison would let you in.

Crito: He knows me, because I often come, Socrates; moreover, I have done him a kindness.

Socrates: And are you only just arrived?

Crito: No, I came some time ago.

Socrates: Then why did you sit and say nothing, instead at once awakening me?

Crito: I should not have liked myself, Socrates, to be in such great trouble and unrest as you are—indeed I should not: I have been watching with amazement your peaceful slumbers; and for that reason I did not awake you, because I wished to minimize the pain. I have always thought you to be of a happy disposition; but never did I see anything like the easy, tranquil manner in which you bear this calamity.[1]

Despite his sense of the presence of the miraculous in the person of Socrates, despite his amazement at the latter's 'peaceful slumbers', Plato shows a curious inability to take in conceptually what he perceives with Crito. Notice the ease with which he humanises Socrates. He allows, with no undertone of irony, Crito to speak of his 'trouble and unrest' and of his not awakening him in order to 'minimize the pain', the pain, obviously, of Socrates. As the dialogue proceeds, Plato, it is true, makes us understand that Crito had falsely attributed trouble, unrest and pain to Socrates, that he was not the like of Crito, Plato and other mortals. Yet Socrates remains a man, does not become 'untruth' or death, neither in *Crito* nor in *Phaedo*. They did not allow, neither the friend nor the philosopher, to let the peaceful and tranquil sleeping body to speak to them. One was too anxious to help Socrates escape from the grip of the laws of Athens, the other too inquisitive to understand the enigma that he was. The body lay as a revelation, the man died as disclosure of truth but the restless humanity, well meaning and intelligent, could not catch the truth.

1. Jowett's translation.

What possible explanation could philosophy give of that miracle of peace and fearlessness that Socrates was? All mortal men, our observation reveals, fear death and love life. Socrates was a man but he neither loved life nor feared death. The only possible explanation of his fearlessness of death could be his vision of the immortality of soul. So would argue the philosopher. Plato would ignore Socrates's observation that life was a disease. He would forget that if it was a disease here it would be a disease in the other world too. This truth we mortals do not easily grasp; so blindly are we attached to life that death holds only horror for us but no meaning and no mystery. For Socrates, on the contrary, death and nonbeing hold the key to our redemption, our salvation, our release from the disease. He would not be interested in prolonging this disease birth after birth as the author of the *Phaedo* was.

For Plato, death remained an evil. He wrote the *Republic* to evolve a *polis* which would utilise the services of a Socrates rather than offer him a cup of poison. From our human point of view, Plato's horror of Athenian society was fully justified. No society that killed a Socrates could possibly retain its human face. The social thinker has almost all the points in his favour, irrespective of the soundness or otherwise of the alternatives he suggested. The work, however, shows how blind Plato was to his own insights, how he could not understand the things that the artist in him saw with a clarity truly breathless and startling.

Plato's theory of forms shows his full revulsion for untruth, nonbeing or its human expression, death. Whether forms be interpreted as metaphysical principles or logical essences, they embody Plato's—and man's—thirst for stability. Our world, our own selves are too unstable, too much of the nature of flux to be intelligible. Forms turn the flux into intelligible phenomena and selves. Only the form of the Good seems to beckon Plato on to untruth, for as the teleological principle it seems to disown all its incarnations, all of its embodiments. Those who would identify it with the plan of the universe as a whole hardly save it; for the whole of the universe is as unintelligible as its telos. You cannot perceive the whole nor conceive it, much less its plan. Whatever you can perceive or conceive has to be relational, finite and tentative, not absolute, infinite and final. The form of Good as the teleological principle disowns the world, disowns all immanence, it operates as mortality in creatures and as time in the world; it reduces our identities, our forms, into uncertainties and the forms of things into fragilities. It makes of us creatures and the world a creation, the embodiment of disinheritance. The form of Good, in one word, disowns the theory of forms as metaphysical principles or logical essences. To give it a Hegelian shape would mean not only violence against the artist in Plato, it would also mean reducing it to absurdity.

Plato, I should like to emphasise, came, to an extent, near his artistic vision of Socrates in his formulation of the form of the Good, but only to an extent. The form of Good, as a negation of phenomena, remains relational, it is not absolute untruth or nonbeing. It ever remains negation of embodiments, its expressions; beyond and above them, it has no being of its own. It is a transcendence that is immanent. It is not death that Socrates had come to be.

Plato's influence on Western philosophy speaks of the latter's insensitivity to the artist in Plato. It is only in the realm of theory of forms and social structures that his influence is pervasive. For Sophocles, the saviour of the *polis* was an outcast, Oedipus. Even the remains of his body could protect the *polis*. The real man was not the *zoon politikon* but the man who had exiled himself from the *polis*. For Plato, the philosopher who did not take part in the affairs of government was not a responsible man in the strict sense of the term. Reading of the *Republic* gives the impression as if the philosopher acquired wisdom only to serve society, society seemed to have precedence over truth. So man becomes, in a way, the measure of value. A philosopher's wisdom had no meaning outside the social context. This view has been almost an assumption for most of the influential thinkers of the West. In fact, Hegel's thought is Platonism in a modern garb and his *Geist* is the form the Good in a new dress, if the latter be interpreted as the plan of the whole of the universe. The solitary self is a fiction for the majority of Western thinkers. Man as a being-with-others, a being-for-others, a communality, a participant in creative and communicative action, a participant in language games and forms of life, a link in the historical process, whether universal or local and episodal, are some of the legacies of Plato regarding the ontology of man. His theory of forms has, of course, been most influential. But neither those who are Platonists nor anti-Platonists are alive to what Plato saw; they are, in truth, more blind to his vision than was Plato himself.

That neither Plato nor the majority of philosophers after him had the power of *tapas*, of ardent contemplation, to look into the so-called trances of Socrates, trances which most people in India would equate with the state of *samādhi*, can easily be gathered from the following description of the 'trance' from the *Symposium*.

> One morning he was thinking about something which he could not resolve; he would not give it up, but continued thinking from early dawn until noon—there he stood fixed in thought; and at

> noon attention was drawn to him, and the rumour ran through the wondering crowd that Socrates had been standing and thinking about something ever since the break of day. At last, in the evening after supper, some Ionians out of curiosity (I should explain that this was not in winter but in summer), brought out their mats and slept in the open air that they might catch him and see whether he would stand all night. There he stood until the following morning; and with the return of light he offered up a prayer to the sun, and went his way.[1]

Both Plato (it is obvious he identifies himself with the narrator, Alicibiades, in the matter) and the curious crowd assume that Socrates was thinking, 'fixed in thought'! None has the peace of mind, neither Plato nor the members of the crowd, to spare a moment for the expression (or lack of it?) that must have appeared in Socrates's face at that time, when he stood, in one posture, for the length of full twenty four hours. If they had that *schole*, that leisure, they would have understood the 'meaning' of 'the trance' better. A thinker is a restless person, his limbs, his gestures, his expressions speak more of the pain of search, the anxiety of expectations, the despair of not finding than of peace and stillness. You do not stand still for twenty four hours while thinking, that simply does not happen, cannot happen. The toil and the torture would not allow you to do so. How wide of the mark are Plato's interpretations of his own language, of his own report. He sees more than he understands, like most of us. The peace of the man, his fearlessness, his state of being lost inspire our thinker to weave theories of the immortality of the soul, they do not beckon him to be absored in that peace, that *samādhi* and its deep impersonal expression. Plato remains an onlooker, he does not become a participant in the life of his mentor, does not lose himself in the sight, that of Socrates standing all oblivious of the body and the world around him. If he had done that, he would have been usurped by the sight, by the impersonal face and figure and would have known what it means to be untruth, nonbeing. As an outside observer, he made theories, influential and thought provoking, which generation after generation of thinkers admired and debated but, alas, with no sense of their loss, not even a suspicion of it.

One may, of course, say that Śaṅkara too speaks of the Upaniṣadic revelation as an outsider. He too draws inference of the existence of Brahman from the truth of the fearlessness of a seer of Brahman. There is no invoking of that fearlessness, no presentation of it, not to speak

1. Jowett's translation.

of participation in it and losing oneself in it. Superficially speaking, this criticism is valid. But Śaṅkara knows how to disown such inferences, how to find them only tentative, mere stepping stones to the sacrifice of the ego-self, to the redemptive loss of oneself. This we do not generally find in Plato if we exclude for a moment his form of Good. The main stream of Western philosophy is not a meditation on death, it is, despite its impressive complexity, an insult to death. Meditation on death has been the prerogative of mystics, tragic artists and certain religious thinkers in the West, not, generally speaking, of the famous names in philosophy.

Meditation on death leads one to detachment from the narcissistic concerns of the ego-personality. It makes one a serene witness of one's own thoughts, desires and passions, turns one into a calm passivity, a nothingness before which thoughts 'come like shadows and so depart'. As long as one lives as the body self, the fear of death persists unabated. What we call life is, for most of us, a mere struggle against death. It was so for the majority of the people in the premodern times, it is so even now for most of them in the third world. They live a life prompted, so to say, by death. Death is the source, the sustaining principle of their miserable life. Those who live above the subsistence level, think of their ambitions, their goals, their ideals. But whatever their ambitions, their goals and ideals, they are negated by the transcendental thrust operating in them, the thrust that finds the fulfilment of every ambition a frustration, the attaining of goals a preparation for further goals, attaining to ideals a mere disillusionment. Realisation of the futility of one's efforts is almost as painful as the realisation of one's mortality. Brahman thus makes its presence felt in our life in two ways: as death for the body ego and as eternal frustration, as, that is to say, the all negating transcendental thrust for the mind ego.

Negation in the form of death and in the form of transcendental thrust, negation as Brahman the immanent principle, does not let beings remain what they are or what they come to be. Men of the world would forget this negation in their varied pursuits, even in their miseries but when pursuits and ambitions come to a naught, when one's misery appears meaningless and chillingly unredemptive, that is the moment when one feels the presence of negation most poignantly. If one can summon up the courage to pay, in such dark and inhuman moments, heed to the negation, then will one experience that death, that negation as untruth, [an] untruth, [a] nothingness without limits and without end. And experience it one will in one's body, this little, fragile, unclean and corrupt body. That is the promise that the Upaniṣads make to man. If he dives deep into that nothingness, that peace, then alone will he know, the Upaniṣads assure him, the secret true of death, of death that is the fount and inbeing of life. This nothingness the Upaniṣads term eternity for the benefit of timid mortals. For those who die into it, terms like eternity, knowledge and infinity will appear profane and useless. This the Upaniṣads themselves say recanting their own revelations.

Chapter 8

1. **bhīṣāsmād vātaḥ pavate. bhīṣodeti sūryaḥ. bhīṣāsmād agniś cendraś ca. mṛtyur dhāvati pañcama iti. saiṣānandasya mīmāṃsā bhavati. yuvā syāt sādhu yuvādhyāyaka āśiṣṭho dṛḍhiṣṭho baliṣṭhas tasyeyaṃ pṛthivī sarvā vittasya pūrṇā syāt. sa eko mānuṣa ānandaḥ. te ye śataṃ mānuṣā ānandāḥ.**

For fear of him blows the wind, for fear of him rises the sun, for fear of him runs the fire and Indra and death the fifth.
This is a consideration of bliss:
Suppose there is a young man, a good young man, learned, most agile, firm and strong, all this earth, full of wealth, his possession. He will measure one human bliss. A hundred such human blisses . . .

ŚB For fear of him blows the wind, for fear of him rises the sun and for fear of him runs the fire, Indra and death the fifth. The wind, the sun, the fire, Indra and death are great adorables, are gods themselves. Yet even they do their highly strenuous activities, do them in accordance with a certain law. They could not act in this disciplined way if there were no ruler over them. Therefore, there is a ruler over them to cause fear in them. And that ruler, that cause of fear, is Brahman. Out of fear of that Brahman do they act as a servant would out of fear of his king. That Brahman, the cause of their fear, is of the nature of bliss.

Śaṅkara's commentary does not bring out the force of the verse in question. The fear that dwells in man is not a mere psychological fear, it is anthropocosmic fear. Fear we associate with humanity, with animals, sometimes, to an extent, with plants. We do not, however, associate fear with the sun, the moon, the wind and the fire. These are inanimate phenomena for us, totally incapable of human emotions. Yet the Upaniṣads associate fear with these phenomena. They do not, however, indulge in anthropomorphism, for these phenomena are not, as they are for us, inanimate things for them, they are gods, as immortal as the world is. Their fear cannot, therefore, be like our fear. Our fear is, basically, the fear of death. This fear of mortals cannot inflict the immortal sun, the moon, the wind and the fire. The sun does not live in fear of death as I do. But he too is ever active, ever on the move, ever restless. What is it that compels the sun to be ever on the move, indeed the whole universe? There seems to be an unappeasable transcendental thrust at the heart of the universe that never lets things to be themselves, neither man nor beasts nor things inanimate nor gods. Our ontological ground, the world, is itself ungrounded. As I never come to be myself so the world too never comes to be itself. There is no identity, no essence that man would not disown, that the world would not disown. In this respect the sun is as far away from being itself as I am from being myself. A universal, all-pervasive nothingness seems to inform each and every being of the world, be it a being living or nonliving. This nothingness resides in me as my self, it resides in the sun as its self. What we call our knowledge of things, knowledge of things as distinct identities is a false knowledge. Every being will disown that knowledge, every thing will. The only truth about things is their untruth which appears death to interpreted and interpreting things but truth to those who have the daring to die into it. It does not allow the sun to be itself, it does not allow the moon to be itself, it does not allow the universe to be itself. When they cease to be themselves, they attain to truth as man becomes his self, his true self, when he ceases to be man.

ŚB There is a consideration of the bliss of Brahman, an assessment of it. What is to be considered about bliss? Whether the bliss in question springs from the contact of the subject and the object, as is the case with the bliss the people of the world experience or it is something self-existent. This is what one should consider about the nature of bliss.

The bliss experienced by the people of the world is measured in terms of the concurrence of subjective and objective means and in terms of their plentifulness. The more plentiful they are and the more in concurrence, the greater will be this bliss. This bliss is introduced here to enable one to know what that bliss called Brahman is. This familiar bliss will enable man to know the bliss that one can attain to when one's intellect has been freed from all objective orientations.

The worldly bliss is also a particle of the bliss that is Brahman. That bliss turns into worldly and ephemeral bliss when ignorance comes to cover up knowledge. When that ignorance thickens, each of creatures from Brahmā downwards finds itself endowed with a particular kind of consciousness and in contact with such means as objects. The mode of their consciousness and the contact with means is determined by their past deeds. Contemplating that bliss with this consciousness and through these means, they find it as worldly and unstable. The bliss that creatures from man to Brahmā experience is, thus, [an appearance of] the self-same bliss that the man endowed with wisdom experiences, he who knows the Vedas and is free from desire. That bliss increases hundred-fold at each place of existence from that of man-

gandharva up to that of Brahmā. It does so because at each successive place there is a corresponding thinning of *avidyā*, false knowledge, of desire and action. When the distinction between the subject and the object, the distinction set up by ignorance, comes to be eliminated by wisdom, then that bliss becomes the intrinsic bliss, bliss full on every side, and one without a second. In order to highlight this point, the *śruti* says:

Suppose there is a young man, a young man in the prime of life, not merely a young man but a good young man. There may be a young man but he may not be a good man. Equally, there may be a good man but not young. To eliminate such alternatives, the *śruti* qualifies 'a young man' with 'a good young man', the latter expression serving as it were as an adjectival phrase. The *śruti* asks us further to imagine that good young man as well versed in the Vedas, as most agile, most firm and most strong—to imagine him, in one word, as endowed with a rich personality. Let it also be supposed that all the earth is his, the earth full of wealth, full of all the means of enjoyment and profusely endowed with all the means necessary for doing all the necessary acts, secular as well as holy. Let him, in short, be a king, a master of the earth. The bliss of such a young man would count as one human bliss, as one supreme human bliss.

2. sa eko manuṣyagandharvāṇām ānandaḥ. śrotriyasya cākāmahatasya. te ye śataṃ manuṣyagandharvāṇām ānandāḥ. sa eko devagandharvāṇām ānandaḥ. śrotriyasya cākāmahatasya. te ye śataṃ devagandharvāṇām ānandāḥ. sa ekaḥ pitṝṇāṃ ciralokalokānām ānandaḥ. śrotriyasya cākāmahatasya. te ye śataṃ pitṝṇāṃ ciralokalokānām ānandāḥ. sa eka ājānajānāṃ devānām ānandaḥ.

[*A hundred such human blisses*] *are one bliss of human* gandharva. *And of the one who has heard the Word and is not smitten with desire. A hundred such blisses of human* gandharvas *are one bliss of the divine* gandharva. *And of the one who has heard the Word and is not smitten with desire.*

A hundred such blisses of divine gandharvas *are one bliss of the fathers of the long lasting worlds. And of the one who has heard the Word and is unsmitten with desire.*

A hundred such blisses of fathers dwelling in their long lasting worlds are one bliss of ājānajāḥ, *of gods born in* ājāna, *heaven. And of the one who has heard the Word and is unsmitten with desire.*

ŚB A hundred such human blisses constitute one bliss of human *gandharvas*, men, who as a result of the holy acts and meditation, attain, after their death, the status of *gandharvas*, divine singers. Their bliss is a hundredfold the bliss of man. These singers are endowed with subtle bodies and subtle senses and have the power to become invisible with the result that they have to face few obstacles and have the strength and the means to overcome the pairs of opposites that fall in their way. Virtually unopposed and, when opposed, confident of his strength, a human *gandharva* lives with his mind at peace. The peace that is so conditioned, the peace peculiar to him, manifests bliss too as so conditioned, bliss peculiar to him. Each of the successive planes of being manifests a hundredfold the bliss pertaining to the preceding one. This becomes possible because each plane is conditioned by the peace peculiar to it.

The *śruti* says that the man who has heard the Word and is unsmitten with desire obtains the bliss peculiar to each plane of being except the bliss peculiar to the human plane. Since such a man is not tortured by desire and enjoyment, his bliss cannot be called human bliss, it is hundred times as much as the human bliss and is comparable to the bliss of human *gandharvas*. It is to emphasise this fact that the *śruti* does not mention him in the context of human bliss. It may be noted that Vedic studies and sinlessness are mentioned even in the case of the human youth. These two qualities may be taken to apply to all the happy beings at varied planes of being. What is peculiar to the man of wisdom is his desirelessness. It is desirelessness that determines how rich one is and to what extent one's riches make one happy. It is for this reason that 'the man without desire' is mentioned as partaking of the bliss of every plane. He who is free from the desire peculiar to each plane will have bliss a hundredfold the bliss peculiar to it. The *śruti* shows this relationship between joy and desirelessness in order to enjoin upon man that he free himself from desire if he would attain to supreme bliss. For that alone is the way to it.

The other words have already been explained.

Divine *gandharvas* are born as such. Fathers dwell in long lasting worlds. Hence the qualifier: 'of the long lasting worlds'. *Ājāna* is the world of gods. Gods born in *ājāna* are called *ājanajāḥ*. Men who do the good deeds prescribed by traditional wisdom are born in *ājāna*.

3. śrotriyasaya cākāmahatasya. te ye śatam ājānajānāṃ devānām ānandāḥ. sa ekaḥ karmadevānāṃ devānām ānandaḥ. ye karmaṇā devān apiyanti. śrotriyasya cākāmahatasya. te ye śataṃ karmadevānāṃ devānām ānandāḥ. sa eko devānām ānandaḥ. śrotriyasya cākāmahatasya. te ye śataṃ devānām ānandāḥ. sa eka indrasyānandaḥ.

And of the one who has heard the Word and is unsmitten with desire. A hundred such blisses of the gods born in ājāna *is one bliss of the gods that are gods by acts. And of the one who has heard the Word and is not smitten with desire. A hundred such blisses of the gods that are gods by holy acts is one bliss of the gods. And of the one who has heard the Word and is not smitten with desire. A hundred such blisses of the gods is one bliss of Indra. . .*

ŚB Men who reach the status of godhood through the performance of fire worship and other holy Vedic acts—through these alone—are called gods by acts. They partake of the holy oblations and are thirtythree in number, with Indra as their lord and Bṛhaspati as their teacher.

4. śrotriyasya cākāmahatasya. te ye śatam indrasyānandāḥ sa eko bṛhaspater ānandaḥ. śrotriyasaya cākāmahatasya. te ye śataṃ bṛhaspater ānandāḥ. sa ekaḥ prajāpater ānandaḥ. śrotriyasya cākāmahatasya. te ye śataṃ prajāpater ānandāḥ. sa eko brahmaṇa ānandaḥ. śrotriyasya cākāmahatasya.

And of the one who has heard the Word and is unsmitten with desire. A hundred such blisses of Indra are one bliss of Bṛhaspati. And of the one who has heard the Word and is unsmitten with desire. A hundred such blisses of Bṛhaspati are one bliss of Prajāpati. And of one who has heard the Word and is unsmitten with desire. A hundred such blisses of Prajāpati are one bliss of Brahmā. And of one who has heard the Word and is unsmitten with desire.

ŚB Prajāpati is *Virāj,* the Cosmic Self with the three worlds—earth, interspace and heaven—as his body. Brahmā is at once all and each, pervading the *maṇḍala* of the universe. In him these blisses become one, in that Golden Germ, the dwelling place of righteousness, the cause of bliss and of consciousness that knows that bliss and desirelessness unsurpassed. This his bliss is also the bliss of one who has heard the Word, who has freed himself from sin and desire—he perceives it directly and everywhere. This should show that holy learning, freedom from sin and from desire constitute the triple means to bliss. Holy learning and freedom from sins remain constant at every plane but not desirelessness, it increases progressively at every plane of being. For this reason, they know it to be the best among the three means.

There is the bliss supreme of which the bliss of Brahmā is a mere bit, a mere particle. This we learn from another *śruti* text: 'On a bit of this very bliss live other beings' (BṛU 4. 3. 32). The hearer of the Word [alone] has a direct experience of that bliss, but only when his desirelessness reaches its acme, its perfection. As spray parts from the sea to return to it, similarly bits of joy part from that supreme bliss but only to become one with it. That supreme bliss is the bliss that resides as one with Brahman, since that bliss is the bliss nondual, the bliss that is its own enjoyer.

The Creator has heard the Vedas, so have gods and so have men. And yet they do not know the true bliss, only a semblance of it, though they know that semblance in vastly varied degrees and ways. Sinless, of course, they all are but not desire free. Even the Creator is not. This means that sinlessness and hearing change their miens, their forms at different planes of being. What is sinlessness for man is not exactly sinlessness for Brahmā, the Creator, for in his case the desire to create itself will be considered a sin. This point Śaṅkara himself makes in his commentary on *Īśa Upaniṣad* 3. So Saṅkara's words that sinlessness and hearing remain the same at every plane of being should not be taken at its face value. The 'sinless' young man will hear the Vedas from his teacher but from whom will Brahmā the Alone hear them? Will words have the same ontological status for him as they have for the 'sinless' man? And what about hearing of the seer of the nondual bliss? Words will not remain words for him nor the hearer hearer.

The man who truly hears the Word is the man who truly knows Brahman. Man becomes the true hearer when the Word speaks to him without the mediation of a speaker, human or divine. When the speaker becomes the Word, the hearer too becomes the Word. With his becoming the Word, he becomes the bliss supreme. To say that he 'experiences' that bliss will be an outrageous joke. For we can experience only the other, and the other is our misery, our fear. As bliss, it is our death. Will it mean anything to say that with my coming to rest, there will still remain bliss? Can I say when the hearer is not and the speaker is not, there is still the Word? Yet the commentator calls it bliss supreme, this state where there is neither the enjoyer nor the enjoyed. Is it anthropomorphic superimposition, a false attribution which will subsequently be recanted?

If we are talking in terms of concepts, then *paramānanda*, bliss supreme, is only a false attribution. At the experiential level, the moment of immersion of the enjoyer into bliss is indeed the moment of ecstasy. When, however, the enjoyer is lost in the bliss, then the bliss too would not remain bliss. Bliss, the supreme bliss, is the last remnant of what we may call experience, a state of being this side of truth or untruth. That is all that man can aim at, can experience, can recollect, can report. Not the final plunge, the beatitude proper, the release, the *mukti*. That will not admit even bliss as its description, it smacks too much of the worldly mode of being.

ŚB Now the final result of the consideration of bliss:

5. sa yaś cāyaṃ puruṣe yaś cāsāvāditye sa ekaḥ sa ya evaṃvid asmāllokāt pretya. etam annamayam ātamānam upasaṃkrāmati. etaṃ prāṇamayam ātmānam upasaṃkrāmati. etaṃ manomayam ātmānam upasaṃkrāmati. etaṃ vijñānamayam atmānam upasaṃkrāmati. etam ānandamayam ātmānam upasaṃkrāmati. tad apy eṣa śloko bhavati.

He that is here in this person and he that is there in that sun are one. He who knows this attains, after departing from this world, this self made of food, this self made of breath, this self made of mind, this self made of knowledge, this self made of bliss. As to this, there is this verse:

ŚB 'He', *saḥ*, refers to him who dwells in the secret place within the *parama vyoman*, the highest heaven, dwells there after transforming himself into creation as would a cause into its effect, into creation ranging from the ether of space to the self made of food. Who is that dweller? The bliss supreme that is here in this person and that is there in that sun, the same bliss of which the hearer of the Word, the *śruti* has already said, has a direct and immediate vision, a small bit of which can sustain the life of beings that deserve to be happy, beings like Brahmā and others. It is this bliss that is presented here as residing in the sun. As the ether of space within different pots is the same ether of space, so is this bliss one though residing in many different loci.
Doubt: 'He that is here in this person' is too general a description of the embodied individual soul. The better description should have been [the more specific]: 'He that resides in the right eye'] (BṛU 2.3.5; 4.2.2; 5.2.2) For that is how it is generally described.
Answer: Your objection is misplaced. The *śruti* here speaks of the supreme self and not of the embodied individual soul. 'The invisible, the selfless', 'For fear of him blows the wind,' 'of this bliss is the consideration' have relevance in relation to the supreme self alone. It is no use bringing in irrelevant matters. The *śruti* here is concerned with the revelation of the supreme self. And it is of that self alone that it speaks in terms of oneness, oneness of the self in man and of the self in the sun.
Objection: The context here is the consideration of bliss [and not revelation of the person residing in the sun]. When the *śruti* is concerned with the

revelation of the different planes of bliss, it is quite in order that it should end up by a statement of the highest bliss, the final end, the culmination of the consideration. That nondifferent and intrinsic bliss is the supreme self itself, it is not born out of contact between the subject and the object.
Mediator: This means that the statement: 'He that is here in this person and he that is there in the sun' is in accord with what you say. For this statement denies that different loci could create any difference in that bliss.
Objection: Even then it is useless to bring in the sun.
Answer: The sun is brought in to do away with distinctions between the higher and the lower. The sun embodies the highest reach of duality, duality consisting of the formed and the not-formed. But when man has undone 'the man' in him, then [his]bliss comes to be the same as that which abides in the sun, it comes to be the supreme bliss itself. For him there remains, then, no distinction between the higher and the lower. He attains the state fearless. The statement in question highlights this point and is, from this point of view, quite relevant.

Bliss is not merely human, it is divine, a vast difference obtaining between the two, with varied states occurring inbetween. Does it mean that the supreme bliss too is merely the culminating point of the calculus. If so, then whatever the difference between divine bliss and the supreme bliss, it would be calculable, conceivably calculable. The supreme bliss is not, however, calculable, and it is incalculable precisely because no one can experience it, neither man nor god. That bliss manifests itself when man dies as man and god as god. It will then be 'found' to dwell in man with all its fullness, so will it be in the sun and so in the universe. In each will it be as full as in all.

Already, we have used such expressions as 'manifests itself', 'will be "found" and so on despite the earlier assertion that there can be no enjoyer of this bliss, neither god nor man. The bliss that can be talked about this way can only be the prelude of this bliss, the ecstasy that kills the enjoyer, absorbs him into itself. The 'nomenclature' of bliss for what ensues when the enjoyer of bliss comes to die is an attribution of what precedes it. Like Dante, one can talk about what precedes the darkness of unknowing and what succeeds it, not about that untruth, that nothingness.

The sun is the symbol of perfection, the meeting place of the formed and the not-formed, what the Upaniṣad calls truth and untruth, the cause of truth. Calculation cannot go beyond the sun, the home of life and death, the centre from which varied phenomena of the world emanate to come back to it. In relation to those phenomena, the sun is all light, the ultimate formed revealing all other forms. When it gathers into itself all the rays, all the phenomena, when it turns all phenomena, all formeds into unformeds, then it too turns into the unformed. The informing principle is also the unforming principle, the source the end.

This source and the end of the world is, however, as much dependent on the world as the world is dependent on it. And both depend for their being on man, the world and the sun—the god—as man is dependent on them. When man dies into the supreme bliss, then God too will die into it and also the world. The way to the supreme bliss does not lie through higher states, one after the other; that is the way to death, to worldly mode of being. The way lies through undoing oneself, through putting an end to the journey.

It is evident that 'the supreme bliss' anthropomorphises the 'untruth', another instance of anthropomorphisation. One can talk only in terms of symbols, from one to the other. What I seek I call supreme bliss if I find myself unhappy, I call truth when I find myself ignorant. I call it 'untruth' when I find that no concept in terms of which I can visualise 'truth' can be applicable to it. This home of the banished seeker will accept any name that the seeker may give it, for that name describes the state of the seeker, describes it truly. It has the generosity to accommodate our fall, our degradation. It does not hesitate to fall with us, suffer with us, this god supreme and bliss supreme.

ŚB The question as to the existence or nonexistence of Brahman was raised after the teacher had finished his instruction to the disciple. That question has now been answered. That beings do have bliss to enjoy, that they breathe the breath of life, that they fear and transcend their fear are effects that speak of their cause, of Brahman from which have proceeded the ether of space and other phenomena of the world. Two other questions too had cropped up regarding the attainment of Brahman by the man of wisdom and its nonattainment by the man of ignorance. The last of the three questions was concerned with the fate of the wise man—whether he could or could not attain Brahman. To answer this last question, the *śruti* says, 'He who knows this attains, after departing from this world. . . .'. The answer to the question regarding the fate of the unwise is implicit in this answer. So no attempt is made to answer it explicitly.

Any person who gives up all thoughts of the higher and the lower and knows himself to be nondual Brahman, described as truth, knowledge and infinity, attains to the self made of food. 'This' in 'He who knows this' refers to Brahman, the subject matter of the discourse. He attains the aforesaid self made of food after departing from this world, this mass of phenomena seen and not-seen. *Departing* here has the connotation of desisting, isolating, nondependence. When man dies this way, when he dies unto the world, the totality of objects, both seen and unseen, he attains to the food self, attains to a state where he will see no difference between the body made of food and the entire phenomenal world, will perceive all the gross phenomena as his own food-self.

Inside all the selves made of food he perceives the self undivided, the self made of breath. Afterwards he attains the self made of mind, the self made of knowledge and the self made of bliss, one after the other. Lastly, he attains the state fearless in the invisible, the selfless, the unsayable and the nestless.

Who is he who knows this? And how does he attain these states? Is he different from the supreme self or is he that self itself? These questions demand our attention.

Opponent: What purpose will this serve?

Answer: To say that he who attains these states is different from the self is to contradict the *śruti*. Witness what it says: 'Having created it, he entered it' (TaitU 2.6.1); 'He who says that he is one and I another, does not know' (BṛU 1.4.10); 'One alone without a second' (ChU 6.2.1); 'Thou art that' (ChU 6.8-16). To say, on the contrary, that it is the supreme self that attains the self made of bliss is to say that it attains itself—surely, an absurdity. Add to it another absurdity: The fall of the Supreme into the worldly state of being or its negation as the Supreme.

Opponent: If either position is faulty, it is useless to speculate who attains the blissful self—the supreme self or someone other than that. Any position that proves faultless—whether one of these two or a third—should be considered as intended by the *śruti*. So no purpose will be served by your speculation.

Answer: No, I raise the questions to come to a decisive conclusion. True is it that the fault cannot be set right by accepting any of the two positions. If there had been a third position free from the flaws mentioned above, there would have been no need to raise the questions concerned. But no such position is in sight. It is necessary, therefore, to consider the questions raised to ascertain the meaning of the Upaniṣad.

Objection: To think about the texts is fruitful only if it leads to a decisive conclusion about that meaning. But you merely think! The meaning escapes you!

Vedāntin: Is there any Vedic commandment to the effect that one should not try to arrive at conclusive interpretation of Vedic statements?

Opponent: No, there is none.

Vedāntin: Then, why should not one try for one?

Opponent: Because of the large number of your opponents. You, as a follower of the Vedas, believe in the doctrine that reality is one. But there are many who do not follow the Vedas and, as a result, believe in pluralism. They are opposed to you in their beliefs. In view of this fact, you will, I fear, fail in your attempt.

Vedāntin: I feel privileged that you call me a monist with many pluralists pitted against me. I'm sure, I shall conquer them all. Let me then commence the discussion.

That which attains the blissful self is none else than the supreme self itself. For that self indeed does he become who attains it. This is precisely what the Upaniṣad wants to impart. The knower of Brahman, we have been told, attains to the supreme. Through these words, the Upaniṣad intends to teach that knowledge of the supreme leads one to become the supreme. This only means that he who attains to Brahman is none else than Brahman itself, otherwise he could not become Brahman—one thing simply cannot become another thing.

But to say that one becomes oneself too is, you may object, an absurdity. My reply to this would be that this talk about becoming the self through knowing it is meant only to undo the sense of identity one has with the phenomena which primal ignorance has generated in one. When the Upaniṣad says that one attains to the self through *brahma-vidyā*, knowledge of the Absolute, its purpose is only to negate the self made of food and also the other selves made of breath, mind, knowledge and bliss. These distinct 'selves' are set up by ignorance and are really not-selves onto which the idea of the self has been superimposed.

Opponent: How do we gather that this indeed is the purpose of the *śruti* when it says that the knower of Brahman becomes Brahman?

Answer: We know this because all that the Upaniṣad calls upon man is to know the self. And knowledge is meant to dispel ignorance, that alone is its function. That very knowledge is described here as the means to the attainment of the self.

Opponent: The *śruti* instructs man about self-knowledge as one would instruct a man about the way to his destination. Self-knowledge thus is only a means to reach the self. Instruction about it cannot turn the instructed into the self. A traveller instructed as to the path leading to a village does not turn into the village. The village would not travel to itself.

Answer: Your analogy is misplaced. Your traveller is instructed about the path to the village, not about the village. Here one is instructed into knowledge of Brahman, not about any means leading to attainment of Brahman.

Objection: Brahman-knowledge owes its birth to the holy acts mentioned earlier. This knowledge is enjoined only as a means for the attainment of the supreme self.

Answer: We have already refuted this position through our contention that liberation [which is the same thing as attainment of Brahman] is ever attained. The *śruti* too reveals the identity of the self immanent in creation with the supreme self when it speaks of the latter's entry into creation (2.6). The fact that man can attain to fearlessness also shows that the self of man is the same as the supreme self. For fearlessness of the man of wisdom implies that he sees nothing other than his self. The other always causes fear and fearlessness means its absence. Absence of the other could not, of course, be revealed by wisdom, if it were not an unreal set up by ignorance. As for the clear eyed vision, the truth about the two moons is their oneness, similarly, for the man of true vision the truth about the other is that it is the self.

Opponent: The eye cured of the disease called *timir* sees two moons as one. But where is the vision that sees no duality?

Answer: The man asleep does not see it nor does the man in the yogic state of *samādhi*.

Opponent: A man preoccupied with something else does not see the thing before him. Is not this the case with the man asleep?

Answer: In sleep nothing whatsoever is perceived. The question of preoccupation does not arise in its case.
Opponent: Duality is a fact of our experience, of our dream experience as well as our waking experience. Its truth is, therefore, beyond question.
Vedāntin: No. Dream and waking states are creation of ignorance. Whatever is experienced as the other in these states is set up by ignorance. When ignorance ceases to be, dream and waking phenomena, too, cease to be.
Opponent: Nonperception in sleep too is a product of ignorance.
Vedāntin: No. Nonperception is not a product of ignorance, it is in the nature of the self not to perceive. The truth about a thing, its own native truth, is a truth that does not owe its being to anything else. For this reason, it never deviates from itself, from its true, native being. Not to deviate from itself is thus the truth of a thing. For only that aspect of a thing changes which is caused by factors other than itself. Not its own real being which does not owe its being to agencies external to it, the thing itself. It is, however, these adventitious agencies that turn what is into a particular qualified by attributes [into, that is, a percept], but a particular ever subject to change and modification. This is precisely what happens in the two states of waking and dream. Perceptions that one finds there are such particulars, caused by the other, they are not native to the self and, for this reason, are not constituents of its being. They do not survive when the factors responsible for their being [i.e. the states of dream and waking] disappear. This kind of conditioning of what is, this its particularisation, does not happen in sleep as it does in the other two states. For in that state the self reverts to its natural state of nonperception.

Nonperception of the other is common to both sleep and the state of self-knowledge. In this sense, the state of sleep is an image of the latter, a revelation, in a sense, of the self, a foretaste of self-realisation. In our waking life we live as embodied individualities. These individualities are constituted by the other, are what may be called borrowed ontologies. Denuded of the other, what remains of these individualities is only a frightening nothingness. In sleep, however, I survive despite the fact that the other deserts me. Does not this survival show that I have a being independent of all my conditioning factors and a being, moreover, that is full of repose and bliss? Sleep, however, only indicates my true being, it does not truly reveal it. For selfhood remains intact in sleep, though it does not get affirmed in it as it does in the states of dream and wakefulness. The other is not there to make self-affirmation possible in the state of sleep. In self-knowledge you do not perceive the other because the other has become the self. Nonperception in sleep, on the contrary, is the product of ignorance, of unawareness.

This passage makes, in the original, difficult reading. The translation had to be somewhat interpretative.

ŚB But those who imagine the Lord and creation as other than the self will never find their fear come to rest. For the other gives rise to fear. And since the other [according to you] is an existent, there will never come a moment when it will cease to be the other [will cease, consequently, to cause you fear]. [Nor can you say that the other was not there before creation and only after creation did it come to be to give rise to fear, for] if it had been nonexistent, it would never have come to be.
Objection: We do not fear that other, the Lord, in and by himself. We fear him in relation to something else [in relation to our deeds].
Answer: What we have said about the other applies to this something else too. If the other becomes the cause of fear in association with another auxiliary cause, permanent or nonpermanent, auxiliary cause in the form of good or bad deeds, then our fear will never come to end. For, the auxiliary cause in question will be of the nature of an existent and an existent never ceases to be. If we imagine such a cause to cease to exist, then the real will turn into the unreal and the unreal into the real. That will mean total chaos. However, if one accepts oneness as truth, then this difficulty will not arise. In that case, the world will be found as set up by ignorance and so will be its cause. If you see two moons because of a defect in your eyes, you will not speak of the second moon in terms either of its coming to be or of its ceasing to be.
Objection: But *vidyā* and *avidyā*, knowledge and ignorance, are attributively related to the self [and are, for this reason, inseparable from it].
Answer: This cannot be so, since these are perceptible phenomena: one can directly perceive discrimination and nondiscrimination as attributes of the mind, perceive them belonging to the field of objectivity as much as do the phenomena of the senses. As colours cannot be the attributes of the self simply because they are perceptible, so can't be knowledge and ignorance. 'I am ignorant,' 'my knowledge is indistinct' speak of the fact that one can cognise one's ignorance as an objective fact, describe it to oneself. Similarly, one can experience knowledge also as something distinct from oneself. That knowledge is different from the self is borne out by the fact that people can communicate their knowledge to others and others too can comprehend it. Thus knowledge and ignorance belong to the realm of names and forms, and names and forms do not constitute the attributes of the self. This truth is described by the *śruti* in these words: 'That which they call space brings about the manifestation of name and form. That in which they abide is Brahman' (ChU 8.14.1). But this too is mere imagination. The truth, the truth absolute, is that names and forms no more abide in Brahman than do day and night in the sun.
Objection: If the self and Brahman were nondifferent, then the distinction between the subject and the object implied in the text: 'He attains that blissful self' (TaiU 2.8.5) will be reduced to an absurdity.
Answer: No. For attainment of Brahman is nothing else than knowledge or realisation of it. The *śruti* does not ask man to attain it the way, e.g., a leech may be said to attain, to reach, its object. Attainment here means only knowledge, not reaching.

Objection: The word *upasaṃkrāmati* (he attains) used in the text connotes 'to go near'. Should we, then, not take the *śruti* at its word and interpret it literally?
Answer: No. Man does not reach even the food-self in the literal sense of the word. He does not go from this external world to the food self as would a leech move from one place to another. Nor, for that matter, in any other way.
Objection: The mind self may be said to move out into external phenomena and come back from them into itself. Similarly, one can speak of the going out and coming back of the self made of knowledge.
Answer: This talk about coming back to oneself is absurdity itself. One cannot be the object of one's reaching. You started your thesis by saying that someone other than the food self attains the food self, implying thereby a distinction between the one who attains and that which is attained. Now you say that the mind self reaches itself and also the intellect self. This way you contradict you own position. The bliss self too cannot reach itself. Therefore, *saṃkramaṇa*, approaching, cannot, in the present context, connote attainment. None of the five sheaths can attain itself. Attainment can only mean realisation, realisation of these selves by someone other than these selves, of the selves ranging from the food self to the self made of bliss.

When the self is attained, when, that it to say, dawns the awareness that the self is different from all that falls within the field of knowledge, then is eliminated the delusion that the not-selves, from the food sheath to the bliss sheath, are the self. For this delusion arises from the association of the self with the hidden place within the heart. But the self that resides within the sheath made of bliss resides within all. It created the entire creation from the ether of space to the sheath made of food, and having created it, entered it. The coming to end of this delusion that the all-pervading self is the individual self is figuratively termed as attainment of the self. There is no way to reach the all-pervading self, if one takes 'reaching' in its literal sense.

There is another point to consider. Everything is the self, there is no thing which is not the self. So there is no point in saying that the self attains the self. The leech, as the saying goes, attains to the other, not itself. The myth about Brahman becoming the many, about its entering its own creation, about the attainment of bliss and freedom from fear, and about its attainment, reaching, by man is woven with one purpose that one may realise Brahman defined as truth, knowledge and infinity. The varied activities attributed to Brahman in this myth have become possible only by assuming it to be something empirical. This could not have been possible if Brahman had been taken to be what it really is, the reality beyond all thoughts and all conditions.

When man reaches the unconditioned self this way, passing through varied states, when he thus comes to know it, he ceases to have any fear from anything. He attains to the state of fearlessness. With regard to this, there is this verse, the *mantra* that summarises in brief all that has been revealed in this section on bliss.

Chapter 9

1. yato vāco nivartante aprāpya manasā saha. ānandaṃ brahmaṇo vidvān na vibheti kutaś caneti. etaṃ ha vāva na tapati. kim ahaṃ sādhu nākaravam. kim ahaṃ pāpam akaravam iti. sa ya evaṃ vidvān ete ātamānaṃ spṛṇute. ubhe hy evaiṣa ete ātmānaṃ spṛṇute. ya evaṃ veda. ity upaniṣat.

Wherefrom returns speech finding nothing along with the mind, knowing that bliss of Brahman one fears not anything. Not for him the remorse: Why did I not do the good? Why did I do the ill? Truly do these two release him who knows this way, truly do these two release him who knows this way. This, verily, is the redemptive teaching.

ŚB *Wherefrom returns speech. Wherefrom,* from the unconditioned self, from the self free from every thought, which the Upaniṣad has defined for us. From Bliss the nondual returns speech, names that have determinate objects for their referents. Speakers use these words for expressing the nature of Brahman the nondual and the unconditioned as if it were of the same nature as are determinate things. But speech returns from that Brahman without revealing it, returns deprived of its power to express and denote.

And along with the mind does it, speech, return from Brahman. Mind here denotes concept, cognition. Whatever the word would name, the mind follows suit to reveal it, even though the referent might be something supersensuous. Conversely, wherever there is cognition, there is speech too. The word and the concept, speech and mind always operate together. Men use speech to reveal Brahman which no concept can encompass, no word can name, which is marked by such traits as invisibility etc. From this Brahman speech, however, returns along with the mind, along with conceptual knowledge, knowledge which can reveal everything [else]. But of him who has heard the Word, who is cleansed of sin, whom no desire can assail and no craving is that bliss of Brahman the *ātman,* the self. This bliss is not contingent on contact of the subject with the object, it is native to the self, is eternal and indivisible. He who knows that supreme bliss of Brahman, knows the way described by the Upaniṣad, will have nothing to fear, for the very cause of fear will have disappeared for him. There will remain no other thing for him, for this wise knower, nothing different from him to cause him any fear.

Avidyā generates difference and even a trite of difference, the Upaniṣad has said, causes fear. For the man of wisdom, however, there remains no *avidyā* to cause any difference. It disappears with the rise of *vidyā* as does the second moon when the eye has been cured of its disease. When this happens, there can remain, rightly says the Upaniṣad, no fear for the man of wisdom.

That the bliss called Brahman is beyond the reach of speech and thought is a recurring but widely misunderstood theme of the Upaniṣads. Śaṅkara's commentary on the *mantra* in question should, I believe, be of help in removing that misunderstanding. For Śaṅkara, the word and the concept, speech and mind always operate together. They are inseparable but not, be it noted, one. *Vāc* and *manas,* word and thought, are accepted as separate *padārthas,* categories, in the Indian tradition. *Vāc* belongs to the sphere of the sense and thought to mind, the former to the domain of space, the latter to that of time. *Vāc* is the dispenser of identity, *manas* of subsistence or duration. Things are perceived neither as pure identities nor as pure duration but as identity–duration polarities and ambiguities. Śaṅkara, however, equates mind with concepts and cognition. Cognition could, of course, be interpreted as identity-duration ambiguity but not concept. If mind were to be equated with concept then the age old distinction between sense and thought would become redundant. This Śaṅkara, the interpreter *par excellence,* would not countenance. So what could be his meaning in reducing mind to concept? Has concept a being distinct from word?

Plato, I believe, would not equate form with word. The stability that the word provides to sense-continuum could only be an appearance of the stability that the form provides it, a mere semblance of it. Many a modern thinker would deny this Platonic distinction and would equate the concept with the word. Śaṅkara would avoid both these extremes: he would grant they are inseparables but would not admit clear cut distinction between the two nor would he identify them. Concept, he would say, belongs to *buddhi,* the determinating faculty, the intellect, and word to the organ of speech. The distinction between word and concept is thus to be sought in the distinction between *vāc* and *buddhi,* speech and intellect. Human speech is the speech of an embodied, communal and world-situated being. *Buddhi* is interior to the body, to thoughts and feelings. It is the faculty of knowing through concepts, the faculty that makes phenomena intelligible, unifies the manifold into a whole. Phenomena are thus perceived as informed by concepts of *buddhi,* are perceived as wholes. As a matter of fact, a phenomenon is endlessly divisible. *Buddhi* puts a check to this process of divisibility and conceives of a thing as if it were a real whole. There is an element of temporality in every phenomenon but *buddhi* ignores it to make one feel as if the phenomenon in question were an actual *presence.* Concepts of *buddhi* thus operate ignoring these counter facts about phenomena, which ignoring practically turns it into *avidyā,* ignorance. It superimposes its concepts on phenomena which ever and always disown them.

Concept, thus, is the sense of the whole with regard to an object, something which is superimposed on to it. Concept as mere wholeness is not, however, the whole story. There is also the story about class. Concept represents a class of wholes. The moment a whole gets associated with a class, it becomes linguistic. *Vāc,* language, thus is the provider of class, not of individuality. To superimpose individuality on to—is the function of *pratyaya,* bare concept. To reach the Real(?) one has to give up the secure intelligibility associated with class and come to be bare individuality. This, however, is a hard task beyond the reach of even many a philosopher. Witness how the Naiyāyikas thought of propositional perception—*savikalpa pratyakṣa*—as a sort of more evolved form of perception than the nonpropositional perception—*nirvikalpa pratyakṣa.* We also know how for many a modern philosopher a concept is practically a word. To be an individual one has to give up one's relationship with the class one belongs to, one has, in other words, to delinguise oneself. When you cease to belong to a class, you cannot retain your consciousness of being an individual. For you can retain that consciousness only as a member of a class, as a being-with-others and as a being-for-others. This means that *buddhi* cannot articulate its wholes without language, without social relationships. Without language *buddhi's* concepts remain inarticulate, *nirvikalpāḥ,* mere potentialities.

From the real, *vāc* returns along with *manas,* speech along with mind, because whatever speech–mind posit and articulate are mere superimpositions on to what is. Phenomena of the world that speech and mind articulate are ridden with contradictions, they ever and always refuse to coincide with articulate concepts: their transcendental thrust never owns up these concepts. Our interpreted world thus turns out to be adventitious to truth, not native to it. For the inhabitants of the interpreted world, going beyond it seems impossible. The way to truth does not, of course, lie through disowning language and concepts. All that one has to do is to give oneself up to the bare *this* that one finds oneself to be. This giving up, this passive surrender will open out limitless depths in one's individuality, in one's body. To surrender oneself in desire-free passivity to what one is: this alone is the way. *Vāc* and *buddhi* melt away through this surrender to their creation, not through rejection of it. This paradox shows us the way to truth, this self-submission to *avidyā,* ignorance.

ŚB In the chapter relating to mind-sheath, too, this *mantra* was invoked. Mind, we know, is the means wherewith one attains *brahma-vijñāna*, knowledge of Brahman. Accordingly, the Upaniṣad spoke of mind as if it were Brahman itself and hailed it as the sheath where man's fears came to rest. But only fears, not their cause. In the present context devoted to the revelation of the nondual real, 'one fears not anything' carries the connotation of the cessation of the very cause of fear, not merely of fear.

Objection: Even for the wise man, there will remain the cause of fear, fear of omission and commission, omission of holy deeds and commission of sinful acts.

Answer: Not so. And why this omission and commission do not cause fear in the man who knows this way the bliss of Brahman, the *śruti* explains for us. The *śruti* says in quite emphatic terms—note the use of *ha* and *vāva*—that a man of wisdom can have no regrets for the good deeds he failed to do and no remorse over the sins he committed. When the hour of death approaches, men are often filled with such regrets and remorse. They fear that the sinful deeds they committed, the deeds forbidden by scriptures, will throw them into the tortures of hell. Great is their fear, their misery, regarding what is in store for them. No such regret and no such remorse torture a man of wisdom.

Why don't these torture him? Because he knows, he who has come to realise Brahman the way the Upaniṣad has described for us, that both virtue and vice lead man to grief. This realisation strengthens his self, delights it. It strengthens his self because it enables him to look upon the two, both virtue and vice, as the supreme self. Since they are of this nature, the wise man divests them—these that are the *ātman* itself—of their distinct identities through looking upon them as the *ātman*. This way he strengthens the self itself, he who knows Brahman the nondual, the bliss. Since he looks upon virtue and vice this way, they cease to torment him and lose the power to cause further births.

This is the secret instruction, *brahma-vidyā*, revelation of Brahman, disclosed in this part, of all wisdoms the most secret. The most secret because in it lies the way to the ultimate good, to liberation.

For every civilisation, distinction between virtue and vice is an important distinction, what, that is to say, the civilisation in question considers virtue and vice. To lose the sense of this distinction will mean ceasing to be civilised, it will mean sinking to the level of the barbarian, the nonaryan, the uncivilised, the beast, creatures who have no place in civilisation. No civilisation can afford to do away with this distinction unless it wants to do away with itself. This distinction is, however, not a blessed distinction, it causes pain to 'civilised' people, gives rise to a sense of unnerving guilt in them, to a disabling discontent. Conscience, the super ego, has been the bane of many; it is a moot point whether the guilt of the fallen man is more painful or the discontent of the man of conscience. Add to this the disturbing question if the virtuous man is really as virtuous as he appears to be. In what sadistic pleasures he may seek compensation for his good deeds one cannot say. There is indeed a cold, sinister aspect to every good deed. At any rate, human goodness is too fragile a thing to inspire much faith in itself. Civilisations are not as 'civilised' as fanatics take them to be. When one realises this aspect of virtue, when one realises that civilisations have only let loose the beast in man against himself, then the sharp distinction that civilisations draw between what they call virtue and vice begins to fade out. There is, however, one merit in virtue that sin does not have. It is the virtuous alone, or he who aspires to be so, who can see through the veil of virtue. The sinful man is often blind to the ambiguities of virtue unless he has the courage and the insight of a tragic hero. But then his sin will not be without virtue.

To see virtue as an ambiguity is not common among men and women, vain creatures that they are. When, however, they come to have this rare insight, they become humble enough to get disillusioned with their acts. Often they let themselves act out of serene melancholy and compassion and not out of well-considered resolutions. The paradox about such men and women is that their acts are almost always prompted by concern for others. There is an unobtrusive spontaneity about their righteousness, and not resoluteness, the mark of the self-righteous, who can be good in pain alone, the pain speaking their inner sinfulness. This spontaneity in goodness ends up in innocence of their own goodness, in the death of the ego of the good man.

Only such a man without the ego of the doer in him can be free from regrets and remorse.

Part 3

Bhṛguvallī

Chapter 1

ŚB Brahman, the truth, knowledge and infinity created the effects from the ether of space to the body made of food, and entered them to appear marked by distinctions as it were. This would argue for the transcendental nature of that bliss and of its nonphenomenal character and all that goes with such a character. This bliss should one realise as one's very self and identity. For that verily was the purpose of Brahman's becoming the immanent principle—to make creatures realise that it alone was their identity and their self. He who realises this truth is never born again, his deeds, whether good or bad, do not lead to rebirth. Such was the theme and tenor of the Part on bliss. With the conclusion of that Part, the Upaniṣad has revealed all that was to be revealed about the nature of Brahman. There remains, however, the means for the realisation of Brahman to be revealed, means like *tapas*, concentration and meditations on food and the like, meditations not touched upon earlier. This the Upaniṣad now proceeds to do in this part which commences with these words:

1. bhṛgur vai vāruṇiḥ. varuṇaṃ pitaram upasasāra. adhīhi bhagavo brahmeti. tasmā etat provāca. annaṃ prāṇaṃ cakṣuḥ śrotraṃ mano vācam iti. taṃ hovāca. yato vā imāni bhūtāni jāyante yena jātāni jīvanti. yat pryanty abhisaṃviśanti. tad vijijñāsasva. tad brahmeti. sa tapo'tapyata. sa tapas taptvā ....

Bhṛgu Vāruṇi, verily, approached Varuṇa, his father, to make him a request, 'Teach unto me, revered sir, Brahman.' To him did he teach that food [is the way to Brahman and so are] breath, eye, ear, mind and the word. Then did he say, 'From whom are born these beings and by whom, when born, they live and into whom they enter after death—him do you desire to know. That is Brahman.' He performed tapas, *practised meditation. And having practised it . . .*

ŚB That a father instructed his son in this knowledge highlights the importance of this knowledge. The form of the story is resorted to for this very purpose—to praise this knowledge. The word *verily* in 'Bhṛgu Vāruṇi, verily, approached Varuṇa, his father' recalls to one a personality famous and well known, namely, the famous sage called Bhṛgu, the son of Varuṇa. He approached Varuṇa, his father, as a seeker of Brahman and requested him, in these sacred words, 'Teach unto me, revered sir, Brahman.' To him, who had approached him in the way laid down in scriptures, his father spoke these words: 'Food, breath, eye, ear, mind and speech.'

'Food' here means the body. In the body moves breath, the eater. Eye, ear, mind and speech are the means of cognition. These are, he said, the doors that open out to Brahman. Having taught him that these food, breath etc. are the doors that open out to Brahman, Varuṇa defined Brahman for Bhṛgu. What is that definition, he proceeds to say:

From whom are born these beings—all beings from Brahmā the Creator to a clump of grass; and by whom, when born, do they live, breathe and grow; and towards whom, at the hour of death, do they proceed and move to enter into and become one with—who, in one word, ever remains their self, their being, be it the time of creation, of existence or dissolution—that is Brahman. . . . This, then, is the definition of Brahman. That Brahman should you desire to know, know well. Know him through food and other doors of knowledge, know Brahman defined thus. 'Those who know the breath of breath, the eye of eye, the mind of mind, know Brahman the ancient, the primordial' (BṛU 4.4.18). These words of the *śruti* show how breath and others are the doorways to Brahman.

When Bhṛgu had learnt from his father the doorways to Brahman and also the nature of Brahman as defined by the latter, he resorted to *tapas*, concentration, a means for the realisation of Brahman.

Objection: How could Bhṛgu think of *tapas*, concentration, as a way to the realisation of Brahman when no one had told him any such thing about it?

Answer: Because of the incompleteness of the instruction he had received from his father. All that Varuṇa had told him was that food, breath, eye, ear, mind and speech were the doorways to the revelation of Brahman, and how Brahman was to be defined in terms of the origin of beings, their sustaining principle and their ultimate *telos*. This evidently is not enough; this does not point out Brahman directly, immediately. Varuṇa should have taught Brahman in a different way to his son, a true seeker; he should have pointed out the real nature of Brahman to him. This he did not do. He chose to speak in incomplete terms. Evidently, Varuṇa expected his son to resort to some other means too to qualify for knowledge of Brahman. Bhṛgu chose *tapas* as that other means because it is the best of all the means [for the purpose in question]. The world knows how of all the means that relate to definite ends, *tapas* is the best. So Bhṛgu resorted to it for attaining to the knowledge of Brahman, even though Varuṇa had not asked him to do so. *Tapas* means concentration of outer and inner organs, for that is the doorway to the revelation of Brahman:

> Concentration of the mind and of the senses alone is the highest austerity. It exceeds every other *dharma*, every other virtue, this what they term the highest *dharma*.

Thus the *smṛti* (MB *Śānti Parvan* 250.4). Having practised this austerity. . .

The language of the Upaniṣad becomes here aphoristic, almost enigmatic. Food, breath, eye, ear, mind and speech are mentioned but not related to Brahman, neither in terms of identity nor difference nor, for that matter, as means for its realisation. The commentator, however, takes them as means for the realisation of Brahman. Furthermore, the revelatory language of the Upaniṣad, the *śruti*, does not care to reveal Brahman, to point it out, in direct and immediate terms. Instead it proceeds to define it once again, not, as earlier, in terms of perfections but in relation to creation, in terms, that is, of imperfection. Bhṛgu, in other words, is vouchsafed only a discourse about Brahman, not its disclosure. We can understand Brahman only in relation to creation, in terms of our existential situation, not in terms of what it in itself is. All answers to questions about the nature of Brahman can be given in terms that relate to that which is other than Brahman, in terms, in other words, of *avidyā*, of superimposition, of false attribution. No discourse can be complete, can be true. The Upaniṣad shows forth the incompleteness of its answer, its ultimate falsity, not through rejecting, in explicit terms, what it says but through what it does not say. The unsaid becomes a part of the said, of the text, to deepen the meaning of what is said. The incompleteness of syntax makes it imperative that what is said should not be taken at its face value.

The name *Bhṛgu* itself, to invoke a term which I should like to avoid because of its vulgarisation, deconstructs the words attributed to Varuṇa. That Bhṛgu should resort to *tapas*, should burn bright in it, to unveil the mystery is quite natural. For it is in his nature to burn bright, his name being derived from *bhrāj*, to shine. The mythical beings who bore the name were closely connected with fire, they in fact brought fire to mankind for their good as the *Ṛg Veda* (1.58.6) would tell us:

dadhuṣṭvā bhṛgavo mānuṣeṣvā
rayiṃ na cāruṃ suhavaṃ janebhyaḥ,
hotāram agne atithiṃ vareṇyaṃ
mitraṃ na śevaṃ divyāya janmane.

The Bhṛgus established among men for men'
like a treasure, beauteous and easy to invoke,

> Agni, *thou offerer of oblation, the best of guests,*
> *as an auspicious friend of the shining race.*

They established communion between mortals and immortals through the holy fire, the mediator, at once human, cosmic and divine. *Agni,* the burning flame, is the link between man and god, the promise of man's redemption into godhood. That fire burns in man in the form of *tapas,* the purifying heat. In the body it burns in the form of austerities, in the senses in paying heed to and getting concentrated on their objects, with no thought of enjoying or doing, in dwelling in them to the extent of dwelling as them. At the level of the mind, *tapas* burns in the form of living the moment before one, to be it here and now, to live, in one word, as space and time. This deep concentration is called *tapas* because it involves burning of desires and ambitions. This moment, this thing, when approached this way, becomes the doorway to what we call the Real and the Upaniṣads the *ātman* or Brahman.

That Bhṛgu, the sage, should partake of *tapas* is indicated, as we have seen, by his very name, that embodiment of the purifying fire. His father Varuṇa, the all enveloping sky, the presiding deity of the night, is the giver of intimations, intimations of what we mortals can only call immortality, so different it seems from all that we are and all that we know. Yet the intimations that the vast dome of the sky at night can give are only intimations, they do not turn into revelations until we undo ourselves through *tapas.* It is in the nature of Varuṇa that his voice should remain mere intimation and it is in the nature of Bhṛgu that he should transform those intimations into full revelation through *tapas,* through a burning that sanctifies the instructed into godhood.

Chapter 2

1. **annaṃ brahmeti vyajānāt. annād dhy eva khalv imāni bhūtāni jāyante. annena jātāni jīvanti. annaṃ prayanty abhisaṃviśantīti. tad vijñāya purnar eva varuṇaṃ pitaram upasasāra. adhīhi bhagavo brahmeti. taṃ hovāca. tapasā brahma vijijñāsasva. tapo brahmeti. sa tapo 'tapyata. sa tapas taptvā...**

He came to know that food was Brahman. For truly from food are born these beings, by food, when born, do they live, and into food do they enter at the time of dissolution. Having known this, he went again to Varuṇa, his father, and said, 'Instruct me about Brahman, revered sir!' To him he said, 'Through tapas *do you seek to know him. For he is* tapas, *the burning ardour.' He performed* tapas, *and having performed* tapas . . . .

ŚB He came to know that food was Brahman. For food indeed met the definition that Varuṇa had given of Brahman. For truly from food were born these beings, by food, when born, did they live and into food did they enter at death. Since this was the case, it was right that food be equated with Brahman. Having practised *tapas* this way and having known, on the basis of the definition given and also on the basis of what his own reasoning told him, that food was Brahman, he went back to Varuṇa, his father, full of doubt and again requested him to instruct him about Brahman.

He was assailed by doubts regarding the equation of food with Brahman because food has its origin [whereas Brahman is eternal].

The *śruti,* through repeated mention of *tapas,* calls upon the seeker of truth to resort to it because it is the primary means whereby one may attain to truth. *Tapas* alone is your resort until the definition of Brahman admits of no extension, until your desire to know ceases. Through *tapas* alone do you seek to know Brahman. This, in brief, is what the *śruti* intends to say. The rest of the text is easy to comprehend.

Human beings usually seek only that truth which they have already 'defined'. Not for them is possible patient waiting for the disclosure of the unknown, the undefined truth, the mark of a true seeker. This propensity of the interpreting creature that man is the Upaniṣad takes due notice of. For this reason, and as a concession to man who fears the uncertain and undefined, the Upaniṣad defines the ultimate truth and asks him to find it. There is something in phenomena, some informing principle that exceeds them, precedes and succeeds them. That excess, that more, is what gives phenomena their identities, that is the truth, theirs as well as man's. That is what man should seek and find.

If that is our truth, mine as well as yours, then food, the most proximate thing among the observables, meets the criterion as well as the most mysterious entity. Of food indeed is man a creature, is sustained by it and eventually becomes its victim, becomes food of food. Man and earth, man and matter thus relate to each other as eater–eaten ambiguities. This is what Bhṛgu learns from his *tapas,* from the penance he does when he deliberately ceases to be a consumer and burns himself in hunger. To live as eater–eaten duality, to live as a mortal, is the first step towards enlightenment and this step Bhṛgu, the living flame of *sattva,* has taken. Instead of seeking life, he has chosen to lose it in order to find its being, its truth.

Yet, at its first flush, this vision dawns upon man not as a redemptive vision but as a tragic vision. The redemptive possibilities of this vision do not unfold themselves all of a sudden, not before a long and watchful probation. What the definition of Brahman prompted man to seek was the anchor of his being, an anchor more stable than his world and his own person. Man indeed lives by food and dies into it but this food is as much informed by a lack, a want as man is. His world is as poor in terms of truth as he himself is and so is the eater–eaten duality, the man–world. Not only is the security that the man of the world seeks through food and possessions a fake security but also the truth of sacrifice, the truth that man comes to know when he becomes eater–food duality. So food–eater duality does not meet the definition of Brahman given by Varuṇa. It cannot be the ground of man's unhappy being, despite its promise.

Chapter 3

1. **prāṇo brahmeti vyajānāt. prāṇād dhy eva khalv imāni bhūtāni jāyante. prāṇena jātāni jīvanti. prāṇaṃ prayanty abhisaṃviśantīti. tad vijñāya punar eva varuṇaṃ pitaram upasasāra. adhīhi bhagavo brahmeti. taṃ hovāca. tapasā brahma vijijñāsasva. tapo brahmeti. sa tapo 'tapyata. sa tapas taptvā . . . .**

Breath is Brahman, he came to know. For verily from breath are born these creatures. By breath, when born, do they live, and into breath do they enter when they die. Having known that, he returned to Varuṇa, his father, to request him to instruct him about Brahman. To him Varuṇa said: 'By tapas *seek to know Brahman. For* tapas *is Brahman.' So he performed* tapas *and having performed it . . . .*

Life as food-vision gives place to life as breath-vision. Food-vision is a tragic vision until man steps out of victor–victim duality. This becomes possible only through living his tragedy, not through escape from it. Men and women would escape from it through appropriating for themselves the impossible role of the victor and eater. All their life is wasted in trying to undo the other that would undo them. The man who can see through this vain endeavour, can have the clarity and the vision to accept and live his tragic truth, will step out of his thoughts, his visions and his ambitions. He will become witness to his breath current, will serenly flow out and flow in with it. It is when he comes to die with the incoming breath and with the outgoing breath that he will know the living face of death, of ceasing to be. He will accept himself as the eaten, as food, for he will move, in serene surrender, from life to death and from death to life, from the motion of breath to its cessation and from its cessation to its motion. That is the vision, the vision of the ebb of his life and its flow, that will reveal itself before him when he performs *tapas* in the form of this yoga of *apāna* and *prāṇa*, of flowing out and flowing in, with full concentration, with the current of breath.

Chapter 4

1. **mano brahmeti vyajānāt. manaso hy eva khalv imāni bhūtāni jāyante. manasā jātāni jīvanti. manaḥ prayanty abhisaṃviśantīti. tad vijñāya punar eva varuṇaṃ pitaram upasasāra. adhīhi bhagavo brahmeti. taṃ hovāca. tapasā brahma vijijñāsasva. tapo brahmeti. sa tapo 'tapyata. sa tapas taptvā . . . .**

Mind is Brahman, he came to know. For, verily, from mind are born these beings and by mind, when born, do they live and into mind do they enter when they die. Having known this, he went back to Varuṇa, his father, to request him to instruct him about Brahman. To him Varuṇa said, 'Through tapas *seek to know Brahman, for Brahman is* tapas.*' He performed* tapas *and having performed it . . . .*

Tapas is a continuous process. The incomplete sentence at the end of every passage shows that no state reached through *tapas* is the final state. Every destination points towards the beyond. *Tapas* in the form of identification with breath leads to identification with the Word, into coalescence of all with each. There will be moments when the flow of thoughts will come to cease and man and his world merge into peaceful emptiness, the source true of both mind and the world. Let us not, however, anticipate what the Upaniṣad is going to state in the chapters to come.

Chapter 5

1. vijñānaṃ brahmeti vyajānāt. vijñānād dhy eva khalv imāni bhūtāni jāyante. vijñānena jātāni jīvanti. vijñānaṃ prayanty abisaṃviśantīti. tad vijñāya punar eva varuṇaṃ pitaram upasasāra. adhīhi bhagavo brahmeti. taṃ hovāca. tapasā brahma vijijñāsasva. tapo brahmeti. sa tapo 'tapyata. sa tapas taptvā . . .

Vijñāna, *knowledge, is Brahman, he came to know. For truly from knowledge are born these beings and by knowledge, when born, do they live. And into knowledge do they enter at the time of death. Having known that he returned to Varuṇa, his father, and requested him to instruct him about Brahman. To him said Varuṇa, 'Seek to know Brahman through* tapas. *For* tapas *is Brahman. He practised* tapas *and having practised it. . .*

In the silent peaceful depths, abysmal and without end, lies the source alike of mind and of the world. That *śūnya,* that nothingness, that anonymous peace without limits is the source and the sustaining principle of our interpreted world. A ripple of thought, a scarcely felt trace of it, changes that peace into a faint sensation, into a sort of pre-body as it were, which pre-body changes into body proper the moment the ripple of thought changes into full thought. With the rise of these, thought and body, rises the world. Such is the plenitude of that nothingness, that *śūnya* but only for those who have died into the Word. However, even this depth is torn by division, division between it and consciousness of it. This consciousness, this knower of the *śūnya,* is the primordial *pratīka,* mien, of what the Upaniṣads call the self, the last veil which no effort can tear apart. Man has to accept this consciousness as his ultimate truth and live outside the margins of its sacred shrine. How the peace, the source of the world and man, will merge into this consciousness, no one knows. One has to accept this banishment, this not to be oneself as one's final lot, accept it without question. This is the last *tapas* one has to do, for there is, can be, no further definition of the self which one may strive to attain. Here *tapas* as striving gives place to *tapas* as acceptance. With this acceptance, man the disowned, the banished will, at long last, be, the *śruti* says, owned up and accepted. The creature will be transformed into god if he does not quarrel with his disinheritance.

Chapter 6

1. ānando brahmeti vyajānāt. ānandād dhy eva khalv imani bhūtāni jāyante. ānandena jātāni jīvanti. ānandaṃ prayanty abhisaṃviśantīti. saiṣā bhārgavī vāruṇī vidyā parame vyoman pratiṣṭhitā. sa ya evaṃ veda pratitiṣṭhati. annavān annādo bhavati. mahān bhavati prajayā paśubhir brahmavarcasena. mahān kīrtyā.

Bliss is Brahman, he came to know. For truly from bliss are born these beings and by bliss, when born, do they live and into bliss do they enter at the time of death.
This wisdom of Bhṛgu and Varuṇa is established in the highest heaven. He who knows this is securely established. The possessor of food does he become and its consumer. Great in progeny does he become and in cattle, in the splendour of holiness and in renown.

ŚB This way Bhṛgu, purified by *tapas*, did not find all the characteristics of Brahman in any of the selves, from that made of food to that made of knowledge. Slowly did he proceed inwards to find the inmost bliss that is Brahman, proceed towards it through *tapas*. Those who would realise Brahman should therefore resort to concentration of external and internal organs, the senses and the mind. That truly is the highest *tapas*. This, in brief, is the gist of this part of the Upaniṣad.

The *śruti* now discards the narrative form and speaks in its own voice to state the gist of the story. This, it says, is the wisdom that Bhṛgu received and Varuṇa taught, the wisdom that commenced with the self made of food and culminated in the supreme, nondual bliss that resides in the highest heaven. The highest heaven is the cavity, the secret place, lodged in the ether of space within the heart. Any other person who follows in the footsteps of Bhṛgu and enters, through the efficacy of *tapas*, one self after the other, will also finally know the bliss that is Brahman, will be firmly established in this wisdom to be firmly established in that bliss, in the supreme Brahman. He will, in sum, become Brahman itself.

The *śruti* also tells us what visible results follow from one's establishment in the nondual bliss. A man established in this bliss becomes, the *śruti* says, possessor of food, plenty of food. Everyone possesses food. Mere possession of food will do no credit to knowledge. Therefore, possessor of food should be taken to mean possessor of plenty of food. He will also be a consumer of food, will have good digestion. And he will become great, great in progeny, in sons and the like, great in cattle, in cows, horses and the like, great in the splendour of holiness—in the splendour that springs from calm of mind, restraint of the senses, from spiritual knowledge. And he will be great in renown, in fame, earned through virtuous life.

Since bliss and Brahman are equated, bliss is not to be taken in the psychological sense. Brahman is bliss because in it the divide between what one is and what one would be is healed, in this plenitude of being. In Brahman one's struggle for being comes to end, the struggle that is otherwise so hopeless, so tragic. It comes to end not through self-enrichment but through self-extinction, through what the Upaniṣads call *tapas.* The hope for self-enrichment is a vain hope, every endeavour for it a futile endeavour.

The Upaniṣads often promise food for a man of wisdom and a good power of digestion. Does this mean the continuation of the Vedic view which found the fulfilment of even ordinary needs as the result of divine favour? And also success of every effort? Or does this recurrent reference to food and eating of food show hard times when food was scarce and health of people indifferent, even bad? Or do these words admit of symbolic interpretations? One need not choose one possibility to the exclusion of others. All these possibilities may be in order—together. Symbolically, the reference to food and eating of food implies that only the knower of Brahman becomes the eater of food, of the world, and can digest it, make it one with himself. Only he can turn the other into the self. The violent tragedy of creatures becomes in his case the ecstasy of bliss.

Chapter 7

1. annaṃ na nindyāt. tad vratam. prāṇo vā annam. śarīram annādam. prāṇe śarīraṃ pratiṣṭhitam. śarīre prāṇaḥ pratiṣṭhitaḥ. tad etad annam anne pratiṣṭhitam. sa ya etad annam anne pratiṣṭhitaṃ veda pratitiṣṭhati. annavān annādo bhavati. mahān bhavati prajayā paśubhir brahmavarcasena. mahān kīrtyā.

Let him not disparage food. Be this his vow. Breath, verily, is food. The body is the eater of food. In breath is established the body and in the body is established breath. So food is established in food. He who knows that food is established in food himself is firmly established. Of food does he become the possessor, of food does he become the eater. In offspring does he become great and in cattle, in the splendour of holiness and in renown.

ŚB Since through food has he realised Brahman, through that doorway to it, let him not disparage food as one would not disparage one's spiritual preceptor. For the knower of Brahman, the *śruti* lays down this vow. The vow highlights the value of food. Food partakes of this praise because it is a means for the realisation of Brahman.

Breath, verily, is food. It is food because it dwells within the body. That which dwells within one becomes one's food. Since breath dwells within the body, therefore breath is food and the body is the eater of that food. Likewise, the body too is food and breath its eater. *This* because the body is established in breath, is sustained by breath. Therefore, each of these two—body and breath—is both eater and eaten. Each is the food of the other because they are both established in each other, and each is the eater of the other because each is the base of the other. Therefore, each of the two is both the eater and the eaten—the body of the breath and the breath of the body.

He who knows, this way, food as established in food is firmly established as eater–eaten. And of food does he become the possessor and eater. These words, as also what follows them, have already been explained.

Creation is an eater–eaten duality and so is man. Man would consume the earth, the earth man, the body breath and breath the body. The entire creation is a dance of plunder, of prey and cruel violence. For me it is a cruel creation if I appropriate to myself the role and status of the eater, of the eater alone and reduce others to the level of the eaten, of food. For the narcissistic creature that I am the world is indeed a cruel tragedy. But if I, through a lucid insight, recognise my status as that of an eater–eaten ambiguity, then this very cruel world will change into a redemptive *yajña*, sacrifice. I will not then fear it and avoid it through narcissistic pleasures, sadistic cruelties, masochistic pains. For I will then know what these are, these pleasures and pains—illusory, painful, tragic. To be only the eater is, however, the governing passion of most of us, the cause primal of our tragic lot. To have the capacity, the meekness, the generosity to be the eater–eaten ambiguity is the mark of the few, those who can perceive the redemptive possibilities of our colossal tragedy.

A man informed by this vision will not disparage food because he perceives himself in it and it in himself. For food too is an eater like him and he too is an eaten like food. This acceptance of one's mortality and of the world unfolds the vision of the world as as *madhu*, as honey, the paradisal drink of immortality. Only a man of this vision can be the possessor of food, he who knows himself as the eaten. For only he knows the joy, the ecstasy of creation as *yajña*, not self-centred creatures who ever remain starved of being and of life. And only he can eat in abundance, only his hunger is fully appeased. Only he has the capacity to eat the entire world, make it his own, turn it into the self.

Chapter 8

1. annaṃ na paricakṣīta. tad vratam. āpo vā annam. jyotir annādam. apsu jyotiḥ pratiṣṭhitam. jyotiṣyāpaḥ pratiṣṭhītāḥ. tad etad annam anne pratiṣṭhitam. sa ya etad annam anne pratiṣṭhitaṃ veda pratitiṣṭhati. annavān annādo bhavait. mahān bhavati prajayā paśubhir brahmavarcasena. mahān kīrtyā.

Let him not despise food. Let this be his vow. Waters, verily, are the eaten, light the eater. In water is light established and in light the waters. So food is established in food. He who knows that food is established in food is firmly established. Of food does he become the possessor and eater. Great does he become in progeny, in cattle, in holy splendour and in renown.

ŚB Let him not despise food, let him not discard it. 'Let this be his vow' are, as in the preceding chapter, words of praise. Thus food is praised and made great. It is not to be despised through thoughts of good and bad. The sentences to follow—commencing from 'waters, verily are the eaten, light the eater'—should be interpreted the same way as 'breath is food, the body the eater' etc. were interpreted earlier.

The eater–eaten duality extends to include waters and light, i. e., fire. Water flows on earth, the flame of fire leaps upwards. Water is the *rajas* principle, fire the *sattva* principle. *Sattva* is the urge for transcendence, *rajas*, the urge to act, to change, to improve. You want to change because you find the present state of being inadequate. This feeling of inadequacy is common to every state of being, whether inherited or brought about through praxis. So one has, ultimately, to pay heed to the call of transcendence, that of *sattva*, the call which demands of creation to undo itself into the plenitude of being the Upaniṣads call *ātman* or Brahman. So let waters, *rajas*, be the food of fire, of *sattva*. But if one would embrace *sattva* alone and would discard all states of affairs, one would do it out of conscious choice and that would mean remaining a prisoner of the thought of giving up, of discarding. So let man offer the urge for transcendence inherent him, too, as food to the urge to act. Let him act but without the passion to bring about the desired change. Let him not shun his status as eater–eaten ambiguity, let him remain it, live it. If man lives this status of mortality this way, without fret and without vanity, he will turn his tragedy into redemption, his bondage into release.

Chapter 9

1. annaṃ bahu kurvīta. tad vratam. pṛthivī vā annam. ākāśo 'nnādaḥ. pṛthivyām ākāśaḥ pratiṣṭhitaḥ. ākāśe pṛthivī pratiṣṭhitā. tad etad annam anne pratiṣṭhitam. sa ya etad annam anne pratiṣṭhitaṃ veda pratitiṣṭhati. annavān annādo bhavati. mahān bhavati prajayā paśubhir brahmavarcasena. mahān kīrtyā.

Let him produce food in plenty. Let this be his vow. The vast domain, earth, verily, is food, the sky is the eater. The sky is established on the earth and on the sky is established the earth. Thus food is established on food. He who knows that food is established on food comes to be firmly established. Of food does he become the possessor, of food does he become the eater. Great does he become in progeny, in cattle, in the splendour holy and in renown.

ŚB The vow to make food in plenty is meant for one who worships water and light as eater–eaten dualities as mentioned in the preceding chapter.

How does one make food in plenty by worshipping water and fire as constitutive–negating dualities? Worshipping these two this way, and not as polar opposites, implies that one live as a mortal, as one who owns up to one's mortality, does not fight against it nor try to transcend it. While *techné* may produce more food or so may faith, for faith, they say, can move mountains, what is there in the man whose only virtue is his deep realisation that he is a mortal, practically a nothing? Will this earth respond to his needs, and the vast dome of the sky?

When man owns up to his mortality, earth and sky no longer remain objective. It is only the me as presence that finds the cosmos—earth and sky—as objective reality. When the me as presence lives as a mortal, it flows with the flow of time. For this flowing me, earth and sky lose their status as objective others, they too turn temporal, they too mingle with the flow of thoughts to become the flow. When space thus mingles with time, matter into mind, then the entire world turns into food for consciousness. Everything, every moment, every atom merges into consciousness. With consciousness turning contentless and unintentional, it too ceases to be consciousness, it too turns into food. This is the moment of *ānanda*, of bliss absolute. But even before this death of consciousness, there is the state of plenitude, when the other is there but on the point of mingling with consciousness. This point of being is the moment of plenty, of ecstasy, of joy, for it is the state when all is food for oneself, all is on the point of being swallowed up by oneself. This is the meaning of having food in plenty—at the symbolic level.

Whether such a man can produce food in abundance in the ordinary sense of the expression, whether the earth and the sky will literally respond to his prayers, is a question which should be left for the consideration of *yogins* and mystics. Do they acquire the power to perform miracles when matter turns, for them, into mind? Is faith that can move mountains the same thing as the state of the eater, the state in which 'man' can digest the entire cosmos? Only prophets can answer these questions.

But what does the *śruti* mean when it says that earth and sky too are eater–eaten dualities as are water and fire? Earth and sky are objective realities but only for the man who is earthly. *Pṛthivī*, earth, means vast domain, it means space. For a situated being, the cosmos is indeed the other, not the self. But the moment man tries to interiorise sky into himself, the moment he lets its infinity sink into him, then spatial relations tend to melt away. Man does not remain here, nor the sky remain there, man comes to dwell there and the sky comes to dwell here. The presence of the body becomes vague and faint, the flow of thought is suspended, or almost suspended. The entire man–world turns into one peaceful being, a whole almost without parts. The earth is there and the sky is there, the moon is there and the stars are there but all phenomena are overpowered with a sense of the whole, earth mingling into the sky and the sky mingling into earth, each sustaining the other, and yet, in a sense, negating the other. For the sky does not remain the sky and the earth does not remain the earth. There is neither east there nor west, nor north nor south, nor above nor below. Everything is on the verge of a wished for collapse, on the verge of an ecstatic death. Yet how calm is that vision, how inarticulate and yet meaningful, a nothing which is everything. This, I believe, is the meaning of earth and sky being related to each other in terms of food and the eater of food. It is not merely a matter of matter collapsing into mind or space into time when we experience earth and sky as eater–eaten dualities, it is also a matter of time and space, matter and mind being overpowered by a nothingness. Who could imagine that unreality can be so beautiful, so rich and so unnervingly bewitching!

Chapter 10

1. na kaṃcana vasatau pratyācakṣīta. tad vratam. tasmād yayā kayā ca vidhayā bahvannaṃ prāpnuyāt. ārādhyasmā annam ity ācakṣate. etad vai mukhato 'nnaṃ rāddham. mukhato 'smā annaṃ rādhyate. etad vai madhyato 'nnaṃ rāddham. madhyato 'smā annaṃ rādhyate. etad vā antato 'nnaṃ rāddham. antato 'smā annaṃ rādhyate.

2. ya evaṃ veda. kṣema iti vāci. yogakeṣema iti prāṇāpānayoḥ. karmeti hastayoḥ. gatir iti pādayoḥ. vimuktir iti pāyau. iti mānuṣīḥ samājñāḥ. atha daivīḥ. tṛptir iti vṛṣṭau. balam iti vidyuti.

3. yaśa iti paśuṣu. jyotir iti nakṣatreṣu. prajātir amṛtam ānanda ity upasthe. sarvam ity ākāśe. tat pratiṣṭhety upāsīta. pratiṣṭhāvān bhavati. tan maha ity upasīta. mahān bhavati. tan mana ity upāsīta. mānavān bhavati.

4. tan nama ity upāsīta. namyante 'smai kāmāḥ. tad brahmety upāsīta. brahmavān bhavati. tad brahmaṇaḥ parimara ity upāsīta. paryeṇaṃ mriyante dviṣantaḥ sapatnāḥ. pari ye 'priyā bhrātṛvyāḥ. sa yaś cāyaṃ puruṣe yaś cāsāvāditye sa ekaḥ.

Let not man deny hospitality to one who comes to him for shelter. Let this be his vow. Let him, therefore, obtain, by whatever means, plenty of food. Of the one who comes for shelter, they say: Food is ready for him. If food is prepared in an excellent way for the guest, it will be prepared in an excellent way for the giver. If it is prepared in a mediocre way for the guest, it will be prepared in a mediocre way for the giver. If it is prepared in a wretched way for the guest, it will be prepared in a wretched way for the giver. (1)

He who knows thus [he gets the same reward promised to the seer of eater–eaten dualities].

In speech is he present as preservation, in outgoing breath and incoming breath as acquisition and preservation. In the hands as action, in the feet as motion, in the anus as evacuation. This is the human form of meditation. And now the divine.

In the rain he is satisfaction, in the lightning is he energy. (2) in the cattle he is glory, in the stars he glimmers as light. Procreation is he in the genitals, and immortality and bliss. Let man worship him as foundation and foundation shall he have. Let him worship him as maha *and great shall he become. Let him worship him as* manas, *mind, and mindful shall he become. (3)*

Let man worship him as adoration and desires shall come to adore him. Let man worship him as Brahman and of Brahman shall he become the master. Let him worship him as Brahman's destruction and die shall his envious adversaries and kinsmen he does not like.

That who is in this person and that who is yonder in the sun are one. (4)

ŚB Let not the man who worships earth and sky as eater–eaten dualities refuse hospitality to any who comes to him for shelter, let him not turn him back. If you give shelter to one, you must provide food also to him. Let man, therefore, obtain, by whatever means, plenty of food, let him store it in abundance. Since well provided men given to meditation do not refuse food to a hungry guest, rather welcome him by saying: 'Food is ready,' let them, for this reason of their hospitable disposition, procure food in profusion. This is how '. . . food is ready for him' should be connected with 'Let him . . . obtain plenty of food.'

Now the Upaniṣad tells us what reward shall he reap who thus gives food to a guest. The way he gives food the same way shall he get it and the time he gives it, the same time shall he get it, it says. The *śruti* elaborates this for us:

He who prepares food for the hungry guest *mukhataḥ*, at an early age or in an excellent way, with feelings of regard and veneration, the same way shall he receive it—either at an early age or in the best way. As he gives it, so shall he receive it. This shall be his reward. '. . . prepares food,' of course, implies giving it. Similarly, if the time of giving is middle age, he shall receive it in the middle age, if the manner of giving is mediocre, he shall receive it in the selfsame manner. The same is the case with old age or the wretched way, i.e., with contempt.

Man is born as a guest of the earth, she is not his permanent home, only a mortal home. Yet this pilgrim, this sojourner receives a treatment like that given to an inmate. Earth is almost kind to him and his family more than kind. It is proper, therefore, that he give to the unknown guest the same treatment that he receives from earth and those he calls his. A guest is a symbol of mortal man's place in the world. A traveller, he is a seeker of temporary shelter and a few morsels of food. Nothing belongs to him, all that he calls his is only a gift. That is his life, his being, the being of a constant traveller, his home far away and unknown.

Let him care for the guest in all stages of life, from youth to middle age to old age. And let him honour him well, be obliged to him, not hold him in contempt. That should be his vow, his holy undertaking. For the law is that he will receive but what he gives. Even the time of giving will be reciprocated, not merely the manner of giving. Faith in this law has produced high cultures and civilisations. This faith is now deserting us, has, almost, deserted us. It is difficult for most of us to be humble and obliged towards those who need our help. We would be indifferent, and if not indifferent, then vain and self–righteous. Without faith in the goodness and generosity of their gods, men tend to be small minded. It is, however, easier to believe in the goodness of God than in the goodness of vain men, only a thin line divides them from the frustrated and the unfeeling.

Can we regain faith in a moral order of the world? We are accustomed to look upon the world as a repository of our rational–manipulative thought. We believe we can understand it to an impressive extent and control and manipulate it. We do not, however, think that for our feelings and moral aspirations the world has any place. So we have changed the content of our feelings and aspirations; instead of peace we seek power, instead of well being we seek money. Our better sentiments we have reserved for our families. Our society, which is geared to controlling nature, has, therefore, not much room for our 'sentiments'. All holy feelings with regard to nature are out of the question. We may demand of our artists to express, on occasions, such feelings for us, for we realise, however vaguely, that feelings of this sort are necessary for our mental health and even for the survival of our civilisation. We, of course, indulge in such feelings for what may be called curative purposes, to restore our health and our efficiency. When it comes to brass tacks, we would, however, resort to rational investigations, serious, tentative, open–ended; we would not dream of either prayer or contemplation. Feelings that would convert this earth into *our* earth, our home and our god, we reserve for moments of sophisticated pastime. We would inoculate these feelings into our psyche in order to escape from the dangerous malady of schizophrenia. It is no use saying to modern man: You care for the stranger, and this earth, this symbol of appalling otherness, will suddenly turn alive to your life and your aspirations. We live in an age in which we would not even think of refuting such views, so absurd they seem to us.

There is, however, something in us that revolts against this attitude. Take a man who does not have the temperament of a scientist, who cannot understand the world the way science understands it. Should he be supposed to be a part of the blue print that technocrats have devised for our life? Those who believe that our world embodies only a part of us, only the reason in us, those who deny that there are dimensions in the world correlative to moral and spiritual dimensions in us would expect man to live the way technology has chalked out for us, however sophisticated, however 'nonsimplistic' their articulation of this expectation might be. For the man who matters for theorists of this kind, the man who is relevant is one who can identify himself, as far as possible, with reason. That is, in essence, our belief, inspite of all the qualifications we may add to it.

It is hard, really hard, in this our 'successful' age, to have trust in earth, faith in her. But we who swear in the name of humanity, could listen to the Upaniṣads. They ask us to have care and concern for the guest, for the man we do not know, who cannot do any 'good' to us, and for other creatures. If we have concern and care for man and beast, then earth will be more kind to us than we could ever be kind to men and beasts; it will reveal more than its human face for us, it will reveal it divine face. It will not let us remain human beings, when it unveils its divine visage before us, it will turn us into gods. Less than the god it will not tolerate in us. Earth is a stern other for us because we act as the other to human and other beings. When we shed that otherness, earth will not, of course, be generous to us the way we want her to be generous; she will not replace our technologies. She will become divine to make us divine.

ŚB He who knows thus, knows thus the greatness of food revealed earlier, and of giving away food, will find the reward mentioned earlier.

The *śruti* next proceeds to reveal another form of meditation on Brahman in 'In speech is he present as preservation. . . .' Preservation means preservation of a thing already in one's possession. Brahman is present in speech in the form of preservation. Thus should it be meditated. In outgoing and incoming breaths, it is present as preservation and acquisition, acquisition of that which is not already in one's possession. Preservation and acquisition are possible only when outgoing and incoming breaths, *prāṇa* and *apāna*, are in motion but these breaths are not their causes. Only Brahman is the cause of preservation and acquisition. Brahman is present in outgoing and incoming breath as preservation and acquisition and should be meditated as such.

How is Brahman present as *kṣema,* as preservation, as safety in speech? No phenomenon can exist as itself without being informed by language. Language may be said to preserve it, preserve its identity. Many a modern thinker will agree on this point. The Upaniṣad, however, speaks of a deeper informing principle than language. Language can speak only of the *kind* of the phenomenon in question, of its *class.* It is not the individuating principle. The individual is the referent of the subject term, it is not encompassed by the predicate terms that turn it into an interpreted, linguistically informed, phenomenon. The anchor of *this,* the referent of the subject term, is Brahman. Without this informing principle, I am not there to be interpreted as a man, as a teacher, as a student. So when I *stay* as *man,* I stay, prior to *man,* as *this.* This *this* reveals itself when the act of predication ceases to operate, thought process comes to a standstill and even the motion of breath is scarcely felt.

What one preserves and what one acquires depends on the motion of breath. Life that is mere breathing consists of merely acquisition and preservation, a sleeping over the teleological thrust that informs our life. Until my breath stops moving, I continue to preserve my interpreted identity, identity that is not *me,* my self, but a mere public label. This self is a dissatisfied self because it tends to throttle my real self, which rejects it. No linguistic label can really catch me, for I constantly disown it through my mortality, through, paradoxically enough, my breathing. To meet this disowning that will not rest until it undoes me, I acquire other things, other labels to be a different self. So the process continues, the useless process of being a being. But even this acquiring and preserving are not the functions of my breath, my life, but are dependent on Brahman.

I preserve my identity, linguistically informed identity, through Brahman. And whatever I acquire, whatever I become, too, derives its being from Brahman. Before that being comes to be interpreted, it is an *it,* a *this,* not the class that language would equate it with. The motion of breath leads me from one interpretation to another interpretation but this comes to be possible only because I am already an *am* and what I acquire and what I come to be is already an *is* to be called a class. Mortals find Brahman as *is* or *am,* of the nature of being, but can grasp it or be it as other than *is* or *am,* as the undoing of *is* or *am.* The undoing is frightening for them, hence their interpretations and their actions. Until they accept that undoing, until they live their mortality, they will not escape this tragic dichotomy. They can also escape it if they have the courage and endurance to be the *is* in them and disown the undoing. Either way, they can die into their being, their life, where dualities like identity and process, being and becoming will not obtain.

ŚB Similarly, Brahman should be meditated in each of the other forms the *śruti* will mention. Thus all action comes to be possible because Brahman is there to be the act each and every. Thus Brahman should be meditated as action in the hands, as motion in the feet, as evacuation in the anus. Such are the human forms of meditation, perfect meditations of Brahman as the varied functions of the organs of the human body.

Now the *śruti* will mention meditation of Brahman in varied divine forms. Brahman should thus be meditated as satisfaction in rain. Rain brings about satisfaction through food, etc. That satisfaction is Brahman. It should be meditated as such, as satisfaction that rain brings about.

It should be meditated the same way in other phenomenona, too—-as their self, their essence. Thus it should be meditated as energy in lightning, as glory in cattle, as light in the stars, as procreation, immortality and pleasure in the genitals. [Pleasure and procreation need no explanation]. As to immortality, it falls to the lot a man through his discharge from the debt he owes to his ancestors through begetting a son. Pleasure, procreation and immortality, the continuation of one's line, are possible through the genitals. Brahman is present in the genitals in these forms and should be meditated as such.

The secular and the holy, the physical and the spiritual are not two different realms. The physical is spiritual, the secular holy (though the spiritual will not consent to be the physical and the holy secular). You see the clouds gather in the sky to cool and soothe the earth parched with the pitiless heat of the summer sun. Their rain falls on the earth to make it productive, to make its fields green and rich. Their promise of a good harvest makes the race of men smile with satisfaction. This smile of satisfaction is Brahman, the result of a theoanthoropocosmic act. For gods of rain, earth and sky, men and oxen have joined to produce the harvest. And also the sacrificial offerings to gods. The smile is not merely human, it is the smile of man, of beasts, of earth, of air, of clouds and gods. It is a smile of the universe, of the known and the unknown, of what has come to be and of what is yet to be. In one gleam of that smile you can see all the smiles, of that which is the world and that which is beyond the world.

When rain comes to bless, thunder and lightning also appear to smite and destroy. Mortals can, in certain fortunate moments, participate in that smile but they find it hard to participate in the terror and destruction. The coappearance of the smile and the terror is symbolic of the coappearance of life and death for the creatures of the world and coappearance of *Virāj* and the *avaykta* for the man on the path. The cosmotheandric smile, the smile of *Virāj*, is also the terror of the *avyakta*. Man has to accept both, to be blessed by both, he cannot have one and reject the other. The joy of being all is a prelude to the 'bliss' of being a nothing.

There is, to move on to the next meditation, the vault of the starry sky, vast and infinite, with stars glimmering without number. Yet the *light* that emanates from the awesome galaxies is dim and useless, useless for the doer in us. This seemingly useless light is also, let the busy man remember, the supreme Brahman, this all-pervasive, scarcely visible light. Let man meditate this light-in-darkness, the light that only makes, to borrow a phrase from Milton, darkness visible. Let this light steal into your mind, let it make your ideas vague, your thoughts indeterminate, your sensations faint and your desires weak. You will find 'untruth' steal into you with this light. You will find your personality fall off from you and all its weary weight. You will find yourself free from the bondage of existence, from the threat of the other. You will find death in what you have all along called life and life in what you have called death.

Wealth through security and sex through the touch of the other's body make one feel that one is a being with a self, a soul, that one is a being, not an event among other events. The family provides a prop to this feeling. Wealth, sex and family sabotage the truth of one's mortality, they make man sleep over it. This sleeping over, however, reveals what man seeks through them, what he is in search of. It is being that he seeks through them, the being that ever remains being, the being that is Brahman. Let man, therefore, meditate on wealth and sex as Brahman. For that end, he is to turn his wealth into glory. Let him not degrade it into a mere means of self-preservation, let him turn it into glory by giving it to others. Let him turn it into glory by sharing the insecurity of others, symbolised by the traveller, hungry and lonely. And let his narcissistic sex turn into the joy of belonging, to the joy that one feels through relating to others, through relating to the family line, the joy of receiving and bequeathing. You feel yourself immortal because you help create the immortal family line, a family line that goes back to the dead ancestors, to the land of the dead. When you thus become a part of life and its source that now belongs to death, when you live as a receiver and a giver, as a creature and a creator, as alive and as dead, then you contemplate sex act as Brahman. Of time is your pleasure then and of timelessness, of being is it and of nonbeing, of truth and of untruth.

ŚB *Sarvam,* all, dwells in the ether of space. As Brahman should all that be worshipped. The ether of space too is Brahman, the ether of space that is the support of all that exists in it. Therefore, Brahman should be worshipped thus, as the support of all. By worshipping Brahman as the support of all shall man be blessed with support. What is true of this meditation is also true of other meditations mentioned earlier. Whatever fruit a thing can bear, Brahman verily is that fruit. When man meditates on that fruit as Brahman, its master shall he be. Let him understand this. The *śruti* says in another context: 'In whatever form man worships it, that very form does he become.'

Thus he becomes great if he worships Brahman as great, if as thought, he becomes a man of thought, capable of thinking. [3]

Man is, basically, a doer. When doing turns, as it has done in our age, into the act of comprehending and mastering nature, then the doer gives place to function, a function in the collective effort. The individual disappears in the practice, so do his instruments of understanding, his concepts and categories, even Nature that was the original object of the theoretico-practical practice. For in this practice, there remain no given truths or beings, truths are to be forged and so are beings. Practice turns into history and history into a forge, a workshop. A time comes, however, when the truth of the forge itself is in question; in this limbo of tentativities, even history is not spared, it too turns into a tentativity.

The *śruti* asks man to do solitary contemplations to encompass the other, to make it turn into his self. This approach has no meaning for our contemporary attitudes. These attitudes have, however, eroded values and hopes. The man to be forged has no being and no truth to be protected; he has no given values that could be cherished or pursued. He has no aims and objectives that humanity could endeavour to realise in the course of history. This is the irony of our age: history itself has undone history.

In our confusions we have forgotten that we are not doings, we are doers. A doer cannot be pinpointed, cannot be identified. He is a contradiction, a self-negation. But he cannot be wished away, he cannot be reduced to an unstable act, a mere function. In every practice, he remains there to make his presence felt. For collective effort is not a mere succession of events, it is a move towards a goal, whether the goal is final and necessary or tentative and contingent would not make much of a difference. History as a universal phenomenon or as a local phenomenon are not important distinctions from this point of view. In both the cases, things and beings are forged, concepts employed and categories used. You may replace these categories by others but when you are immersed in the act you cannot do without them. No understanding is possible without them and no action. To say that concepts and categories, beings and things, emerge in the process of practice itself is a contradiction in terms. For no practice can be cognised or imagined without them. Practice is a doer–doing, concept–process ambiguity, it is not a doing, an unambiguous doing, which somehow gives rise to concepts and beings.

Those thinkers who equate man with the material act thus reduce, perhaps unintentionally, man into a mere tool of productive practice. It is no use bringing in the concept of 'communicative action' to redeem man from this wreck. For unless and until you find the man you cannot possibly speak of his contribution. Man is not a contribution, he is a contributor. Even though you do not find, cannot identify, the doer, you cannot eliminate him.

Kant may have been, was, wrong when he talked of given categories. Perhaps even his concepts were not *a priori*. Categories change and concepts break down but they are indispensable. The contents of concepts and categories do undergo revision, sometimes even radical disruptions but they ever remain tied up to thought, categories as such and concepts as such. You simply cannot think without them, nor can you comprehend nor perceive. Neither can you do without what Kant called the unity of apperception. One cannot, however, predicate anything of the unity of apperception; you cannot even call it unity of apperception. To predicate anything of it will mean reducing it into a phenomenon, to call it unity of apperception would mean making it relational to phenomena. It is unity of apperception only in relation to phenomena, the way it integrates 'them' into intelligible wholes. I put *them* within quotes because one cannot say what things are prior to being made intelligibles. To us they are revealed as already intelligibles.

So the truth of man is the unity of apperception but before it comes to be 'the unity of apperception'. The unity of apperception is mere *avidyā*. What is it that it unifies? There can be no raw material which has not already been forged into unity by the unity of apperception, there is not even a before without it. What it presents as truth is a hopeless confusion; its intelligibility is only apparent, not real. Yet this concealment is our truth, our being. We have to own it up, this confusion and confusion making power, this nothing that brings about everything. We have to accept ourselves as individuals and look on the world as *alones*. The alone can only pray and, if he is calm and detached enough, meditate; he cannot act the way the communality acts. He cannot reduce himself into a bare function.

There is the world before him, before this alone. What is he to do with that world? There is the sky before him. What shall he do with the sky? He walks all alone without an aim—for all aims are *their* aims. What is he to make of the walking? The *śruti* asks him to contemplate all the functions, all the phenomena, within the body and outside the body. What shall he find them to be?

First to take up the words we speak, the words we take to be mere instruments of expression. We pick them up as if they were there around us, as we would pick up tools. We do not try to see how they, in fact and in truth, relate to uṣ. We do not pause to feel and contemplate the deep mystery of the *vāc*, of the word, to find how the being of all dwells in it as the preserver, as the sustainer of our life and being. We need to listen to the Vedas [*Ṛg Veda* 10.71][1] to feel the mystery and have a glimpse of the truth:

uta tvaḥ paśyan na dadarśa vācam
uta tvaḥ śṛṇvan na śṛṇoty enām,
uto tvasmai tanvaṃ vi sasre
jāyeva patya uśatī suvāsāḥ. (4)

Seeing, one may not see the Word
Hearing, one may hear her not.
To some the Word disrobes herself freely
as to her husband' a fair mantled bride.

In the world of man, the Word is used, not loved. That is the reason why men fail to see her true form, her splendid body, the restless race of men and women ever anxious to utilise and to exploit. For she will reveal that form, that body, only to an ardent husband tied to her by bonds sacred and unbreakable, not to one who would reduce her to a mere tool. How to relate oneself to her through the sacred and holy bond so that we may know what is her truth and being, the Vedas would reveal to us:

yas tityāja sacividaṃ sakhāyaṃ
na tasya vācy api bhāgo asti
yad īṃ ṣṛṇoty alkaṃ ṣṛṇoti
nahi praveda sukṛtasya panthām. (6)

The man who gives up a named-alike
in the know of the named-alike,

1. The *sūkta* has been analysed in full, pp. 117-25. Here we have another look at some as its verses.

shall have no share in the vāc, *in the Word.*
Whatever he hears, he hears in vain.
Never shall he know the path to the good.

The named alike is the sharer of the same name with you, he is your friend indeed. If you break this holy bond of sharing, if you abandon a true friend, the Word too will abandon you. You will cease to be man when you betray your friend. For you are what you are, a friend, because of the sharing in the Word. The name informs the other as much as it informs you, it shows itself forth only in sharing, not in isolation. A self-centred man will not find the Word, the Word as his sustaining principle, for it will be only a name. Only a being-with-others can know how the word the tool is really and truly the Word the soul. When you freely flow to others and let them flow to you, only then will you know what it is to have a share in the Word. And this flowing is not to be confined to mankind alone, for when you have flowed enough to beings who share the same name with you, you will know that your name is but one manifestation of the same Name, that sharing in the Word as such is common to all that is. When you have vision of this common sharing, only then will the Word reveal itself, the word as Brahman. Only then shall you know and recognise in speech the sustaining principle, of yours and of all that is. It is in and through love, the first *mantra* of this *sūkta* tells us, that sages name things. To name a thing is to lend your identity, your self, your *ātman* to it. It is through this sacrifice that one comes to find the Word, disrobed and in itself. Thus:

yajñena vācaḥ padavīyam āyan
tām anvavindann ṛṣiṣu praviṣṭām,
tām ābhṛtyā vyadadhuḥ purutrā
tāṃ sapta rebhā abhi saṃ navante. (3)

The trace of the Word they followed through sacrifice,
and found her reposing within the seers.
They brought her forth to reveal it to many
Seven are the singers to sing her together.

The Word has deserted our world because we have forsaken each other. If we do away with our narcissism, sacrifice it, we shall be able to find her. We shall find her entered in among the *ṛṣis,* seers of *vāc,* of the Vedic *mantras.* Those who love all, who perceive their common ontological sharing, live as stillness in stillness. To them alone the Word reveals herself, to them alone does she speak. To such seers should men resort to find the Word, to find themselves. For the seer as one with the Word speaks the Word, not its shadows as we do, miserable creatures who love only ourselves, not others. When we receive the Word as fit recipients, when, that is to say, all the seven seers, seven senses, in us sing her praise, only her praise, then we too shall save the world from death. We shall reveal the Word to many, to make the shadows come back into life. The seven singers are the two eyes, the two ears, the two nostrils and the mouth.

Meditation on breath has occupied our attention many a time. Breath is the process of acquisition, acquisition in the form of inhaling. Inhaling, however, is impossible without exhaling, receiving without giving. So Brahman is receiving that is also giving. It should be meditated as this spirit of acquisition, as receiving that is also giving.

When we do an act with our hands, our attention is so much focussed on the act and the things associated with it that we forget our hands, do not take notice of them. We identify ourselves so deeply with our hands that they get isolated from the world of objects, cease to be things among things. We have to release them, free them into the world of objects to which they belong. To do this, we must look at our hands when they are engaged in the task in question. At this moment, when I am writing, I allow my hands to get back to the world, to get back their status as objects. I send them to the *kṣetra*, to the objective sphere. This sending back does not interfere with my writing. My writing continues but I become aware, when I see this movement of my right hand, when I feel the pressure of the pen on my nervous thumb and fingers, that there is something in me that is not the hand. My hand stops moving, my eyes close and I see an amassed something in the head which soon envelops my body, turning it into a presence, dark and endless. What horizons ring this presence I cannot see or feel. To contemplate this presence is, paradoxically enough, to dissociate oneself from it. What is that self which contemplates it I do not know, for that never turns into an object. That, the Upaniṣads say, is the infinite, that is Brahman, this *sākṣin*, this witness of the darkness in me.

Similar revelation will occur if I see with concentrated attention the motion of my feet. To concentrate on every step I take is to extricate myself from the interests I have in walking, whether to reach a particular place or do my daily exercise. How restless are morning walkers, not to speak of those who are on a journey! Let *me* move with each step I take, be as it were that step. The traveller will, before long, halt, overwhelmed by the same dark peace which swallows the contemplator of the motion of the hand. The interiority that contemplates, without knowing that it contemplates, that dark interiority I cannot be until I too contemplate what I call me with thought-free concentration.

Men and women nauseate at the very mention of the word 'anus'. It is not a word that should, they feel, be uttered in polite society, in the house of god, in legislative assemblies, in courts. You may contemplate the sun, the moon, the sky or the earth, you may contemplate your breath, your pain, your anguish but certainly not anus, much less the act of evacuation. This seat of narcissism is indeed filthy. But contemplation of the anus in the act of evacuation distances man from the body. It reveals, in the first place, what man receives from the earth and what he gives back. The resultant injury to self-esteem is not, of course, the end. The end is handing over the body back to the world and the contemplation in question is the first step towards this end. The contemplation reveals how this body is an object, empty from the throat to the anus. You can feel that emptiness most immediately, can live it to become, eventually, the *avyakta*, the unmanifest.

We have already deliberated on the nature of satisfaction, the smile that appears in the face of man when he perceives, all happy, the rain falling on his fields. The seeker of truth is asked to focus his attention on this feeling of satisfaction. This focusing will exteriorise his satisfaction, make him distant from it, from this theoanthropocosmic satisfaction. His self will reveal itself if he contemplates this satisfaction, provided his attention is exclusively, spontaneously and, more importantly, innocently concentrated upon it. He will feel the presence of that self as the deepest interiority, he will never know it as he knows an object, this innocence without name and characteristics.

People fear lightning, they cannot, dare not, think of meditating it. In ancient India, lightning was not merely thought fearful, it was also worshipped as holy. Like *Agni* burning at the altar, it was not merely divine but also a friend to man, 'of many,' says the *Ṛg Veda*, 'the closest friend' (2.35.12). A lonely traveller lost at night in a forest found it a friend and also a young woman going to meet her lover at night, protected from scandal by the dark night and the dark clouds, with lightning showing her the way. A man who feels the deep mystery and beauty of things forbidding and terrible too found it a friend, the most intimate and closest.

The restless line of light among the clouds fascinates the eye, its thunder deafens the ear. It blasts trees, sends down an avalanche of water down the mountain slopes, spares neither man nor beast. This fire in water can also, if one gives oneself up to it, kill thoughts with its thunder. Brahman too undoes man and his thoughts, it too is light and, as *praṇava*, roaring thunder. Lightning is its manifestation, manifestation of its light and thunder. Let man contemplate that beauty and that terror, let him contemplate it in serene unconcern. That flash, implies the Upaniṣad, will turn into revelation and that thunder into *praṇava*, and the possibility of death through one's exposure to it into possibility of salvation. Lightning is a *devatā*, divine light, and divinity favours man through undoing him.

The cattle meant in the days of the Upaniṣads what we now call wealth and bank balance, a wealth visible, living and life sustaining, related to man through bonds of intimacy and affection. Your fame depended not only on the number of cows and bullocks you owned but also on how you looked after them. Each cow had a proper name, each bullock and each calf. Such was your wealth which expanded your human self to encompass the nonhuman world. You cared for these creatures and tended their pastures, relating yourself to earth. You waited for the proper season to sow, you waited for rain and for sunshine, your life assumed cosmic dimensions. That was the *dharma* of the *vaiśya*, the man of wealth: to tend and care for the cattle. The fame he got as a man of wealth spoke of the expansiveness of his soul, of his care and concern. This glory of wealth was also a divine glory, for this expansiveness of the soul also opened out that interiority the Upaniṣads call the *ātman* or the self. For deeply serene is this expansiveness which, when exteriorised through contemplation, leads to the revelation of the self. One steps out of it, out of this glory, to be the self.

The contemplation of the sky and the starry heaven has had our attention, we need not pause at this sublime contemplation.

We shall pass on to the generative organ, to the phallus, man's torture. An appendage as it were, this organ does not integrate with the body. It would go out of it as it were to rest somewhere else. The phallus and its female counterpart make of men and women householders and open out all the redemptive possibilities in that station.

It is as a householder that man comes to give up his narcissism that he inherits from the womb. There he was the world and the world was him. Here the genitals compel him to seek his life, his being, his joy in the other, in *human* space, in woman, and in *human* time, in the family line. [Needless to add that what is true of man is also true of woman]. A householder is always a being-with-others, he is a *Mitsein*. That is what his gentials make of him, these divinities. They also alienate him from earth. A householder is an inhabitant of home, not of earth. So much of narcissism he still retains. The deep tragedy of life makes him realise, through a long probation, that he is not a mere householder or a creature of civilisation but a creature of earth. The flow from civilisation to earth, to the cosmos, becomes possible through the gift of suffering. And also his orientation towards godhood. That too is a gift of suffering. A householder is a mortal and a mortal is always unhappy. The mortal becomes the god and the cosmos when he accepts his suffering, when he lives it. That is the promise that a householder's life holds for him.

Sarvam iti ākāse, as all in the vacuity of space.

The all is inconceivable but when imagined as existing within the empty space, it becomes conceivable. The infinitude of space setting limits to all also makes itself imagine-able in the process of making the all conceivable. The all–space is the face of Brahman, its revelation to man. Imagine the world existing within space. The space will appear endless, boundless and the world, however vast and huge, will be a tiny thing within the infinite space. The world, the all will be just like me. As I am a small thing living in space, so will be the world. From the standpoint of the former, there will be little difference between me and the world. When I imagine myself within the infinity of empty space, I fade into that emptiness, become that emptiness, emptiness without limits. Infinite do I become then, as infinite as space, larger than the world, the all, stretching beyond its horizons. I become space within a corner of which exists all that we call the world. I become Brahman, the conditioned Brahman, not Brahman the Absolute, for no meditation can lead me to it, not even the meditation of all within space.

Meditation of Brahman as the support of the all: Brahman can be meditated as the all within space or as empty space to which limits are set by the all or by me. To fade into the infinity of space is to become infinitely more than the all. But even this infinity, the infinity of space, exists within what we mortals call consciousness. Awareness, consciousness *is* there; even the infinite, *my* infinite, what I call infinite, admits of this schism within itself. This infinite needs a support and has it in the form of consciousness of it. I call it consciousness but it does not admit this nomenclature; it does not admit it because it never shows forth, never becomes a knowable. I as an individual set limits to the world but this what I call consciousness does not do so because it is not a being, a thing like me to violate the infinitude of space without me. It is merely a peace without a name, a *śūnya,* a nothingness. Yet the fact of its being there is there; it is there as my self, as my being; it is not the me they call the individual. This nothingness which is different from the me they know, this nothingness that never asserts itself, this unknowing knower, this *sākṣin,* the witness is the support of the infinite, this nothing.

I cannot become this nothing until I become innocent of the infinite before me, until I cease to know it. I become this nothing when my contemplation of the infinite comes to cease. The state of *dhyāna*, of contemplation, has to give place to *samādhi*, the state of innocence absolute. As innocence, as nothing alone can man become the support of the world and of its noninterpreted state, the amassed being, the *avyakta*, the unmanifest. This alone is *mūla avidyā*, primal ignorance, this nothingness, this peace infinite. It is *avidyā* precisely because one is aware of its presence as the self. Not to know even this nothing is *vidyā*, enlightenment.

ŚB Let man contemplate it as adoration, as one whose attribute is to bend low [before others]. If a devotee contemplates it this way, all that he desires will bend low before him, obedient and all-humble. And let him contemplate it as Brahman, the Supreme. And his shall be that supremacy; he will be a partaker of the attributes of Brahman. And let him contemplate it as death, as destruction ordained by Brahman. Lightning dies into which and so do rain, the earth, the moon and the sun—that into which die these five gods is called 'death around Brahman'. That death, the death of these five gods, is air as the *śruti* elsewhere confirms.[1] This air is one with the ether of space; therefore, the ether of space is Brahman's destructive power. Let man worship the ether of space as death ordained by Brahman, the ether of space that is of the nature of *vāyu*, air.

If a man knows this, if he worships Brahman's destructive power this way, his envious adversaries will die all around him. Not all adversaries but only those who are envious of him. And so shall the kinsmen he does not like, envious, though, they not be of him.

Earth dies into water, water into fire, fire into air and air into *ākāśa*, into empty space. Such is the process of destruction ordained by Brahman. The other gods too, the moon and the sun, the two eyes of the world, dissolve into the empty space. Let man contemplate this process of destruction, let him contemplate the death of all, including himself, into space. Let him, in other words, contemplate space empty of all content, all objects, all beings, all gods. If he can let himself die into the space, if he can let all that he beholds fade into it, he will find no adversaries around him. Only those who cling to life have enemies, not those who are dead.

ŚB From chapter 8 to chapter 9, the *śruti* has revealed the entire creation, from the body to breath to the ether of space, as of the nature of eater–eaten duality.

---

1. ChU 4.3.1.

Opponent: Yes, it has. What do you want to infer from that?
Answer: From this it follows that the world constituted by eater–eaten dualities belongs to the sphere of the effect, not to the self, the cause of the world. It is superimposed onto the *ātman* through delusion.
Opponent: The *ātman*, too, is an effect of the supreme self, is evolved out of it. It is therefore right to say that it too is immersed in the world, in the recurring cycle of birth and death.
Answer: No. For the *śruti* speaks of the nonworldly entering the world, not of the worldly. 'Having created it, he entered into it.' (TaitU 2.6.1): in these words, the *śruti* speaks of the nonworldly supreme self, the cause of the ether of space and other phenomena, entering into creation. Therefore, the living being that has entered the body is no one else than the supreme self, the nonworldly self, itself. 'Having created it, he entered into it' shows the identity of the one who created the world and the one who entered it. Otherwise the expression 'having created' would not make any sense.
Opponent: On entering creation, the supreme, unworldly self does not remain itself, it undergoes change.
Answer: No, for we have already refuted this possibility by pointing out that Brahman entered into creation for a different purpose (*vide* 2.6).
Opponent: There is a *śruti* that specifically speaks of Brahman entering creation in the form of the individual (*vide* ChU 6.3.2). Now, this would argue for a change in its nature in the process of entrance, change from a nonworldly nature to a worldly one.
Answer: No, for the *śruti* reiterates the identity of the embodied soul with the one *ātman* in the words: Thou art that.
Opponent: 'Thou art that' is meant for contemplation so that the embodied being into which Brahman has changed may regain his lost status by negating his present state of being.
Answer: 'That is real, that is the self, that thou art' (ChU 6.8-16) speaks of the identity of truth, of *ātman* and the embodied being; it does not countenance the change you attribute to the self in the process of its entry into the world.
Objection : The worldly nature of the embodied being is, nevertheless, a fact of life and experience. You cannot deny this.
Answer: No, for he who perceives cannot be perceived.
Objection: But we do experience the self as conditioned by the worldly state of being; worldliness is the constitutive attribute of the embodied self.
Answer: Constitutive attributes are inseparable from what they are attributes of. If worldly nature is a real attribute of the self, it cannot be perceived by the self, the perceiver. To perceive it would be like heating the heat and illuminating the light.
Opponent: We do find the self subject to fear and other maladies. From this fact we cannot but draw the inference that the self is subject to pain and sorrow.
Answer: The very fact that we can perceive fear, sorrow and other maladies shows that they cannot be the attribute of their perceiver.

Opponent: If you think that sorrow and fear and other maladies cannot touch the self, then your views about the matter in question run counter to what Kapila has expounded in his system of *Sāṅkhya* and Kaṇāda in his system of logic.
Answer: This does not affect the soundness of what we say. The systems of Kapila and Kaṇāda do not have a sound foundation. They contradict the teachings of the Vedas (the Upaniṣads). They are therefore unsound and erroneous. That the self is nonworldly is a truth revealed by scriptures and supported by reasoning. And also because it is one with the supreme self. If Kapila and Kaṇāda do not agree on this count, so much the worse for them.
Opponent: How is the self of man one with the supreme self?
Answer: That is stated in: 'That who is in this person and that who is yonder in the sun are one.' This has already been explained (*vide* Tait U 2.8.5)

Traces of absence have been inscribed on each and every thing, each and every being of the world. The entire world is a paradise lost and left behind, tells a tale of ontological fall. You do not know a thing unless and until you know the cause behind it. The world also cries of the loss, of depredation, of having been deprived. To go back to its cause will, however, mean to reduce the cause too to the status of the world, it would mean to rob it of its plenitude. The cause cannot be a worldly cause, wailing for its own cause. The cause has to be nonworldly. To talk of that plenitude, that fullness in terms of cause and effect would, however, mean to deprive it of its fullness, its plenitude. Things of the world produce effects, not that which does not belong to the world. Yet we who live as deprivations in a world that is a deprivation cannot but talk of the cause. We who are not beings but only creatures must, have to, talk about the creator, though the creator cannot be the creator, he can be the creator or the father only in relation to us, to us who are children of impoverishment, ontological impoverishment.

So the cause of the world, the creator, the father is the cause, the creator, the father because we make him so, because our world is an effect, and we are creatures and children. It is because we superimpose our own derivative nature onto him that he becomes the cause, the creator, the father. Not that he is the cause, the creator or the father. Some among us, some who are fascinated by logic and consistency, declare our creator and his creation mere our fabrications and call the world an illusion, and also the act of creation. But these acute thinkers too fail to account for the rise of illusion, the cause of this fabrication. Others, the more serene, the more 'passive', the more innocent, the more open can however find the world as 'full' , as *pūrṇa,* as its supposed cause. They do not draw a distinction between the world and Brahman, creation and the creator, the effect and the cause. They speak of the sameness, of *samatvam*, between the world and Brahman and not of *ajāti*, nonbirth. This is the conclusive view of the wise Gauḍapāda, the well known expounder of *ajāti*:

> The designation of *ātman* as unborn too is the work of imagined concealment. For in its real being, the *ātman* is not even unborn. Concealment which other schools generate through their philosophical positions conjures up the spectre of the birth of the self [and our doctrine of the unborn self is advanced only to refute that position and not to speak the truth about the self]. (GK 4.74)

This kind of talk is possible only for those who have dissolved their personality into the self. Until this dissolution, the self reveals itself as the interiority absolute, as the *śūnya*, as the peace that passeth understanding. Even talk about it as the knower of the field is a superimposition because it knows not that it knows. It disowns, is distant from all the attributes we normally associate with what we call our self, the person that we are. It is the absolute 'knower' which no object, no known can profane. In relation to it, even the epithet 'knower' smacks too much of the known, of the *kṣetra*, the field of knowledge. One can only die into this peace, one cannot talk about it. That would be a sacrilege, a sin.

5. sa ya evaṃ vit. asmāl lokāt pretya. etam annamayam ātmānam upasaṃkramya. etaṃ prāṇamayam ātmānam upasaṃkramya. etaṃ manomayam ātmānam upsaṃkramya. etaṃ vijñānamayam ātmānam upasaṃkramya. etam ānandamayam ātmānam upsaṃkramya. imāṃl-lokān kāmānnī kāma rūpy anusaṃcaran. etat sāma gāyann āste. hā vu hā vu hā vu.

He who knows this, having departed from this world, having attained to this self made of food, having attained to this self made of breath, having attained to this self made of mind, having attained to this self made of knowledge, having attained to this self made of bliss, roams over these worlds, eating the food he would eat, assuming the forms he would assume. Still he abides, singing this sāman, *this song ecstatic: O wonder! O wonder! O wonder!*

ŚB From the self made of food, he attains to the self made of breath, to that made of mind, of knowledge and, lastly, of bliss. Still he sits, singing this *sāman*, this mystic chant.

The second part of this Upaniṣad, the part devoted to the exposition of bliss, explained, in elaborate terms, the *mantra* of the *Ṛg Veda,* viz., 'Brahman is truth, knowledge and infinity.' The said part may be considered a commentary on this *mantra.* However, what fruit he reaps who knows Brahman thus defined was mentioned but not explained in details, the fruit enshrined in, 'Hidden in the heart who knows him, in the heaven highest,/obtains he all that one could desire,/obtains them all together along with Brahman the wise' (TaitU 2.1.1). What are his desires and what he desires and how he obtains them all together with Brahman still remains to be shown and the *śruti* now proceeds to do this in what follows.

In the story of the father and the son, of Varuṇa and Bhṛgu, a supplement to the knowledge revealed earlier in Part 2, *tapas,* concentration,was taught as a means whereby one could have knowledge of Brahman. The *śruti* then revealed how all created phenomena, from breath to *ākāśa,* ether of space, relate to each other in terms of the eater and the eaten. Thereafter, the *śruti* treated of the various ways Brahman could be contemplated. The *śruti* has also revealed all the blessings that contemplation of the varied phenomena of creation, from the ether of space downwards, may bring about. There are many ways to reach those joys, appropriate ways to reach each of them. If, however, the self is admitted to be one, then there can be no object of desire nor one who desires, since all diversity, including the desirer and the desired, will be one, one self. This being the case, how will a knower of Brahman, as one with Brahman, attain all that one could desire, obtain them all together? Because, we reply, he becomes the all.

How does he become the all? The *śruti* replies: He sees the self that dwells in man and the self that dwells in the sun as one. Blessed with this knowledge, he discards all thoughts of the inferior and the superior, this seer of oneness. Passing on from one self to the other set up by false knowledge, from that made of food to the one made of breath, of mind, of knowledge, and of bliss, he attains to Brahman, to the goal final and ultimate. The Upaniṣad has described that goal as truth, knowledge and infinity, that Brahman which none can perceive, such is its nature [being the self of all]. It is not made of bliss, that Brahman, but is bliss itself, bliss being its very own being. Unborn is it and immortal, beyond fear and nondual. Having attained Brahman of this nature, he wanders about in worlds (connect *imān lokān* with *saṃcaran*) from earth to heaven, experiencing, as the self of all, these worlds as his self, eating food to his fancy and assuming forms to his fancy. And abides he in stillness, singing this *sāman,* this song exalted, this mystic chant.

Brahman itself is *sāman* because it is *sama,* because it abides self same in every thing, abides as nondifferent from it. He, the man of wisdom, abides singing the *sāman, sāman* which is nondifferent from all, proclaiming to the world the oneness of the self, proclaiming this oneness as a favour to it and as celebration of the fulfilment, the absolute fulfilment, it brings about. How does he sing? In extreme wonder, for that is what *hā vu hā vu hā vu* express.

What kind of wonder is it, the *śruti* expresses in the *mantra* to follow:

6. aham annam aham annam aham annam. aham annādo'ham annādo 'ham annādaḥ. ahaṃ ślokakṛd ahaṃ ślokakṛd ahaṃ ślokakṛt. aham asmi prathamajā ṛtāsya. pūrvaṃ devebhyo 'amṛtasya nābhāyi. yo mā dadāti sa id eva mā 'vāḥ. aham annam annam adantam ādmi. ahaṃ viśvaṃ bhuvanam abhyabhavām. suvarna jyotīḥ ya evaṃ veda. ity upaniṣat.

I am the eaten, I am the eaten, I am the eaten. I am the eater, I am the eater, I am the eater. I bind these together, I bind these together, I bind these together, the eater and the eaten. I am the first born of ṛta, *of truth, of that which has come to be; before the gods came I, the centre of immortality. He who gives me to another, alone protects me. I, who am food, eat the eater of food. The whole world have I overcome. Like the sun is my [lit. our] light and of him who knows this. Such is the* upaniṣad.

ŚB I am the *ātman*, the self, unstained and nondual. Despite this, I am the eater and also the eaten and also the one that binds these two together, the conscious binder. Or, to interpret this in another way, I bring together, integrate into unity, all food, which is meant for other than itself, for the eater of food, and is, for this reason, diverse in nature. The threefold repetition is an expression of wonder at the nondual self being, at the same time, the eater–eaten duality.

I am the first born of *ṛta*, of 'truth', of what has come to be, of the world, formed and not-formed . Before the gods came I. The centre of immortality am I, in me is centred the immortality of creatures. He who gives me to the seekers of food, tells them that I am food, he protects me intact and as I am. But he who does not give food, at the right time, to those who need it and ask for it and himself eats it all, becomes food of food, of me that am food.
Opponent: If this be so, I fear this liberation, this becoming the self of all. Let me be born again and again and die again and again, if to be liberated means to be the food of food.
Vedāntin: Let there be no fear on this count. All desirables belong to the world of experience set up by ignorance and so do their enjoyments. A man of wisdom transcends this world constituted by eater–eaten dualities projected by ignorance. His knowledge, his wisdom, makes him one with Brahman. Not for him exists the other to cause him fear. Why, then, this fear of liberation?
Opponent : If so, why say, 'I am the eaten, I am the eater'?
Answer: The eater and the eaten belong to the realm of empirical dealings, to creation, not to the truth absolute but to the truth experienced [in terms of categories set up by ignorance]. Even though the phenomenal world, the

world experienced, is of this nature, the *śruti* wants to emphasise that it originates from Brahman and has no being apart from it, and that to know Brahman is to be Brahman. 'I am the eaten, I am the eaten, I am the eaten. I am the eater, I am the eater, I am the eater' is thus at once an assertion and a celebration of this unity of the world and Brahman, of it and its knower. Therefore, for the man who has undone *avidyā*, false knowledge, and has, as a result of its eradication, become Brahman itself, there cannot be even a hint of fear and other maladies which *avidyā*, attribution of ideas to truth, gives rise to.

As the Lord Supreme I overcome the entire world, the ontological ground of beings, from the creator downwards, the world they would share in and enjoy. This, etymology tells us, is the meaning of *bhuvana*, the word for the world. Like the sun shines our light, ever bright and luminous.

This is the *upaniṣad* imparted in the two parts of this text, the second and the third, the *upaniṣad* that is knowledge of the supreme self. If a man resorts to *tapas*, great as that of Bhṛgu, resorts to it calm in mind and restrained in senses, from passion free and full of patience, with attention all focussed on truth—if a man of this sort knows this *upaniṣad*, this wisdom, he too will reap the same reward, he too will be liberated [as was Bhṛgu].

'I am the eaten, I am the eaten, I am the eaten' is at once a celebration and a deploration : celebration, ecstatic celebration, of our mortal lot and deploration of our pathetic struggle against it. 'I am the eater, I am the eater, I am the eater' highlights our joyous participation in the *yajña* that the world is and mocks at our petty virtues, the expression of our self–esteem. Man is, the *mantra* says in effect, at once a sacrificer and the sacrificial victim. His frightening world of plunder and prey turns into holy sacrifice when man sees, in himself and others, both the eater and the eaten. When he does this, he turns into the other and the other into himself. That is the first step towards realisation of the all as the self, the realisation that all are alike in their sin and their pain, that our happiness is born out of our sadism *vis-a-vis* others and others' happiness out of their sadism *vis-a-vis* us, that we are all alike in the meanness of our pleasures and the pain our mean pleasure gives rise to.

This realisation makes us distance ourselves from our sick selves and makes us realise that there is a pre-person in us which is common to all, to me as well as my adversary. To be that pre-person means celebration of our violence against each other, to be the realisation that I kill the me in the other and the other his *me* in me. My sin, my meanness and his sin and his meanness turn into glory when I become the self that that pre-person is. I become then the first born, I become *Hiraṇyagarbha*, the not-formed creator of the formed world.

I live, then, as the world, the world that is sacrifice, the sacrifice in which everything is the eater as well as the eaten. To be this sacrifice is to be the centre of immortality. For to eat with the eater and to be eaten with the eaten is to be 'untruth', to be the not-mortal, the untruth that at once creates the world and overwhelms it, creates it as its self and overwhelms it as its self. Destruction is as much a joy for it as creation is, they are the celebration of its being, the manifest proof of its truth and reality.

This is all that human language can say about 'the self,' the 'untruth', this is all that man can think about it : in terms of his experience, in terms of the categories that make that experience intelligible to him, make it what it is. The Upaniṣad uses our categories paradoxically, negating them through each other, the negation negating us and our world. This negation does not, cannot, however, turn 'untruth' into truth for us, does not reveal it but only suggests it. To this extent, even this mystic chant, this joyous celebration of our death and the world's death, is a false attribution, attribution of our condition onto our being, onto what the Upaniṣads term, for our convenience, our self, our true self that is Brahman the Absolute.

Peace Chant

aum! śaṃ no mitraḥ śaṃ varuṇaḥ. śaṃ no bhavatv aryamā. śaṃ na indro bṛhaspatiḥ. śaṃ no visṇur urukramaḥ. namo brahmaṇe. namaste vāyo. tvam eva pratyakṣaṃ brahmāsi. tvām eva pratyakṣaṃ brahmāvādiṣam. ṛtam avādiṣam. satyam avādiṣam. tan mām āvīt. tad vaktāram āvīt. āvīn mām āvīd vaktāram.

aum! śāntiḥ! śāntiḥ! śāntiḥ!

For translation see page 91

AITAREYA UPANIṢAD

An Upaniṣad of the *Ṛg Veda*

AITAREYA UPANIṢAD

Invocation

aum! vāṅ me manasi pratiṣṭhitā mano me vāci pratiṣṭhitam āvir āvīr ma edhi. vedasya ma āṇīsthaḥ śrutaṃ me mā prahāsīḥ. anenādhītenāhorātrān sandadhāmy ṛtam vadiṣyāmi. satyaṃ vadiṣyāmi. tan mām avatu. tad vaktāram avatu. avatu mām avatu vakrāram avatu vaktāram.

aum! śāntiḥ! śāntiḥ! śāntiḥ!

Aum. *Established in my mind is my speech and in my speech my mind. To me be manifest, O thou Manifest. When the Vedas move unto me, for ever stay, my mind and my speech, with their axle. And forsake me not what I have heard. Together do I join the day and the night through this my study. Of the right shall I speak, of the true shall I speak. May that protect me. May that protect the speaker. May that protect me, may that protect the speaker, the speaker.* Aum! *peace, peace, peace.*

Mind is thought process, speech is arrest of that process, an uneasy precarious arrest. Speech is mind tied to the world, it is spatialisation of time. When speech and mind rest in each other, time and space come to coalesce, the mind and the world. I do not then flow with thoughts and desires cut off from the world. I flow into the world, into space and become it, become space. And space too flows into me, to become me. I become spatialised and space becomes temporalised.

Man lives alienated from the world because he isolates his body from the world, an isolation that enslaves him to the world and its laws. The transformation of mind into speech is the result of this isolation and the resultant slavery. The flux has to solidify in order to grasp the nonfluid, the solid; the mind has to turn into speech, the fluid into the nonfluid. The body has to be handed back to its right place, the world, for speech to turn back to mind. Man has, in other words, to acknowledge his mortality, existentially acknowledge it, to make his speech go back to mind.

When the body is seen as a thing among things, then alone does the miracle happen. Things, then, come to be dominated by space and so does man. He no longer stands *here* to set limits to it, nor does any other thing. Things become space, man becomes space without distinctions, without the sense of here or of there. East no longer remains east, nor west west. Space itself disappears, what we, the intruders into it, call space. All becomes one, one without parts, without bounds.

The mind becomes, in this state, still, almost perfectly still, a bare awareness-of-the-boundless. Thoughts disappear into this stillness, and so do time and space. This is the revelation given to one whose speech has coalesced with his mind, this intermingling of space and time, this stillness that is presence and this presence which is stillness, this peace that swallows all.

Yet this revelation is also a concealment. For too often and too soon this peace turns into pain, the still presence into time and space, the calm into the tumult of thoughts and senses. Even when this peace stays, the tumult is only distant, perhaps absent but not nonexistent. It is there somewhere threatening intrusion. The presence does not reveal itself so as to heal the divide between itself and the world. The individual's efforts are of no avail here, the body-sense is too indistinct for those efforts. The fear arises, vague and nameless, to undo the peace, and with that arises speech. Speech, in that state, arises as prayer, prayer to the presence that it reveal what it conceals. For even that stillness is experienced as a veil, a concealment. For this purpose is said the prayer, 'To me be manifest, O thou Manifest.'

If the prayer succeeds, if one stays still as stillness, deaf to the call of security and knowledge, the still silence will change into the Word, the Word as revelation, the Word they term the Veda. The Word changes into the self, the self as Brahman, if mind and speech remain tied to its axle, to the axle of the Word, move with it, become one with it. They are not to forsake the revelation by asserting themselves.

This revelation has another counterpart, the coalescence of the day and the night. The shadows of this coalescence we can see in the dawn and the dusk, its symbols, the moments when time becomes holy, ready to reveal its redemptive truth to anyone who lives as those shadows, those symbols, adores them, does not insult them, is not deaf to the call they make. Many are there who would term the coalescence of the day and the night, whose shadows are the dawn and the dusk, *eternity* and would interpret it as something opposed to time, not as the truth of time, the being of time. But he who has heard the Word will find the very truth of time in this their intermingling, in the cessation of the divide between the two. The day and the night come together, become one moment, when the Word has swallowed our words and our concepts when, to speak in the vein of mystics, all time becomes a moment and all space an atom.

The other requisite for this coming together of day and night, this coalescence, that is, of all the concepts that make our world intelligible, is that I speak of the right and of truth. Truthful speech is the undoer of all clear cut concepts, those indispensables for the doer. It erodes the distinction between me and others as against untruthfulness which sharpens that distinction. The right I speak is also closely linked with truthfulness, it is, basically, nonselfcentredness. Concepts, selfcentredness and the not-right go together. Righteousness is flowing out, so is truthfulness and so is innocence as opposed to conceptual thinking. Without this self-offering to the human other, I cannot become space, to turn the latter into peace, that reposeful quiet in which the Word speaks to undo all distinctions, symbolised by the distinction between day and night.

And, lastly, the prayer is for protection. Protection of whom and by whom? The protector is not named. The roaring Word—*pra-ṇava*—has undone me, me the individual, me the consciousness of the bare presence that the world has become, has undone this consciousness along with the presence. I have mingled with the Word and so has the presence. This coming together of the Word, consciousness and presence is the Nameless. Men debase that Nameless when they call it *ātman* or Brahman, the self or the Absolute. That Nameless is to protect me, me who has become one with it. The prayer is for the final merger, for *mokṣa,* for *nirvāṇa.* The mortal me can never be protected, it is born only to perish. The prayer is not for its protection. The prayer is, in fact, for the non-reemergence of this me, this death, this tragedy.

The prayer is also made for the protection of the speaker, the teacher. Let him, too, speak as *That,* as the Nameless. Let him not speak as man. Let not the Word that the teacher is, the Word that is more than the teacher, turn into speech, into language, into the word that *avidyā* makes of it.

To reduce this prayer into realistic interpretation will be problematic. The very first line will make no sense for those who are anxious to retain distinctions.

AITAREYA UPANIṢAD

Part 1

Chapter 1

ŚB Holy acts together with knowledge, contemplation of lower Brahman, constitute the theme of the ritualistic portion of the Vedas. With the end of that portion[1] ends that theme. When man duly performs the holy acts enjoined in the Vedas and combines them with meditation, he is vouchsafed the vision of *uktha* verses. That, verily, is the highest reach of holy acts–contemplation combine, this vision of *uktha*, the verse chanted [as against the *yajus*, the sacrificial formula muttered and the *sāman*, the verse sung]. The ritualistic portion ends at this note. [Equating the *uktha* with breath,] it was said there: 'Breath is the name given to this Brahman, this truth;' 'this alone is *deva*, the shining god;' 'Of this breath are all the gods manifestations, of this breath alone;' 'When this breath becomes his self, into all the *devas* shall he merge, into all the gods.'

Uktha is, as noted above, the verse chanted as distinct from *sāman*, the verse sung and *yajus*, the sacrificial formula muttered, neither sung nor chanted. In the *sāman*, the tonal rhythm dominates, breath is only a means at its disposal. In muttering the prose formula, breath is held in check. In chanting, it is controlled and regulated, it and the verse move as one movement, the *mantra* controlling breath and breath the *mantra*. In chanting, one does not rush to the concluding word, as one does in muttering, one lingers on syllables, even on pauses. This lingering on implies words becoming part of the breath movement. In singing, both words and breath give themselves up to the note, its pitch and duration. It is the mind as idea, as the musical idea that controls and regulates the word and breath. In chanting they mingle with each other.

When chanting becomes spontaneous, when you do not do it but it is done for you, then occurs some kind of distancing between you and it. At that moment, chanting tends to become interiorised, continuing without actual articulation. It is at this point of meditation that you have the vision of *uktha*, of the chant. The senses, the words, the words as thought leave you to be *there*, to become a sight. You surrender them

1. The *Aitareya Upaniṣad* is a part of the *Aitareya Brāhmaṇa* consisting of chs. 4-6 of the second *Āraṇyaka* of the said *Brāhmaṇa*.

to their rightful place, the world. Identification with the body is then revealed as an act of stealth, it is revealed as *avidyā*, this setting limits to the world by the body that actually belongs to the world, not to you. What am I when I distance myself from the tongue that moves, from the words it utters, from the thoughts enshrined in those words? I am then, in that moment of distancing, breath, only breath. That alone becomes my self, my *ātman*. It is for this breath self, this tranquil moving that knows not itself, that verses become the sight, but not merely the verses of the Vedas. Of other verses, which were nowhere before, too, it may have the vision. This self, however, is the seer of *ukthas*, of chants to be uttered, of prayers and hymns but not of *mantras* that reveal and of sacrificial formulas that lead. Leading verses come later and later still the revelatory verses. *Uktha* belongs to earth, it is the burning flame rising upwards from earth, a distancing from it.

When one has attained this distancing, when one has become the seer of *Uktha*, one enters *antarikṣa*, the region of air, of breath not regulated and controlled but free. There the muttered *yajus*, the *yajus* suppressed on earth, reveals itself. One, as free air, reaches all, one becomes the way, the path, the breath that is the way, that is the path. *Devas*, those that shine, the gods that guide, are nothing else than this liberated breath, this air. One attains them, enters into them, enters into all the gods, those guides to truth.

The three sentences Śaṅkara quotes here I have not been able to trace in the pre-Upaniṣadic texts.

ŚB For some this merger in the gods is the final goal of human life, this alone is liberation. And this merger, they say, is to be attained through holy acts combined with contemplation of gods, the way they have been combined in the ritualistic section preceding this Upaniṣad. They cannot look beyond this merger, that alone being the ultimate for them. The Upaniṣadic text to follow rejects this their view. In its very first sentence, it proclaims the self to be the primal truth. And the final truth too, for it calls upon man to know that self, that self alone.
Opponent: What are the grounds of your assertion that the text enjoins self-knowledge, exclusive and unrelated to holy acts?
Vedāntin: I say this because this text, this Upaniṣad, yields no other meaning. There is another point also to consider. The gods, the objects of worship for the *Brāhmaṇa*[s], are presented here as creatures of the world subject [like mortals] to such maladies as hunger and thirst. 'He visited him [the Cosmic Person] with hunger and thirst' (1.2.1)—this is how the Upaniṣad will speak about these gods. Those who are subject to hunger and thirst are subject to death after death, birth after birth. Of the supreme Brahman alone, of the Absolute alone, the *śruti* speaks in terms of its freedom from hunger and thirst and of no one else.

Opponent: Knowledge of [the all as] the self may lead one to liberation from recurring deaths and recurring births. But you cannot, surely, maintain that the nondoer of holy acts alone is eligible for this vision of all as the self. Nowhere does this Upaniṣad specifically mention this, nowhere does it speak about the renunciate, the nonperformer of holy acts, alone qualifying for the vision of the all as the self. There is also the fact that the text[1] moves on, from the presentation of the rite called *bṛhatī-sahasra*, straightway to the presentation of self-knowledge, the theme of the Upaniṣad. This would rather show that in the view of the *śruti* the man of piety alone is qualified to receive instructions in self-knowledge.

Furthermore, we have to consider another point about the text in question. The Upaniṣad sums up its teaching in the same vein as the *Brāhmaṇa* preceding it. The *Brāhmaṇa*, the part dealing with ceremonial piety, tells us how the man of piety comes to be, as identified with the sun, the self of all beings, whether those that move or those that do not move. This conclusion of the *Brāhmaṇa* is supported by the *mantras* too in, for example, these words: 'The sun is the self of all that moves and does not move' (*Ṛg Veda* 1.115.1). In the same way will speak the *Aitareya Upaniṣad* about the man of wisdom. *Mantra* 3.1.3 of this Upaniṣad begins by affirming that all beings are the self alone. 'This one is Brahmā, the Creator, this one is Indra,' is its first sentence. And it concludes on this note, 'Whatever inert there be is impelled by consciousness. . . .'

This way we find that piety leads man to the same goal as does self-knowledge: to the realisation that all that be is the self. In view of this, your position that revelation of all as the self has nothing to do with piety becomes unsustainable.

To reiterate this point we have also the authority of the Upaniṣad of the *Saṃhitā*. That which 'the followers of the *Ṛg Veda* deliberate in the *uktha*, the hymn, called the *bṛhatī-sahasra*' (AitĀ 3.2.3.12), the *Saṃhitā Upaniṣad* equates with Brahman. 'Of it alone do they speak as Brahman dwelling in all that have come to be.' This is what it has to say, by way of conclusion, about the self related to rituals. And also: 'That which is this self, bodiless and conscious' 'is verily one with that which dwells in the sun. Let man know this.'

This Upaniṣad, too, we shall see, will equate the self that one worships through the act of introspective contemplation, the self as consciousness, with Brahman, the Absolute. For it begins chapter 3 with the question: What is this self that we contemplate? And its answer is: 'Consciousness is Brahman' (3.1.3). In the face of these words, you cannot say that self-knowledge and piety have no connection with each other.

Counter Objection: If what you say is true, if the Upaniṣad merely states what has already been stated in the pre-Upaniṣadic texts, then this Upaniṣad will become redundant. If the *ātman*, the self, has already been declared to be breath: 'I am, O Seer, breath itself': by the *Brāhmaṇas*, and if it has already been equated with the sun by the *mantras*: 'The sun is the *ātman*': then there

1. We should recall that the *Aitareya Upaniṣad* is the concluding part of the *Aitareya Brāhmaṇa*.

is little point in asking the question, 'What is the self that we contemplate?' as does this Upaniṣad. For you do not seek to identify the already identified. And equally useless is its answer to the question that all this is the self. The pre-Upaniṣadic texts, both the *Saṃhitā* and the *Brāhmaṇa*, have already, as you have shown, revealed this much.

Opponent: I would not rush to this unwarranted conclusion. For the Upaniṣad will reveal that about the self, the self they worship through acts and through meditation, which neither the *mantras* revealed nor did the *Brāhmaṇas*, neither the hymns nor the texts about rituals. What it reveals is that the very self of the pious and the contemplator is the creator of the world too and also its sustainer and destroyer. Revelation of qualities like these is the prerogative of the Upaniṣads alone. One cannot, therefore, lay the charge of repetitiveness against them. It is also possible that this description of the self-same self as creator, sustainer and destroyer is meant to present before us *bare* contemplation of the self, contemplation unrelated to anything else. When the Vedas expounded the holy acts, they commanded man to worship the self in and through these acts alone. The self the doer was to be worshipped only through deeds, not outside them. Here the Upaniṣad emphasises that the same self can be worshipped without those rituals. The self is to be worshipped both as other than oneself and as one with oneself. In the context of ceremonial piety, the self is looked upon as different from oneself, in the absence of that context, that very self comes to be worshipped as nondifferent from oneself. This is what the Upaniṣad reveals to us. So where is the alleged repetitiveness?

That the self is to be worshipped in both these ways, as other than oneself as well as one with oneself is, according to those who adhere to the *Vājasaneya* branch of the Vedas, the theme of the Upaniṣads. 'Knowledge and ignorance,' they quote, 'knowledge and ignorance, he who knows the two together, through ignorance shall cross death and through knowledge become immortal' (ĪśaU 11) and 'By performing rites should one seek to live here a hundred years' (ĪśaU 2). The life of mortals does not span beyond a hundred years. If they have to perform, as the *Īśa Upaniṣad* commands, holy acts all these years, when will they renounce these acts to do contemplation? Six and thirty thousand days are, says the *Aitareya Āraṇyaka*, allotted to man. And these, the *Īśa Upaniṣad* commands, he is to live doing holy acts. Holy acts thus pervade his entire life span of a hundred years. That this has really to be the style of his life, many texts, other than the *Īśa Upaniṣad*, would also reiterate. '*Agni*, the Fire, does he worship as long as his life lasts,' says one text. 'Let him sacrifice unto the moon when it appears anew and also when it appears full. Let him do this as long as he lives,' says another. 'Together with the sacrificial vessels do they cremate him,' yet another. Add to these the *śruti* texts that call upon man to pay the three debts—to gods, the fathers, to seers (Tait Saṃhitā 6.3.10). There are, of course, several *śruti* texts to consider, texts replete with the the thought of renunciation, for example, the following one:

> Having known this very *ātman*, this very self, knowers of Brahman rise above desires for son, for wealth, for worlds, living the life of mendicants . . . (BṛU 3.5.1 4.4.22).

Texts like these are either eulogies of self-knowledge or injunctions for those who are not qualified to perform the holy acts [widowers and others].

Holy acts, to speak from the point of view of the opponent, are nothing else than worship of the self. When the day dawns and the fire divine burns in the east, man offers oblations into the fire that burns at the altar, the earthly symbol of the divine fire that burns yonder in the east. The offering symbolises the offering of all that man is and has. The same act he performs again in the evening. One of the names of the sun is *āditya*, derived from the root *ad*, to eat. He is the eater principle and whatever man offers, including himself, to the sun is his food. Fire-worship thus is the worship of the eater, the eater as the sun and the fire. For me, the man, the eater is only myself. The pious act of fire worship reveals this eater as the eaten. The true eater in me is, therefore, not what I deem myself to be but what eats me up, the *Aditi* in me, the mother of *Āditya*, the eater as the sun. There is the self in me, the self that I ordinarily deem myself to be, that eats other things, but there is also, reminds the fire worship, another self in me, the self like the sun and the fire, that burns me up, eats me up. That is my true self, the self that is the same as the self that dwells in the sun, the universal eater. This is the vision that Vedas reveal to man, according to the opponent, the vision of the self in man and the self in the sun as one.

The *Brāhmaṇas*, he maintains, interiorise this Vedic vision. They identify the self with *prāṇa*, with breath, the sun in the microcosm. *Prāṇa*, as the outgoing breath, as exhaling, is the eater of *apāna*, the incoming breath, inhaling. *Apāna* too is the eater of *prāṇa*. Each becomes the other to be itself and to sustain the life process. *Prāṇa*, the paradigm of *yajña*, of sacrifice is the process that reveals the other, the negating other as the self and the self as the other. The opponent, conceding the possibility, even the desirability, of contemplation and eventually of identification with *prāṇa*, the process of being the other and from being the other to being oneself, warns against the possibility of fall and reminds the *Vedāntin* of the necessity of piety as a safeguard against the fall. He is, as far as he goes, faithful to the Vedic tradition. The self as the other is the sun, for the sun sustains the other by shining on phenomena other than itself, but the self as the sun, as the perpetual sacrifice is not the self supreme but a step towards it. Hence the Vedāntin's rejoinder.

ŚB *Vedāntin* : [Your contention that holy acts should continue along with contemplation is no doubt right up to a point but does not square with knowledge of the true self.] When man comes to be blessed with knowledge of the true self, he finds no acts bearing any fruit for him. Seeing them of no use, he gives them up. Let me disillusion you about your belief that the doer of obligatory deeds can have knowledge of the self and that this knowledge is related to those deeds, has any connection with them. For when man finds himself as Brahman, ever fulfilled and pure, no pollutions of the world ever touching him, when he thus realises that he is the Absolute itself, what purpose will any action serve for him, whether already done or to be done? Can he possibly do any action, he who sees it as bearing no fruit for him?

Objection: Actions may turn as of no account for such a man but even he performs the ordained deeds in view of the command of scriptures.

Answer: One who has come to have the vision of the self, comes ever to abide in it is beyond the reach of every commandment. If a man wants to have something or avoid something, he will seek every means to attain his purpose. For such a man alone scriptural commandments have any meaning. This is a matter of common observation. This is, however, not true in the case of one who ever abides in Brahman the Absolute, who finds his self and the Absolute as one. If even he is not to be an exception, if even he is ever under painful obligation to abide by injunctions, then there will be no respite for any one from them. All, without exception, will be ever obliged to perform all acts, without exception. This will not be a happy situation. No one can lay down instructions for the seer of the self, not even scriptures. For they are his emanations, the scriptures. Commands that spring up from the depths of his knowledge have no binding force for one who is none other than that knowledge. Masters that know much do not obey their servants who know little.

There is a tradition, long and well established, that considers the Vedas nonoriginary and *apauruṣayāḥ*, authorless. Neither man created them, it says, nor god. Here, however, Śaṅkara seems to suggest that the Vedas are not merely the creation of enlightened souls but also a mere partial manifestation of their wisdom. It is the Vedas that are servants of men of wisdom, not they of theirs. In the sentence to follow Śaṅkara will also concede the eternal status of the Vedas. How are we to reconcile these two, apparently, contradictory views?

The reconciliation we seek is not, however, far to find. For who is the man who is blessed with the knowledge of the self? It is the man whom holy acts turned into a sacrificial victim, to the eaten, meditation into the act of sacrifice. There was the self that witnessed the victim in his martyrdom and the act in its serenity but itself remained distant alike from agony and from serenity. In it, in that witness, there was neither the tumult of the one nor the harmony of the other. Since we mortals of the world find it the witness of our thinking, our martyrdom, our being as the act, we call it consciousness. What, however, is left of the self that has disowned the thinker, the martyr, the joy? Can it remain consciousness which must link itself with something other than itself to be consciousness? The witness of our thoughts, the witness absolute, cannot be consciousness in and for itself. It is only we who are tied to thoughts that call it *śūnya*, a nothingness that knows all but not itself. It is that unknowing wisdom, that dark fount of nonbeing that is the source of being and of revelation, of the Vedas.

So the Vedas as revelation originate from these impersonal depths. For us men of the world, the Vedas seem to originate from human beings at particular times and particular places. To the seer of the revelatory words himself they have no human author and no date, for in the peace from which originate the Vedas and the world neither man is nor time is. Man dies when revelation comes and so does the world.

The Veda, revelation, however is eternal. The Veda is eternal because it originates with creation. The moment beings come into being, they find themselves creatures, their creator, their being, their home lost to them. As ontologies of loss do they live, as seekers of their cause. All knowledge they have or they seek has its moment of 'inspiration' in this dejection, in the feeling that their birth is a deprivation and their life a seeking. So much of the Veda, so much of wisdom, is ever known to creatures, whether they try to undo their ontological penury through possessions and pleasures or through renunciation and serious reflection and meditation. They also know, despite their obsessions and vanities, that whatever they do or find will not undo the primordial poverty. This much of the Veda too is revealed to all human beings, sleep as they may or will over this truth. Add to this their conceptual awareness of their death, notwithstanding their existential ignorance of it. To recognise, existentially recognise, the fact of original penury, the futility of desires that would sleep over that poverty and the ultimate truth of death is to know the Vedas; to accept and live these facts, these truths is to be the Vedas, to be the truth ultimate. Scriptures call upon man only to recognise and accept what he already knows, but knows only at the margins of his consciousness. Their truth is his truth, the truth of creation itself.

The Veda is eternal because it is immanent in the world. Every revelation has to meet this criterion. The Hindus believe that the books called the Vedas articulate in human language this immanence. There will be many who will question the validity of this claim *vis-a-vis* the entire corpus of the Vedas. It will, however, be difficult to reject this claim *vis-a-vis* the Upaniṣads, the crown of the Vedas.

ŚB *Objection*: The Vedas are eternal and are, for this very reason, autonomous: they owe their being to no being. Their commands are, therefore, universal commands that admit of no exception.
Answer: We have already stated how this kind of universal obligation has unhappy implications. That every man, without exception, should ever be doing each and every prescribed act, again without exception, is surely not a desirable state of affairs. And your argument has unfortunately led you to this very sorry state! So the point of our criticism persists unrefuted.

There comes a time in the life of man when his life becomes weary of itself, his body of its functions, his mind of calculations. A time comes too when his piety becomes a burden, his meditation a drudgery, his ideals nonentities. Advocates of piety are often insensitive to this truth, so are, in our time, historicists and so are, I am afraid, those who find the truth of man, his being, in action, material action or communicative action. Those who found man's being in history turned out to be enemies of mankind, those who advocate theories of material action or communicative action unwittingly reduce man to a productive factor. Advocates of piety have often sacrificed man, the individual man, for the sake of the sacred cause, have often turned him into a fanatic, a crusader, a murderer. I fail to see how advocates of theories of material action or communicative actions can save mankind from destructive wars any more than advocates of the theory of historicism could. It is not necessary that destructive wars may take the shape of wars among nations, they may well be in the shape of conflicts between one set of people and another set of people, between, for example, the mafia and the masters of information and technology.

The *śruti* projects ideals before man so that he may think beyond what his inherited dispositions, dispositions, that is, of the natural man projected before him as truth. Acts of piety enable him to outgrow his self-love and meditation enables him to distance himself from what his desire has woven as truth for him, namely, his body and the world. But to be ever pious and meditative is to ontologise the natural man into a precondition, an indispensable precondition, of ideals, of acts of piety and of meditation. It is to give him the privilege of having the last laugh, thereby establishing what he deems to be reality as *the* reality. Ideals will, in that situation, turn into mere existential necessities to give our life a semblance of purposefulness. Cynicism or consumerism often overwhelm those who would be ever pious, who would be mere 'contributions' to progress.

Ideals, good acts and solitary meditation can have lasting meaning only for man the mortal, not for man the contribution or for man the piety. A mortal being is neither a part of the world nor of history. He is alone, all alone. Born as related, he dies isolated. Ideals, good acts, meditation are there to find meaning in this tragic situation. If they fail to do so, they will have no real relevance for man; he will not, cannot, continue with them for their own sake if he will not sleep over the truth of his mortality. This latter thing a genuinely creative soul finds it hard to do. It cannot but take its ideals seriously because it cannot but take its mortality seriously.

ŚB *Objection*: The call to seek self-knowledge too is given by scriptures. The man who is commanded to do holy deeds is also commanded to seek self-knowledge.

Answer: This is untrue. For scriptures would not ask man to seek contradictory goals. They cannot instruct a man that he do certain acts and not do certain others and, at the the same time, ask him to dissociate himself from all acts. These two instructions cannot go together *vis-a-vis* the same person. You cannot instruct a man to be a doer of deeds and knower of the self at the same time. It will be like making fire feel both hot and cold.

Moreover, it is not true to say that scriptures call upon man to seek what he deems to be good and avoid what he deems to be not good. The desire to seek one and avoid the other is universal. It is not the prerogative of only the learned to nurture this desire, even cowherds do that, innocent though they be of scriptures. Scriptures instruct man only how to get that which is not available on its own. [Self-knowledge is one thing which scriptures alone can generate: it does not dawn on him on its own]. If once they have generated self-knowledge in a man, knowledge that is opposed to thoughts of all duties, all acts, done or to be done, how would they lead him back from the former to the latter, from the state of self-knowledge to that of doing? That would be like making fire cold and the sun dark.

Objection: Scriptures do not generate self-knowledge in man.

Answer: You are certainly wrong here, for they invariably conclude on the note of self-knowledge. Examples: 'Let him know thus: He is my self' (KauU 3.9); 'Consciousness is Brahman' (AitU 3.1.3). These, of course, are not the only examples, many another text has the same refrain, e.g. 'He knew only himself' (BṛU 1.4.9) and 'Thou art that' (ChU 6.8-16). Once this knowledge comes to dawn, the knowledge that the self is the Absolute, then nothing can eliminate it. For this reason, it cannot be said that it cannot dawn or that it is illusory or erroneous.

Objection: If a man who has realised all as the self has nothing to do with acts, he has equally, as the traditional wisdom would inform us, nothing to do with not doing either (*vide* BG 3.18). In view of this, those who advocate renunciation after the dawn of knowledge of Brahman are equally at fault as are those who insist on ceremonial piety. For want of purpose is applicable as much to the one option as to the other.

Answer: What you say springs from lack of understanding regarding the true nature of renunciation. Renunciation is that state of being where no activity obtains; it is a state of actionlessness. [To explain:] It is *avidyā*, false knowledge, that prompts one to have a thing; there is nothing in the thing itself to do do this prompting. This fact can be observed in the behaviour of all creatures. Their desires are prompted by *avidyā* and their actions by these desires, be they actions of their body, of their speech or of their mind. The *Vājasaneya Brāhmaṇa* in *Bṛhadāraṇyaka Upaniṣad* brings home this truth at 1.4.17: 'He said : let me have a wife' and at 3.5.1 and 4.4.22: 'These two are only desires.' These texts clearly affirm that the fivefold act, the act in which wife, son, divine wealth and human wealth and holy rites enter, is all prompted by desire.

In the man of knowledge, there remains neither ignorance nor desire to prompt his mind, his speech or his body to do the fivefold act. His renunciation is merely this state of no-action. It is not something that he could accomplish, something 'positive' like sacrifice. Not to be active is the very being of the man of enlightenment. It is no use associating purposes with him. In darkness one may stumble into a pit, into a swamp or into thorns. Not when the day has dawned. Will it, then, make sense to ask: What purpose has he in not stumbling into these?

Objection: In that case, renunciation cannot be enjoined, it being inherent in self-knowledge. You cannot ask a householder to renounce his home and family if he happens to be blessed with self-knowledge. He will stay there passive and unmoving.

Answer: No. Man becomes a householder because of desire, as the *śruti* will tell us in unmistakable terms. See what it says in this regard:

> In the beginning, all this was but the self, one only. He desired: 'Let me have a wife so that I may be born. Let me have wealth so that I may do the holy deeds.' This much is the range of desire (BṛU 1.4.17).

And:

> Having known this very self, they give up desire for sons, for wealth, for the worlds and live on alms, those who come to abide in Brahman. The desire for the son is verily the desire for wealth, the desire for wealth is the desire for the world, for both these are only desire (BṛU 3.5.1., also 4.4.22).

One relates to one's son, to wealth and other things because of desire. Renunciation means merely absence of these relationships, these creations of desire; it does not mean leaving home, sons, wealth and other things. For this reason, for the reason that all desire and all activity has come to end in his case, the man blessed with knowledge cannot stay at home. Not for him is even the service of the teacher or, for that matter, even *tapas*, penance or contemplation.

However, those who live tied to home and family life cannot bring themselves to lead a beggar's life. The insecurity and humiliation that go with this kind of life are too much for them. Men of this sort, therefore, propose a different style of life for the man of wisdom, rejecting what we have said about it. In support of their proposals, they advance arguments that are apparently quite appealing. Scriptures, they argue with all apparent wisdom, call upon man of knowledge to observe certain rules while begging food or other things for the sustenance of his body—for even he, we know, is obliged to sustain it, at least his bare life. This he can do while living at home. With all his desires for means and ends having come to a naught, let him stay at home reducing his needs to the bare minimum of food and clothing to keep his life going.

This contention of theirs is, however, a baseless one. We have already pointed out that only a man of desire will ever care to have his own home, not a man without desire. The latter cares only for the bare minimum of food and clothing, just sufficient to sustain his life. With the desire for home dead in him, a beggar's life will come naturally to him.

A beggar's life is enjoined for the man whose desires have been burnt up, for whom there is no other to desire, for whom all has become the self. No thoughts stir up in him, no perception, no desire, no tendency to act. *Yogins* give the name of *samādhi* to this state, tortured people call it peace absolute. When man has become this peaceful all, where can there be any need to sustain the body? For even the body turns, in that state, into the self as does everything else. The answer to this very legitimate question is given in the Vadāntic and other traditions on the following lines.

Man and, for that matter, every other creature, the tradition says, lives burdened with a beginningless past. As the world has no beginning, as it is *anādi,* so are creatures; they have lived in the world as long as the world has existed. No beginning can be traced of their fall into it, no point of time. Each of their births is the result of merely a small slice of what they have done or not done, thought or not thought in their past lives. This slice is called *prārabdha karmans,* acts that have started bearing their fruits, their results. When, however, the vision of all as the self is revealed to man, there remains no past for him nor future, neither the past deeds with their burdens nor desires and their tensions. The deeds he did in the past, deeds other than the *prārabdha karmans* are, to use a well known phrase, all burnt up with the rise of knowledge and so is the possibility of further action. But the *prārabdha karman* remains intact to visit him with rewards and punishments. It is the *prārabdha karman* that forces the *yogin* out of his *samādhi* into consciousness of his body and its needs. For destroy the body he cannot; he has not left in him the will to do this. So he lives accepting the body and its needs as his *prārabdha karman* will dictate, lives, to use a well known metaphor, as a withered leaf at the mercy of the wind, falling now here, now now there as the wind would decide. The Vedas command a man of wisdom of this sort to live a beggar's life as long as his *prārabdha karman* lasts. So much of limitation he will have to bear, so much of bondage, until his body does not mingle with the elements.

It is, however, possible that somebody's *prārabdha* may force him to live an active life. But that life will be a mere appearance. He will remain passive even when active; actions will be done for him, he will not do them. He will be their witness, a passive witness, not a restless doer of them. The truth is that a man of wisdom can neither truly beg nor truly act. There will be no ego in him, neither of the beggar nor of the doer of holy deeds. He will be all passivity, all renunciation, with no desire either to live or to die. The opponent's view that for the sustenance of his body it would be better for him to live at home than to wander about homeless is a false view. For he eats not because he has a desire to live, he eats because he has no desire to die. His apparent desire to live is only an indication of his passivity, his renunciation.

ŚB *Objection*: Scriptures have laid down rules about the way a man of wisdom is to beg his food and keep himself clean. These rules, of course, apply to the wise man the renunciate, not to the wise man the householder. The latter, though freed from every desire, may continue doing the acts of piety because scriptures command man to do them till the end of life and also for avoiding the evil that falls to the lot of those who forsake the obligatory acts.
Answer: We have already refuted this point of yours when we said that a man of enlightenment is beyond the reach of scriptural injunctions. There are no imperatives for him to obey and follow.
Objection: Then vain will be scriptural injunctions like the one that calls upon man to perform the holy deeds all his life.
Answer: Commandments like the one you have referred to are not given in vain. They have their relevance for all those who live ignorant of their self. As for the rules about the way a man of wisdom is to beg, they are only regulative principles. They regulate the activity he is called upon to do by his *prārabdha karman*; they do not prompt him to act. They are like rules regarding ceremonial sipping. Since sipping has to be done for a man engaged in a holy act, scriptures tell man how he would do it. Sipping in accordance with these rules will not produce any other effect on the sipper than normal drinking of water does, namely, quench his thirst. Holy acts, on the contrary, are prompted by desire, they are not 'given' acts, acts that fall one's way either by the force of *prārabdha karman* as acts of begging are, or

as necessary prelude to the act of sacrifice as acts of sipping are. [For this reason, a man of wisdom will not perform them; he will not have the requisite desire for doing them.]

There are acts that man finds himself destined to do, acts which are thrust upon him. A man who has the vision of all as the self, who sees no other to desire or to appease, to hate or to avoid, will find no occasion to act, no need even to think and contemplate. Yet, as long as his body lasts, it will, when pangs of hunger and thirst become strong, thrust itself upon him. The rewards and punishments his *karmans,* his *prārabdha karmans,* have decided for him he cannot avoid, the burden of this much of *avidyā* he has still to bear and endure. Totally unfit to act as a member of society, dead to its honours and its humiliations, he lives outside the boundaries of a village or a town in the midst of beasts and birds and goes back to the habitats of civilisation only for a few morsels of food. Recognising the needs of his body, scriptures have laid down rules for begging. These rules do not apply only to the beggar, some of them apply to the giver as well. Let not the giver imagine that a sage who comes to beg at his door is a burden on him or on society, for he comes in the guise of a beggar to bless the giver, to protect him, to save him. His act of begging is, in every truth, an act of blessing. Without the desire to live, he lives helpless, a beggar at your door, an embodiment of self-effacement. Serene, calm and forgiving, he reveals to you what it means to live distant from the body, from its life and its death. You will see his body all aglow and soft, the home not of man but of the absence of man; in it you will find the visible face of what the Vedas can only call 'who?', that which men and women ever seek but find not, neither in their acts nor in their desires nor in the fulfilment of these desires. Neither, for that matter, in their thoughts, however deep, however sublime, however beautiful. This body he will save for you alone, for you the giver, not for himself. For life is too poor a thing to give him anything worthwhile.

Yet he does not remember that he breathes for others, eats for others, begs for others. The body comes, on occasions, to present itself before him and he lets himself be led by it. He begs as, the Indian tradition says, the Lord, as incarnation of the Lord, to speak the Word, the Word they call the Vedas, his 'servant'. The rules for his begging sustain others, not him, the ever-sustained and ever-sustaining. There is no revelation as proximate, as immediate as a sage at one's door. In him one beholds one's being, one's very life. In giving him, one gives up one's selfhood, one's bondage, one's sin.

This act of begging leaves no trace behind, no germ for further acts. When the act is over, the benign seer returns to his self. His return from *samādhi*, from the self to the world is, in every truth, the act of incarnation.

ŚB *Objection*: If begging on the part of a man of wisdom is spontaneous and automatic, regulations about it would serve no purpose. Why indulge in this useless exercise?

Answer: A man blessed with self-knowledge follows regulations about begging as a matter of habit, a habit nurtured by past practice before the rise of self-knowledge. Violation of these regulations would, in fact, require strenuous effort on his part. Scriptures merely reiterate, through injunctions, what comes naturally to him, namely, renunciation. This gives them the status of being obligatory for him.

This obligation to renounce is also applicable to the seeker of liberation, to him who is yet to know his self. We know on the authority of the *Bṛhdāraṇyaka Upaniṣad* (4.4.23) how self-knowledge is possible only for those who are peaceful and self-controlled, patient and concentrated. Traits of this kind can be cultivated only in the stage of renunication, not in the earlier ones. Time and again the *śruti* makes this evident :

> By the power of meditation and the grace of the Lord, the wise Śvetāśvatara spoke in the way proper about Brahman, the pure and supreme, to those who had gone beyond the stages three, about what the seers of the Word in earnest seek.

Thus the *Śvetāśvatara Upaniṣad* (6.21) and in the same vein speaks the *Kaivalya Upaniṣad* (2)

> Not by holy deeds, not by offering, not by wealth but by renunication alone did a few reach immortality.

And reiterates the *smṛti*, the traditional wisdom:

> After knowing it, let him stay passive.

And:

> Let him dwell in the stage of life conducive to the knowledge of Brahman.

The last quotation implies that celibacy and other virtues that gives rise to self-knowledge can best be practised by a renunciate, even up to the level of perfection. That perfection is simply out of the question for a householder. And imperfect means, we all know, never lead to the realisation of ends. It is true that holy acts which a householder performs do lead him to some kind of knowledge but that knowledge is only god-knowledge, absorption in *Hiraṇyagarbha*, the Golden Germ. That verily is its highest reach, but it is a reach within the range of the world and its cycle of recurring deaths and recurring births. The text preceding the Upaniṣad, the text concerned with

ceremonial piety and contemplation, concluded at this absorption, the absorption in the Golden Germ. If it were possible for a man of piety to attain to knowledge of the self, it would not stop at absorption in the god as it did, the absorption that is very much within the worldly mode of being.
Objection: Absorption in *Hiraṇyagarbha* is the product of some subsidiary factor associated with self-knowledge.
Answer: No, this cannot be. For absorption in the self and absorption in *Hiraṇyagarbha* are two opposite states. Knowledge of the self relates to that self which is the supreme reality—nameless, formless, devoid of all activity, knowledge which makes one immortal. If this knowledge has some subsidiary result associated with it, then it cannot reveal the reality devoid of all distinctions, the reality called the self. This would be unwelcome to anyone who believes in the authority of the Vedas. For the *śruti* speaks in contradictory terms of the two states, that of the man who knows the self and that of the man who does not know the self. For the man 'for whom all has become the self' (BṛU 2.4.14) has no actions to do, no auxiliaries to depend upon and no fruits to reap. The *śruti*, in short, denies all empirical dealings in the case of the man of knowledge. On the contrary, for the man who does not know the self, for whom 'there is duality as it were' (BṛU 2.4.14), there is a world to perceive, a world in which obtain action, auxiliaries, and fruits of these actions. This is what we learn from the *Vājasaneya Brāhmaṇa*.[1] Having said whatever was to be said about absorption in *Hiraṇyagarbha*, the state worldly and inflicted with hunger and other needs, the *Aitareya Brāhmaṇa* too proceeds, in its Upaniṣadic section, to speak about that knowledge which relates to the Real that is the All, the knowledge which leads one to immortality.

There are indeed debts to be discharged before one can attain, after death, the worlds of man, of fathers, of gods. Different debts for each one of these three worlds. But these debts are to be discharged by those alone who do not perceive all as the self, not by those who perceive it as the self.

> This world of man is to be won through the son, through him alone and not through any holy act; through holy acts is to be won the world of fathers. And the world of gods through contemplative wisdom (BṛU 1.5.16).

Thus have been laid down the means for the attainment of the three worlds. But these means are meant for the ignorant, not for those who seek to know the self. The latter have no such debts to discharge:

> Brahmins, those belonging to the highest caste, seek to know it through the study of the Vedas, through sacrifices, through chastity and through fasting. By knowing it, indeed, does one become a sage. Desiring it alone as their world, renunciates wander forth. They do this because the ancients did not desire offspring. 'What shall we do with offspring,'

1. i.e the *Bṛhadāraṇyaka Upaniṣad* which is a part of the said *Brāhmaṇa*.

> they said, 'we who have attained this self, this world?' They, it is said, rose above desire for sons, for wealth, for worlds to lead the life of a mendicant (BṛU 4.4.22).

And also the texts of the Kauṣītaki branch:

> So the ancient seers, the Kāvaṣeyas, who knew the self, said: 'Why should we study the Vedas?' (Untraced).

> Knowing this, the ancient seers did not perform the fire sacrifice (Kauṣītaki U 2.5).

Objection: This would, then, mean that until he has paid back the debts, no man, with the exception of the enlightened ones, can renounce the world. *Answer*: No. There are no debts for one who has not entered the householder's life. Only when you live this mode of life are you obliged to pay back those debts. To expect people to discharge responsibilities where there are none would be tantamount to inflicting a misfortune on them. This way you will reduce every man into a debtor—a very unhappy situation indeed! As a matter of fact, if a householder is seized with the desire to realise the self, the *śruti* asks him to forthwith embrace *saṃnyāsa*, renunciation, the means proper for self-realisation. These are its sacred words:

> After he has completed the life of a student, let a man become a householder. And let him afterwards be a forest dweller and, then a homeless wanderer. Otherwise, let him renounce even when a student or a householder or a forest dweller (*Jābāla Upaniṣad* 4).

The latter option shows that the discharge of debts is not absolutely indispensable. Of course, if a man is not insightful enough to long for liberation, there can then be no option for him except to obey the scriptural injunction relevant for him, the injunction that he perform the holy acts all his life. Not, however, if he has the requisite insight. The latter kind of persons, the *Chāndogya* says [in some recensions], should perform the holy act of fireworship for twelve nights and then give it up altogether.

To your contention that only those who are disqualified to perform the holy acts [as a result of the death of their wives or an injury to their persons or some other factors] are to take to renunciation, we shall only say that you are absolutely wrong in making this contention. We say this on the basis of a specific injunction, namely:

> He whose fire has become extinct or who has not lighted it up shall give up home the day his desires come to cease.

One could add that in the matter concerning renunciation, the *smṛtis* too echo the *śrutis*. They too give man the option either to proceed on to *saṃnyāsa* step by step or to move on to it in one step from any of the earlier three stages.

You also made an observation to the effect that it makes no difference whether an enlightened man stays at home or in a forest. The reason you gave for your view was the spontaneous occurrence of renunciation and, consequently, of its being beyond the purview of scriptures. This view of yours, I repeat, is not a sound one. For the very fact that his renunciation is a natural occurrence and not a voluntary act, speaks of its being out of step with the life associated with the other three orders which, as we said earlier, are informed by desire and action. Renunciation means rising above these two, desire and action, it means their absence.

This should not, however, be taken to mean that a man of wisdom will act out of a perverse self-will. That is the prerogative of the foolish and stupid. When even scriptural acts are too much for this passivity, what will he do with perverse acts, the result of total inability to know the right from the wrong? When the maladies of mind and vision are cured, you no longer perceive the way you did as their victim. Similar is the case with actions, they do not survive self-knowledge, neither perverse actions nor holy nor, for that matter, any other. Renunciation alone is the mode of life meant for him.

Mantra 11 of the *Īśa Upaniṣad*: 'Knowledge and ignorance, he who knows the two together, through ignorance shall cross death and through knowledge become immortal': should not be taken to mean, as some have, that these two, knowledge and ignorance, codwell in a man blessed with self-knowledge. Quite the contrary. The *mantra* denies, in every truth, the possibility of their codwelling in the same man and at the same time as one would deny the possibility of the same man calling the same thing silver and nacre at the same time. For 'distant opposites are they and divergent, that which is ignorance and what they know as knowledge . . .', the *Kaṭha Upaniṣad* tells us (1.2.4). Where there is knowledge, there cannot possibly be ignorance.

What, then, is ignorance which the *Īśa Upaniṣad* would combine with knowledge, and, what is that knowledge? Ignorance there means holy acts like penance, i.e. concentration'; the means to self-knowledge as the *Taittirīya Upaniṣad* (3.2) would say: 'Seek to know Brahman through *tapas,* concentration'; it also means serving one's teacher with devotion and other acts that purify the mind. These acts are constituted by *avidyā,* ignorance. Hence their equation with it. These acts help one cross death, death in the shape of desire, by generating self-knowledge in one. When man becomes free from desire and passion, he attains to immortality through knowledge of Brahman born out of the death of desire. This is the meaning of the *mantra* in question.

In his commentary on the *Īśa Upaniṣad,* Śaṅkara interprets this verse in a slightly different way. There he equates ignorance with holy acts as he does in the present context. But, unlike in the commentary on the *Aitareya Upaniṣad,* he equates knowledge there with god-knowledge, with meditation on gods. Immortality there means status of godhood, here it means liberation.

One need not draw hasty conclusions on the basis of this apparent inconsistency. In the commentary on the present *Upaniṣad, tapas* may be taken to take the place of *vidyā,* knowledge, of the *mantra* in question of the *Īśa Upaniṣad.* So as holy acts and meditation on gods could go together there, concentration and holy acts may be said to go together here. Only the term 'knowledge' has been interpreted as self-knowledge here, since concentration has been included in the category of holy acts. Substantially, the position remains the same: Concentration/meditation and holy acts supplement and reinforce each other, self-knowledge leaves both far behind.

ŚB You also said that the entire span of man's life was permeated by ceremonial piety. You invoked *Īśa Upaniṣad* 2 in support of your contention: 'By performing holy rites should one seek to live a hundred years here. For such as you, a man, there is no other way to remain clean of the stain of rites.' We rejected this view of yours by pointing out how this injunction was meant for the man who did not know the self; it could not possibly be meant for the man of self-knowledge. Still another of your views that the text to follow [comprising the *Aitareya Upaniṣad*] was in no way different from what precedes this text in view of the fact that the result that ensued from holy acts was identical with the result that ensued from self-knowledge, and, for this reason, self-knowledge was not opposed to ceremonial piety—this view of yours too was refuted by pointing out how piety [joined with meditation] leads to the realisation of the conditioned self and *jñāna*, knowledge, to the realisation of the unconditioned self. This point will be reiterated in our explanation of the *Aitareya Upaniṣad.*

Now is being commenced the text which is devoted to the revelation of that vision in which the passive Absolute and the self of each and every creature will be found to be one and identical.

1. aum! ātmā vā idam eka evāgra āsīt. nānyat kiṃcana miṣat. sa īkṣata lokān nu sṛjā iti.

In the beginning this was only the self, one and absolute. There was no other to blink, none whatsoever. He thought, 'Let me create the worlds.'

ŚB The word *ātman*, the self, is derived from the root *āp*, to pervade or from *ad*, to eat or *at*, to move on continuously. *This* means what they call *this world*, the world that has been rendered into a multiplicity by the diversifying factors consisting of names, forms and motions. This world was only the *ātman*, the self, one and absolute in the beginning, before its creation. It was that one self, that supreme self that knew all, that wielded all power, that knew neither hunger nor thirst, that had no characteristics of the world, none whatsoever, that was ever pure, ever conscious, ever free, the self birthless, undecaying, immortal, immortality itself, the self without a second. *Objection*: Is it not the case that what the Upaniṣad terms *idam*, this, still remains one, even after creation?
Answer: No.

Objection: Why should the *śruti* then use the singular number, why should it say '[This] was' and not '[these] were'?
Answer: It is indeed true that the referent of 'this' even now subsists as one reality. There is, however, a difference. Before creation, names and forms were not manifest and so were not the distinctions they connote. The world then subsisted as one with the self. One could call that state 'the self' and think of it as the self. One word and one concept could be said to encompass it, namely, the *self*. Now, however, names and forms are manifest and so are the distinctions they create. Consequently, the world can now be talked about and conceived in terms of 'many' and, of course, in terms of 'one self' too.

Before the manifestation of the name and form of foam, foam is all water. You call it 'water' and think of it as water. When, however, it appears with its own name and form, as distinct from water, then it is either talked about and conceived in terms of foam–water or simply as water, as one–many or as simply one. Similar is the case with the world. Before creation it is simply one, after creation, it is one–many.

Our world is a world of diverse forms. I cannot, however, perceive any form without giving it a name, a common name. My perception of, say, a leaf, is really a recognition as well as a cognition. Naming individualises and relates at the same time, perceives and conceives simultaneously.

What is it that the name names? Not the form before me, not the leaf before me, for the form, the leaf does not appear before the act of naming. Naming, of course, is other-oriented, but the other cannot be the leaf of our example because our leaf is already suffused with the name. So what I name has to be the 'form' preceding the form, the leaf before the leaf I experience. That form preceding the form would not be related to other preforms in terms of any categories of thought because relations obtain within the domain of the already named, not between the named and that which is yet to be named. Kantianism would obviously be out of place here. What, then, is that opaque being which is the other for the act of naming?

I use the expression 'naming' or 'the act of naming', not 'the name'. I use it because name as an object of my cognition, as what we call an item of language, is a phenomenon of the named world, obtains within it. It cannot be conceived as obtaining outside it. Before I move on to further consideration of naming and its object, I shall dwell a little on our concept of the world. The concept of the class implied in cognition of an object leads, eventually, to the concept of the world, to a whole net of relationships between things and their classes, between classes and classes, a net apparently countable but actually countless, potentially knowable but always unknown, the place in which our percepts obtain. This complex of relationships, which we ever seek to know but, as a matter of fact, never come to know is our world. Not something we perceive or can perceive but something that the act of naming, each and every instance of it, points to. The act of naming thus precedes the world, though not the name, not language which obtains within this world.

So those who would equate language with the informing principle do not run their full race. The name as the object of cognition has the same status as the object it names. But what we know as a name merely names the already named. The language we use is only referential not informing. It operates within an already named world.

But what is the act of naming that seems to turn its other into unity–multiplicity complex, into leaf–leaves–world complex? What is the status of what we call language when it functions, so to say, as a part of that act? What, furthermore, am I, the speaker in that state? I cannot obviously be what I am now, a being placed–deplaced, placed in the world, yet pitted against it. As a being deplaced, my words do not have the power to create, they only refer [to]. Yet the world I find myself living in is already a named world. So what was this world before it came to be named, what was it, to use the Upaniṣadic phraseology, in the beginning?

The world denuded of the name is bare presence, man denuded of the name is bare awareness of the presence. As bare awareness of the presence, he is bare temporality and the world it, that bare temporality, experiences turns into what we have termed bare presence, eventless and nontemporal as it were. It becomes what the Upaniṣad has called *idam*, this, the referent of all our names and the ground of all our shapes, shapes we experience. In our named world, *this* remains fully intact as the ground of our meanings and interpretations, even the ground of the totality of meanings and relationships. The totality of meanings and relationships could not acquire the status of a 'real, objective world' without the *idam* for its ground.

When bare awareness of the presence remains bare, it cannot distinguish itself from the presence, it remains suffused with it, one with it. The moment it becomes self-aware, the moment it turns from awareness-of-presence into awareness *of* presence, it turns linguistic. This becoming aware *of* the presence is the act of naming, it is *avidyā*, false knowledge, ig-norance. It conceals what we call *idam*, this, into this–world duality.

ŚB And there was nothing else that blinked, was active. Nor was there anything other than the active. The followers of the *Sāṅkhya* system believe that the world before its manifestation existed as *pradhāna*, as primordial

nature in and by itself, something that belongs, in their reckoning, to the category of the not-self. The followers of Kaṇāda would invest atoms with this kind of status. The *śruti* has nothing to do with views of this kind. Nothing other than the self, it says, existed then, only the self. Despite this, despite the fact that it alone existed, only it and nothing else, the self 'thought', 'thought' because it is in the nature of the self to be omniscient.
Objection: There was neither the body before creation, nor the senses. How could it, then, think?
Answer: It could think because it is by nature omniscient. 'Without hands and without feet,' says the Vedic *mantra*, 'does he grasp and go' (ŚveU 3.19). What did he think? Let me create worlds like *aṃbha* and others wherein creatures dwell to reap the fruits of their deeds.

The *śruti* weaves myths to lead man to truth. The myth mediates between what is intelligible to man and what is not. Before creation, the world was only the self, says the myth. Now 'before' and 'after' belong to the discourse that has the world for its subject matter, not what was before the world. Before–after relationships obtain within the world, there alone, not to what does not occur in it. We seek to know the before(s) of things because, as mentioned earlier, all that we are and all that we experience live destitute of being, of *ātman*. We seek effects or fabricate them also for the same reason. Engaged in this pursuit of finding causes and producing effects, we do not realise that the world we live in, our ontological ground, is itself a poor thing, as deprived of truth or the *ātman* as is our own poor life. When, however, the poverty of the world dawns upon us, we start thinking of the cause of the world itself, the cause which is *pūrṇa*, full of being, something of the nature of plenitude as against the destitution that characterises us and our world. In this kind of thinking we, of course, hold on to our old ways of thinking, of seeking befores and afters of things. Disillusioned, we still stick on to our illusions.

The myth in question appeals to this our ambivalent attitude. The cause of the world, it says, is all plenitude but to find that cause, we have to lose ourselves. For to move to the cause of the world would mean not only that I leave behind the world but also that I leave behind myself, the seeker and finder. This loss is not a loss but a finding, finding of the being I sought in befores and afters, whether of myself or of the world.

The argument that since cause–effect relationship obtains only within the world, we should not speculate about the cause of the world but rather confine our attention to the study of causes and effects that obtain within the world, is an argument that is conceptually sound but existentially absurd. It sleeps over the reason that prompts us to seek causes and work for effects, namely, our sense of inadequacy with regard to our situated mode of being. The mood of *vairāgya*, the mood in which we become existentially aware of our mortality, shows us the truth about our search for causes and effects, it reveals the truth of our loss and the possibility of regain. Seeking the cause of the world ends in undoing our seeking in terms of causes and effects, which means undoing our world and our situated mode of being. For the world exists for us only as a system of causes and effects at varied levels, depending on the kind of discourse we resort to or the mode of life we lead. So to ask about the cause of the world is the only genuine question about the cause. To say that we should restrict ourselves within the sphere of the world while discussing in terms of cause and effect is to ontologize an illusion, to mistake a mistake for truth and the object it mis-takes for reality.

The myth thus takes up our discourse, our discourse in terms of cause and effect, to undo all discourse and the world it sets up. It reveals how discourse projects the real that is our truth as well as the world's truth into the *other* with all the miseries that the *other* inflicts upon us.

That self, our primordial being, is presented as thinking, thinking the way we do, and creating worlds, all kinds of them. Our thinking, says the commentary, is not possible without the senses and the body. We think only as embodied, situated beings, situated in a world and society, two of the constitutive others of us as thinking beings. As isolated from this context, the context consisting of the body, the world and society, we cannot retain our status as thinking beings. The self, however, says the commentator, could think because it is omniscient. And it could also, the quotation from the *Śvetāśvatara Upaniṣad* adds, go and grasp. Another instance of mysticism? We who can think, the *advaitin* would say, know little, if what we think can at all be called knowledge. The truth is, he would add, our belief in our knowledge is little else than illusion, for only omniscience can be knowledge, less than that is ig-norance. Omniscience comes to be possible when I am freed from the bonds of the body, the senses and the mind, including the intellect. For then will all become me and me all. This self, this self that knows all because it is all can, says Śaṅkara, think as well as know, it can also do. It will think, it will know, it will do without the instruments that mediate our knowledge and reduce it to *alpam*, to knowledge small and insignificant.

When I am freed from the bondage of these instruments of knowledge that limit my knowledge, my consciousness, my thinking, my actions attain to what they seek. As a situated, embodied being, I feel that action without these instruments is impossible, and so is thinking. Indeed, I cannot be conscious without these instruments, I shall protest. If our thinking is fruitless, thinking done through these instruments, then fruitless thinking is all that we can do. Scriptures, too, I may add, describe the state of freedom in terms of passivity, in terms of cessation of all thinking. How is it, then, that thinking and action are now being associated with that state?

Let us try to see what kind of thinking comes to be possible for me when I progressively discard these instruments. When I live identified with the body, I think *about* things, when I live identified with the senses, I think *of* things. As the body self, I think about what I can do with the things in question, as the sense-self, I become a bare, passive percipient. This passive perception becomes possible when I am so much absorbed in the object that all self-consciousness of the body goes into the background.

Discarding the senses will mean transformation of the body and the world into events, into liquidity. I have described experience of this kind on earlier occasions. What I wish to emphasise here is the proneness of the passive contemplative sense self to articulate what it perceives, thereby sliding back into the body self. The liquid self, the self that reveals itself when the senses have been discarded is a silent self but it tends to slip back into the sense self rather quickly and too often in order to articulate, in retrospect, what it could not do as itself. However calm and placid, this self has strong links with the sense self.

There are moments of desire-free peace, when this liquidity will sink into indolence, into silence so deep that even the trace of what we call the human self disappears and every thought, every memory of the world. Yet this nothingness can speak again, can revive into man and his world, to add to them a meaning and a beauty they never had before. This is the utmost limit of man's adventure into nothingness, testifying to the truth of its creativity. When the senses are forgotten and the mind ceases to operate, the inner creative springs commence their outflow to fertilise our stale world. But this limit, this human limit, is not, the Upaniṣads say, the end of our pilgrimage. There is the further step to take, the step towards merging into this nothingness. Only the man who has done *tapas*, who has burnt himself up, is admitted into this nothingness as its inmate, neither poets nor artists nor visionaries, who remain mere visitors to it. Only the *tapasvin* can lose himself into it, can become it. When this happens, when man becomes nothingness, only then does he become the creator, the Great, the Word, the Golden Germ. He the innocent absolute knows all because he can will all into existence. All lies in him because he is their germ. He knows all because there is nothing else for him to know, all is he and he all. The world that we perceive is his creation, his doing. All doing takes place in the world, that is in him. There is no doer which is not him and no doing which is not him.

How he creates the world, the *mantra* to follow will explain and the commentary on it.

ŚB Having visualised, having thought, thus,

2. sa imāṃl lokān asrajita. ambho marīcīr maramāpo'do 'mbhaḥ pareṇa divaṃ dyauḥ pratiṣṭhāntarikṣaṃ marīcayaḥ pṛthivī maro yā adhastāt tā āpaḥ.

He created these worlds: ambhas, *the worlds of celestial waters,* marīci, *the world of shining rays,* mara, *the world of death and* āpaḥ, *the world of waters below. With heaven for its support is the world of celestial waters, the world up there beyond heaven. The space inbetween, between heaven and earth, is the world of shining rays. The vast domained earth is the world of death. And below the world of death is the world of subterranean waters.*

ŚB That self created these worlds: It created these worlds as a wise architect would create palaces and other buildings—with a lot of premeditation. *Objection*: Architects and others build palaces out of some material whereas the self has no material at its disposal. How can it create these worlds? *Answer*: In the beginning, names and forms lie unmanifest in the self, as one with it. They are, in that state, referred to as the self itself, so indistinguishable from the self are they in that state. They could very well be the material cause of the world. The relationship of foam, in its unmanifest and manifest form, with water could serve as a good analogue in this regard. The omniscient creates the world out of names and forms that lie dormant in it as one with it. So there is nothing wrong if its act of creation is compared with that of an architect.

There is, however, another explanation that can meet the demands of reason better than the one given above. And the explanation is that the omniscient and omnipotent god, the great magician, transforms himself into another self, viz., the world just as an intelligent public hypnotist transforms himself into another self. One can see this second form of him moving about in the sky even when the real public hypnotist keeps standing on the earth. And he performs this feat without the aid of any material whatsoever. Similar is the case with the self, the material cause of the world. This explanation avoids nihilistic positions, positions that would reduce the cause as well as the effect into absurdities. In fact, it dismantles them altogether.

Advocates of rigorous thinking do not feel satisfied with analogies, they ask for conceptually precise and intelligible arguments. The comments made by Śaṅkara in the present context will not satisfy them. They need some reformulations.

We daily observe things originate from their causes and produce effects of their own. This observation makes us believe, some empiricists say, that there is a law of causation operating in the world. We believe we know a phenomenon when we can place it in the causal link. 'How' and 'why' constitute what we call knowledge, even our scientific knowledge.

A philosopher would not care to defend this kind of belief. He will question the truth of the law of causation and the legitimacy of our attempt to make it a guiding principle of our investigation. Induction, he would say, cannot generate a ground for our belief in the necessity of a given principle.

Thinkers like Nāgārjuna will question not merely what may be called the objective validity of cause and effect but the very legitimacy of talking in these terms. For, in their view, cause and effect cannot even be conceived. As interconstitutive of each other, they can claim no independent status for themselves, neither cause nor effect.

The Upaniṣadic myth will be sympathetic with the sceptical strain of a Hume and more than sympathetic with Nāgārjuna's critique of our conceptual frameworks. It speaks about the cause not of this phenomenon or that phenomenon but of the very framework of our perception, our thinking, our action. The world as a totality is only that framework; it is neither an object of our perception nor a precise object of a concept nor the objective of our practice. It is the place where all these occur. But it is not really a place, not the ground of our being, not the world as the world. It is only, as I said above, the correlate of our theoretico-practical dispositions. If the dispositions are undone, the world too will be undone. But only as the correlate of our dispositions. For the place will remain, place denuded of the world as the framework. That will survive the death of the world. We seek the cause of the world when we become aware of the inadequacy of our theoretico-practical concerns, when we become aware that our concepts/percepts do not coincide with that ground and that whatever our practice might bring about will also remain adventitious to that ground. Those who uncritically accept their concepts and practices, men of thought and practice, do not become aware of the ground of the ground, of the ground of the world.

Seeking the ground of the world, thus, is to concur, to an extent, with sceptics and interconstitutionalists. The latter are convinced that there is no such thing as the world that our theories would build and our practice would master. The myth too finds the world, ontologically speaking, too poor to equate it with the ground of our being. It does not, however, rest content with this position. If the world is not the genuine ground we seek, we have to find the real ground beneath, the ground where we do not find any inadequacy, the ground which is suffused with being, suffused so deeply with it that we do not feel the need to seek a cause beyond it.

Names and forms, whether manifest or unmanifest, cannot survive the critique of interconstitutionalists. The seeming dependence of phenomena on their others does not, however, establish the ontology of the ambiguous, it points to something more primordial than either or both. This becomes evident to man when he realises the nature of his dependence on things around, things that he terms 'objective', 'real', 'material'. His preoccupation with them saves him from the agony of finding himself a mere instability, a being without a place, without an identity, a constant displacement. To be a constant displacement is his horror, of him who would live secure and happy, with an identifiable nature, a reliable character, a person with a self. That is his nature, to be this anguished inconsistency. To strive to attain to the unattainable state of being is his tragedy. There is, however, another dimension of his life. In order to escape from this anguish, he steals as it were his body from the world and turns it into an instrument to acquire and enjoy things around him. As an instrument, the body turns into a 'stable' entity and so do the things of the world when I move and stay identified with the body. The being of things as entities is thus dependent upon me but me as displacement. For the other me that I am, the nondisplacement, the being stable and placed is dependent on the things I see around. So when we talk of ontological interdependence of things, we have to identify the me on which the things around me are dependent and the me which is dependent on those things. The two are not exactly alike.

We confuse these two aspects of ourselves and couple one with the other because we do not wish to own up to our constant displacement; as thinkers, we disown it through concepts, as doers and enjoyers, through things. Thus I conjure up the illusion of stable things through my identification with the body. When, however, I look at the body as an object, I find it turn into a mere succession of sensations. But then thoughts of things do not occur to me nor desires for them assail me. It is at that moment when I live as emptiness that the illusory nature of things *as* entities reveals itself to me. In such moments of lucidity I truly come to know how my interest in understanding things in terms of why and how is itself an attempt at rationalising my concealment of truth as displacement; it is, in truth, not knowledge that I seek through my intellectual endeavours but augmentation of my delusion. It is also in such moments that the need to know the true ground of me, of my being, dawns upon me, for I know with utmost clarity that the ground I have pitched my tents on is nothing but an illusion.

So interdependence of things does not establish them either as ambiguities or as unrealities; what it establishes is the reality of the ground of phenomena. It is that ground that this Upaniṣad is going to reveal through the myth of creation, the myth necessitated by our poverty and of all that we perceive. It is that ground, that self that has transformed itself into us and our world. The change and transformation does not, however, change and transform it. This last point will be dwelt on in due course. At present, we should let the myth speak for itself.

ŚB Which were the worlds that it created? The *śruti* counts them as follows: *ambhas, marīcīḥ, maram, āpaḥ*. The first element it created was *ākāśa*, the ether of space. Then followed the cosmic egg in due order. Having created these, it created the worlds, *ambhas* and others. The *śruti* itself explains, what *ambhas* and other worlds are. The world named *ambhas* is the one that lies up there beyond *dyu*, beyond heaven. It is called *ambhas* because it carries *ambhas*, waters [clouds] with it. Heaven is the support of this world of waters. *Marīci* is what lies below heaven, the world of interspace. Interspace is one world but the *śruti* uses the plural *marīcīḥ* (= *marīcayaḥ*) because interspace has diverse spaces constituting it, each different from the other. There could, however, be another explanation for the use of *marīcīḥ*. And that is: This world of intermediate space between heaven and earth is the space of *marīci*-s, of shining, bright rays. *Mara* is the world of death; earth is that world, this place of mortals. The worlds below this home of mortals are called *āpaḥ*, the worlds of waters. The word is derived from *āp*, to attain. [These worlds are worlds which creatures merely fall into—attain—without striving for them. They are the natural worlds of the fallen, fallen below the level of mortals, of creatures devoid of the *ekstatic* urge].

The worlds from the highest to the lowest are constituted by the five elements, sky, air, fire, water and earth. Yet it is water that dominates over all the other ones. Hence the use of *ambhas, marīcīḥ, maram, āpaḥ*—all synonyms of *āpaḥ*, waters.

All the worlds, from the highest to the lowest, are constituted by the five elements. The five elements, however, manifest themselves in different ways in each of the worlds mentioned above. This means that heaven, earth, the space inbetween and the world below are the different miens of the same reality. These worlds are not topographies but different appearances of what really is. The world below is the absolute given, the world open to those who are, almost completely, at the mercy of their blind urges, devoid of creative participation. Heaven is the world of light where the percipient freely flows into it to become one with it. Here the sun god *Āditya* flows out to all that is, freely and without interruption, and the essence of all, their water, evaporates to reach the sun to be absorbed by it. It is the bright world sustained by sacrifice—the sun spending itself into things and things evaporating into *Āditya,* the eater. This is the world of waters, the home and destination of the life of things, of their waters. The intermediate region, the region bright with rays, too is the home of waters, for these rays are the *waters* of creatures, their life, waters as offerings of things to the sun and as offerings of the sun to things. The earth on which these rays fall too is, thus, the home of waters, waters that will rise up again to move to the sun. The worlds below are called the worlds of water proper, for these are the fallen worlds in which the tendency to rise up, to evaporate, is almost dead. This is hell, the home of darkness, where no redemptive fire seems to burn. This hell is not, however, eternal, for with the death of the creator, it too will die. Moreover, this world too is *watery,* of the nature of activity, not of inertness, though its waters, its activities, lie arrested in stale stillness. It has the potentiality, though not the ability, to change and rise up. *Sattva,* the force of transcendence, lies suppressed in it but is not altogether dead. The presence of water everywhere shows that the possibility of evaporation, of transcendence, is present in all the worlds, though in different degrees. In the worlds below it is present as dominated by *tamas.*

ŚB Having created these four worlds, where creatures reap the fruits of their actions and which themselves are those fruits:

3. sa īkṣteme nu lokā lokapālān nu sṛjā iti. so'dbhya eva puruṣaṃ samud-dhṛtyāmūrchayat.

He thought: These, now, are the worlds. Let me now create of these the guardians. From the waters did he take out the person and gave him a shape.

ŚB He, the Lord, thought again : These worlds, *ambhas* and others, that I have created may perish if there are no guardians to protect them. Let me, therefore, create guardians for the protection of these worlds. Having thought thus, he took out a semblance of the person, endowed with hands, feet, etc., from waters, from, that is to say, the five elements dominated by water, the same he had created the worlds with. This semblance of the person was to the person as a lump of earth is to the post that a potter shapes out of it. To this he gave a shape, endowing it with limbs.

The Lord is the self of man, his inbeing. The world emerges out of that self but man, who finds himself placed in the world, does not remember the Creator that he is. This does not mean the fall of the god—the myth does not speak of it—though he has transformed himself into the worlds and their enjoyers/sufferers. The god is the enjoyer as well as the enjoyed, he eats as man and is eaten as the earth, he kills as earth and is killed as man. As *devas* he lives as harmony, as *yajña*, embracing alike both life and death. As creatures of the underworld, of the world of waters below, he suffers despair, the loss of hope. Darkness is he and light, heaven is he and hell, with the hopefuls he hopes, with the despondents he despairs. Consciousness is he and matter, life is he and death, evil is he and good. The entire world is honey for him, he himself is honey, to borrow an image from the *Bṛhadāraṇyaka Upaniṣad.* With creation he does not fall, with its dissolution he is not redeemed, this perpetual *status quo*, blessed in damnation, fallen in redemption.

Creatures of the world, who suffer with god but do not know his joy in suffering, have only to share this *samatvam*, this being-ever-alike, of the god to be the god. For he is not a person as we are, he is only this *samatvam*, this alikeness. When man comes to be alikeness, he will find no difference between creation and no-creation, between fall and redemption. The myth in question is the myth about *samatvam.* It has no theological or philosophical assertions to make.

4. tam abhyatapat. tasyābhitaptasya mukhaṃ nirabhidyata yathāṇḍam. mukhād vāg, vāco'gnir nāsike nirabhidyetām. nasikābhyāṃ prāṇaḥ, prāṇād vāyuḥ, akṣinī nirabhidyetām. akṣibhyāṃ cakṣuḥ, cakṣuṣa ādityaḥ. karṇau nirabhidyetām. karṇābhyāṃ śrotram, śrotrād diṣas tvaṅ nirabhidyata. tvaco lomāni, lomabhya ośadhi-vanaspatayo hṛdyaṃ nirabhidayata. hṛdyān manaḥ, manasaś candramā nābhir nirabhidyata. nābhyā apānaḥ, apanān mṛtyuḥ śiśnaṃ nirabhidyata. śiśnād retaḥ, retasa āpaḥ.

He brooded over him, the person. Of him thus brooded on, the mouth parted as would an egg. From the mouth came out speech, from speech fire. [Then] were parted the nostrils. From the nostrils came out

> *breath, from breath air. The eyes parted. From the eyes emerged sight, from the sight the sun. The ears parted. From the ears hearing, from hearing quarters of space. Then was separated out the skin. From the skin came out hair, from hair herbs and plants. The heart was separated out. From the heart came out the mind, from the mind the moon. The navel separated out. From the navel emerged the incoming breath, from the incoming breath death. The organ of generation separated out. From it emerged semen, from semen water.*

ŚB He did *tapas* with regard to that mass that resembled the person—contemplated it, brooded over it. That, in every truth, is the *tapas*, the austerity of the Lord, that contemplation, as the voice of the *śruti* will itself proclaim:

> He who is all knowing and all wise, whose ascetic austerity is knowledge . . . (MuṇḍU 1.1.9).

Of him thus contemplated, of him over whom the Lord brooded, did his *tapas*, ascetic austerity that was knowledge itself, of that mass was parted the mouth, a mouth-like hole. It parted as would a bird's egg. Out of that parted mouth came the organ of speech. And from speech came out fire, the presiding deity of speech, one of the guardians of the world. Likewise emerged nostrils, from nostrils emerged outgoing breath, from outgoing breath air. Here too, as in other cases, the first to emerge was the seat of the organ, then the organ and then the presiding deity. Thus the eyes, the ears, the skin and the heart should be taken as the respective seats of the organs of sight, of hearing, of touch (touch associated with hair) and of the internal organ of desire, volition, aversion, etc. What the text calls the mind is this very internal organ. The navel is the point to which all the [five] breaths are tied. [They originate from here and come to repose here]. The organ of ejection is called *apāna*, the incoming breath, because of its association with this breath. From this breath emerged its presiding deity, death. As in other cases, the seat of the organ of generation separated out. The organ itself has been termed semen. This because of its association with semen. From the organ of generation emerged water.

To many in our times this description will appear fanciful, even puerile. What could be the equation between human speech and cosmic fire? Between outgoing breath and air, the eye and the sun, the ear and space, the incoming breath and death? It is, one may object, one thing to say that man has his other in the world, it is quite another thing to enumerate this otherness organ by organ. Speculation has indeed, he may conclude, run wild here!

To people of this sort a reply would be that myths in the Upaniṣads are ways, doorways, to truth, they are not truth itself as realists would understand the term. The man of faith, of course, accepts the myth as truth but in a different way. He will, for example, look at the sun as the cosmic–divine counterpart of the eye, its presiding deity, the giver of light to it and its sustainer. He will look at it, meditate it, with this sense of intimate relationship, of affinity. If the eye can absorb the sun as its self and being, if man's entire attention and being is focussed on the sun, absorbed in it, the revelation is not far away, the revelation that the person here (to use the language of the Upaniṣads) and the person there in the yonder sun are the same. But this truth would be revealed only when the golden vessel that the shining orb is is removed and so is the bodily eye. The two coalesce, the sun with the eye and the eye with the sun. With this coalescence the face of truth is revealed. This is what the *Īśa Upaniṣad* says towards the end:

> The face of truth is covered with a golden vessel. Uncover it, O Sun, that I who am truth itself may see it.
>
> Sustainer! Solitary Traveller! Controller! Sun! Creator's Son! Remove your rays, gather up your splendour! I see your splendid form, most benign! He who is there, the *puruṣa*, the Person, that very Person am I!

For Plato, the eye–sun simile remains only a simile; it does not become a symbol of truth, its partaker, its sharer. That is the bane of transcendentalists. In the Upaniṣads, however, the truth enunciated is only a symbol but a symbol suffused with the truth it symbolises. One has only to self-submit to the symbol to find that truth. The truth of the myth thus is the truth for meditation, it is not a conceptual truth, the truth of philosophy as the term is understood in contemporary academic world.

Similarly, the breath–air image is also suggestive of meditation. It indicates the yogic meditation on breath, breath which goes out to die in the cosmic air to be reborn as incoming breath. You die into air to come back to life, you who live as breath. *That,* you see, is your origin and your end, the air you breathe. This way the *yogin* becomes *virāj,* the cosmotheandric god, to eventually die into truth.

Other images could also be seen to work as meditative truths. Thus hearing and quarters of space are represented as another duality, with hearing having precedence over quarters. This, one can easily see, is a meditative truth, not a propositional one. The voice I hear points out the direction from where it comes—from east or west, north or south, from above or from below. The eye can reveal only what lies in front of me but the ear can 'register' each and every quarter. To me, a being fallen into a situated mode of being, the ears can only point out quarters, the latter do not emerge from my organ of hearing, as the Upaniṣad would say. How can I reduce these presiding deities of my ears to emanations of my ears?

Once again I have to submit myself to the process of hearing, contemplate it without comment or judgement. I hear the tick of a clock on the wall. I notice the direction from where it is coming—from the wall in front of me. The monotone continues: tick, tick, tick. . . . I notice it is not a monotone, for the tick before registers itself more distinctly, more intensely, than the one succeeding it. The sound continues. There are, of course, regular intervals. Are they empty of all audible content? No. For, I hear a faint hum in the ears during those intervals. It spreads slowly in the region of the brain which seems to me, at this moment, all empty, devoid of flesh and bones. The hum concentrates in the crown of the head to become a continuity, uniform and even. This continuum of sound spreads, gradually, from head to foot, to arms and fingers. The entire body reverberates with it to bring all thoughts to extinction. As for the tick of the clock, it is heard no more. No sense of quarters remains, neither of east nor of west. It is only when the sound becomes indistinct and my hearing returns that I become aware of east or west, north or south.

As one entrenched in hearing, I find *diś*-es, quarters of space, 'more real' than me, I find myself placed in their midst, find them preceding my birth and I can also imagine that they will continue to be after my death. They are the presiding deities of my hearing, its guardians. But the hum within undoes these *diś*-es, undoes them after undoing my hearing. This undoing of them, an undoing after the undoing of hearing, shows their being as dependent on that of the organ of hearing, the faculty of hearing. It is this yogic truth which the Upaniṣad is hinting at; it is not a propositional truth that it states.

The navel–incoming breath–death trio might appear to many as more puerile than any other in the list. The navel is the seat of the organ, the incoming breath the organ itself, and death the presiding deity. The breathing creature who inhales breath down to the navel to exhale it back is a mortal creature, his life a prey of death. With every breath he inhales, the breath he takes to be his life, he moves towards death. Escaping death through 'breath of life', he, in every truth, goes near it. Through breath does death kill him. Death is indeed the presiding deity of his life. But one must add a little rider to what has been stated. Breath that moves towards the navel to die there gives birth to *prāṇa,* the outgoing breath. It is the breath of mortality, not death itself. But breath as the organ of excretion is death itself. We receive breath to give it back but we receive food only to absorb it.

What we give back is only waste. When man gives back the breath he received, he is vouchsafed new breath, instead of the stale breath he receives fresh and life-sustaining breath. When, however, he gives waste to earth, he isolates himself from it. Earth is not as prompt as air is in responding generously to his offerings. Earth is generous enough, forgiving enough, to transform his waste into manure but it will also demand strenuous labour from him to get back food from it. Without that labour, man lives isolated from earth, lives in hunger, that killer image of isolation and of death. Hunger is the killer *par excellence*, it kills all that one turns into food but refuses to be appeased until it has killed the eater. He is its ultimate victim. But how many it undoes before it finally claims him!

Chapter 2

1. **tā etā devatāḥ sṛṣṭā asmin mahaty arṇave prāpataṃs tam aśanāyāpipāsābhyām anvavārjat tā enam abruvann āyatanaṃ naḥ prajānīhi yasmin pratiṣṭhitā annam adāmeti.**

Into this great ocean fell the gods thus created. The Self then decreed that with hunger and thirst be endowed the man to be. 'Find us an abode,' said the gods unto him, 'wherein dwelling may we the eaten eat.'

ŚB Those *Agni* and other gods that God had created through the power of thought, those guardians of the regions, fell into this great ocean of the world: the ocean filled with the waters of suffering, that creature of ignorance, desire and action. Many a sea monster infests this ocean—in the form of maladies severe and painful, in the form of decay and death. No end has this ocean nor a beginning, boundless does it stretch, giving no promise of an anchor near or afar. The only pleasure this world can promise is the mean pleasure of the sense, ephemeral and momentary, the only respite from pain available here.

Desire for the objects of five senses, that generator of evils in their hundreds, is the tempest that ever assails this ocean with unabated fury. Overwhelming are the evils it generates—like the high and mighty waves stirred up by it. Hells in numbers large abound in it, with cries of despair ever emanating from them and shrieks of pain. So great is the tumult of that agony that no part of the ocean is bereft of it.

There is, however, a raft to take one across this sea of misery. And that raft is the raft of knowledge. There have, of course, to be provisions for the voyage towards the goal. These consist of truth and simplicity, charity and compassion, care and concern for creatures and the resolve never to do them any injury. Restraint of the senses too is an essential part of that provision and peace of mind and patience—these and other traits that sanctify the heart. The course that the raft follows is marked by holy association and renunciation absolute. As for its shore, the end of this course, it is *mokṣa*, liberation.

Into this great ocean fell the gods, the presiding deities of the regions. That the gods lie fallen in this ocean of misery shows that those who seek to merge into them, into *Agni* and others, will not reach the true goal; not for them will be the end of sorrows and sufferings that go with the worldly mode of being. We have already had occasion to dwell on this aspect of *devatāpyaya*, merger into gods, what it can promise and what it cannot, along with its nature. Meditation on gods and holy acts cannot however promise more than this kind of merger. For the end of the sorrows of life, for their absolute cessation, one must realise Brahman the supreme, that self of one and of all. Of that Brahman and its qualities the Upaniṣad will speak presently, the self-same Brahman that the *śruti* has introduced as the creator, the sustainer and the destroyer of the temporal world. The Vedas emphasise this point in words like these:, 'This, verily, is the path, this is the holy deed, this is Brahman, this is the truth' (AiĀ 2.1.1). And they do so because, for them, there is no way to liberation other than realisation of Brahman, the Absolute, as the self:

> By knowing him alone does one pass over death.
> No other path is there for going forth.

Thus the *Śvetāśvatara Upaniṣad* (3.8):

[To come back, however, to the words of the text:] The creator endowed that lump-self, that man-to-be, that first born person, the source of seats of organs, of organs and of the presiding deities—the creator endowed him with hunger and thirst. With him, the cause, inflicted with these pollutions, the gods, the effects, too got inflicted with them. Tortured with them, these gods said to the creator, the grandsire: Find for us, provide for us, an abode wherein dwelling we may eat food, be able to eat it.

Gods that we worship with meditation and holy deeds are themselves creatures of hunger and thirst, the creations of man himself, not of man the dweller in space and time but of man as he was before that placement, before even coming to be of space and time, for these emerged along with placement. What was man before that placement, before even the birth of gods? He could well be imagined man without name and form but the Upaniṣad speaks of the shape given to him even before the emergence of organs, of gods, of time, of space. He had a shape like a lump of earth to be wrought into a pot. He was the material cause of the world, the man–world–gods in potentiality. This potential man–world–gods, this cosmotheandric being, this lump, this person, was itself a creation of the creator. The creator had transformed himself into this person, the material cause, with himself emerging as the efficient cause. Thus did the *causa sui* divide himself into the material and the efficient causes. The material cause was then transformed into the world. The world is nothing else than senses and mind but senses and mind as placed and also oriented towards and subject to gods. Space, time, the sun, the moon, death and others are gods. In other words, the temporal–spatial world is the god of the fallen man. The varied phenomena of the world are the others of the senses, their constitutive and regulative others. The world thus has no being apart from the body and yet the body lives as subject to the world, its god.

When does man reach the level of that lump, that form of the body which projects itself, manifests itself, as body–world duality? As placed in the spatial–temporal world, the body has a temporal–spatial form but that, obviously, cannot be the form of the lump. That [pre-]form of the body can be realised only when man contemplates gods after purging himself of his self-orientations through participatory acts. This contemplation free of self-reference leads to one's merger in the sun or space or time or breath. Contemplation of death can also undo the narcissistic tendencies in man. When he thus becomes one with the sun, with space or time or when he comes to live death, he as well as his god dies into the impersonal self called the lump, the person, the material cause of the world, of man–world–gods. He (it) is the cosmotheandric being, he is the *puruṣa,* the person, the lump that contains in himself/itself *sarvam,* all that is.

To be that preperson is however only a step towards the realisation of all as the self. For this preperson, this man impersonal, has all the potentialities of the fall.

2. tābhyo gām ānayat tā abruvan na vai no'yam alam iti. tābhyo'śvam ānayat tā abruvan na vai no'yam alam iti.

He brought for them a cow. 'Verily,' said they, 'this is not enough for us.' He brought for them a horse. 'Verily', said they, 'this is not enough for us.'

ŚB When the gods requested him thus, he brought for them a cow. This cow he brought forth from the waters as he had brought forth [pre-] man from them. It was a lump resembling the form of a cow. He gave it a shape and brought it to the gods to show it to them. Seeing this cow-like form, they spoke to him, 'This lump is certainly not enough for us. It cannot be the anchor of our being, we cannot eat our food with this lump for our body: it is not adequate for that purpose.' When they thus rejected the cow, God brought for them a horse. But they found that too inadequate. Their words regarding the horse should be interpreted the same way as their words relating to the cow.

3. tābhyaḥ puruṣam ānayat tā abruvan sukṛtaṃ bateti. puruṣo vāva sukṛtam. tā abravīd yathāyatanaṃ praviśateti.

He brought for them a man. 'Well done,' said they, 'truly man is made well.' Then he unto them: Enter, then, into your abodes, each into each.

ŚB When gods had rejected all other forms, God brought man for them, man their source. Seeing him, they felt happy, for they found that abode well made, beautifully made. Man is well made because he is the source of the noble and holy deeds. Or because it was the Lord who fashioned him all by Himself, by the power of his own *māyā,* his divine magic.

The Lord thought that the gods liked man for their abode. All beings love their source and so, in this matter, did the gods. He said to them, 'Enter into your abodes, each into his. Enter into that where you can do your respective functions—speaking and others.'

4. agnir vāg bhūtvā mukhaṃ prāviśad vāyuḥ prāṇo bhūtvā nāsike prāviśad ādityaś cakṣur bhūtvākṣiṇī prāviśad diśaḥ śrotraṃ bhūtvā karṇau prāviśann oṣadhi-vanaspatayo lomāni bhūtvā tvacaṃ prāviśaṃś candramā mano bhūtvā hṛdayaṃ prāviśan mṛtyur apāno bhūtvā nābhiṃ prāviśad āpo reto bhūtvā śiśanaṃ prāviśan.

Fire, becoming the organ of speech, entered the mounth. Air, becoming the organ of smell, entered the nostrils. The sun, becoming the organ of sight, entered the eyes. The quarters of space, becoming the organ of hearing, entered the ears. Plants and herbs, becoming hair, entered the skin. The moon, becoming the mind, entered the heart. Death, becoming incoming breath, entered the navel. Waters, becoming semen, entered the organ of generation.

ŚB 'Be it so', said the gods when they were permitted by the Lord to enter the lump-like form of man as would enter commanders a city when so commanded by a king. Fire, the god that identifies himself with the organ of speech, entered the mouth, its source. Similarly did the rest. Air entered the nostrils, the sun the eye, the quarters of space the ears, herbs and plants the skin, the moon the heart, death the navel, the waters the organ of generation.

The myth seems here to enter almost the domain of unintelligibility. The primordial man was, we may recall, the source of the world of time and space. From his organs had sprung the cosmic gods, who, before coming into being of the cosmos, felt themselves deplaced and sought to be *placed.* That is the meaning of their hunger and thirst. To appease their ontological hunger and thirst, they entered their respective seats once again, not the seats located in the body of the primordial man but in the seats located in the body of the fallen man, the man who found himself situated in the world of time and space. Our senses, the myth implies, have their respective counterparts in the world, what is there in the sun is also here in the eye, what is there in space is also here in the ear and so on. In short, the body of man and the universe are, in every truth, dualities-in-unity. The whole world, with its extension into the past and its projection into the future, is the function of the body. It emerges with the emergence of the body but emerges as the other, not as its emanation. The primordial man creates the world as his emanation, mortal man finds it as the oppressive other.

To find the world as his emanation, mortal man has to find himself as the primordial man. He has to lose himself in the sight to find himself. He has to lose himself in the sounds coming from various quarters to find himself. And in the breath, incoming and outgoing. He has also to feel the touch of plants and herbs and reciprocate that touch. We touch with warmth the living, even animals, because we feel the reciprocal tactual response. When we can give the same kind of touch to plants and herbs, when, in other words, we feel the same breath of life in them as we feel in ourselves, then the world will well be on its way to transform itself into our emanation.

When I touch the woman I love, I feel the touch of her life, not the touch of my life in her. So much of otherness is there in every human love-relationship. But to feel the warmth of the leaf is to give myself up to it, it is to let it affect me on its own. When I touch it, I must feel that it is the leaf that is touching me, not I that am touching it. When I forget my touch of it and remember only its touch of me, I shall change from mortal man to the primordial man.

Seeds of nonmoving beings have no water in them; seeds of moving beings have it in them. That makes the difference between these two kinds of beings. The seed in man relates man to woman, makes him *move* towards her and, through her, to his children, to other beings in his group. It is the function of water to make one move to the other and, also, to move *into* the other, as it would make a seed to move, to be transformed, into a plant. The watery seed in man too makes him move towards others and into others. Water means life-in-relationships. And so does the human seed.

The fallen man finds his water not the water of relationships and of self-transformations but destructive of those relationships and a hindrance in the way of self-transformation. The sadistic–masochistic tendencies of sex drive are well known. To perceive water in semen is to perceive woman as an emblem of relationships, not an object of sadistic–masochistic pleasures. To sprinkle the seed in woman is to relate to future as one's forefathers related to one, it is to acknowledge one's mortality, one's affinity with the dead, one's forefathers: it is to count oneself as one among them. It also means to recognise the fact that one's being is a being-in-displacement, to be ever to be someone else. This the fallen man is not ready to accept, despite the force of waters in him, the force of sex-drive. Thus breed perversities. To perceive the truth of the seed as water is to accept one's lot as other-related. This other-orientation does not, however, save man from death. Not until man lives as a mortal will he regain his primordial manhood. This brings us to death as the guardian spirit.

Death guards over the motion of our breath. The breath that we breathe is the breath of a mortal frame, we breathe ourselves out of life. Yet this breath of mortality can lead us to the primordial man if we do not spend our breath but live it, each and every moment of it. Unless we have breathing trouble or do some exercises relating to breath, we do not pay attention to breath, not to speak of participating in it. Only a *yogin* participates in its motion, only he lives as breath. And only he steps out of it to become the person, the primordial man.

Perhaps a few words on moon–mind identity may also be in order. The moon waxes into fullness and wanes into darkness to be reborn as the new moon. Thoughts too rise to collapse and collapse to rise again. The nothingness into which thoughts die to be reborn is not noticed by *kṛpaṇāḥ*, miserable creatures that live deprived and in fear. They believe that thoughts are a part of a continuity, of thought-process. Now, what continues is not thoughts but what may be called awareness of thoughts, their witness. Men and women are so much in the grip of their desires and thoughts that they cannot, do not have the patience and the leisure to distinguish between their thoughts and their awareness of them. If ever they could summon up the calm and the leisure to perceive the comings and goings of their thoughts, they would not fail to perceive, with utmost clarity, the difference between the thoughts that come and go and awareness of these, awareness that stays stable and unchanging. If they do that, they will soon find their thought dying into bare consciousness, the source of the primal person.

Alternately, man may, if he cannot summon the detachment enough for this inner contemplation, concentrate his attention on the moon, contemplate it with steady and exclusive attentiveness. Let him carefully locate the new moon in the sky and see how it slowly waxes, digit by digit, every night until it attains to fullness. Let him also see it fade out, again digit by digit, until it disappears into darkness. Let him live that darkness too, the darkness with its own shape, its form, benign and serene at one moment, dangerous and frightening at another. Let him allow this darkness, this dread, the very image of his death occupy him, kill his thoughts, his concerns, his ambitions. If he renews this encounter month after month, the man in him will give place to the primordial man and the cruel world will become his emanation.

5. tam aśanāyāpipāse abrūtām āvābhyām abhiprajānīhīti. te abravīd etāsveva vāṃ devatāsvābhajāmy etāsu bhāginyau karomīti. tasmād yasyai kasyai ca devatāyai havir gṛhyate bhāginyāvevāsyām aśanāyā-pipāse bhavataḥ.

To him said hunger and thirst, 'Think for us, too'. Said he to them, 'Among these very gods I assign you a place, with them I make you both the partakers.' Therefore, for whatever god they take up an offering, of that become hunger and thirst the sharers.

ŚB When gods had thus found each their place, hunger and thirst still remained homeless. The two, therefore, said to the Lord, 'Think of a place for us too to abide in, ordain one for us too.' 'You two,' said he, 'are mere feelings. You can't eat food until you abide in some conscious being. Therefore, among these very gods, *Agni* and others, I assign you a place. Among these shall you dwell, among these in the body [where they dwell as senses, breath, death etc.] or among these as divinities proper. There shall you find your living. Thus do I bless you two. Whatever is the share of gods, whatever is offered to them, of that I make you two also the sharers.' Thus did the Lord ordain in the beginning of creation. Therefore, for whatever god a man takes up as offering porridge, cake or any other suitable thing, of that become, along with the deity in question, hunger and thirst the sharers. This is as true today as it was before.

Impoverishment is the mark of creation. Even gods live in unrest, even they seek their being in the other, their food. Since hunger and thirst are unappeasable, there is no true sustenance for both mortals and immortals. Not until man dies as man and gods as gods will their hunger be appeased and their thirst slaked. This is as true of other beings as of man and his gods.

Chapter 3

1. sa īkṣateme nu lokāś ca lokapālāś cānnam ebhyaḥ srijā iti.

He thought, 'These, then, are the worlds and the guardians of the world. Let me now create food for these worlds and these guardians.'

ŚB The Lord thought: These, then, are the worlds and the guardians of the world. I have created them and filled them with hunger and thirst. They cannot live without food, these creatures replete with hunger and thirst. Let me, therefore, create food for these worlds and these guardians.

Thus do those in power have the authority to dispense favours or disfavours. This is what we see happening in the world. The same holds true of the Great God, too, that Lord of all that is.

The worlds, of course, are the senses and the mind and the guardians are their divine correlates.

2. so 'apo 'bhyatapat. tābhyo 'bhitaptābhyo mūrtir ajāyata. yā vai sā mūrtir ajāyatānnaṃ vai tat.

He brooded over waters. Out of these thus brooded over was born a form. That verily is food, that form born out of waters.

ŚB When the Lord thus desired to create food, he brooded over the self-same waters over which he had brooded earlier when he thought of creating the worlds and their guardians. From those waters, the material cause, thus brooded over, was born a form. The form was of the shape of a mass, could provide support to others and had the characteristics of both the moving and the nonmoving, the sentient and the insentient. That form was indeed food itself, that which appeared as a form, had a likeness to it.

The source of man and his gods, of those who eat, is the same as that of what they eat. Out of waters, out of the primal material cause, are they born, that other of the primal efficient cause. Their ultimate source is Brahman as the self, all-as-the-self. The eater eats, in every truth, only himself. For there is no other to eat. In order to highlight this point, Śaṅkara calls the enmassed form both sentient and insentient, living and nonliving. Living beings eat the dead or the nonliving; they cannot swallow them alive because they, their food, will turn the swallowers into their food if they live and breed in the eaters' bellies. Men and gods thus are partakers of violence and of sin.

To mitigate this sin, man does not eat animals the way the beasts do. A tiger may eat an ox even when the latter is bellowing in agony. Men kill before they eat. To swallow life itself is not their *forte*, exceptions notwithstanding. This much of sense and sensitivity they do have. The thing in which one sees some affinity with oneself, one cannot turn into food. Civilised human beings do not eat other human beings, nor, generally speaking, other things alive, for life in me and in others appears so deeply alike to them. Many turn vegetarians for this reason. Those who seek self-knowledge, those who would see the other as the self, do not, could not, eat meat. It is not out of mere sentiments that pious and orthodox Hindus are vegetarians.

When this sense of affinity becomes deep and immediate, man finds himself eating only himself. He becomes, then, the primordial man, violent but only to himself. In him human violence turns into self-sacrifice, human sin into divine glory.

3. tad enat sṛṣṭaṃ prāṅatyajighāṃsat tad vācā'jighṛkṣat tan nāśaknod vācā gṛhītum. yad dhainad vācāgrahaiṣyad abhivyāhṛtya haivānnam atrapsyat.

This food, which the Lord had created, turned back and sought to flee away. With speech the Person sought to catch it but could not. If he had caught it with speech, mere utterance of the word 'food' would have appeased one's hunger.

ŚB This food, created for the worlds and for their guardians, created in their very presence, turned back and sought to flee away from those eaters, began to run away from their presence, as a mouse would from a cat, thinking the latter to be its eater, its death.

That mass of the worlds and their deities, that body–sense lump, knew what was the intention of food. Being the first born, he found no other eaters around and sought to catch that food through speech, through utterance itself. But he did not succeed this way in his purpose. If he, the first embodied, had succeeded in seizing the food, then every creature would have been appeased by merely uttering the word 'food', for these creatures are only transformations or modifications of the first-born. But that does not happen to be the case. This would show that even the primordial person, he who was the first to be born, did not succeed in seizing the food through speech.

The *mantras* to follow too should be understood the same way.

4. tat prāṇenājighṛkṣat tan nāṣaknot praṇena grahītuṃ sa yad dhainat prāṇenāgrahaiṣyad abhiprāṇya haivānnam atrapsyat.

He sought to catch it through breath but did not succeed in catching it through the breath. If he had caught it with breath, then mere smelling of food would have appeased one's hunger.

5. **tac cakṣuṣājighṛkṣat tan nāśaknoc cakṣuṣā grahītuṃ sa yad dhainac cakṣuṣāgrahaiṣyad dṛṣṭvā haivānnam atrapsyat.**

He sought to catch it with the eye but did not succeed in catching it with the eye. If he had caught it with the eye, mere sight of food would have appeased one's hunger.

6. **tac chrotreṇājighṛkṣat tan nāśaknoc chrotreṇa grahītuṃ sa yad dhainac chrotreṇāgrahaiṣyac chrutvā haivānnam atrapsyat.**

He sought to catch it with the ear but did not succeed in catching it with the ear. If he had caught it with the ear, mere hearing of food would have appeased one's hunger.

7. **tat tvacājighṛkṣat tan nāśaknot tvacā grahītuṃ sa yad dhainat tvacāgrahaiṣyat spṛṣṭvā haivānnam atrapsyat.**

He sought to catch it with the skin but did not succeed in catching it with the skin. If he had caught it with the skin, merely touching of food would have appeased one's hunger.

8. **tan manasājighṛkṣat tan nāśaknon manasā grahītum sa yad dhainan manasāgrahaiṣyad dhyātvā haivānnam atrapsyat.**

He sought to catch it with the mind but did not succeed in catching it through the mind. If indeed he had succeeded in catching food with the mind, mere thought of food would have appeased one's hunger.

9. **tac chiśnenājighṛkṣat tan nāśaknoc chiśnena grahītuṃ sa yad dhainac chiśnenāgrahaiṣyad visṛjya haivānnam atrapsyat.**

He sought to catch it with the organ of generation but did not succeed in catching it with the organ of generation. If he had caught it with the organ of generation, mere emission would have appeased one's hunger.

10. tad apānenājighṛkṣat tadāvayat saiṣo 'nnasya graho yad vāyur annāyur vā eṣa yad vāyuḥ.

He sought to catch it with the incoming breath, and grasp it did he. Of food is that breath the grasper. The breath living on food is, verily, this breath.

ŚB When he, the primordial man, could not succeed in grasping food with the outgoing breath or with the eye, the ear, the skin, the mind or with the organ of generation, when the functions of these organs failed to perform the function of eating, he sought to grasp it with the incoming breath—through the mouth. He succeeded in grasping it, eating it. For this reason, the incoming breath is the eater of food. That breath which is known as dependent on food, living on it, is this very incoming breath.

For the primordial man, what we call the world is an emanation of his senses; they do not have the isolation that would make them seekers, make them hungry. His breath, the incoming and outgoing, constitutes him as sacrifice, as ecstasy of life through death. But for man, that creature of hunger, the incoming breath is the eater. Through it does he inhale and eat. But he eats not to give back what food gives him, his life. He would retain it, keep it to himself as if it were his life alone and not the life of man–world. He would remain the eater alone and that means his death.

11. sa īkṣata kathaṃ nvidam mad ṛte syād iti sa īkṣata katareṇa prapadyā iti. sa īkṣata yadi vācābhivyāhṛtaṃ yadi prāṇenābhiprāṇitaṃ yadi cakṣuṣā dṛṣṭam yadi śrotreṇa śrutaṃ yadi tvacā spṛṣṭaṃ yadi manasā dhyātaṃ yady apānenābhyapānitaṃ yadi śiśnena visṛṣṭam atha ko'ham iti.

He thought: How indeed could this be there without me? Through which way should I enter?
He thought: If speech is there to speak and breath to breathe, if the eye is there to see and the ear to hear, if the skin is there to touch and the mind to think, if apāna, *the incoming breath, is there to draw in and the genitals to emit, then who am I?*

ŚB When the Lord had made the world–guardians complex thus dependent on food for their life as is a city, its citizens and its protectors, he thought unto himself: How could indeed this body–sense complex function without him, its master? For its functions, which the Upaniṣad will enumerate presently, are functions for another. As citizens bring their offerings in vain and bards sing to no purpose in the absence of their king, so the organ of speech will speak in vain, will, in truth, not speak at all, in the Lord's absence. So let me, the Lord thought, be its master supreme, its ruler, the witness of the good it does and the evil, and dwell in it as enjoyer and sufferer. The Lord thus thought of becoming unto that complex what a king is unto a city.

The body–sense complex functions, in every truth, for another, its master, as a city and its citizens work for their king. The complex needs the conscious Lord in order to function. The Lord dwells in the complex as sufferer and enjoyer. As a dweller of this fort he too needs these functions, cannot be [a] sufferer–enjoyer without them. To imagine the body–sense complex functioning without the Lord is to imagine a city state without its ruler. If it could be imagined functioning without the Lord, then who will he be, of what nature, and whose Lord? No one will then think of the Lord, no one will say: he is the truth, the real and of this nature. So the Lord thought of entering the body–sense complex to witness speech speak, the eye see, the mind think, to witness all its functions as a king would enter a city to take stock of what his officers do and don't do. This is how they will know him: the witness of the functions of composites like speech and other senses and organs, the witness who knows them in the form of 'this', as obtaining in the domain of objects, the witness who is of the nature of truth and consciousness. They will know that all the functions of the body–sense complex are meant for him only, for that conscious witness, that Real just as pillars, walls and other constituents of a palace are there to serve the purpose of someone else, a conscious being who is not a part of the palace.

Having deliberated this way, he thought of the gate through which he should enter the body–sense complex. Two ways were open to him: the forefront of the foot and the crown of the head. The lower way of the forefronts of the feet he rejected, for that is the way meant for *prāṇa*, breath, the Lord's deputy, whose duty it is to do everything on his behalf. He, therefore, thought of the other way, the crown of the head. 'Let me,' he thought, 'pierce it to enter the body–sense complex.' Thus did he deliberate as a human being would do before he acts.

12. sa etam eva sīmānaṃ vidāryaitayā dvārā prāpadyata. saiṣā vidṛtir nāma dvās tad etannāndanam. tasya traya āvasathās trayaḥ svapnāḥ, ayam āvastho'yam āvastho'yam āvastha iti.

Having pierced this end, he entered the body–sense complex through this very door. Vidṛti, *the pierced one, is the name of this door. Bliss is it, this door. Three are its abodes, three dreams: this one, this one, this one.*

ŚB That Lord, that creator, pierced this end, made a hole into that end where the hair comes to part. Through this door did he enter this world, this body–sense complex. This is the well known door through which the Lord entered the complex. It is the well known door because when you apply oil on the crown of the head, you feel its taste in the mouth. This door is famous as *vidṛti,* the pierced one, because of the fact that the Lord pierced it.

Other doors are there: the eyes, the ear, the nose, the mouth, the genitals and the anus. But they are secondary ones, subordinate to this door. They are not perfect nor do they lead one to bliss. This door is of the Lord Supreme, of him alone. For this reason, this door is bliss itself. *Nāndana* is the Vedic form of *nandana,* bliss. Through this door, one attains to the Supreme Brahman to revel in it.

The Lord thus entered the body having created it as would a king his city. He entered it as the individual soul to dwell there in three abodes. In the waking state, he dwells in the right eye, the seat of the sense of vision; in the dream state, the mind inside is his abode; in sleep, it is the space within the heart. Or the three abodes may well be the body of the father, the womb of the mother and one's own body proper. These the Upaniṣad will elaborate in due course.

The three dreams are the three states: Waking, dream and sleep. Some find the waking state as the state in which obtain cognitions of real things and would not, for this reason, equate it with dream. But they are mistaken. In this state there is no awareness of one's own self, the self that is supremely real. Whatever awareness is there, it is of unreal things, as it is in a dream.

Of these abodes, the right eye is the first one, the inner mind the second one and the space within the heart the third one. The repetition of 'this one' recounts only what has already been mentioned [namely, the three abodes]. In these three abodes sleeps, as one with them, the embodied soul one after another, sleeps the sleep of ignorance, long and deep. Calamities in their hundreds of thousands fall upon its head, their blows painful and crushing like those of a heavy club. Even these fail to wake it up. Such is the depth of *avidyā,* of ignorance.

The body is called a city with nine gates—two eyes, two ears, two nostrils, the mouth, the genitals and the anus. Through these gates, the world and man 'enter' into each other. But this interflow never comes to be a real interflow. Man and the world, though essentially one, remain outsiders for each other, despite these gates and despite the continuous traffic through them. This is the state of *avidyā,* of ignorance, of finding what is not other as other. The gates ensure only narcissistic possessions or enjoyments, not smooth flow of the world into man and of man into the world, flow of the self into the self. Man and the world, the senses and their objects, live in each other and for each other. Yet a heavy and crushing sense of *other* one has of the world. That is our tragedy, of us mortals. The world is this my body itself and yet how vast is the world and how small is the body!

This predicament falls to my portion because the nine gates are too narrow for our intermingling. There is another gate, the Upaniṣads say, at the crown of the head, the tenth gate, the gateway to bliss, to beatitude, to merger of *piṇḍa* and *brahmāṇḍa* into each other, of the body into the universe and of the universe into the body. This tenth gate is the yogic gate to truth. The path to this gate starts from the navel to the heart to the place between the eye-brows to the head to, ultimately, the crown. It is there that man comes to escape from the confines of the body to become one with all that is.

The nine gates open out to a false appearance of the Absolute, the tenth to the Absolute itself. There can be no real communication between man and the world through the nine gates; in fact, the greater the coming and going through them, the greater will be the alienation between man and the world. Time and again have we dwelt on this aspect of modern civilisation, its exclusive dependence on the nine gates. A warning is implicit for our civilisation in this seemingly naive myth. And, of course, against the narcissism of the man of the world which we so obsessively exalt and idealise.

Some other points made in the commentary too call for a brief comment. When man lives as the sense-self (lives in the 'right eye'), he finds himself an inhabitant of a 'real' material world. The spiritual counterpart of this self is *Virāj*, for whom the world is only his emanation. Our mind-self experiences a world, the world of dreams, which for us embodied selves is only a phantom but which for the genuine mind self, for what the *Māṇḍūkya Upaniṣad* would call *Taijasa*, is all harmony. There is a yogic counterpart of our narcissistic sleep too as there are for our waking and dream states. That is the state of *samādhi* where all is realised as the self. Its place of experience is said to be the tiny space within the heart. The tenth gate leads one to that space.

As long as the tenth door does not open for him, man will continue to live in the three states, the three fallen states, that is to say. As sense-self he will live as a fragile, unhappy individual, as mind-self as a dreamer of phantoms, as the heart-self as narcissistic isolation. Such will be the enormity of his deprivations.

This myth reveals in a few words all that Gauḍapāda and Śaṅkara had to say in their exposition of the *Māṇḍūkya Upaniṣad*.

13. sa jāto bhūtany abhivyaikhyat kim ihānyaṃ vāvadiṣad iti. sa etam eva puruṣaṃ brahma tatamam apaśyat. idam adarśam itī.

Having been born, he manifested all the bhūtas, *all that have come to be. Of what else here would one desire to speak? This very person did he perceive as Brahman, the all-pervading. 'I have seen it,' he said.*

ŚB Having been born, having entered the body as the individual soul, he manifested all *bhūtas,* all beings. A time approached when a teacher, all compassionate, came unto him to sound in his ears the notes of the mighty drum that wake creatures into themselves, into their self. The notes that sounded in his ears were the great sayings we find in the Upaniṣads. When he, the embodied man, had been thus awakened, he saw this very person, the person that the *śruti* has revealed as the originator of creation, the person that resides in the city, in the body, as the self of man—he saw this very person as Brahman *tatam,* as Brahman the all pervading (read *tatam* as *tatatamam*), Brahman the Great, the most full. Like space did he pervade all, this person that sleeps in the space within the heart of man. Full of wonder was this vision of his own self as the full, as the Absolute. *Idam adarśam itī,* 'I have seen it', expresses this thought of wonder. For *i* in *iti* is here lengthened into *ī* to make it *itī.* This is done, according to the rules of grammar, to indicate thought, deliberation.

The things of the world appear only when the individual appears. The world is, ever and always, the other of the body. Not that it is the creation of the individuated being, but the way reality manifests itself before him. Man emerges as man–world duality; in fact, each and every creature is such a duality. He is not described as creating beings but as manifesting them. The moment man finds himself as man, as an embodied being, he will also find himself placed in a world, its creature and, ultimately, its victim. That will be his fate, of one who merely asserts, 'I am'. And that comes to be the fate of the creator too, to become the victim of his own creation, its helpless prisoner (though in this very helplessness lies, as we have pointed out, his glory as *yajña,* a glory which the individual does not care to share).

Man requires the word of revelation to redeem him from his tragedy. The redeeming feature of this his fallen state is that with the manifestation of the world, there also occurs the revelation of the redemptive word. No one can become aware of a thing without a simultaneous awareness of the beyond. Everything points to something beyond itself. An interpreted thing is always a being-towards . . ., the whole world is a being towards . . .. So the moment the world gets articulated, the beyond too gets articulated. The Vedas are the voice of the beyond resonating in the language of the fact.

When this resonance becomes loud and irresistible, a teacher comes to articulate it in human, communicative speech. The faithfuls explain this mystery by invoking the concept of the act of grace. God sends, they would believe, a messiah, a prophet, a guide to those who would escape from the forest of the night. The mystery is, however, deeper. A scientist finds the world responding to his discourse, finds it embodying, to an extent, the principles he can understand and communicate. Not fully, of course. For the force of the beyond renders all principles tentative. Still the world embodies what he thinks enough to render his disposition into discovery. Similarly, when the beyond comes to live in man as tangible anguish, the world will manifest itself as embodying what he seeks. That manifestation will be the prophet, the guide, the *guru.* That is the fate of the embodied soul: his truth, his ideals, desert him to dwell in the world. He lives an ontological bankruptcy.

The teacher will communicate the voice of the beyond to him to make him realise that his creator is his self, his own self. Notice how to the embodied soul the creator is another, *etam, this.* The creator has become the creature but has also kept himself intact as the creator. Becoming the effect, he nevertheless remained the cause. This cause, as cause, is subject to fall, an apparent fall. When the embodied man finds his life an insupportable agony, when this appearance of man finds his pain as absolutely real pain, then does he wake into his status as the creator, the creator as the thrust for the beyond. To live this thrust is to die into what the religious minded call 'life'. The unhappy call it bliss or liberation, thinkers the truth absolute. These words, however, speak more of their dispositions, of the nature of their discourse and their seeking, not what they come to be. The disillusioned often call it final extinction of man. This too reflects a particular state of being, a disposition.

14. tasmād idandro nāmedandro ha vai nāma. tam idandraṃ santam indra ity ācakṣate parokṣeṇa. parokṣapriyā iva hi devāḥ parokṣapriyā iva hi devāḥ.

For this reason, Idandra, idam-dra, *'the seer of this' is his name. That verily, came to be his name:* Idandra. *Him who came to be* Idandra, *they call* Indra *indirectly. Indirect names are as it were dear to gods, are as it were dear to gods.*

ŚB Within each and every being does Brahman dwell as direct and immediate presence. This Brahman [he] perceived as 'this', as im-mediate presence. Since that is so, since the supreme self perceives 'this', therefore it is called *idandra*, the seer of 'this'. That is how they of the world call the Lord. Since he came to be Idandra, they, the knowers of Brahman, give him the name Indra, a name that denotes him indirectly. This they do for the sake of the world. For they fear to name the Lord directly, address him through a direct name, the Lord they adore most. Gods are fond as it were of indirect names, more so the Great Lord, the God of gods.

The repetition of the last sentence in the *mantra* indicates the end of the Part in question.

[The embodied soul] perceived Brahman as *this* and, with this perception, itself came to be Brahman, for Brahman is the seer of *this*, of *this* unmediated by anything else, by a concept, a word or a class. We perceive a thing mediated by a word, a class, relationships of part and whole, cause and effect, contexts of here and there. Our *this* is never a *this*, it is a constant shifting, a displacement. He who can purge himself of these adjuncts and can bring himself to the perception of *this*, of *this* alone and absolutely nothing else, will turn into Brahman. For finding the *this* is to find the self. This *this* will be all and so will be the perceiver. This is self-knowledge, Brahman-knowledge, this concentrated innocence.

Yet knowers of Brahman proclaim Brahman to the world, not as the knower of *this*, but as the Lord, not as *Idandra* but as *Indra*. For men and women of the world cannot feel the presence of the real in unmediated terms. They like mysteries, complexities, ambiguities, depths. Truth resides, for them, in these and not in what lies immediately before them. Not in this sheet of paper but in all the words in my shelves and other people's shelves. Not even there, perhaps beyond man and his world. Our gods cannot, therefore, be gods whom we can describe in immediate words. Something in them should exceed the sense we give them through names. They must appear mysterious, ineffable. That is their glory. But the wise innocence finds *this* itself as the truth, the most immediate as the most ultimate.

Part 2

Chapter 1

ŚB The teachings of the first part of the *Aitareya Upaniṣad* which constitutes the fourth chapter of the *Aitareya Āraṇyaka*, could well be summarised as follows. He who created the world, sustains it and will destroy it is himself not of the world. Omniscient is he and omnipotent, and all-wise. He created this entire world out of himself, without resort to any other material or means. He created it in due order ranging from the ether of space to things gross and tangible. And having created it he entered into bodies instinct with breath. and the like. This he did in order to know himself. There he came to know his true self as Brahman, and knew this immediately, directly. Therefore, he alone dwells within all the bodies as the self and no other.

As the creator realised himself as Brahman, so should creatures. Let each one of them know that it too is the self that dwells self-same in all and that this self is Brahman itself. This the Upaniṣad has taught us in *mantras* like the following: 'In the beginning, this was but the self, one and absolute' (1.1.1) and 'This very person did he perceive as Brahman, the all-pervading. "I have seen it," he said.' (1.3.13) In the same vein speak other Upaniṣads too.

Objection: That one is all-pervasive, the self of all that is. There is nothing he has not entered, not even the point of a hair. How could he enter the body the way this Upaniṣad describes—by piercing the crown of the head as an ant would a hole?

Answer: Your objection touches mere margins of this account of creation. The account describes the creator as thinking without organs, creating the world without means, taking the person out of the waters to give him a shape, his brooding separating out the mouth and other organs of the person. It also describes fire and other guardians emerging out of these organs and becoming inflicted with hunger and thirst; their prayer for an abode, the presentation of the bodies of a cow and a horse, the entry of these gods into their respective abodes. Then there is the description of created food running away and the desire of speech and other organs to take it. All these events are no less incredible than the entry of the Lord into the body by piercing the crown of the head.

Opponent: Then let us take it that the entire account is an absurdity.

Answer: No hasty conclusion, please! The myth has woven these seeming irrelevancies only for one purpose: to make man wake up to the truth of his self. Perhaps, a still better explanation could be offered. The great magician, the omnipotent and omniscient Lord, created the world as would a human magician create his magic show. To make this mystery easily accessible to people, this myth is recounted. In our ordinary life, too, we adopt the same device—of expressing abstruse matters through a story. To interpret this myth as a bare account of creation will be of no use. But its symbolic import that there is but one self that dwells in all and the all is that self—blesses man with life immortal. This is the focus of the Upaniṣadic teaching, including the one under discussion. And so of the *Bhagavadgītā* and other works of traditional wisdom. Thus the *Bhagavadgītā*:

> He who sees the Lord Supreme dwelling alike in beings each and every, he *alone* sees, this seer of the immortal in the mortal (13.27).

Objection: There are as many as three selves. One, the self that does many an act and gathers the fruit of those acts in terms of happiness and sorrow, pleasure and pain. The world knows of it and scriptures proclaim of it as the self ever tied to the cycle of birth and death. Then we have the self that one can infer, scriptures say, from the effect, the universe. The universe is an ordered universe. Innumerable creatures are born here to act according to their propensities and to reap the fruit of those acts. They have bodies suitable for this purpose and also the worlds with their varied localities. Now, this kind of universe argues for the existence of its maker, the omniscient Lord, as a house and a city show forth their designer and their architect—skilful and knowledgeable. So the creator of the universe is the second self. And, lastly, we have the third self, the person ineffable of the Upaniṣads, the person celebrated in such of their words as, 'from where speech returns without finding anything along with the mind' and 'Not this, not this' (TaitU 2.4 1.& BṛU 3.1.26). These three selves are thus distinct from each other. How can one possibly know that there is only one self, unworldly, one without a second?

Vedāntin: Out of these three, how does one know the individual self?

Opponent: Is he not known as the one who hears, who thinks, sees, commands, speaks, perceives and knows?

Vedāntin: 'Unthought he thinks, unknown he knows,' (BṛU 3.8.11) speaks the *śruti* about the one who knows, hears, thinks, etc. It also says, 'You could not think of the thinker of thought, could not know the knower of knowledge' (BṛU 3.4.2). Is it not, then, self-contradictory to speak of the hearer in terms of the heard, of the knower in terms of the known?

Opponent: Yes, it would be self-contradictory to speak of the self as if it were an object of perception. One could not know it as one would know, for example, a phenomenon like pleasure. Texts like, 'You could not think of the thinker of thought' (BṛU 3.4.2) deny the possibility of knowing the self the way one could know an object of perception. But, surely, you could infer the self from the facts of hearing, thinking, etc. This won't involve any contradiction.

Vedāntin: Even the indicatory sign of hearing and other activities cannot possibly lead you to infer the self. For the moment of its hearing cannot coincide with the moment of thinking or knowing. the former moment will be an exclusive moment rendering any thought or knowledge of the self or, for that matter, of anything else impossible. The same is the case with the moment of thinking and others. Moreover, hearing and thinking are object-oriented, not self-oriented. You cannot hear the hearer nor think the thinker.

Opponent: Mind can think of any and everything.

Vedāntin: True. But the mind cannot think of its object without the thinker.
Opponent: What do you want to suggest?
Vedāntin: Only this much. The thinker of all will ever remain the thinker, he will never be the object of thought. There cannot be another thinker of the thinker. The thinker himself cannot of course think about himself. You require two thinkers to think about the thinker—one that thinks and the other that is thought of. Or the self will, like a bamboo, divide itself into two to perform this act. Neither of the two situations is possible. As one lamp cannot illumine another lamp—being of the same nature—so can't one self another.

The thinker's thinking is thus ever and always object-oriented. There never occurs a moment of self-oriented thinking in the process of thought. To infer the self from the indicatory sign [of hearing, thinking, etc.] too involves two selves as we mentioned earlier—the self as thinker and the self as the object of its thinking. Or the self itself will get divided into two. So the inferential knowledge of the self implies the same difficulties as its perceptual knowledge.
Objection: If the self can be known neither through perception nor through inference, then why is the injunction, 'Let man know: He is the self' (KauU 3.9) and why is the self called hearer and thinker?
Vedāntin: The self is known as hearer, etc. and also as not-hearer, etc. What inconsistency do you find in these two descriptions?
Opponent: You may find this all consistent but not I.
Vedāntin: Why so?
Opponent: When it is hearer, it is not thinker and when it is thinker, it is not hearer. From one point of view, it is, therefore, hearer and thinker but from another it is neither one nor other. The same is the case with regard to other traits. That being so, it is natural that doubt should arise as to whether the self is a hearer or not a hearer, is a thinker or not a thinker, has other sense-qualities or is devoid of them. To predicate, as you do, hearer and not-hearer of the self will naturally involve inconsistency but you don't feel it! When Devadatta walks, he will be called a walker when he doesn't, he will be stationary. You can characterise him as a walker or as stationary alternatively but not simultaneously. The same is the case with the self with regard to its traits.

The followers of Kaṇāda speak in the same vein with regard to the self *vis-a-vis* its traits. The self, according to them, is a hearer, thinker, etc. incidentally, not in essence. Knowledge comes to be born, they say, when mind and senses come into contact, but moments of knowledge occur successively, not simultaneously. When mind, they argue, is inattentive one cannot perceive an object even when it lies before the eye. This, they say, indicates how self-cognitions cannot arise simultaneously: they have to wait for the attention of the mind. Their argument has the force of logic behind it. And we should accept it, Any objection?
Vedāntin: If it is acceptable to you, let it be so. But the *śruti* will not countenance it.
Opponent: Does not the *śruti* accept implicitly that the self is hearer, thinker

and agent of other such activities related to the cognitive and motor organs and to the internal organ, their mind?

Vedāntin: No, for it declares the self to be neither hearer nor thinker nor the agent of any activity of the body–sense complex.

Opponent: But you have refuted this description of the self by saying that it is on one occasion hearer etc. and on another not-hearer etc.

Vedāntin: No, this is not my position. For me the self is the eternal hearer, eternal thinker, eternal speaker, etc. Not of the hearer, declares the *śruti* (BṛU 4.3.27), is there ever the loss of its hearing.

Opponent: In that case, the self will know all kinds of things at the same moment. This, you know, will not tally with our daily experience. Moreover, this will also imply absence of ignorance in the self. And this, you know, no one will accept.

Vedāntin: Neither of these objections is valid. The Upaniṣads declare the self to be the hearer of hearing, the thinker of thought, the seer of seeing and so on. The gross senses, the eyes and the like, are impermanent and so are their objects and the act of perception, which last occurs when these senses come into contact with their objects as does fire with hay or other kinds of fuel when it burns into flames. This perception cannot occur when there is no contact of the senses with their objects as fire cannot burn when it has no contact with hay etc. The self, however, unlike the senses, their objects and their mutual contact, is eternal, it is not-gross and does not ever come into contacts with anything whatsoever nor does it ever separate from anything whatsoever. It can, therefore, never perceive, as do the eye and other organs, internal or external, perceive as a result of its contact with objects. Its seeing, its hearing, its cognition can never be a transient thing as are those of the eye and other organs. 'There can never be loss of the sight of the seer,' says the *śruti* (BṛU 4.3.23). There are, therefore, two kinds of sight, the transient sight of the eye and the eternal sight of the self. Similarly, there are two hearings, the transient hearing of the ear and the eternal hearing of the self. Likewise, there are two kinds of thinking, external and internal. This way alone can the words of the *śruti* become meaningful, viz., 'The seer of seeing and hearer of hearing' (BṛU 3.4.2).

The power of the eye to see can be lost, can also be regained. And so can be the power of the ear to hear and the power of the mind to think. We know how the eye loses that power when it is inflicted by disease and regains it when it is cured of that. The sight of the self, however, is never lost, it is eternal. That is why, even a blind man can 'see' in dreams. We hear a man, whose eyes have been plucked out, talking of his having seen his brother in a dream. So can a deaf man hear *mantras* in that state. If the eternal power of seeing of the self were dependent on the eye, it would cease with the cessation of eyesight. In that case, a blind man could see no dreams and the words of the *śruti* that the seeing of the seer is never lost (BṛU 4.3.23) would be rendered false and so would its other saying: 'That verily is the eye with which man perceives things in a dream.'

The eternal sight of *ātman* is the seer of the external sight of the eye. This external sight of the senses comes to be and ceases to be. To be fragile and ephemeral is its nature, its native characteristic. Creatures of the world confuse, through delusion, this sight with the sight of the self and superimpose its traits onto the sight of the self, the traits of coming to be and ceasing to be. This is how the confusion can validly be explained. The explanation would find support in what happens when one fixes one's attention on a moving thing like a firebrand. The motion of the latter seems, in that case, to belong to the vision of the eye itself. The *śruti* also speaks of this superimposition of the traits of the senses and the mind onto the self when it describes it in such terms as the following: 'It thinks as it were, shakes as it were' (BṛU 4.3.7).

There can thus be no question of simultaneity and nonsimultaneity with regard to the eternal vision of the self.

It is natural that men of the world and logicians should cherish the illusion that the vision of the self is a transient vision. Men of the world do so because they superimpose the transient vision of the senses onto the self, the logicians because they think outside the Vedic tradition. The distinctions that men of the world and logicians draw between the individual being, God and the self supreme too have their origin in this very reason. And so have such distinctions as 'is' and 'is not' that mind and speech conjure up. These distinctions dissolve themselves into unity in the self, the object of eternal and unconditioned vision, the very essence of that vision, the vision that perceives only itself, not the other.[1] Of that vision and of its object which is but itself, one cannot think in terms of 'is' or 'is not', of one and many or that it has attributes or is without attributes. One cannot even say of it that it knows or it does not know or that it acts or does not act, or that its acts bear fruit or do not bear fruit, or that it has a cause or no cause. It is neither happy nor unhappy neither inside nor outside. Nor can it be called *śūnya*, nothing, nor *aśūnya*, not-nothing, neither me nor other. Beyond speech is it and all its concepts. He who would imagine it in terms of such concepts may as well roll up the sky as one would a roll of leather, or think of just striding up to it! To trace the footprints of birds in the sky would be easier or the path of the swimming fish. Of that Real the *śruti* can speak only in terms of 'Not this, not this' (BṛU 3.9.26). 'From that speech,' it says, 'returns along with the mind' (TaitU 2.4.1). The *mantras* too speak in the same voice:

> Who really knows? Who shall here proclaim
> from where was it born?
> From where is this creation?
> Gods came later than its creation;
> Who then knows from where has it come to be? (*Ṛg Veda* 10.129)

Opponent: How, in that case, can that be realised as one's self. Tell me, how shall I know that as my self?

Vedāntin: They narrate a story in connection with this matter. An idiot once committed a crime to receive a reprimand: 'Fie on you! You are not a human

1. The vision that perceives only itself, not the other. This according to Ānandagiri.

being!' To be reassured, he approached another man and said, 'Tell me, Sir, who am I?' The other understood that the man before him was an absolute fool. 'I shall, ' he said, 'tell you by and by.' He told him he was not an inert thing. 'You are, ' he concluded, 'not, then, a not-man.' The idiot was not satisfied with the answer. He wanted from his instructor an explicit statement to the effect that he was a man. You too speak in the same way. He who does not understand that he is a man when he has been assured he is not a not-man, will likewise not know his human identity even when he is told that he is a man.

As the man was instructed about his human identity *via negativa*, similarly, scriptures too follow the same method. That alone is the way to know the self, the way of 'Not this, not this', the way scriptural. There is no other way than this way, as there is no other means to burn hay than fire. With 'Not this, not this', scriptural instructions come to end, with this scriptures come to be silent. Other scriptural statements too show that scriptures lead man to his self *via negativa*, statements like the following: 'Without an inside, without an outside' (BṛU 2.5.19, 3.8.8); 'This self is Brahman, the all-perceiving. This is the teaching' (BṛU 2.5.19); 'You are that' (ChU 6.8-16); 'But when unto him all has become the self, then what shall he perceive and with what?' (BṛU 2.4.14; 4.5.15).

As long as man does not realise this way the self described, so long will he mistake the external and transient sight of the senses and the mind as his own self. He will take the attributes of that which is an adjunct as the attributes of his self. This he shall do because of *avidyā*, false knowledge. And as long as this disposition lasts, as long as he, through primordial ignorance, superimposes on to his self the attributes of an adjunct and, thereby, becomes a victim of desire and bondman of action, he will continue to be reborn in various forms—from that of Brahmā, the creator, to those of gods, of men and women, of animals and of even stationary things like a clump of grass. Thus does one move on from one embodied state to another, from one birth to another. This process continues unbroken as does the flow of a river. And one passes through many states of being in it. Of these states, the Upaniṣad is now going to speak so that man may lose all interest in them.

The myth calls for an interpretation, demands it. Man seeks the cause of things because the thing before him points out, ever and always, to something other than itself. So does the world. Within the world, effects can be traced to causes but along with causes, material causes, one also finds some auxiliary factors, instrumental causes, for example. In this chain of causes and effects, people sometimes find a teleological urge also, some purpose or goal. When it comes to the question of the cause of the world, instrumental causes lose their relevance. Phenomena of the world are contextualities, you find many factors responsible for the being of a thing besides its material cause. In the case of the cause of the world, when you try to think about it, you simply cannot bring in contextualities. The cause of the world has to be material as well as instrumental. There could, however, be a purpose behind creation. That purpose might be called self-knowledge. The creator creates the world in order to know himself.

That creator is what may be called consciousness. For that is our ultimate, the final reach of our investigation. Most people imagine that the senses perceive and mind conceives or imagines, that our perceptions consist of sense–concept combine and mind of thought-process. But neither perception nor thinking is possible without nontemporal consciousness. I perceive things, I also know my perception of things. I think, I also know my thoughts. I can step back from them, from my perception as well as from my thoughts. There is something in me that is neither my perception nor my thoughts. Many thinkers posit this something, this witness consciousness of percepts and thoughts because they find that memory remains unaccounted for without positing this eternal consciousness. There can be no recognition without this witness consciousness, they say, and, hence, no fully articulate perception. Some may go even further to say that no cognition whatever is possible without it, for even the atomic constituent of a percept or a thought requires integrating activity: there being no ultimate facts, no atomic givens.

Such arguments lead one to a state where all explanations of a perception or a thought become impossible. For these arguments do not explain how nontemporal consciousness comes to integrate with temporal percepts and thoughts. As a matter of fact, the rise of percepts and thoughts itself becomes, in this hypothesis, unintelligible. They are, no doubt, inconceivable without nontemporal consciousness but, then, we do not know how they could be there. The more austere among thinkers would declare them to be unreal and allot the concept of reality only to eternal consciousness. The world then becomes an illusion and reality becomes this eternal consciousness.

This is how many theoretical Vedāntins have interpreted their tradition and even the teachings of Gauḍapāda. These thinkers have to explain how they arrive at the concept of nontemporal consciousness. Could they ever stumble into it if they did not have temporal thoughts or percepts to investigate? It is these temporal thoughts and percepts that 'demand' eternal consciousness for their being, rendering it dependent on themselves. These two concepts, that of the eternal and that of the noneternal, are, however, so divergent that they simply cannot coalesce. Percepts and precepts are, however, such impossibilities. You may lend these impossibilities some respectability by calling them 'ambiguities' but the fact remains they cannot be turned into ambiguities. These concepts simply cannot make percepts and precepts intelligible.

What is this green thing I see before me, the thing they call the plant of the rose? I cannot explain it in the realistic vein nor in the idealistic vein nor in the vein of ambiguities. I cannot say that the rose I see is a reflection in the brain of the rose-in-itself, for the brain, the eye and the optic nerves and the current are as much problematic, epistemologically speaking, as the rose. The rose as an 'idea' too is problematic as we have seen earlier. So too are sense-impressions and thoughts and, for that matter, nontemporal consciousness. The way out of this impasse lies in *living* our impressions, our thoughts and awareness of these. I see the rose before me but I do not, because of my preoccupations, let the rose occupy me. If I let it do to me what it can do to me, if I let it displace my thoughts and possess me, I will step out of it, out of the rose that has become me, to become mere passive awareness of it. I shall find myself melting into a silent, wordless, thought-free quiet, so shall I find the rose; it too will become the quiet that I have become. Can I call that what I have become eternal consciousness? The thought of eternity will sound as blasphemous in relation to that state as the thought of transience. The Upaniṣads try to bring man to that state *via negativa* but the way of negation is not a conscious, deliberate way. You do not negate a thing through denying its existence; you negate it by being it. Things of the world are anchors of our selfhood. We affirm and assert them in order to affirm and assert ourselves. When I calmly become the rose before me, the me–rose will cease to be, so will sensations, so will thoughts when I become those sensations and those thoughts. With their cessation, I too will cease, the embodied and worldly *I* that I am.

Some maintain, as we noted above, that the Lord created the world to know himself. The Lord knows himself in two ways: as an embodied individual and as the self. When he knows himself through the world, he becomes a mortal. To say and know that *I am* means to become an embodied individual. The individual *knows* himself but at the cost of a giant ignorance. For his knowing is only being conscious of himself; it does not mean knowledge of what he truly is. It is only when his harsh world takes away all his props that he truly comes to be himself. He has to become things, he has to become the world to know himself. This way self-knowledge is brought about by the world.

Does it mean, then, that God 'in the beginning' is ignorant and that he creates the world in order to know himself—not, of course, as the Hegelian *Geist* but as the humble nothing? Yes and no. It is true that self-knowledge comes to be possible through the harsh schooling of the world. There has to be ignorance in order that knowledge may rise; we the inhabitants of this earth cannot think of knowledge without ignorance, of blessedness without fall and misery. Not, however, the Lord. The Lord 'willingly' becomes ignorant in order to be enlightened. He sets up ignorance as the *arché* and knowledge as the *télos* and moves on from error to error, from death to death, until he finally dies into self-knowledge. For us this is a grim and appallingly costly venture. But not for the Lord. To lose himself in ignorance is his glory, glory which is nothing else than self-extinction. He dies into the other and dies as the other to become himself, truly himself. That is his nature, his *līlā*, his play, his truth: to be a perpetual sacrifice. And that is his immortality, this his sacrifice. He kills with the killer and dies with the killed. For him all is his self. Every pain is his ecstasy, every death a redemption, every sin a holy act. What the Lord always is, man has to become; he too has to die with all and live with all. Then will the difference between bondage and liberation, Brahman and *māyā* come to an end. Scriptures teach him that he realise his self, they tell him how bondage is his curse and liberation a blessing, *the* blessing. However, when he reaches the goal, he finds that what they call bondage is itself liberation, what he shunned as pain was itself joy. Truly, there is no scripture which is not untruthful.

1. puruṣe ha vā ayam ādito garbho bhavati. yad etad retaḥ tad etat sarvebhyo 'ṅgebhyas tejaḥ saṃbhūtam ātmany evātmānaṃ bibharti. tad yadā striyāṃ siñcaty athainaj janayati tad asya prathamaṃ janma.

In a man himself is this first conceived. That which is semen is the splendour come out of all the limbs. In himself, indeed, he bears this self. He causes it to be born when he pours it into a woman. That is his first birth.

ŚB Man lives as one with *avidyā*, primal ignorance, and with [its creatures] desire and action. As a being inflicted with this ignorance, he performs many acts, sacrifice and others. These holy acts lead him, after his death, from this world to that of the moon through regions replete with smoke and other pollutions. There in that lunar world, he dwells as long as the merit earned through his holy acts lasts. When it is spent out, he falls back into this world again. He falls as rain drops to turn into food. This food is poured as a libation into the fire called man. There, in man, this worldly being turns into the juice of food to be conceived, first, as semen. *Yad etad retaḥ*, that which is semen, refers to this process.

That which is this semen is the splendour come out of all the limbs of the body, limbs like the juice of food that flows in the body. This splendour is the very essence of the body, that lump made of food. This semen has been called '*ātman*', the self, of man because that is the being of the embodied being [conceived as *annamaya*, one made of food]. That self, conceived as semen, man holds in his self, his body.

That semen man pours into the fire called woman. When he approaches his wife at the right time, he begets as child this very semen that he bore within himself as self. That is the first birth of the worldly being, this flow of the semen from man into woman. For it is the worldly being himself that flows out in the form of semen. This first birth is his first manifestation 'This self' offers this self to that self'—these were the words that the text [in the section preceding the Upaniṣad] used to express this process.

2. tat striyā ātmabhūyam gacchati. yathā svam angaṃ tathā. tasmād enāṃ na hinasti. sāsyaitam ātmānam atragataṃ bhāvayati.

Into the woman it flows to become one with her as if it were a limb of her own. Therefore, does it not hurt her. She nourishes as her own this his self in her.

ŚB The semen poured into the woman becomes one with her as it was one with man. And it becomes one with her as are her breasts and other limbs. That is why, the foetus does not hurt her as would, for example, a boil. As her own limbs do not hurt her, so this too, as one with her, does not hurt her.

The woman feels that the seed of her husband in her womb is the very self of his. She, therefore, nourishes and protects it with care, taking only those things that nurture the foetus and avoiding those that could harm it.

3. sā bhāvayitrī bhāvayitavyā bhavati. taṃ strī garbhaṃ bibharti. so 'gra eva kumāraṃ janmano'gre 'dhi bhāvayati. sa yat kumāraṃ janmano'gre 'dhi bhāvayaty ātmānam eva tad bhāvayaty eṣāṃ lokānāṃ santatyai. evaṃ santatā hīme lokās tad asya dvitīyaṃ janma.

She, the nourisher, is to be nourished. The woman bears him as the embryo and, in the beginning, the man protects the child before its birth and after. In protecting the child before its birth and after, he, these worlds perpetuating, verily, protects himself. For this is the way these worlds are perpetuated. This is his second birth.

ŚB The woman bears in her womb the self of her husband to nourish and protect it. For this protection she gives to the foetus, she is to be protected. For all relationships flourish in the spirit of give and take. The woman protects the foetus before its birth, protects it through all the precautions mentioned above. And man protects the child before its birth and after. *Before its birth and after* means here: as soon as it is born. He protects the child, as soon as it is born, through the natal ceremonies. This ceremonial protection of the child before its birth and after, at the very moment of its birth, is verily his own protection. For he himself is born as the son. The husband, it is said, himself enters the wife (see Manu 9.8).

Why does man protect himself thus, protect himself born as his own son? The answer is: For the continuation, for the perpetuation, of these worlds. For these worlds could not endure if men would not beget [and women would not bear]. Since this is the case, since these worlds cannot endure, cannot flow continuously as do waters, if humanity would not perpetuate itself, it is incumbent upon man that he procreate. This procreation can, however, only perpetuate these worlds, it cannot bring him liberation.

This delivery of the child from the mother's womb is the second birth of this worldly being, second relatively to the first one in the form of semen.

4. so'syāyam ātmā puṇyebhyaḥ karmabhyaḥ pratidhīyate. athāsyāyam itara ātmā kṛtakṛtyo vayogataḥ praiti. so itaḥ prayann eva punar jāyate tad asya tṛtīyaṃ janma.

Man makes this self of his take his place to do the deeds holy and sacred. Then this his other self departs, having done what he was to do and having reached age. That very moment is he reborn, the moment he departs from here. That is his third birth.

ŚB Then this self of man, this his son, is established in his place to do the holy deeds, deeds ordained by scriptures. He succeeds him to do all that his father was expected to do. In the *Bṛhadāraṇyaka Upaniṣad* too we find the same thing *vis-a-vis* father–son relationship. In the section dealing with *saṃpratti vidyā*, father's benediction and transmission of charge, we find the father passing on his sacred responsibilities on to his son. When he has received the charge, the son says, 'I am Brahman, the sacred knowledge, I am *yajña*, the holy sacrifice . . .' (BṛU 1.5.17).

When thus he has passed his responsibilities on to his son, man, that other self of the son, dies, having done what he was to do and grown old and decrepit. 'What he was to do', relates to discharge of threefold debt—to gods, to seers and fathers. The moment he departs from here, the moment he gives up his body, he attains another body, the effect of his deeds here. Like a leech he moves on from one body to another, is, that is to say, reborn immediately [without gaps or interruptions]. This is his third birth, the birth he gets after death.

Two accounts of rebirth have been given here. The first speaks of the pious man's departure from the world and his return to earth when his piety has spent itself out. The other account describes rebirth as an immediate occurrence. The first account, the faithfuls would say, relates to a man of piety, the other to an ordinary man, partly pious, partly not pious. The accounts could also be looked at as reflections of two dispositions. The first account reflects what may by called realistic or objective disposition. Here the process of rebirth is given in objective terms. The world and its regions—earthly, lunar or solar—are accepted as realities existing independently of an embodied being. The other account reflects the teaching of this Upaniṣad. The world, this Upaniṣad implies, is the other of the body and the senses. As long as desire to act and to enjoy the fruits of acts persists, the embodied mode of being will continue and so will continue the world, its other. The death of man is not the end of his pilgrimage. The end of the journey will come about when the end of his desire to act and to enjoy the fruit of his acts will come to end, not before. Those who believe that death will put an end to all their miseries and desires are victims of a *naïveté*. They believe themselves to be independent realities—though short lived—and also the world. They forget that their being lies in the world and the world's in them. Such is the depth of our self-centredness that we cannot, even for a moment, flow out of ourselves into things to realise how deep is our mutual relationship. Not to speak of common people, even philosophers are obsessed with the idea of 'the external world'. They do not care to investigate how I could set a limit to the world, could withdraw myself from it, when I am only a creature of it, a tiny part of it. It is this withdrawal, this narcissistic isolation that creates our problems—existential, epistemological, ontological. How many centuries have been spent on the problem of my knowledge of the table before me? Do I know the table in itself or only a reflection of it? Where is the locus of this reflection? What is the status of the reflector? What is the relationship between the noumenon and the phenomenon, language and its referent, mind and body, me and the world?

There are no convincing answers to these questions because the questioner will not question himself. He does not have the calm and the patience to flow into things and be those things. If perchance, he is allowed some moments of release from himself, from the cave of selfhood, he recollects such moments as, no doubt, happy moments but not as real moments. He would welcome them as happy diversions, even as lucid revelations but not as reflecting what he would call reality. For us, prisoners of the cave, reality can consist of only trivialities. We think we can be serious only when we are neurotics, not when we are serene and at peace with all that is. To be isolated, to be mean and acquisitive sum up our seriousness. To open out, to be generous to things, to be accommodating to them is to be mad. We will accommodate ourselves but we will not accommodate things. We do not even suspect that we have space enough to accommodate the entire world, even what lies beyond it. Such is the enormity of our bankruptcy! This is how the Upaniṣadic vision will assess our civilisation.

The world as the other, then, is only the other of my body, of, that is to say, my passion to be. Until I am purged of this passion, the body will be there and so will be the world. My death will not be the end of my tragedy, only the death of my narcissistic passion will be. Such is the nature of the vision that reveals man and other creatures as moving on from death to death. Our tragedy is too deep for death to undo it. And precisely because it is too deep for death, it is not too deep for us. I *can* undo my narcissism and my tragedy.

ŚB *Objection*: The first birth of this creature that moves continuously from birth to birth and from death to death is in the form of the semen that man sprinkles into woman. His second birth takes place, according to the Upaniṣad, when the mother delivers the child. Now, when the turn comes for the description of the third birth, the Upaniṣad does not speak of the third birth of the self-same child.

Answer: The Upaniṣad describes the rebirth of the father as his son's because as creatures of recurring birth and death, there is nothing to distinguish one from the other. The son too will entrust his responsibilities to his own son as did his father to him. He too will depart to be reborn immediately thereafter as did his father. For the *śruti*, what is the case with one is the case with the other too. That is why, what it says of one, it takes as said of the other.

Thus does a creature move on from birth to birth and from death to death when it takes the three births, finding itself lost in the ocean of the world, with no sense of its whereabouts and of direction. There may, however, come a moment of realisation, realisation of the self the Vedas proclaim, the moment of release from the ties of the world, the moment of attaining all that is to be attained.

The *ṛṣi*, the seer, speaks to the same effect, the *ṛṣi* that is the *mantra* itself, the sacred hymn itself:

5. tad uktam ṛṣiṇā
garbhe nu sann anveṣām avedam
ahaṃ devānāṃ janimāni viśvā.
śataṃ mā pura āyasīr arakṣann

adhaḥ śyeno javasā nirdīyam iti.
garbha evaitac chayāno vāmadeva evam uvāca.

This has been said by a seer:
'While still in the womb, all the births of these gods I already knew. Though a hundred iron citadels guarded me, and held me down in the worlds below, with swiftness have I come out, with the swiftness of an eagle have I come out.' In the womb itself thus lying spake this way the seer Vāmadeva of times ancient.

ŚB While still in the womb of his mother, Vāmadeva, the seer, already knew all the births of these gods, of speech, of fire, of others. This knowledge he earned when the meditations he had practised in many a life earlier came to mature. The indeclinable particle *nu* in the the text indicates this thought [the thought about the reason why Vāmadeva could know, even when he lay in the embryo, all the births of gods]. These words resonate his happiness at the success of his long endeavour. Many iron citadels were there to guard him, hundreds of them to keep him down in the worlds below. Impregnable were these citadels, these bodies, for the bodies indeed were those citadels that kept him a prisoner and would not allow him to free himself from the fetters of the worldly mode of being. But now, he says, he has torn open the worldly net as would an eagle tear open the net spread out for it, and has come out of it with the latter's swiftness. With the power born out of self-knowledge has he come out with that swiftness.

6. sa evaṃ vidvān asmāc charīrabhedād ūrdhva utkramyāmuṣmin svarge loke sarvān kāmān āptvāmṛtaḥ samabhavat samabhavat.

He, knowing thus and ascending aloft after his body had come to disintegrate, obtained all that one could ever desire in that world of heaven, and became immortal, became immortal.

ŚB That seer, Vāmadeva, came to know this way the self as described and ascended aloft when his body came to disintegrate, to end. The body-series is impregnable like an iron fortress set up as it is by primal ignorance. Hundreds of evils is it subject to, evils like births and deaths. Only he can undo this chain who has drunk in self-knowledge, that drink of immortality. Only the power this drink can generate can undo it. For it destroys the very seed out of which is born the body, the seed called the primal ignorance. With the death of that cause comes about the death of the body [-series]. When Vāmadeva thus rose above after the death of the body, when, that is to say, he rose above the worldly state of being and came to be the self supreme, that self of all, alight with knowledge and pure, he obtained in that world of heaven all that one could ever desire. *Heaven* here means the self-same self which neither decays nor dies; immortal is it and fearless, all-knowing, with neither a before nor an after, neither an inside nor an outside. Consciousness ever the same is that self, consciousness that is immortality itself. In that heaven, in that his own self, he became extinct, was blown out like the flame of a lamp. He blew out to become immortal in the self, his own being. That knowledge of the self had already made him an *āptakāmaḥ,* one whose desires have all been fulfilled. He, this way, had attained all that one could desire, even before the death of his body. The repetition at the end of the *mantra* bespeaks of the conclusion of this disclosure of self-knowledge and the fruit thereof and the illustrations used in the process.

Part 3

Chapter 1

ŚB One comes to be the self of all through *brahma-vidyā,* knowledge of Brahman. This truth the Vedas have revealed to us and has been kept alive by a succession of teachers like Vāmadeva and others. This truth is a celebrated one among the councils of those who know Brahman and is known to Brahmins of our times too, to those who would know Brahman and would attain liberation. They would keep themselves at a distance from this transient world, this world of ends and means and from the embodied mode of being. For this purpose, these discriminators of truth from untruth, ask one another, 'Who is this self that we worship?' That question the *śruti* enunicates for us this way:

1. ko'yam ātmeti vayam upāsmahe. katarah sa ātmā yena vā paśyati yena vā śṛṇoti yena vā gandhān ājighrati yena vā vācaṃ vyākroti yena vā svādu cāsvādu ca vijānāti.

Who is the self that we worship? Which one is the self? That by which one perceives or that by which one hears, that with which one smells scents or that by which one utters speech, or that by which one discriminates the sweet and the unsweet?

ŚB The *ātman,* the self, that we meditate in such direct terms as 'This self', who is this *ātman*? The *ātman* that Vāmadeva worshipped in the same direct terms to become immortal, that very self do we worship. Who, in truth, is that self? Thus did seekers of liberation ask each other, eager to know. While they thus questioned each other, there arose in them memory of what the *śruti* had taught them—remembered it because what they had heard was concerned with a distinct and definite subject and had not failed to leave behind its impression in their minds. What they remembered concerned the entry of Brahman into the person, the entry through, first, the two ends of the feet and, secondly, through the crown of the head (*vide* 2.1.12). From this account it appeared as if there were two Brahmans, one opposed to the other. Each seemed to dwell there as the self of the person. They thought that only one of these could be worshipped as the self. Which of the two was to be worshipped, then? Thus did they ask each other again and again, thinking; ask each other, seeking a clear and unambiguous answer.

While thinking thus, there occurred to them a thought regarding the specific matter they were enquiring about. Two things, they thought, were to be found in the body: (1) the instruments of cognition, of diverse and varied kinds and (2) the cogniser, who is alone and one. That the latter exists can be inferred from the following fact. One perceives an object with one organ but recognises it as the self-same one when memory, a function of another organ, calls it up.

Of these two, the instrument of cognition cannot be the self. Who, then, is the cogniser? To this question, the *śruti* gives the following reply. That which as the eye perceives colour, as the ear hears sound, as the sense of smell smells scents, as the organ of speech speaks the word—utters names like 'cow', 'horse' and the like, or calls something good and another evil. And that which as the sense of taste knows the sweet and the unsweet.

I see an orange, perceive its colour, its shape with the eye, smell its scent with the nose, have a taste of it with the tongue. I also know the soft feel it gives. Later on, I only have a smell of it in the dark and yet, its colour, its shape, its taste and its soft touch immediately rise up in my mind to get integrated into one thing, the orange. This only shows that I who put together various reports of the senses to integrate them into a whole, into a percept and can also recall it, am different from the senses, something more than these.

When I see a thing, I become the eye, when I hear something, I become the ear. Similar is the case with the other senses. When I perceive a thing, I am conscious of the thing before me but not of the sense with which I perceive it. It is only when I am thinking, when I become thought, that I remember that I saw the thing in question with my eyes, smelt it with my nose or heard it with my ears. As one with thought, I become aware of the senses, not when I am one with the senses. This fact, the fact that I can identify myself now with the eye, now with the ear, now with the mind and so on shows that I am different from the senses and the mind.

ŚB Who is that which is one but becomes many organs? That one is now being described in the following words:

2. yad etad dhṛdyaṃ manaś caitat. saṃjñānam ājñānaṃ vijñānaṃ prajñānaṃ medhā dṛṣṭir dhṛtir matir manīṣā jūtiḥ smṛtiḥ saṃkalpaḥ kratur asuḥ kāmo vaśa iti sarvāṇy evaitāni prajñānasya namadheyāni bhavanti.

That which is the heart is, moreover, the mind. It is consciousness and the power that rules; it is knowledge of the things of the world and the power that is equal to any situation; it retains whatever it has learnt; it is perception, steadfastness, thought and the ability to think independently;

it is suffering, memory and conception; it is comprehension, life, desire and passion. All these are but the names of consciousness.

ŚB It was said earlier that the essence of all creatures is the heart and the essence of the heart is the mind, from the mind sprang the waters and Varuṇa, from the heart came the mind and from the mind the moon. That heart is the mind. The one has become multiformed. There is but this one internal organ that, as one with the eye, makes one see, as one with the ear, makes one hear, as one with the organ of smell, makes one smell, as one with the organ of speech, makes one speak, as one with the organ of taste, makes one taste, as one with itself, that is, the organ of deliberation, it makes one deliberate and as one with the heart [intellect], it makes one determinate. It is but this one organ that acts for all organs when they reveal their respective percepts for the percipient.

To the same effect are these words of the *Kauṣītaki Upaniṣad*, too: 'When one mounts on speech through consciousness, one obtains all names. When one mounts on the eye through consciousness, one obtains all forms' (3.6). And also the *Vājasaneyaka*: 'With the mind one sees, with the mind one hears' (BṛU 1.5.3); '. . . one knows the forms through the heart' (BṛU 3.9.20). Therefore, the internal organ called the heart and mind alone is the means of every perception and cognition. Breath too has its being in it, as the *śruti* would inform us: 'That which is breath is verily consciousness, that which is breath is verily consciousness' (KauṣU 3.3).

While commenting on the dialogue between breath and other organs (BṛU 1.3, 6.1. 7-14; PrU 2), we said that the vital force is the integral whole consisting of organs. Since this is the case, the Brahman that entered the body through the feet cannot be the Brahman that one could worship as one's self; it being the means of cognition for the cogniser, not the primordial cogniser himself. Therefore, the knower for whose cognitions the heart and the mind function as instruments, that knower alone is to be worshipped by us. This was the conclusion of their deliberation, of the seekers of truth of those days.

Of the mind and heart, the *śruti* proceeds to state the functions. The functions of the internal organ relating to phenomena, subjective and objective, bear witness to the cogniser, to Brahman. Brahman as cogniser is consciousness but only when it is conditioned by the conditioning adjunct of the internal organ. Those witnessing functions are now being stated. They are consciousness, the state of consciousness, the state of being the ruler, the lord; knowledge of the things of the world, knowledge of the arts, etc.; presence of mind, ability to comprehend books and to retain whatever one has learnt; perception of the phenomena of the sense, steadfastness that stimulates the drooping body and the senses into alertness: 'By fortitude they stimulate the body into activity' they say; thought, the ability to think independently; suffering caused by diseases and other factors; memory; conception, to conceive things, e.g., colours as white or black; comprehension, life, functions like breathing and others that sustain the life-process; desire for things not within one's reach; passion, sex desire.

These functions of the internal organ bear witness to the cogniser, mere consciousness. These are therefore the conditioning adjuncts of Brahman, of Brahman in the form of pure consciousness. Consciousness and other names are, therefore, not the names of Brahman as it really is but of Brahman as conditioned by adjuncts, not of Brahman the primary but of Brahman the secondary, the derivative—mere secondary names of secondary Brahman. These names are but the names of consciousness, not of Brahman itself. To this effect speaks the *śruti* too: 'When it breathes, it is called breath' (BṛU 1.4.7).

Many functions and dispositions constitute man's personality, many thoughts and many experiences, outward as well as inward oriented. Behind the body–mind complex that the human person is there is consciousness. Consciousness is always consciousness of something, it is ever and always object-oriented. Accordingly, many conceive of it as of the nature of a relationship, an opening out, an orientation, an *ekstasis*, a moving towards, not an entity, a thing. Yet it is inconceivable how consciousness would be subjected to this kind of reduction. All phenomena, all that we can know, perceive or conceive, are of the nature of flux, including the so-called 'material' phenomena. And mere flux or process cannot be opening outs, relationships, moving towards, for the latter also imply dimensions that are other than flux, other than process. I could not have related various reports of the senses into an integral whole if I were mere flux. Nor could have I subordinated the parts to the whole, or related a given phenomenon to its class and differentiated it from other phenomena belonging to the same class or other classes. Every percept is a construct, every cognition a recognition. I have to be something more than temporal thoughts to do all this. Moreover, even my awareness of the succession of thoughts in me shows this me to be more than this succession. So consciousness cannot be reduced to mere flux, which means it cannot be a phenomenon, something that I can know, think about, conceive or imagine. For all that I know, imagine or think about is of the nature of flux. Consciousness cannot be identified with thought-process.

Can we, then, call it eternal or permanent? No, for then it could not have related itself with thoughts and perceptions. It resists imposition of every conceivable concept onto it, this nonphenomenal thing called consciousness. The Upaniṣads call it the knower, the cogniser of all cognitions. Since it is the cogniser, it cannot be the cognised, cannot know itself, cannot become a phenomenon. You cannot know it even as the cogniser, for that will mean reducing it to the cognised. Nor can we call it eternal. As observer of the succession of thoughts I, no doubt, find myself something out of that succession, something nontemporal. Yet my awareness of the temporal succession too is an event. I could not therefore be something absolutely nontemporal. There seems to be something of a confluence of the temporal and the eternal in me which is, of course, an impossibility.

Can I, then, call it consciousness at all? It is not mere flux nor something nontemporal, nor a phenomenon, it cannot be a relationship, an opening out, for all these traits belong to the sphere of the known or the knowable, not to the knower, the cogniser. Nor can it be absolutely unrelated to phenomena, for then it would cease to be consciousness. So consciousness is a phenomenon and yet it cannot be a phenomenon; consciousness is and it is not. Our concepts are hopelessly adventitious to it, they cannot grasp it. Can we then equate it with an ambiguity? No. We cannot truly perceive a thing as an ambiguity when we talk about it as an ambiguity. To talk about ambiguities means, in effect, reducing things to the level of language. When the name and the named are truly held in balance, when we truly live as ambiguities, when we do not allow the name to appropriate the named or the named name, we are so suffused with what lies before us that we cannot have enough of the thinker in us to impose any concept on it. That what lies before us will undo us, our concepts, our words, our world, even the concept 'ambiguity'.

Consciousness cannot, therefore, be reduced to the concept 'consciousness'. To be this ambiguity is to undo the concepts that make it an ambiguity. Which means to undo consciousness itself. The real 'becomes' consciousness only when I affirm myself as a knower, a doer, an enjoyer, a sufferer. When, that is, I equate myself with mind, reality turns into consciousness, which, while informing the mind, does not get exhausted by the mind, extends beyond it, exceeds it, rendering all our concepts irrelevant. Some Buddhist thinkers, like many moderns, committed the mistake of reducing consciousness to mind, other conceptualists turned it into the soul. But these are false attributions. Even consciousness is a false attribution. Consciousness is consciousness only in relation to mind, to thought-process. With the mind undone, consciousness too is undone. So will be Brahman and *ātman*, the Absolute and the self.

There is a tendency among moderns, not of course philosophers, to accept the accounts of perception given by science as the final truth. The brain and the nervous system, they say, will take care of our problem of recognition and cognition, relationship between parts and wholes and so on. This is being naive, philosophically speaking. For the ontology of the brain and the nervous system is itself problematic and the epistemological problems afflicting other phenomena afflict these too. And there is, finally, the problem of 'physiological' solipsism to attend to. And also the question of how the brain and the nervous system, these percepts, could be called 'material' things, existing in and by themselves—without an observer, without consciousness.

Refuge in science will not, cannot, solve our philosophical puzzles.

3. eṣa brahmaiṣa indra eṣa prajāpatir ete sarve devā imāni ca pañca mahābhūtāni pṛthivī vāyur ākāśa āpo jyotīṃsīty etānīmāni ca kṣudramiśrāṇīva bījānītarāṇi cetarāṇi cāṇḍajāni ca jārujāni ca svedajāni codbhijāni cāśvā gāvaḥ puruṣā hastino yat kiṃcedaṃ prāṇi jaṅgamaṃ ca patatri ca yac ca sthāvaraṃ sarvaṃ tatprajñānetram. prajñāne pratiṣṭhitam. prjñānetro lokaḥ prajñā pratiṣṭhā prajñānaṃ brahma.

This is Brahman, this is Indra and this is Prajāpati, the Lord of creation, and all these gods. This is the five elements: earth, air, the ether of space, water and light. And this is these creatures together, as it were, with small ones; this is the seeds [of beings] of one kind and another: those born of eggs and of wombs, of moisture and of earth—horses and cows, men and elephants and creatures that move, fly or stay. All these have consciousness for their guide, their eye, and their anchor. Consciousness is the guide of the world, its eye, its netra, *and consciousness is its support. Consciousness is Brahman, the Real absolute.*

ŚB He is the self, that is, consciousness. He that is the lower Brahman, dwelling in all the bodies as their breath, their self in the form of consciousness. He dwells in them as the conditioning adjunct of the internal organ, of the mind, dwells in them as the sun dwells as diversified into many reflections in water. He is *Hiraṇyagarbha,* the Golden Germ, the Breath, the self as consciousness. He is verily Indra because of his qualities [*vide* 1.13-14] or he is Indra, the chief of all the gods. And he is Prajāpati, the lord of creation, the first embodied being, from whom emerged the presiding deities of the organs like Fire and others, emerged when his mouth and other organs parted or came to be formed. And he is also these gods, Fire and others.

And he is these five great elements: earth and others of which are composed all bodies, elements that constitute both the eater and the eaten.

And he is these other creatures, snakes and the like, together with small ones. The indeclinable *iva,* as it were, is meaningless. And he is seeds too, causes as well as [their] others (*itarāṇi*), effects, and others that are to be mentioned in pairs.

Who are these creatures? The *śruti* enumerates them as follows. Those that are born of eggs, the birds of the air and others; those born of wombs, men and animals; those born of moisture, lice and others; those that are born of earth, trees, plants and others. And horses, cows, men, elephants and other living creatures that move and walk on the earth, creatures that fly in the sky and creatures that stay still. All these beings are This One indeed. And all these, all these without exception, have consciousness for their guide, consciousness that is Brahman itself. All thse are anchored to consciousness, to Brahman, ever and always: in birth, in life, in death and dissolution, Brahman is their support. *Consciousness is the guide of the world* should be understood the same way as 'All these have consciousness for their guide.' Or, alternately, *netra* in *prajñānetra* could mean *eye* instead of *guide.* In that case, the phrase would mean: The whole world has consciousness for its eye [revelation]. Consciousness is the support of the entire world. Therefore, consciousness is Brahman.

That Brahman is, in its own being, free from all distinctions that conditioning adjuncts give rise to. It is stainless, it is pure, it is passive, it is peaceful, one without a second. The Upaniṣads describe it in terms of *neti, neti,* not this, not this (BṛU 3.9.26). It can be, they imply, known or realised only when all concepts predicated of it have been depredicated of it. Beyond the reach of words is it and beyond the reach of thought. It becomes omniscient Lord when it is associated with the purest of the conditioning adjuncts, consciousness, to effect the common and unmanifest seed of the world and to assume the name of the Inner Controller, for it is he that controls all, the Lord that dwells within all. Identified with *buddhi,* intellect, that determinating faculty, that seed of the manifest world, it assumes the name of *Hiraṇyagarbha,* the Golden Germ. And it it also the same Brahman that assumes as its conditioning adjunct the body born first in the cosmic egg to become what they call *Virāj,* the Radiant, *Prajāpati,* the Lord of creation. And it is, again, the self-same Brahman that becomes what are called gods, fire and others, the adjuncts emanating from *Virāj* himself. And it is Brahman itself that assumes the names and forms of particular bodies when it gets conditioned by them. The body might be that of Brahmā, the creator, or it might be a mere clump of grass or anybody inbetween.

Thus the One appears many because the adjuncts superimposed on to it are many. All creatures know that one as many and in varied ways because of these adjuncts; all logicians imagine it so for the same reason.

> Some call it fire, some Manu and some Prajāpati,
> some Indra, others breath, and Brahman the eternal others still.

Thus Manu (12.123).

4. sa etena prajñenātmanāsmāl lokād utkramyāmuṣmin svarge loke sarvān kāmān āptvāmṛtaḥ samabhavat samabhavat.

As consciousness from this world ascending, he obtained all that one could ever desire in that world of heaven and became immortal, became immortal.

ŚB This way did Vāmadeva or some other person come to know Brahman the Upaniṣad has revealed unto us, came to know it through the *ātman* that is consciousness. As seers of old became immortal through this self as consciousness, so did he. Through that self he ascended from this world, ascended from it as consciousness. This part of the *mantra* should be understood the same way as was 2.1.6. Ascending from this world he obtained all that one could ever desire in that world of heaven and became immortal, became immortal. Aum!

Invocation

Aum! vāṅ me manasi pratiṣṭhitā mano me vāci pratiṣṭhitam āvir āvīr ma edhi. vedasya ma āṇīsthaḥ śrutaṃ me mā prahāsīḥ. anenādhītenāhorātrān saṃdadhāmy ṛtaṃ vadiṣyāmi. satyaṃ vadiṣyāmi. tan mām avatu. tad vaktāram avatu. avatu mām avatu vaktāram avatu vaktāram.
aum! śāntiḥ śāntiḥ śāntiḥ.

Aum. Established in my mind is my speech and in my speech my mind. To me be manifest, O thou Manifest. When the Vedas move unto me, for ever stay, my mind and my speech, with their axle. And forsake not what I have heard. Together do I join the day and the night through this my study. Of the right shall I speak, of the true shall I speak. May that protect me. May that protect the speaker. May that protect me, may that protect the speaker, the speaker. Aum! peace, peace, peace.

	Absolute', 'The Word without a speaker', not even 'being' or 'no being'.
BRĀHMAṆA-S	The part of the Vedas devoted to rituals.
BRAHMAVIDYĀ	The wisdom of Brahman, revelation of Brahman.
CAITANYA	Consciousness.
CIT	Consciousness, intelligence. One of the three 'expressions' of Brahman, the other two being *sat,* being and *ānanda,* bliss.
CITTA	Mind. Consciousness oriented toward the object.
DAKṢIṆĀGNI	The 'southern' fire, one of the three main fireplaces for the sacrifice. The word acquires deep symbolic connotations in the Upaniṣads.
DAKṢIṆĀYANA	The sourthern way of the sun; the six months comprising *śarad,* autumn, *hemanta* and *śiśira,* early and late winter.
DEVĀḤ	'The shining ones', gods. Not to be equated with *Īśvara,* the Lord. Sometimes *deva* in the singular is used in the sense of *Īśvara.* Human sense faculties.
DEVAYĀNA	The path that leads to the world of the gods.
DHARMA	Cosmic order, religious law, righteousness. In Buddhism the term refers to substanceless quality. Gauḍapāda uses this word which Śaṅkara interprets as connoting being, a living being.
DRAVYA	Substance.
DVAITA	Duality.
DYAUS	Heaven.
DYU	Heaven.
GĀRHAPATYA	The fire of the householder, one of the three main sacred fires. The other fires are lit from it. It too forms a part of Upaniṣadic symbolism.
GĀYATRĪ	A Vedic metre of twenty four syllables. The most sacred *mantra* of the Vedas.
GUṆA	Property. In the Sāṅkhya *darśana,* system, *guṇas* are the fundamental constituents of *prakṛti,* primordial nature. They arc *sattva, rajas* and

	tamas. For an adequate understanding of these *guṇas,* see index to the first and the second volumes.
GURU	Spiritual guide and preceptor. Only he who has become one with Brahman, has realised the all as the self, qualifies to be a *guru.*
HEMANTA	Early winter.
HETU	Cause, reason.
HIRAṆYAGARBHA	The Goldern Germ. The Creator, the divine form of *taijasa,* the radiant, that has dream as its sphere of manifestation.
HOTṚ	One of the four officiating priests. He recites *mantras* of the *Ṛg Veda.* Also priest in general.
HṚDAYA	Lit. heart. Spiritual core of man.
IḌĀ	One of the three yogic nerves.
INDRIYA(S)	Sense organs. Also the presiding deities of the sense organs. They are ten in number, five being organs of cognition and five of action.
IṢṬAPŪRTA	Pious works, Vedic and traditional.
ĪŚVARA	The Lord, the manifest aspect of Brahman. Derived from the root *iś,* to rule, to possess, to be master.
JĀGARITA-STHĀNA	The waking state.
JANMAN	Birth, origin.
JĀTAVEDAS	Knower of all that has come to be, a recurring epithet of *Agni,* Fire.
JĪVA	He who lives. An embodied individual.
JÑĀNA	Derived from the root *jña,* to know. Realisation of the other, of the world, as the self. *Jñāna* dawns when man becomes innocent passivity through holy acts and meditation. The doer and the meditator have to die before *jñāna* shines forth. Not to be confused with rational thinking. In worldly affairs, *jñāna* may be used in the ordinary sense of the word 'knowledge'.
JÑĀNIN	The sage for whom all has become the self.
KAḤ	'Who?', one of the names of *Prajāpati,* the Lord of creation.

KAIVALYA	Aloneness, the state of liberation.
KĀLA	Time.
KĀMA	Desire.
KĀRIKĀ	Verse.
KARMAN	Action, sacred act, sacrifice, noble deeds, moral law.
KĀRYA	Effect.
KṚṢṆAPAKṢA	The dark half of the month.
KṢATRIYA	A member of the warrior class, a hero.
KṢETRA	Field, the entire sphere of the knowable, psychic as well as physical.
KUṆḌALINĪ	Serpent Power. Consult index to the first and the second volumes.
LOKA	World. Derived, according to Śaṅkara, from the root *loka,* to see, to perceive. Where one sees, experiences the fruit of one's past deeds is *loka,* the world.
MADHU-VIDYĀ	Honey-wisdom.
MADHYAMAKA	A name given to the *śunyavāda* of Buddhism. A famous work of Nāgārjuna's is called *Madhyamaka-śāstram.*
MAHĀBHŪTĀNI	The primordial elements: earth, water, fire, air, and ether of space.
MAHĀVĀKYA	Great utterances of the Upaniṣads, meditation on which leads to *brahma-jñana,* revelation of Brahman.
MANAS	Mind, the internal organ of perception and cognition, volition and feeling.
MANTRA	A Vedic verse or text.
MĀTRĀ	Phoneme, letter, sound.
MĀYĀ	A very complex concept. To equate it with 'illusion' will be misleading. All that can be thought, perceived or imagined belongs to the sphere of *māyā,* all the world consisting of names and forms. For an adequate understanding of the concept see index to the first and second volumes of the present work.

MOKṢA	Liberation from the cycle of birth and death.
NĀDA	Sound.
NĀMA-RŪPA	Name and form, the phenomenal world.
NETI NETI	'Not this, not this'.
NIRGUṆA BRAHMAN	The unconditioned Brahman.
NIRVĀṆA	'The blowing out' of the phenomenal world. Liberation.
NYĀYA	One of the six systems of philosophy which believe in the authority of the Vedas, reasoning.
OM	*Aum,* the sacred syllable.
PĀDA	Foot, quarter.
PAÑCĀGNI	Five fires.
PARA-BRAHMAN	Higher Brahman as against *a-para brahman,* lower Brahman.
PARJANYA	Cloud, god of rain and thunderstorm.
PARAMĀTMAN	The supreme *ātman,* Brahman, also God.
PARAMEŚVARA	The supreme god, God.
PARĀ-VIDYĀ	Higher knowledge as against *a-parā vidyā,* lower knowledge.
PARIṆĀMAVĀDA	The view that the effect is only a modification of the cause.
PHALA	Fruit, effect.
PIṄGALĀ	One of the three yogic nerves.
PITṚ, PITARAḤ	Father, forefathers.
PITṚYĀṆA	The way of the fathers (cp. *devayāna,* the way that leads to the world of gods).
PRADHĀNA	The primordial nature in the Sāṅkhya system.
PRAJĀPATI	The Lord of creation.
PRĀJÑA	'The conscious' with the state of sleep as its sphere of manifestation. The third quarter of the self.
PRAJÑĀNA	Consciousness, wisdom. A manifestation of Brahman to be meditated as Brahman itself.
PRAKṚTI	Primordial nature in the Sāṅkhya.
PRALAYA	Cosmic dissolution.
PRĀṆA	Breath.

PRAṆAVA	*Aum* as the speaking word, as *nāda*.
PRAPAÑCA	Phenomenal world
PRAPAÑCOPAŚAMA	Coming to rest of the phenomenal world.
PRṬHIVĪ	Earth.
PUNAR-JANMA	Rebirth.
PŪRĀṆA	Class of literature consisting of myths, legend and history.
PUROHITA	Domestic priest. Lit. 'set before'.
PURUṢA	The Person at once individual and universal and yet asleep to both individuality and the universe. The self.
PURUṢĀRTHA	The goal of life.
PURUṢOTTAMA	The highest person, God.
PŪRVAPAKṢA	The opponent's view as against the *sidhānta,* the correct view.
RAJAS	One of the *guṇas* of *prakṛti.*
RAYI	Wealth, food, matter. *Vide* the *Praśna Upaniṣad.*
ṚK	A Ṛg Vedic *mantra.*
ṚṢI	Seer, sage, seer of Vedic *mantras.*
ṚTA	Cosmic order, sacrifice as the sustaining principle of the world.
ṚTVIJ	The officiating priest. 'He who sacrifices in due season.'
ŚABDA	Sound, word. The manifest Brahman.
SĀDHYAS/SĀDHYA	'Those who are to be attained.' A group of minor deities. Sing. The proposition to be proved.
SĀGUṆA BRAHMAN	Brahman with qualities, lower Brahman.
SAMĀDHI	The state of absorption in the self.
SAMANVAYA	Harmony.
SAṂDHYĀ	Meeting, union, dawn, noon, dusk—sacred times for meditation.
SAṂHITĀ	Collection, the first part of the Vedas.
SAṂNYĀSA	Renunciation.
SAṂSĀRA	The world of death and birth, the phenomenal world.

SAṂSKĀRA	Impressions left by previous lives. Sacrament.
SĀṄKHYA	One of the six schools of philosophy that recognise the authority of the Vedas.
ŚĀNTI	Peace.
ŚARAD	Autumn.
ŚARĪRA	Body.
ŚĀSTRA	Sacred teaching, authoritative texts, holy texts.
SAT	Being, existence.
SATKĀRYAVĀDA	The doctrine that cause transforms itself into effect, that the cause is the effect.
SATTVA	Essence, reality. One of the three *guṇas* of *prakṛti* in the Sāṅkhya.
SATYA	Truth, truthfulness.
SAVITṚ	Divinity related to the sun.
SIDDHĀNTA	The correct view, the view to be established.
ŚIŚIRA	Late winter.
ŚLOKA	Verse of four units each consisting of eight syllables.
SMṚTI	Lit. memory. Scriptures that have human authors. They are less authoritative than the *śruti,* the authorless Word—the Vedas.
SOMA	Drink of immortality, an exalted state of consciousness, moon.
ŚRUTI	The heard word, the Vedic revelation, the Word without a speaker.
ŚŪDRA	A member of the fourth caste.
ŚUKLAPAKṢA	The bright half of the month.
SŪKTA	A Vedic hymn, 'a beautiful utterance'.
ŚŪNYA, SŪNYATĀ	Void.
SUṢUMṆĀ	The principal yogic nerve, the other two being *iḍā* and *piṅgalā.*
SUṢUPTA-STHĀNA, SUṢUPTI	The state of sleep.
SŪTRA	Thread. An aphoristic text.
SVABHĀVA	'Own being', self-nature.
SVAPNA-STHĀNA	Dream-state.

SVAR	Realm of light, heaven. One of the three *vyāhṛti*-s, utterances, by which heaven was created.
SVARŪPA	One's true being, true nature.
TAIJASA	Luminous, radiant. The state of dream.
TAMAS	One of the three *guṇas* of *prakṛti.*
TAPAS	Lit. heat. Spiritual fervour, austerity, penance.
TATTVA	'That-ness', reality.
TAT TVAM ASI	'That thou art', one of the four great *vākyas,* utterances, of the Upaniṣads, meditation on which can lead to revelation of reality as the self.
TRETĀ	The second of the four ages of creation.
TURĪYA, TURYA	The Fourth. The Self.
UCCHEDA	Annihilation.
UDGĀTṚ	The singer, the priest that chants the *sāman* at a sacrifice.
UDGĪTHA	A part of the *sāman* chant. Aum.
UTTARĀYAṆA	The northern way, the six months during which the sun moves towards the north. *Vide the Praśna Upaniṣad.*
VĀC	Word, the Word as the creator, sound, speech, language, the organ of speech, the Vedas.
VĀDA	Debate, discussion, doctrine.
VAIRĀGYA	Dispassion, renunciation. The state of the dryness of the soul before, and as a necessary condition of, enlightenment.
VAIŚEṢIKA	One of the six systems of philosophy which believe in the authority of the Vedas.
VAIŚVĀNARA	The Universal Man, a name of *Agni.* The waking state is the sphere of its manifestation.
VAIŚYA	A member of the third caste, a peasant-trader.
VĀKYA	Sentence, statement.
VĀNAPRASTHA	Forest dweller, the third stage of life.
VARṆA	Lit. colour. Caste.
VASANTA	Spring.
VĀYU	God of air, wind
VEDA	Lit. knowledge in the sense of abiding in the

	object. Knowledge vouchsafed to passive and innocent disposition. Revelation in which one becomes what one beholds; it results in becoming all as each and each as all. Also the name of the sacred scripture known by that name. There are four Vedas, *Ṛg Veda, Yajur Veda, Sāma Veda* and *Atharva Veda.* They include the *Brāhmaṇas, Āryaṇyakas* and *Upaniṣads* too. In the narrow sense, the *mantra* portions of the Vedas, the *Saṃhitās.*
VEDĀNTA	The end of the Vedas, the Upaniṣads as the highest manifestation of Vedic wisdom. The school of philosophy based on the Upaniṣads. It is enshrined in *Brahmasūtras*. Commentators have interpreted the *Brahmasūtras* in different ways giving rise to many sub-schools of Vedānta.
VIDYĀ	Wisdom as revelation. See *Veda.*
VIJÑĀNA	Wisdom, realisation. Also consciousness, mind.
VIJÑĀNAVĀDA	Buddhist idealism.
VIJÑAPTI-MĀTRATĀ	The view that reality is nothing else than consciousness. Lit. consciousness-aloneness.
VIKALPA	Imagination, thought.
VIMUKTA	Liberated from birth and death.
VIPARYĀSA	Error.
VIRĀJ	The all-pervasive self innocent of its all-pervasiveness.
VIṢṆU	The all-pervasive self.
VIŚVA	The first quarter of the self which has the waking state for its sphere of manifestation. *Vaiśvānara.*
VIŚVEDEVĀḤ	All the gods.
VYĀNA	The diffused breath.
VYĀVAHĀRIKA	'Relating to common life'. The theoretico-practical way of viewing reality opposed to *pāramārthika,* which is not a perspective but realisation of one's being, one's self, as the all and the all as the self. *Pāramārthika* connotes innocence of all perspectives.
VYOMAN	Heaven.

YAJÑA	Sacrifice.
YAJUS	*Mantra* of the *Yajur Veda,* sacrificial utterance or formula.
YAMA	The first man to die into immortality. Death.
YOGA	From *yuj,* to join, to unite, to concentrate. Spiritual discipline elaborated in Patañjali's *Yogasūtra,* one of the systems of philosophy, and in other works.
YUGA	Generation, one of the four ages of the world-cycles.

Index

Note : Because of their prevasiveness in the entire text, 'Brahman', 'ātman' and 'māyā' do not, with some exceptions, occur in the Index. So is the care with the frequently occurring with 'śruti' and 'the space within the heart'. The preface too is excluded.